THE
du Pont Family

CHART 1

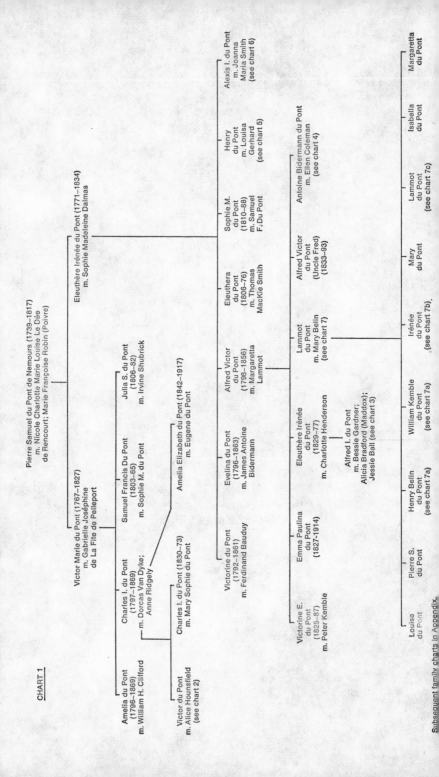

Pierre Samuel du Pont de Nemours (1739–1817)
m. Nicole Charlotte Marie Louise Le Dée
de Rencourt; Marie Françoise Robin (Poivre)

Victor Marie du Pont (1767–1827)
m. Gabrielle Joséphine
de La Fite de Pelleport

Eleuthère Irénée du Pont (1771–1834)
m. Sophie Madeleine Dalmas

Amelia du Pont (1796–1869)
m. William H. Clifford

Charles I. du Pont (1797–1869)
m. Dorcas Van Dyke;
Anne Ridgely

Samuel Francis Du Pont
(1803–65)
m. Sophie M. du Pont

Julia S. du Pont
(1806–82)
m. Irvine Shubrick

Victor du Pont
m. Alice Hounsfield
(see chart 2)

Charles I. du Pont (1830–73)
m. Mary Sophie du Pont

Amelia Elizabeth du Pont (1842–1917)
m. Eugene du Pont

Victorine du Pont
(1792–1861)
m. Ferdinand Bauduy

Evelina du Pont
(1796–1863)
m. James Antoine
Bidermann

Alfred Victor
du Pont
(1798–1856)
m. Margaretta
Lammot

Eleuthera
du Pont
(1806–76)
m. Thomas
MacKie Smith

Sophie M.
du Pont
(1810–88)
m. Samuel
F. Du Pont

Henry
du Pont
m. Louisa
Gerhard
(see chart 5)

Alexis I. du Pont
m. Joanna
Maria Smith
(see chart 6)

Victorine E.
du Pont
(1825–87)
m. Peter Kemble

Emma Paulina
du Pont
(1827–1914)

Eleuthère Irénée
du Pont
(1829–77)
m. Charlotte Henderson

Alfred I. du Pont
m. Bessie Gardner;
Alicia Bradford (Maddox);
Jessie Ball (see chart 3)

Lammot
du Pont
m. Mary Belin
(see chart 7)

Alfred Victor
du Pont
(Uncle Fred)
(1833–93)

Antoine Bidermann du Pont
m. Ellen Coleman
(see chart 4)

Louise
du Pont

Pierre S.
du Pont

Henry Belin
du Pont
(see chart 7a)

William Kemble
du Pont
(see chart 7a)

Irénée
du Pont
(see chart 7b)

Mary
du Pont

Lammot
du Pont
(see chart 7c)

Isabella
du Pont

**Margaretta
du Pont**

Subsequent family charts in Appendix.

THE
du Pont Family

John D. Gates

DOUBLEDAY & COMPANY, INC.   GARDEN CITY, NEW YORK

ISBN: 0-385-13043-0
Library of Congress Catalog Card Number: 78-7754
Copyright © 1979 by John D. Gates

The du Pont family and I first became acquainted in June of 1957, the summer between my graduation from Exeter and my freshman year at Yale. I had been invited to a debutante party in honor of Dedo du Pont, a younger sister of Delaware's present governor, Pete du Pont.

It was not easy to tell me anything in those days, and I drove to Wilmington unencumbered by any specific directions to either Dedo's family home or the house where I had been invited to spend the night. Finding Wilmington was a simple enough proposition, but after driving around the countryside for an hour or more, I realized finding a specific house was another matter.

In the distance, I could see a very large mansion atop a hill and it did not take any particular brilliance on my part to guess that the house must belong to a du Pont. I drove up the driveway, rang the bell, and confided my problem to the butler who answered the door. He gave me directions. I did not know it at the time, but I had just visited Granogue, home of Irénée du Pont, Jr., the ranking member of the family in the Du Pont Company until his recent retirement.

Since that day, I have come to know the du Ponts well. In 1961 I married a woman whose mother was a du Pont. Although we have since been amicably divorced, several of her contemporaries remain among my closest friends. For nine years, until June of 1977, I lived in Wilmington and worked for the newspapers there, where I found myself frequently covering du Pont newsmakers.

The contrast between my attitude toward the family and

that of my fellow reporters was striking. They tended to view the family with a skepticism that bordered on cynicism, even, in some cases, hostility. Perhaps I was naïve in my generally generous, if not always admiring, attitude, but I believe that the basic difference in attitudes was rooted in the two different perspectives involved.

To me, the du Ponts were people, many of whom I saw socially. Maybe they had some advantages they hadn't exactly earned and used them at times in ways the average citizen could not and therefore resented. But they were individuals, personalities. To others at the newspaper, the du Ponts personified many of the inequities in our economic and governmental system. Family members didn't seem to care enough about those inequities or do enough to rectify them. In this view, the family inherited its wealth and power from men who came by it through means not always irreproachable from an ethical standpoint and appeared unconcerned by the fact. I, on the other hand, understood the du Ponts to believe they were playing the game by the rules, then and now. If the rules changed, the du Ponts changed. If they appeared to be ahead, it was not because they had cheated, but because they played better or were luckier.

To put it simply, others tended to make moral and social judgments about the family, and I remained unconvinced they had all the information required to make those judgments. I don't pretend to have all the information, either, and therefore leave the judgments to others.

The du Ponts, with few exceptions, have always studiously avoided publicity. For the most part, they greeted the news of my proposed book on them with something less than enthusiasm. But recent books on the family have left much of its story untold, and some members hoped that a book by someone who knew the family personally—even, in some instances, intimately—might help set the record straight.

As a result, several dozen du Ponts co-operated in the project, granting interviews, talking freely, and suggesting avenues for exploration that had been previously overlooked. While several of the family categorically refused to talk, I believe no book on the family has ever been written, except for a few privately commissioned and privately circulated editions, with comparable family help. Such help, I freely admit, would not have been forthcoming to anyone the family did not feel started from a basically sympathetic position.

A number of books have been published about the du Ponts. Generally they fall in one of three categories—history, historical biography, or socio-economic commentary. In the last category are Gerald Colby Zilg's *Behind the Nylon Curtain* and a book by some protégés of Ralph Nader entitled *The Company State.* Neither flatters the family or the company, and while both reflect massive research efforts, both are less than uniformly accurate in every detail. Generally considered the best book on the du Ponts to date is *Pierre S. du Pont and the Making of the Modern Corporation,* a careful, scholarly business history by Alfred Chandler and Stephen Salsbury. The most readable book on the family is Marquis James's biography, *Alfred I. du Pont, the Family Rebel.* My book, I'd like to think, approaches a portrait of the family not unlike James's portrait of Alfred I., which is largely anecdotal, human, and free of the author's judgments.

I have made every effort to present the facts of the story objectively, but in the last analysis, this book must be considered in many respects a personal view, more concerned with the human than the historical or socio-economic aspects of the du Ponts.

They are, of course, very rich, and how their fortunes were made is an integral part of the book. But they are also very human, and that is equally important. The family today is vastly different from the family that existed two generations ago. That difference is the heart of the matter and of this book.

John D. Gates
8/3/78

Contents

Preface		vii
Chapter 1	Now and Then: An Overview	1
Chapter 2	The Move to America	23
Chapter 3	Building the Business	46
Chapter 4	Two Crises	72
Chapter 5	Pierre: Star of the Show	99
Chapter 6	Two Brothers	126
Chapter 7	Fathers and Sons	146
Chapter 8	Pierre's Other Relatives	165
Chapter 9	T.C. and Family	184
Chapter 10	The Rebel and His Relations	209
Chapter 11	Heirs of "the Boss"	238
Chapter 12	A Diverse Branch	262
Chapter 13	The Underrated Victors	292
Chapter 14	The In-Laws	306
Chapter 15	The Company	327
Chapter 16	A Way of Life	342
Appendix		359

du Pont Family

Chapter One

Now and Then: An Overview

Tall, dark, and not quite handsome, Irénée du Pont, Jr., is a shy, unassuming, conservative businessman whose rise to the penultimate rung of the executive ladder at E. I. du Pont de Nemours & Company cannot be solely accounted for by the similarity of names. He is bright enough and strong, and if his movements reveal a trace of the awkward, his smile is pure, warm, and sincere. People like Irénée du Pont, Jr.

But senior vice-president Irénée du Pont, Jr., retired from the Du Pont Company in the summer of 1978. He will never be president or chairman of the board of the company his great-great-grandfather founded, and those of his relatives who choose to follow his steps are unlikely to go as far as he did. The realization of this was put into writing in April of 1972 in what may be the most dramatic letter in the annals of American business.

Irénée (pronounced "Ear-in-nay") says he does not remember the circumstances surrounding the letter, which he wrote in his capacity as president of the family holding company, Christiana Securities Company, to Charles B. McCoy, chief executive officer of the Du Pont Company. Perhaps he dictated it to a secretary and slipped it into the interoffice mail for the short journey down the ninth-floor hall from his to McCoy's office at company headquarters in Wilmington, Delaware. Or perhaps he composed the letter at home in his sprawling hilltop mansion while an April moon cast silver shadows over the countryside, known to many Delawareans as "châteaux country" because of the du Pont estates that dot the landscape. A poet or a dramatist would surely have savored the implications of the moment. The letter Irénée wrote was rather straightforward.

The du Pont family was quitting, Irénée told McCoy, in effect, and would like the Du Pont Company to consider formally a proposal bandied about for some time now informally —absorption of Christiana into Du Pont through an exchange of stock. On its face, the proposition appeared to be just another large business deal, but just beneath the skin, the pulse of an era was growing faint. It was through Christiana, which held 28.3 per cent of the Du Pont Company's outstanding common stock, that the du Pont family exercised its control of the world's largest chemical company.

Christiana was the base on which the family empire was built, an empire significant enough that Ferdinand Lundberg estimated the family fortune in 1968 at $7.6 billion and called the du Ponts the wealthiest family in America. It wasn't so long ago that he who controlled the Du Pont Company controlled General Motors—at one point, Du Pont owned 38 per cent of GM. It is no wonder that U. S. Attorney General Tom Clark, commenting in 1949 on a government antitrust suit against the family and its company, said: "This case is directed to the breaking up of the largest single concentration of industrial power in the United States."

That case finally forced Du Pont to divest itself of its GM holdings, which amounted to 63 million shares at the time. And now here was Irénée offering to finish the job, as it were, by breaking up the family block of Du Pont held through Christiana.

A generation earlier the suggestion that Christiana ought to be dissolved would have been greeted with derision and scorn by the family. True, the cost of control—the cost of retaining Christiana—was not small. The stock market rated Christiana historically at a 20 to 25 per cent discount to Du Pont, and a lack of liquidity made selling a large block of Christiana a sacrificial undertaking. Then too, there was the intercorporate dividends tax. All were insignificant matters when family control was an active, profitable, exciting reality. What difference did it make at what price you could sell Christiana or how many shares you could sell before the price went down? Who was selling?

In 1972 the principal considerations had changed. Family control was now more in form than in substance. The prospect of selling Christiana to settle estates—in the past, other assets were sold, never Christiana—was growing more imminent. Taxes and marketability were more important to the du Ponts now than control. Once a pendant symbolic of vast powers, Christiana had become an albatross around the family neck.

The du Ponts had dreamed the American Dream. Some years ago, Pierre S. du Pont III, then president of the American Museum of Immigration housed in the base of the Statue of Liberty, was asked how he became interested in the museum and replied, "A lot of people consider the Du Pont Company to be the best example of what an immigrant family has accomplished in this country." Today the family is being shaken awake. For the past quarter century, the present generations of du Ponts have lived with an awesome legacy of personality and achievement. A tough act to follow. The Du Pont Company's current board chairman, Irving S. Shapiro, talks of the great shadows cast by the giants of the previous generation and how those shadows, by keeping out the light, may have contributed to the stunting of the present generations' growth. That is not to say that today's family is a race of pygmies, but only that yesterday's titans may have begotten children merely normal in stature.

In April of 1872, one hundred years almost to the day before Irénée's letter of family resignation, Henry du Pont put together the Gunpowder Trade Association. Soon it would dominate the industry, and Du Pont would dominate the Association. That was important, but it did not make Du Pont a household word. That was a job for the present Irénée's father and his father's contemporary cousins. They managed it well.

In the years between the turn of the century and the Great Depression, the du Ponts, it seemed, could do just about anything. T. Coleman du Pont, boasting of his plan to build a monument one hundred miles high and lay it on the ground, could build the nation's finest highway the length of Delaware, putting up some $4 million back in the days when $4 million could buy something. His first cousin, Pierre S. du Pont, deploring the state of public education in Delaware, could put $5 million into school buildings alone, single-handedly providing modern accommodations for nearly half the state's public school students. Another first cousin, Alfred I. du Pont, could take upon himself financial care of Delaware's elderly needy, setting up an office to scour the state and make a list of those over sixty-five needing financial assistance and then paying up to $25 a month to each person on the list, a project that lasted nearly two years before legislation passed transferring the obligation to the state.

Those were the days. While their company was buying eventual control of General Motors, a family syndicate was purchasing 18 per cent of U. S. Rubber, now Uniroyal. In 1927 the company started buying U. S. Steel, acquiring 114,000 shares, about 1 per cent of the outstanding stock. Shortly after the Justice Department announced it was looking into the transaction, the stock was sold. The du Ponts claimed their company was simply investing surplus cash. The steel stock was sold when the company needed more cash, not because of the antitrust inquiry, the family said. And the company grew through acquisition and invention, bursting forth from its cocoon as the nation's largest explosives maker into a dazzling butterfly, the world's largest chemical company.

When the smooth-running Du Pont Company became boring, Coleman could play a real-life Monopoly game with properties like New York's Equitable Building (then the largest office building in the world), hotels like the Waldorf-Astoria, Philadelphia's Bellevue-Stratford, Washington's Willard, and the Savarin and Louis Sherry restaurant chains.

After a big family scene, Alfred I. withdrew to Florida and built up a real estate and banking dynasty that would own most of St. Joe Paper Company, more than a million acres in Florida and Georgia timberland, and, of course, plenty of Du Pont Company stock. Not to mention a pair of railroads. Estimates of Alfred's estate today range to perhaps $2 billion. Although a large part of the estate is invested in assets that yield virtually no income, the estate has $100 million in cash sitting in the bank.

After Henry F. proved—at least to Irénée Sr.'s satisfaction —that he wasn't going to make it as a chemist and got himself fired from the company, he proceeded to spend an estimated $20 million building what is generally considered the finest collection of American antiques and decorative arts anywhere.

Other du Ponts could branch out in other splashy directions. Francis I., another cousin, started a brokerage firm that grew to be the nation's second largest. E. Paul du Pont started his own automobile firm and later took over Indian Motorcycle Company. His son, E. Paul Jr., became involved in the skytrain, predicting a big future for gliders pulled by airplanes and watching proudly as a prototype flew to Cuba in 1938. Henry B. du Pont, Jr., began Atlantic Aviation and turned it into one of the largest sales and service organizations for private aircraft in the country.

Coleman bought control of the Equitable Life Assurance Society, at the time the nation's biggest insurance company, only to turn right around and mutualize it—sell it to its policyholders—and take a $2 million loss on the deal just because he felt it was the fair thing to do. "I can afford it, I guess," he said.

One branch of the family started All-American Aviation, a company from which Allegheny Airlines was spun off. The family started a bank, the Wilmington Trust Company, and before very long its trust department was among the largest around. Alfred I. bought his own bank when he had his fight with the family. He sold it to his cousin William when he moved to Florida. At various times, various family members held blocks of stock in North American Aviation (now North American Rockwell), American Sugar, Phillips Petroleum, and United Fruit. The family also held large blocks of stock in Hercules and Atlas Powder (now the American arm of Britain's giant Imperial Chemicals). These were the two companies split off from Du Pont as a result of a 1907 antitrust suit and its settlement decree, which by any standard can only be adjudged gentle.

In the 1930s U. S. Senator Gerald P. Nye, chairman of a committee that did its best to crucify the du Ponts over profits from World War I, could honestly inquire, "Are not all members of the family directors or officers of the company?" and not look the complete clown. *Fortune* magazine could write that estimates giving the du Pont family 10 million of the 11 million outstanding Du Pont Company shares are "undoubtedly an exaggeration" with just a hint of an implication that maybe, on the other hand, they weren't.

During the General Motors divestiture suit Irénée Sr. testified that the syndicate formed in the 1920s to acquire stock in U. S. Rubber was mostly family because when you looked for folks with $1.2 million to risk "it just so happened that of that class of people many of them were relatives." He was undoubtedly understating the case.

When the du Ponts entertained, no one worried about where the corners might be cut, the frivolous extra expense spared. When an orchestra hired to start playing at eight-thirty the evening of a party inquired of Irénée—the year was '28—about quitting time, his secretary wrote back: "As to the hour of termination, your guess is as good as mine. My guess would be between three and four o'clock in the morning." Often the hors d'oeuvres would include caviar, smoked salmon, and the like despite a guest list that numbered in the hundreds. Special arrangements were made for the care and feeding of as many as one hundred chauffeurs.

The scale is gone today. The du Ponts hardly play in the minor-monied leagues, but the act of conserving wealth is a different one entirely from that of acquiring it. The players are paler; the movements more restricted. The family is a very different group of individuals today from those who held the stage half a century ago. But if an era has ended, an aura lingers. The public image of the du Ponts has not changed in the last fifty years nearly so dramatically as have the du Ponts themselves. It is really a touch of irony more than a symbol of how little things change that Pierre S. du Pont IV was elected governor of Delaware in 1976.

The glory of the du Pont empire may have diminished in absolute terms, in the eyes of those who sit around the emperor's throne, but to those who reside without the court, the glory is but little dimmed. The name du Pont still conjures up wealth beyond dreaming.

There is, for example, the tale Pierre Coleman (Coley) du Pont tells about his first day on the job. Coley is the son of James Q. du Pont. T. Coleman was James Q.'s uncle. Coley is the only man named du Pont who works for the company. His first job was on the night shift at the Richmond, Virginia, nylon plant. He was told to report on Tuesday. He'd been on the job several days, or rather nights, when a co-worker came up to him in the plant cafeteria during a break and asked to join him. "I hope you won't take this the wrong way," the guy began and proceeded to tell Coley how his arrival had been the chief topic of plant gossip for some time, his being a du Pont and all, and that the fact that Coley had started work on Tuesday rather than Monday had been cause for some speculation and rumor. Among the rank and file, the guy said, the generally accepted rumor was that Coley was sailing his yacht back from the Bermuda race, planning to bring it right up the James River to Richmond, when he got caught by a storm and had to radio the plant he'd be a day late. By both inclination and financial status, Coley is a dinghy man.

Or take the story Alfred Dent—middle name du Pont— grandson of Alfred I., tells about visiting Churchill Downs for the Kentucky Derby a few years ago with a fellow named Baird Brittingham, president of the Delaware Park race track and head of the investment firm in which Dent works, occasionally. After the first few races, it was clearly going to be a banner day. Winners for everyone. Dent suggested they go to Las Vegas after the races. Brittingham went out and checked the airlines. No connecting flights. Dent suggested a hired Lear jet. Brittingham arranged it.

By the time they arrived at the airport, the day had turned a little sour. Winnings had dwindled, and cash was a bit scarce. Not unreasonably, the Lear pilot explained the fare would be $2,500 or something and requested payment in advance. Brittingham pulled some cards, explained he was head of Delaware Park, and asked the man to take a check. The pilot did not seem properly impressed, and Dent, rummaging through a more or less empty wallet, came up with a credit card stamped with his full name. A bell rang in the pilot's head and he excused himself to go and call the home office. Dent was already chuckling. Brittingham could buy and sell him. A few minutes later, the pilot returned and told them to fasten their seat belts. "We're off," the pilot said. "The office says to go with that du Pont guy."

The name provokes different reactions among different people. One young du Pont, who was not ashamed of his name, was picked up for speeding on his way home some years ago. It seems a Pennsylvania state trooper was about to let him off with a warning when he noticed the name on the driver's license. "You one of them Delaware du Ponts?" he asked. "Yessir," came the reply. "Okay, follow me." And for want of sufficient cash and for having a father more amused by than sympathetic to his plight, the young man spent the evening behind bars.

Governor Pete du Pont says some media types—not the same individuals, but more or less the same types—have been asking him the same question since he first went into public life back in 1968. Basically the question is a request of Pete to describe those family meetings where all the big policy decisions are made. "And when I answer that I've never been to one and so far as I know, that's because they don't exist, they don't believe me. They simply don't believe me," the governor says, more amused than perplexed.

Family meetings wouldn't work. The sense of family identity has been fragmented; the vision of family purpose has lost its focus. As Governor du Pont once put it: "The family, the company, and the community interests in the past could have been described as concentric circles, but now those circles have pulled apart. They still overlap, of course, but they are no longer concentric."

Even were there an ideological consensus, a single family voice would present a numbing logistical problem. There were, in the late spring of 1977, 1,905 direct descendants of the original Pierre Samuel du Pont, the fellow who brought his family to the United States back in 1800, and his first wife, Nicole Charlotte Marie Louise Le Dée de Rencourt, according to a study of the du Pont Genealogy Committee. Since only 306 of these had died, that left, not counting in-laws and adopted children, 1,599 living, and these folks were rather neatly spread around the globe. Du Ponts lived in thirty-seven states, the District of Columbia, and ten foreign countries. The Delaware du Ponts dominate. There are more of them and they have more money. In Delaware there are 123 family households. In New York there are 46, with 36 in Massachusetts, 26 in California, 21 in Illinois, 20 in Florida, and 10 each in Colorado and Texas. Mother France heads the foreign countries, with 40 households. Great Britain is second with 22 and Switzerland is third with 6.

It might be argued that many, if not most, of the du Ponts residing outside Delaware and its immediate environs are pe-

ripheral in more ways than the geographical one and therefore need not be a factor in the family decision-making process. Even granting the truth of this does not dilute the
overlying larger truth, which is, simply, that individual family
members have taken to going their own way without consulting the rest of the family. There is no family master plan to
guide its members, be it in choice of career, choice of avocation, or choice of charitable endeavor. The side of the family
that faces the public is a solid front because the family is
loyal, because it is very private, and because public preconceptions would have the family cohesive.

"Anyone who has tried to raise money around here [in
Wilmington] knows the du Pont family is not an entity,"
Lammot du Pont Copeland, former company board chairman, once said. "There's no cohesion in the family whatso-
ever." That is the extreme view from the family side, but
given the public image opposite, it seems the appropriate one
to cite here.

The individuality of the family really took hold around the
turn of the century, when the family was peopled with more
than its share of larger-than-life folk who could not or would
not be squeezed into traditional family roles. The solidarity of
the family was badly dented, if not shattered, in 1915 by the
family feud that developed when Alfred I. took exception to
the manner by which Pierre had acquired T. Coleman's stock
in the company and sued. Family members were more or less
forced to take sides. They tried to hold the ill will of the feud
within the generation directly involved, but things were never
quite the same again. As the family and the company both
grew in proportions that were more geometric than arithmet-
ical, the needs and interests of both expanded and flared.
The company was no longer able to unify the family.

To a surprising degree, the du Ponts today are indifferent
toward family matters. They do not neglect their immediate
families, but things du Pont tend to hold less fascination for
them than for outsiders. Almost to a person, du Ponts say

they do not read the books and articles written about the family, and if they do, pay them little attention. No doubt part of this is due to the fact that recent tales about the du Ponts have been told by those the family considers idiots. Then too, the news the family has made lately doesn't always reflect flatteringly on the name. Young Lammot du Pont Copeland's bankruptcy, which the media called the largest personal bankruptcy ever filed, was a bit of news the family could have done without, for but one example.

Du Ponts seldom get together and talk about the family. Social gatherings are rarely clannish. With few exceptions, individual family members consider themselves individuals first and du Ponts second. They are proud of the family and its tradition, serious about what they see as family duties and obligations, but such things are instinctive more than obsessive, a part of the background fabric.

Many du Ponts want simply to be left alone. Even so public a figure as Irénée Jr., whose civic, charitable, Du Pont, and Christiana activities have made him perhaps the most publicly visible du Pont outside the governor, admits he finds any kind of publicity "embarrassing and offensive." He spent his first day of retirement canoeing on the Brandywine River that runs through his estate and camping out overnight—by himself. Shyness is a family trait Irénée's uncle, Pierre, once attributed to his great-grandmother's side of the family. "To be conspicuous in success or failure has been always distasteful," Pierre wrote.

Such proclivities as individuality were not, of course, absolute. Family groups would gather to discuss and decide immediate or specific concerns. The genealogy committee or the cemetery committee, for example, would hold meetings on a more or less regular basis on broad family matters. But they were broad in that they dealt with the whole family; they were specific in that they were not questions of policy, but ones of mechanical or logistical detail.

In another vein, H. Rodney Sharp III, whose grandmother

was a du Pont, remembered not long ago attending a dinner, probably in the late 1960s, at which nine family members gathered to discuss their careers. They all worked for the company at the time, and the idea was for each guest to talk about his job in terms he felt might be helpful to his cousins. The dinner was billed as the first of many. "It wasn't very successful," Sharp recalled. Of the nine only three still worked for the company at the end of 1973. The first dinner was the last.

The du Ponts are basically soloists when it comes to giving their money away, too. There are literally dozens of family foundations, the majority funded by one individual and administered by his heirs. Some are devoted to special projects. The Unidel Foundation funded by Amy du Pont to succor the University of Delaware is one example. Other, better-known examples include the formal gardens at Longwood, the American decorative arts collection at Winterthur, and the Eleutherian Mills-Hagley Foundation, which supports a business history library and museum. Some are strictly vehicles for charitable donations to such everyday causes as the United Fund. Longwood, with assets in the $150 million neighborhood, is much the largest. In just the branch of the family descended from Longwood's founder, Pierre du Pont, and his brothers and sisters, there are ten foundations listed in the Foundation Center directory with assets of $1 million or more. Their combined value is more than $250 million, and they are, once Longwood and Eleutherian Mills-Hagley have been subtracted, simply representative of the branch's foundation money. Other foundations have less than $1 million in assets; still others have almost no assets but make distributions annually amounting to hundreds of thousands of dollars. Other branches of the family have foundation setups of a similar nature, although Longwood, Pierre's group, is the richest these days, at least collectively.

For most of the family, dispensing dollars through foundations does not dispense the obligations. Worthy Wilmington-area charitable or civic agencies or institutions nearly all have a du Pont or two on their boards, and in some fields, du Ponts are recognized authorities. William K., for example, may have found sophomore year at the University of Virginia an insurmountable obstacle thanks to a somewhat cavalier approach to education, but now, as he nears forty, his life has taken a serious turn. He sits on a number of boards and councils dealing nationally with wildlife and conservation and was chairman of the Interior Department's national advisory council on the subject until he finally managed to have the council abolished. "Advisory councils don't do any good unless someone wants advice," du Pont explained.

Frolic Weymouth—his mother is a du Pont—became involved ten years ago in a concept of marrying art and environment and has raised some $5 million in that period to support the work of the Tri-County Conservancy, whose art adjunct, the Brandywine River Museum, is home for much N. C., Andrew, and Jamie Wyeth work and a haven (perhaps heaven) for name-droppers on show preview nights. The museum's home was purchased when Frolic forgot himself during an auction of the property, but that's another story for a later chapter.

While it would take a hardened cynic to argue that du Pont charities are self-indulgent and frivolous, some are unquestionably more trivial than others. Few du Ponts are so warmly loved or much admired today as Mrs. Emily du Pont, whose community concern is as broad and deep as was the concern of her late husband, Henry B. Jr., considered by many the last of the great movers and shakers in the family. But Mrs. du Pont, who was born a du Pont as well, must still wonder if she will ever live down the title bestowed on her as the result of an SPCA spaying program some years ago. She was dubbed "the mother of birth control for pets."

Another example involves S. Hallock du Pont and the weeping beech tree. Good, pre-Revolutionary weeping beeches are not a dime a dozen, and when Hallock found a particularly fine specimen—reputedly the largest in the Western Hemisphere—not too far away in Pennsylvania, he bought the plot of ground it stood on, tearing down the house and leaving the tree. He delighted in driving out to sit and look at it. After several years, he gave the lot and the tree to his Uncle Pierre's Longwood Gardens, which put a fence around the lot and opened it to the public as a spot on which to contemplate one of nature's marvels.

Hallock was the same fellow who upon hearing that Sergeant Alvin York, America's most famous World War I hero, was living destitute and ignored at home in Tennessee, set up a trust fund for him to allow his life to wind down in dignity. Hallock had been sixteen when York overran a German machine-gun nest and won the Congressional Medal of Honor.

As the du Pont family has dropped out of the company over the recent years, several paths have become well worn as individuals seek some appropriate form of self-expression. Aviation has attracted more than its share of the family. Literally dozens of du Ponts fly airplanes. Henry B. Jr.'s Atlantic Aviation has already been mentioned. Two of his contemporaries, brothers Richard C. and A. Felix Jr., became deeply involved. Richard was perhaps the nation's foremost authority on soaring before he was killed in a glider accident during World War II. Felix was a test pilot for Fokker Aircraft after General Motors bought the company and later was an investor in a helicopter company. In his early seventies, he still flies his own plane. Two younger du Ponts—Richard's son Kippy and E. Paul's son Lex—own and operate their own airfields in the Wilmington area. Another Richard, Hallock's son, was a commercial pilot for a time. In a similar line, although he seldom actually gets off the ground, must fall Brett Lunger, whose mother is a du Pont. He drives the Grand Prix auto racing circuit.

Gardening has been a du Pont family habit from the beginning. The original Eleuthère Irénée, the man who started the company, was an avid botanist. The gardens at Longwood, home of Pierre du Pont while he lived and now a public Eden, are world-renowned, and the antiques and decorative arts within Winterthur are strongly rivaled in their breathtaking qualities by the informal gardens without. It was not for nothing that Harry du Pont, who built the Winterthur museum collections, used to refer to himself as "the head gardener." The formal gardens at Nemours, the house that Alfred I. built, remind visitors of the splendor of Versailles. Lesser formal and informal gardens grace virtually all du Pont homes and make the annual Garden Day tours quick sellouts. National and local garden club boards have been peopled with du Ponts for years.

The museum business is another one toward which family members tend to gravitate. Frolic Weymouth's Brandywine River Museum, for one. Or John du Pont's natural history museum, a rather uninviting concrete box across the street from Winterthur whose exterior belies a delightful, wondrous inside. Perhaps the least well known of the family museums is a place in nearby Pennsylvania called Project 400, a maze of exhibits through which the visitor walks in about two hours, coming out—if he's been paying attention—with a new understanding of the impact of geography on man's development, particularly in America.

While the real presence of the du Pont family—as opposed to the reflected glory of its public image, a carry-over from more halcyon days—continues strongly to influence Wilmington and Delaware, the contributions made to state and community are more modest nowadays. The wealth of the individual family members is less, and therefore the obligation. The problems are bigger and defy one-family, let alone one-man, solutions. The slack that has developed between community problems and the family's ability to solve them has in part at least been taken up by the company. Today the difference between family and company is real.

Company employees may spend up to 20 per cent of their

work time in civic or charitable activities. State and local governments are staffed with Du Pont employees, retired, on leave, or on loan. All manner of public agencies borrow company personnel for specialized assignments and ad hoc committee work. The company employs about 24,000 people in the state, whose total population is only around 600,000. Those 24,000 represent 10 per cent of the state's employment rolls and a third of its manufacturing employment. The impact is inevitable.

Financial policy at the company plays as important a role in the community as does personnel policy. When Du Pont and its two antitrust offspring, Hercules and Atlas (now ICI), all decided to make bonus payments to employees in 1976—they had been eliminated in 1975—taxes paid on the bonuses increased state revenues $10 million. Total state revenues are roughly $400 million. Dividend policy can make a big difference, too. At the end of 1976 the Du Pont Company declared an extra dividend of $.50 a share. According to the company, 23,000 Delawareans own about 19 million shares, some 40 per cent of the outstanding stock. That's $9.5 million extra fattening Delaware wallets and promising more tax revenues, more spending, and general economic happiness. The devastating effect of cutting the dividend or passing up bonuses ought to be obvious. Because local foundations are mostly family foundations and therefore heavily invested in Du Pont and Christiana stock, dividend policy has an added consequence, affecting foundation income and the foundations' ability to fund the various agencies dependent on foundation grants.

In recent years some outsiders visiting Delaware have called sinister the preponderance of company influence on the state, especially where the visitors have adopted the popular misconception that the du Pont family still runs the company. Just too cozy, even feudal, an arrangement. In general, Delawareans are unimpressed with this view. They don't see the du Ponts and their family company as ever and always beyond reproach, but on the bottom line, the ink is black. On a net basis, du Pont influence in Delaware has been positive, they believe.

Suggest a workable alternative, company chairman Irving Shapiro responds to critics of company policy allowing employees to participate in public life. The company employee rolls constitute the state's biggest and richest talent pool. Take it away and what's left? Besides, the notion that Du Pont employees in public roles are automatically operating as company agents is childish nonsense, Shapiro contends. After all, personal integrity and a mind of one's own do not immediately disqualify applicants for Du Pont jobs, do they?

How fickle and fleeting are fame and fortune may be the sigh of a cliché master but it is not without its note of truth. The first fifty years of the twentieth century saw the du Pont family flourish as no other. There was even a small and perhaps self-generated boomlet on behalf of T. Coleman's candidacy for President. In 1929 Pierre paid 1/183 of the total revenues received by the U. S. Treasury from the tax payments of individuals. His brother Irénée spent about $125,000 a year just to run his second home, Xanadu, in Cuba. The family played a crucial role in the design and development of the interstate highway system, and without the efforts of their company, the atom bomb might never have figured as a factor in World War II. (No matter how you feel about nuclear war, producing that first bomb was a Herculean task.)

Gradually, however, the du Ponts have lost their grip. The process began, Irénée Jr. says, with the advent of the graduated income tax and "confiscatory" gift and inheritance taxes. Many consider the death of Pierre in 1954 as tolling the family knell. In his sixty years with the company, its assets grew from $12 million to $2.5 billion. Others mark the date as 1970, the year Henry Belin du Pont died. He was the last of the family with the inclination and resources to effect significant change on his own, but he was already something of an anachronism. Red tape—governmental, corporate, and familial—was stifling individual initiative, and the family fortune was being fragmented as it spread over ever larger numbers with the death of older du Ponts and the coming of age of succeeding generations. Standing alongside the heirs at estate-dividing time was, of course, the ubiquitous Internal Revenue Service.

For nearly 140 years, from the founding of the company in 1802 until World War II, the name du Pont was a prerequisite for holding the office of president in the family company. Since 1940 no one named du Pont has held that office, unless you count Lammot Copeland, whose middle name is du Pont.

The family has not let go entirely. As late as 1960 William du Pont, Jr., paid more than $4 million in income taxes, although he did so not without quibbling about a $32,000 item over which he went to court against the IRS. Ruly Carpenter has taken over operating the Philadelphia Phillies from his father and after years of a severe talent drought, has turned the club into a pennant contender. Ruly is still on the light side of forty. S. Hallock du Pont, Jr., was appointed national commander of the Civil Air Patrol in 1970, a brigadier general while still in his thirties. Young Tony du Pont appears on his way toward making a mark in the aerospace industry; his proud parents contend that a new executive jet recently on the market is basically taken from Tony's design. And Pete is Delaware's governor.

But arguments such as Ferdinand Lundberg makes in his book that the rich are getting richer and more powerful do not survive close scrutiny of, or even a passing glance at, the du Ponts. There may be faster ways to redistribute the wealth, but the current method works. Most people, including some family members, believe the process through which the du Ponts are now going is healthy and normal, socially and economically. The standard in this country is "shirtsleeves to shirtsleeves" in three generations. The du Ponts living today represent the sixth, seventh, and eighth generations. The younger Rockefellers, for comparison, are fourth and fifth generation.

The phenomenon of declining achievement is not particularly mysterious. It has to do with motivation. When you have everything from birth, your acquisitive instincts and competitive drive tend to be retarded. You are afforded the luxury of doing what you want, usually urged by parents only to be good at, to do your best with whatever you choose. And there isn't any hurry. The softness of those early years doesn't help the toughening process later on. Besides, the question arises: What's the point of being tough?

One du Pont in-law has a theory about the shyness of the present-day members of the du Pont family. He is coming to think that the reservation, the lack of communication in the family, veils an inadequacy, a shortage of intellect. "Today's kids are being left a legacy of mediocrity," he says. "They're encouraged to do their own thing but only as long as they don't make waves." The avarice of earlier generations is manifested in the family's penchant for collecting things privately—collections no one ever sees, like Irénée Sr.'s gem collection or S. Hallock's old spice chests. This same in-law views many family father-daughter relationships as "almost incestuous" and suggests that some sons in the family have overreacted in various ways to the legends of their fathers' exploits, particularly with ladies and other women. From within the family, this is perhaps as unsympathetic a view as one could find.

Another view belongs to James Q. du Pont, who wrote and narrated a film about the du Ponts used by the Du Pont Company for public and employee relations purposes. Said he: "Du Ponts have been, I should say, almost passionately fond of education for their children. As a wise and beautiful cousin of ours once said to me, 'Many of our du Pont men are sort of obtuse.' We crave education because most of us realize we're not what you would call brilliant. Other characteristics help to offset this lack of brilliance. One of them is loyalty, a sort of blind admiring for each other and the family when the last cards start to fall. Another is domesticity. A cousin once said, 'You know, Jim, some of you du Pont guys are so domestic you're almost boring.' Another is determination or stubbornness. And we have been dreamers and schemers. I've been brought up on schemes."

Pigeonholing the family just doesn't work. Du Ponts today are coupon clippers, politicians, drunks, working stiffs, artists, athletes, pilots, conservationists, hangers-around, investors, collectors, sheriffs, dreamers, farmers, appliance dealers, car salesmen, lawyers, horsemen, bankrupts, sailors, actors, philanthropists, housewives, scientists, executives, cosmopolites, and provincials. People. People with a leg up on the rest of us as they begin life, perhaps, but the head start is hardly insurmountable.

In an important way, the du Ponts are more real to other people as symbols than as people. Delaware's young U.S. senator, Joseph R. Biden, Jr., remembers when he was just getting into politics in 1969, running for county council and attending one of those meet-the-candidate coffees in a suburban development south of Wilmington. The Democratic committeeman for the district had been urging Biden to hit the property tax issue and how the tax structure forced little guys to pay full freight but allowed rich guys with big estates to get off relatively lightly. Biden did his best politician's shuffle when the question came up. Something along the lines of "Well, if that's something that maybe ought to be looked into, we'll sure see about looking into it." Whereupon a woman piped up and said she certainly hoped Biden wouldn't do anything that might force those wealthy folks over in Greenville (mostly du Ponts) to sell their estates. There was some nodding going on. Obviously the lady wasn't all alone feeling that way. Biden thought he knew, but asked why she felt that way. She told him because on weekends her family would get in the car and go driving through the Greenville countryside, looking at those big houses, escaping, if only vicariously, their own dreary existence for a while, dreaming about what went on and what sort of grand people lived there and remembering—hoping—that in America, with a little luck

and some hard work . . . Biden would readily admit that in the bald telling, the story is hopelessly maudlin, naïve, and corny. But he believes that beneath a surface cynicism toward the system and the establishment in this country, the people nourish dreams of glory. As food for those dreams, the du Ponts are more real, perhaps, to the average Delawarean than they are as, say, fathers and mothers.

The history of the du Pont family differs rather strikingly from that of other wealthy American families. In most cases, it was the work of one or two ancestors that built the family fortune and did it more or less within a single generation. John D. Rockefeller, Sr., for example, or Andrew Carnegie, or J. P. Morgan, or John Jacob Astor. The list is nearly as long as the list of multi-millionaires in the country. The du Ponts, on the other hand, spent more than half a century piling up debt and struggling to keep their business afloat. For another half century or more, they rolled along comfortably but certainly not in the fabulously wealthy strata where ostentation was often mistaken for taste and money was something you made and spent but other people worked for.

When the family fortune finally soared during the post-World War I era, its impact on the family and the family's reactions tended to reflect these earlier conditions. The family had, for example, developed deep roots in the land along the banks of the Brandywine River just north and west of Wilmington. They'd lived and worked and died there for more than a century, and during much of that time, they were a rather isolated clan. Intermarriage was not infrequent. In fact, at one point it became so popular that General Henry du Pont issued a patriarchal ban against it, a ban first broken by his younger son. They belonged to the Brandywine and by extension, to Wilmington and Delaware; or, it could be argued, the Brandywine and environs belonged to the du Ponts. The family has always concentrated its philanthropic efforts in what some might call a provincially narrow area. The du Ponts called it home, and after a time an attitude of let-the-du-Ponts-do-it developed that ensured there would always be a need for du Pont generosity.

Because the family and its company had a long spawning period, the family was already a large one when the real sudden riches began to flow. No one du Pont could take all the credit or blame. No one du Pont could direct the spending of the fortune. The family had already begun to lose its cohesion and singleness of purpose and direction.

These factors, plus a hereditary mistrust of the spotlight, have allowed the du Ponts to remain well in the shadows over the years. The scions of other rich families have fed on fame, and perhaps earlier du Ponts did, too. But there is not much sustenance in reflected glory, and eventually you look elsewhere. The family is getting bigger. A du Pont is born every week. The fortune seems to be getting smaller. How long, one wonders, before du Pont jars no special associations, stirring vague memories of past grandeur perhaps but generally provoking the same reactions at its mention in America as it does now in France, where du Pont is nearly as common as Smith or Jones is in the United States?

Chapter Two

The Move to America

Traditionally—and when one discusses the du Pont family, tradition is not to be lightly regarded—the story of America's richest family begins with Pierre Samuel du Pont de Nemours, the man who in part survived and in part inspired the French Revolution before finally deciding the opportunities in the infant United States exceeded those in France. The decision to move his family across the Atlantic did not come easily to du Pont. He was devoted to France, convinced her former glory would soon return, and hopeful he would share in it, as he had shared in the promise, the agony, and the uncertainty of the years surrounding the revolution. But life in the France of the waning years of the eighteenth century was at best unsettling for a man who had been as prominent and controversial as du Pont, and the Land of Opportunity beckoned irresistibly. Du Pont had always been—an important part of him, at least—a dreamer, and America stirred his imagination.

To begin with Pierre is probably to start a generation early in the history of the family that turned a gunpowder mill into what became in the 1920s the largest concentration of industrial control in the world in the hands of one family. But the temptation is strong nonetheless.

The facile justification is that it was Pierre, after all, who made the decision that brought this branch of the du Ponts to America. Furthermore his connections in high places undoubtedly aided his son's early efforts in the powder business, and the family was very close, with the father exercising considerable influence on the actions and ideals of his sons.

But the real reason for beginning with Pierre is that the man was a fascinating character who played an important role

in a number of affairs that significantly changed the politics
and geography of his day.

Du Pont's father was a Paris watchmaker for whom dreaming was a waste of valuable time bordering on the sinful. Pierre
Samuel was born on December 14, 1739, and his early childhood was something less than idyllic. As an infant he was
farmed out to a nurse, who turned out to be without milk,
feeding him barely enough to keep him alive. A second nurse
was employed. She had a husband sold on the nutritional
qualities of brandy, and soon Pierre was amusing the fellow's
friends by displaying a precocious taste for the stuff.

It was not a life destined to build football players, and
Pierre was weak and thin. At age five, he fell and broke his
nose, an accident of which he was reminded the rest of his
life whenever he looked in a mirror. Finally, as a teen-ager
he contracted smallpox while nursing a victim of the disease,
nearly dying, and leaving himself permanently myopic in his
right eye.

As a scholar, Pierre excelled to the extent that his teacher
hailed him as a prodigy and put him on exhibition, reciting
and answering questions. He was a whiz, which left his father
totally unimpressed. It was time, the old man argued, past
time, in fact, that Pierre learn the watchmaker's trade. His
mother's wiles allowed Pierre some respite from the rigors
and boredom of watchmaking, but his father was a tough task-
master.

The mother, Anne Alexandrine de Montchanin, had been
forced by the impoverishment of her family, which had long
been allied with important French nobility, to work at the
watchmaking trade herself, helping two brothers, but her
genteel heritage was not lost on her and she instilled in her
young son visions of a better life. She was very ambitious for
him and convinced that education was the key to unlocking
important doors. "I owe to my mother all of the little that
I am worth," Pierre wrote in 1792.

When Pierre's mother died in 1756, although still a young

woman, the father-son relationship deteriorated still further. The mother's last wish was that the two men learn to live with each other. It went unfulfilled. Life for Pierre became rapidly so miserable that he apparently decided to end it, but a servant found him about to do himself in with a knife, took it away from him, and reported all to the father. That understanding soul thereupon beat Pierre soundly.

Pierre left home; he was not an instant success. Desperate, he returned to his father's home, quietly tolerating the scorn and abuse his father heaped upon him. In his spare time he dabbled in things intellectual—including a brief fling at the study of medicine—and displayed an uncommonly chivalrous attitude toward the fair sex, including Nicole Charlotte Marie Louise Le Dée de Rencourt. His growing attachment to this particular lady caused her guardian to hasten an arranged marriage for the girl with an older man. Pierre objected, the woman he was growing to love pleaded, and the guardian finally agreed to give Pierre two years in which to establish himself sufficiently to prove he could support a wife.

Meanwhile, du Pont was displaying an increasingly facile bent for the intricacies of economic philosophy and developing notions that eventually led to his association with Dr. François Quesnay, physician to Madame de Pompadour and early articulator of the physiocratic doctrine that all wealth derived from nature, or more specifically, land. Pierre wrote two pamphlets rebutting a controversial tax proposal in someone else's earlier pamphlet; Quesnay was impressed and introduced him to Madame de Pompadour. Life appeared on the upbeat. Quesnay urged du Pont to study and write about the grain trade, liked the work, and suggested it be dedicated to Madame de Pompadour, who died before it could be published. With her died Quesnay's influence at court and whatever promise of a bright future du Pont's association with Quesnay might have held. The grain study was published and acclaimed. One whose interest was stirred was a man named Anne—Anne Robert Jacques Turgot, later Comptroller General of Finances under Louis XVI and undoubtedly the man who most influenced du Pont's later life.

His reputation now on the rise, du Pont was commissioned to do an economic study of the Soissons province. Turgot asked him to do a similar study for Limoges. The money was hopelessly inadequate, but du Pont was eager anyway. However, he still needed a regular job if he was going to marry Miss Le Dée, and time was running out. He was offered the editorship of a journal dealing with the commercial and financial aspects of agriculture, took it in September of 1765, and married the following January after some heavy persuasion finally swayed both the bride's father and his own, from whom he had made a clean, more or less friendly break upon deciding to marry two years earlier, but whose approval was needed in the interests of good form.

The next eight years, du Pont busied himself with a number of projects, not the least of which was the fathering of his two sons—Victor Marie in 1767 and Eleuthère Irénée in 1771. Turgot was the godfather for the latter and is responsible for the name; "in honor of liberty and peace," was the way he put it. Between the births of his sons, he visited Voltaire, with whom he had exchanged a few letters.

When Louis XVI ascended the throne of France, he brought Turgot in, first as Minister of the Navy, then as Comptroller General of Finances, perhaps the most important position in the government. In 1774 Turgot named du Pont Inspector General of Commerce. In 1776 Turgot was dismissed, and du Pont headed for his place in the country, Bois des Fosses, although he continued to get paid as Inspector General of Commerce.

By 1784 life appeared to be agreeing with the du Pont family. Late the year before, Louis XVI had granted Pierre a patent of nobility, which carried with it a grant of a coat of arms. Du Pont had worked diligently for freer trade among France, Great Britain, and the United States and had kept Vergennes, France's Minister of Foreign Affairs, closely informed about his correspondence with an influential Englishman, James Hutton, who was also a close friend of Benjamin Franklin's. There has been some speculation that Hutton's letters were English government-inspired peace feelers and may have, indirectly at least, influenced the conclusion of the Treaty of Paris of 1783 marking the end of the American War of Independence. At any rate, Vergennes apparently interceded with the king on du Pont's behalf. Du Pont, now with his own coat of arms, was evidently quite impressed with the standards of duty and honor he felt went with the privileges of nobility. To accept the honor, du Pont had to take an oath that his religion was Catholic, Apostolic, and Roman, adjectives that described adequately enough his family's religion but hardly did justice to his own.

His religious roots were deeply Huguenot. He was the great-great-great-grandson of Jehan du Pont (1538–1604), one of three brothers who left Brittany to settle in Rouen in the middle of the sixteenth century. Abraham du Pont was Jehan's son. He married a rich girl whose family, in a quaint historical coincidence, was interested in dyes for yarn and cloth, a business that many years later would help the Du Pont Company to prosper. Jean du Pont was Abraham's second son, and Jean had two sons, Abraham (1658–1731) and Jean II. This second Abraham was the founder of the South Carolina branch of the du Pont family. Jean II was Samuel's father and Pierre's grandfather. Jehan and his direct descendants were Huguenots.

Formal religion did not, however, play a particularly important role in Pierre's life, and a slight bending of the truth for the sake of nobility apparently caused no violent pangs of conscience.

Adding to the family's peace of mind in those early days of 1784 was the prospering of their country home, Bois des Fosses, under Mme. du Pont's able management. The family was not wildly rich, but they were comfortable, a pleasant change.

In less than a month, the pleasure drained from their lives. In early August, du Pont's wife complained of feeling ill. It didn't appear serious, and in a letter to her husband in Paris on August 25, she did not even mention her illness. On September 3, at the age of forty-one, she died.

Irénée was now thirteen, time, his father considered, for him to receive the sword his new status as the son of nobility gave him the right to carry. In a formal ceremony that would seem ludicrous today but was undoubtedly not unusual then, Pierre invested his son with a sword, and Irénée and Victor pledged always to look after each other. It may have been, in part at least, this ceremony that Irénée remembered in later years when time and time again he came to the aid of his brother, as unlike himself as night from day and a man seemingly cursed with a reverse Midas touch.

For the next few years the father continued to play an important role in the commercial affairs of France, and in the fateful year of 1789 was a member of the Estates-General and the National Assembly, signing the famous Oath of the Tennis Court at Versailles, in which the signers vowed not to disband the Assembly until France had a constitution. He served as president of the Assembly for two weeks in August 1790. It was in this period that he began to use the "de Nemours" after his name to distinguish himself from several other du Ponts who were also members of the Assembly.

Du Pont's strong belief in the merits of a constitutional monarchy placed him in a precarious position during the coming years, provoking the ire of both royalty and the radical elements of the revolution. When, in August 1792, he was among a small band that defended Louis XVI from an invasion of the Tuileries by the Paris mob—escaping with Irénée only by marching off in the pretense he was part of a regular patrol—du Pont became a liability to the republican element and was forced into hiding. While lying low, he kept busy writing various tracts and pieces, including the beginnings of an autobiography.

In 1794 the order for his arrest was issued and in July he was taken prisoner. According to the account of a granddaughter, Eleuthera du Pont Smith, Fate intervened to save his life. Du Pont was taken to the wrong prison. The very next night, the mob stormed the prison where he should have been, killing the inmates. Some days later the mistake was discovered and du Pont was moved to La Force, where once again his life was in jeopardy. The fall of Robespierre on July 27 allowed him to escape the guillotine. Four weeks later he was released from prison.

The following year he remarried—to Françoise Robin Poivre—and was chosen a member of the Council of Ancients, serving in the summer of 1797 as president of the council for a month. In September another coup d'état resulted in his arrest along with Irénée. The two were released after one night in jail, and du Pont resigned from the council.

It may have been that final night in jail that finally convinced du Pont that France no longer held the promise for him it once had.

Du Pont's sons had not been idle during these hectic years. Not long after his mother's death, Irénée began to show an interest in the manufacture of gunpowder, writing an account on the subject for his father in 1785. Two years later he became a student at the government powder agency of which the famous chemist Lavoisier was director. He then went to work at the government powder plant at Essonnes. In 1791 his father went into the printing business, which Irénée later managed until the family left for America. In November of 1791 he married Sophie Madeleine Dalmas.

Victor began working for his father in 1784 in the Bureau of Commerce, took some time out to tour French manufacturing centers, and late in 1787 became unofficial private secretary to the French minister to the United States. After witnessing the inauguration of George Washington as the new nation's first President, Victor returned to France, where in 1791 he was appointed aide-de-camp to General Lafayette,

commander of the Garde Nationale in Paris. Shortly thereafter he returned to the United States with France's new minister. Back in France in 1793, he married the next year a
marquis's daughter, Gabrielle Joséphine de La Fite de Pelleport. Once again he returned to the United States, and in
1797 was appointed consul general at Philadelphia. Franco-
American relations were growing strained, and he returned the
following year to France.

The planning for and the talk of moving to America was
almost exclusively the father's. Although his elder son had
spent several years in the United States and might well have
been able to offer valuable counsel, there is no indication his
advice was sought. Pierre's friend Thomas Jefferson might also
have been useful in consultation, but again, Pierre was convinced he knew what he was doing and needed no help. His
time was spent cleaning up his own somewhat chaotic affairs
and collaring potential investors for Du Pont de Nemours
Père Fils et Cie., the family company through which Pierre
planned to make his family and his investors rich beyond
imagination.

Pierre planned to capitalize his company at between two
hundred and four hundred shares, selling them for 10,000
francs each. It is a measure of his unswerving optimism that
at one point he drew up a list of likely investors that claimed
three hundred shares were spoken for, even while admitting
that earlier "commitments" had already fallen through.
When the family finally sailed for the United States, Pierre
had managed to raise a few more than 200,000 francs.

It was clear even before the du Ponts weighed anchor that
Pierre's grand scheme to start a new society—Pontiana—based
on his physiocratic principles would have to be drastically
scaled down, postponed, or abandoned completely. Even with
the 56,000 acres of Kentucky land turned over to the company
by the Parisian banker, Jacques Bidermann, the company was
underfunded. Du Pont was undeterred.

On October 2, 1799, du Pont, his two sons, two daughters-in-law, five grandchildren, and several other relatives set sail for New York aboard the *American Eagle*. Her name may have been the most auspicious aspect of this eighty-four-foot ship, whose captain agreed to take the du Ponts at reduced fares after Victor had managed to secure the release of the vessel, captured two years earlier by the French and held in the port of La Rochelle. There was not enough money adequately to repair the ship and her seaworthiness was open to speculation.

Luckily for du Pont's peace of mind, his new wife had gone over several months earlier as an advance guard, primarily to line up a home for the family. The voyage of the *American Eagle* was no vacation cruise. As a later Pierre S. du Pont—he who is generally credited with the making of the modern Du Pont Company—wrote in a letter to a cousin more than one hundred years after the trip: "As the vessel was only eighty-four feet long, it was not equipped with some of the luxuries known to the *Normandie* and the *Queen Mary* of recent years."

Among the missing luxuries was food. Off course most of the time, the ship quickly fell behind schedule. Twice, starvation on the high seas was avoided when passing ships stopped to reprovision the *American Eagle*. Victor was in charge of meat, killing whatever rats he could find and insisting they made very good eating. His father was in charge of soup, varying the menu as best he could. Sometimes he'd scrape the lard from barrels being broken up for firewood and make lard soup. Other times he would gather up the remains of the beans stored on board for the pigs and make bean soup. It was not exactly his fault that the infants on board refused to eat it, and the mothers cried at the sight of the worms rising to the surface during cooking.

In all, a grim trip, with little more than the father's unflaggingly buoyant spirits to keep the family afloat.

The voyage took roughly a month longer than it had taken Columbus to reach the New World more than three hundred years earlier, and when the ship finally did sight land, it was about two hundred miles north of course. The du Ponts got off in Newport, Rhode Island, not New York City.

The first of them got off the night of January 3, 1800. The next morning the rest of the party disembarked, but the day that is celebrated as the anniversary of the family's coming to America is New Year's, the first day of a new century in a new world. On that day they first sighted land. It is a part of this legend that the du Ponts, without a square meal in months, knocked on the door of the first house they came to, found no one home, the door open, the dining table heaped with the makings of a robust meal, and helped themselves, leaving a gold piece and a note of thanks. They had sailed the day after Victor's thirty-second birthday and had celebrated, if that's the word, the father's sixtieth birthday while still more than two weeks from landing. Irénée was not yet twenty-nine.

They must have made quite a spectacle. The trip had surely taken its toll on their appearance; yet their baggage, which was substantial and included such items as pianos, bespoke if not wealth at least considerable comfort. It would have been difficult to guess the father's age. Bald, with rounded shoulders, and suffering from gout, Pierre looked older than his years. But his agile mind, his tireless energy, his infectious optimism were those of a young man. He must have been something of an enigma to those who had known him in France, sometimes brilliant, not infrequently bombastic, unswerving in his loyalty to the principles he believed in, almost mechanical in his attention to tedious detail and his capacity for work, yet with a streak of romanticism in him that often led him to gallant, courageous action.

His two sons stood in stark contrast to each other. The older was tall, handsome, charming. He had in times past frustrated his father by reporting in detail on the parties and night life he had encountered when his mission had been to report on the economy of an area. He probably would have been well suited to the career in diplomacy for which he was being groomed during his early adulthood.

Irénée, with a red birthmark on one of his cheeks and his teeth already falling out, had none of the glamour of his older brother. He was a serious, hard-working type, devoted to his family, supremely conscientious, and not a little boring, if only because he never seemed to have the time or the inclination for witty small talk. He was an unlikely candidate for destiny's call.

By mid-January the family had moved from Newport to a house Pierre's wife had purchased several weeks earlier in New Jersey. Victor, who knew more than anyone else in the family about business in America, moved to New York, where a company office was established. Then he went on a southerly tour to locate what was expected to be the main office near the new capital of the country, finally settling on Alexandria, Virginia.

The father had heard from his friend Thomas Jefferson, and was more than ever convinced that now was not the time to get into the real estate development business. Jefferson wrote of the wild land speculations that made such ventures highly risky propositions, and there seemed but one course to pursue—the commercial brokerage business. Unfortunately Franco-American relations were deteriorating at that point, and business was scarce. To make the profits the du Ponts needed to finance the father's heady schemes would require a volume of business far greater than that being generated in those early days.

By late 1800 Papa du Pont's visions for the business had crystallized into a list of seven specific proposals, mostly involving trade with France, America, and Santo Domingo. That fall Napoleon had signed a treaty with America and relations were looking up. All that was now needed was some additional capital and the signing of some agreements.

Irénée was not a significant part of his father's grand plans. He had not been in America long when a hunting trip with a

French colonel who had served under Lafayette during the American Revolution and chosen to stay in America proved the shortcomings of American gunpowder. Curious as to why his gun had so frequently misfired, Irénée visited a gunpowder mill and found the answer. The production methods were years behind those he had studied in France a dozen years ago. He could make better powder than this without half trying.

Although a gunpowder mill did not exactly fit into the Big Picture as his father saw it, Irénée argued his case successfully enough to have an eighth venture added to the list of prospective business of Du Pont de Nemours Père Fils et Cie. The monumental nature of that offhand decision to devote a fraction of the family capital to the gunpowder business was surely lost on Irénée's father and, undoubtedly, Irénée himself.

Almost precisely a year after they'd landed, Irénée and Victor set sail to return to France. Both hoped to raise money for their respective businesses. Irénée also hoped to learn the latest methods for making gunpowder and to buy the machinery for his mill. Victor hoped to drum up some business as well as some money. That Irénée's trip was shorter and far more successful than his brother's was, in retrospect at least, a sign of things to come.

For Pierre Samuel, however, it was a sign that his own special talents and associations were required in France to further the family company's prospects. Where Victor had failed, his father would succeed, he was sure. Pierre may have been a bit homesick, and besides, his friend Madame de Staël was writing him enticing letters about how Napoleon might consider him for a place in the French Senate if only he would make himself available by returning to France. Pierre hesitated. Would his return to France look as if he was running out on his American plans? By early 1802 du Pont made up his mind: He would return to France, at least for a few months.

Victor set up his own company to run the commercial business, with his father promising a loan from the parent company, whose offices would move with Pierre to Paris. The powder company had already been set up with $36,000—$24,000 from the family company and $12,000 from outside investors, including two Americans, Archibald McCall of Philadelphia and Peter Bauduy of Wilmington, Delaware, where Irénée finally settled to build his mill.

When his friend Jefferson learned that Pierre was planning a return to France, he decided to entrust him with some papers and a letter to the American ambassador to France on the subject of Louisiana, which was rapidly becoming a ticklish one in the United States. Jefferson's attitude was almost bellicose as he warned that America would not tolerate any efforts to limit access to New Orleans and indeed mentioned war as the inevitable result of any attempt by Napoleon to occupy the territory.

At this crucial juncture, Pierre probably made his most valuable contribution to the course of world events, suggesting that the United States negotiate to buy New Orleans rather than fight over it. Later, when the American ambassador expressed pessimism about the progress of those negotiations, du Pont wrote Jefferson a reassuring letter, which appears to have been at least partially responsible for Jefferson's sending James Monroe to France to further negotiations.

When suddenly, almost casually, Napoleon inquired what the United States might be willing to pay for the entire territory, it soon became just a matter of working out the details. Fortunately for the United States, Napoleon was not then in a position to further his schemes of empire, and instead of war, the United States got the Louisiana Territory—with a valuable assist from du Pont.

As Pierre and wife sailed for France in June of 1802, Irénée was already hard at work. It would be nearly two years before the first powder was actually manufactured. Irénée was starting from scratch; powder mills were not built overnight. Had he known the anguish with which the remainder of his life would be filled, he might have tried another vocation. As it was, gunpowder was an odd business for this shy, conservative man to be in. His love of nature was such that on his passport under "Profession" he had written, "botaniste." He loved gardens, trees, all things that grew, and this love was a legacy he left to the du Pont family of succeeding generations as surely as was the gunpowder business.

Although it probably never occurred to him, Irénée was lucky to be alive. Fate first intervened on his behalf back in 1785, when his interest in botany fostered a desire to join an expedition to the Pacific being mounted by Jean-François de Galaup, comte de La Pérouse. His father at first agreed to let him go, but had second thoughts about the prospect of being separated from his son for so long and rescinded his permission. The expedition ship wrecked near the Santa Cruz Islands. Some survivors were massacred by natives; others apparently escaped, but no member of the expedition was ever heard from again.

Just a couple of years after that expedition left without him, Irénée was visiting Essonnes, the French Government gunpowder works, with the Lavoisiers. The workers were refusing to go into the plant because a series of explosions had recently rocked the place. Lavoisier went to the plant himself to encourage the workers. Irénée went with him. When it came time to break for lunch, Irénée wanted to stay in the plant, but Mrs. Lavoisier insisted he join the rest of the party. As they finished eating, a big explosion once more ripped the powder plant.

Surviving the French Revolution as his father's loyal son required its share of good fortune, and completing the voyage aboard the *American Eagle* must have seemed a tenuous proposition at best on occasion. The next thirty-two years would prove no easier.

Irénée was soon on what one company biographer has called "a treadmill of debt." The $36,000 he started with—an amount that wouldn't even put out the Du Pont Company's internal phone book today—wasn't enough. Even before the first powder was made, Irénée was forced to borrow $21,000 from banks in Philadelphia, and when the business began to prosper, it required still more infusions of capital. If Irénée did not increase his production capabilities to meet the demands of incoming orders, those orders would simply be filled elsewhere. The powder Irénée made may have been the best around, but there was plenty of competition.

His brother Victor did not make life easier for Irénée. In 1805 Victor's New York business went under. First the French Government refused to honor drafts of the firm to pay for provisioning French troops and ships in Santo Domingo. Then Jérôme Bonaparte, Napoleon's younger brother, borrowed money from the company to indulge his taste for extravagance. The loans were not repaid. An offer of a loan from Talleyrand came too late to save the firm.

Victor moved to rural upstate New York, ran a general store for a while, and finally moved to Wilmington, where he settled next to his brother on the banks of the Brandywine River. It was late summer 1809. Till now, Victor's troubles had caused Irénée not much more than worry and concern; now they would cost Irénée financially.

Despite his own financial difficulties, Irénée helped set his brother up in a woolen manufacturing business. Four years later Victor branched out into the cotton field. Neither venture enjoyed conspicuous success. Irénée never begrudged his brother anything. Indeed, he seemed genuinely delighted to have the family—at least the American part of it—united on the Brandywine.

By 1810 Irénée's powder works employed thirty-six men, and a visiting Baltimore newspaperman was sufficiently impressed to rave: "He has built a beautiful village. . . . He is a common benefactor to the country about him and beloved by the numerous artisans he employs." Writers on du Pont, family and company, have seldom since lavished such praise unmixed with criticism.

As early as 1802 Irénée's correspondence reveals a preference for French workers. Part of the reason is, of course, that Irénée spoke little or no English. One of the primary factors in his selecting the Brandywine banks on which to build his mill was the small but established French colony already in residence. Irénée felt American workers were generally good but the high price of labor made it difficult to keep them for any length of time, whereas Frenchmen were paid "much more than they could ever hope to get in France" and were therefore more likely to stick around.

Despite the dangerous nature of their work, powder workers were not paid significantly more than workers in other trades. An 1830 study showed the average Delaware worker earned $234 a year. About 25 per cent of Du Pont's employees received more than $200. However, another study, this one in 1810, showed that Du Pont workers had savings that averaged between six months' and a year's wages.

In an undated memorandum, Irénée writes that all workers with families have "from us a house free of rent, a good garden and cow pasture." A few workers even managed to save enough to buy their own farms or migrate west. Savings in the $100 to $200 range aren't too impressive—especially when the workday is twelve hours in summer, nine in winter—but prices were different then, too. Rum, for example, went for $.84 a gallon.

In general, the early du Ponts got along well with their employees. They were neighbors. Their children played together. And when explosions scarred the tranquil Brandywine, the du Ponts were not off somewhere safe sipping brandy. They worked side by side with their employees. Still, altercations did occur. Irénée was once fined $15 for punching a man in a tavern. The man, a former employee, apparently had been trying to lure Du Pont workers and manufacturing secrets away from the Brandywine.

If Irénée generally got along well with his workers, he was less fortunate with some of his shareholders. As time dragged on and the profits of the mill continued to be plowed back into the business, some of his investors grew restless. Two in particular gave him trouble. One was his stepsister, Madame Bureaux de Pusy. The other was Peter Bauduy, his disaffected partner who had become over the years hopelessly disillusioned—as was Irénée—by the relationship between the partners.

Madame de Pusy had become a stockholder in the powder company when, in 1811, Pierre folded the parent company, dividing its stock in the powder works—its only live asset—among the parent stockholders, of whom Madame de Pusy was one, having inherited her husband's stock on his death in 1806. Pierre, attempting naturally enough to put the best possible face on the dissolution of the parent company, had apparently exaggerated the powder company's present worth to Madame de Pusy, who came to America in 1811 determined to find out why the dividends had not been accruing. Irénée's books were not in the best shape at that time because he was busy with other things, like manufacturing powder, but he wanted to do the best he could by his stepsister and put an accountant to work right away. The task of reconciling Pierre's figures on the powder company with his own proved more substantial than Irénée had anticipated, and Madame de Pusy was forced to cool her heels longer than she wanted.

She became easy prey for Bauduy's gossip, which was given further credibility by letters Victor's wife wrote friends in Philadelphia describing her brother-in-law's great successes. After having been enormously helpful to Irénée in the early going, Bauduy had fallen out with Irénée over Bauduy's precise role in the company. Irénée believed Bauduy was a silent partner and that the major decisions of the company were Irénée's alone. Bauduy didn't see it that way. By 1811 the two partners were constantly at each other's throats, and Bau-

duy seldom let an opportunity to criticize Irénée slip by unused.

By 1813 the situation had so deteriorated that Pierre wrote
his two sons threatening to sue them because he felt they
were holding out on the stockholders of the parent company.
In public, Pierre continued to defend the actions of his sons.
Nonetheless, this private threat must have hurt to the quick,
especially Irénée.

It was a bad time. Irénée had pledged his credit to help
Victor start the woolen mill, and while he agreed to take care
of Madame de Pusy's immediate financial needs, raising any
large sums to buy out or pay off dissatisfied stockholders was
out of the question.

When in the fall of 1813 Irénée's daughter Victorine and
Bauduy's son Ferdinand were married, it appeared a reconciliation might be reached. But the Bauduy boy contracted
pneumonia just three weeks after the marriage and died.

The next year Jacques Bidermann, the Paris banker who
had been the largest outside stockholder in the parent company, grew worried enough about his investment that he sent
his son, Antoine, to Wilmington for a firsthand report. This
move may have saved the company. The young Bidermann
was quick to understand the vast problems facing Irénée and
the competent way in which Irénée had been dealing with
them. He wrote his father that they had a potential gold mine
on their hands. Even Madame de Pusy's ruffled feathers were
somewhat smoothed, and she returned to France, still dissatisfied but far more quietly so.

Madame de Pusy never was able to understand that the
profits credited to her shares had been reinvested in the business.

The measure of strain under which Irénée labored is nowhere more poignantly described than in one of his own letters, written on June 20, 1814: "I have spent my life here
building up a very difficult industry. My disappointments
have given me an habitual dullness and a melancholy that

unfits me for society. . . . I now owe $60,000. . . . My debts amount to far more than my profits." Talking about his frequent trips to Philadelphia to renew his notes with banks there, Irénée described himself as "a prisoner on parole who must show himself to the police every month."

The War of 1812 had been good for business. Fixed assets of the company rose from $42,750 at the end of 1809 to $106,300 at the end of 1815. Earlier that year, Bauduy was bought out, and the young Bidermann took his place in the company. In June the mill experienced its first fatal explosion, with nine workers losing their lives, but even this great tragedy could not change the fact that things were looking up.

Back in France, Papa du Pont was having his last fling in French government. The string had just about run out on Napoleon in early 1814, and in April he was deposed. Talleyrand brought his friend du Pont into the provisional government he and his associates were setting up and made him secretary-general, a title rather more impressive than the bookkeeping and document-certifying duties that went with it. Du Pont signed the decree deposing Napoleon. The Bourbon restoration was nearly complete. It lasted less than a year. In February 1815 Napoleon, taking advantage of the general unrest in France, escaped from Elba and headed back to Paris.

Du Pont didn't wait for him. His duties with the provisional government may have lasted only two weeks and his acceptance of favors from the restored monarchy could hardly be termed greedy, but the likelihood that Napoleon would overlook such things was remote. Du Pont determined to return to America. He was delayed for a while in Le Havre, but Napoleon was too busy to worry about him and he sailed March 30 without incident.

Never a robust physical specimen, du Pont was still surprisingly vigorous at the age of seventy-five when he rejoined his sons, who were, despite his recent accusations against them, delighted to see him again. For two years he played the role of family patriarch and played it well. Then in July 1817, on the night of the sixteenth, he awakened to a great commotion coming from the gunpowder works toward the river below his bedroom window. The charcoal house—charcoal was a key ingredient—was burning. If the fire reached the powder magazines . . . Over the protests of his family, the old man joined the bucket brigade battling the fire. Eventually the blaze was brought under control. Exhausted, wet, and blackened by the smoke, du Pont went to bed. He never got up. On August 7 he died.

Greatness always eluded this ambitious man, who frequently speculated about his place in history. But if a man were measured by intentions alone, du Pont would have secured for himself as prominent a position in the annals of man's affairs as even he could have wished.

The du Ponts were a closely knit family at the time of Pierre's death. His grandchildren did not look far afield in seeking marriage partners. The first exception to that attitude ended in tragedy, and since it was the first du Pont marriage to occur on the Brandywine, may well have influenced the attitude. Victor's oldest daughter, Amelia, married a man named William H. Clifford, who had left his family's textile mill in England and had gone to work in Victor's woolen mill. Amelia was no beauty and Clifford seemed a fine catch until he turned out to have another name, a wife, and two children back in England. Confronted with these revelations, Clifford fled the Brandywine.

In 1816 Antoine Bidermann married Irénée's second daughter, Evelina. Discounting the unrealized potential of Ferdinand Bauduy's ill-fated wedding to Irénée's oldest, Victorine, Evelina's was the first of what would prove to be many matches between du Pont women and rising stars in the company. It would not be too long before the first intermarriage in the family would take place between Irénée's Sophie and Victor's Samuel Francis.

The danger that shadowed the du Ponts and their workers

at the gunpowder works was in dramatic counterpoint to the serenity of their home life, where Irénée's love of nature had infected his children, especially Victorine, Eleuthera, and Sophie. "You are aware, my friend, that being without a garden was the greatest deprivation," Irénée once wrote. His children seemed inclined to agree. One of the few non-du Ponts buried in the family cemetery in the woods behind Irénée's home was John Prevost, Irénée's gardener. Always busy with his mills, Irénée had little time for the actual work of gardening, enjoying the planning of gardens and the results of others' efforts.

In the summer of 1823 the family produced a sunflower thirteen inches in diameter and, to judge from correspondence, was mighty proud of the accomplishment.

Botany was not the sole province of Irénée's side of the family. Victor's son Charles was quite an enthusiast. Once while in Paris, he admired a horse chestnut tree he saw and went to considerable effort to obtain seeds that he might grow his own back on the Brandywine. He was perhaps a bit chagrined to learn upon his return that the tree was an Ohio native. It was probably Charles who started the custom of planting a pair of evergreens at the time of marriage. The custom has been carried on by three couples who lived in Louviers, Victor's home—Amy and Eugene du Pont, Eleuthera Bradford and Henry B. du Pont, and the current occupants of the house, Winifred and William Winder Laird, Jr.

Irénée's daughter Eleuthera made a hobby of collecting wild birds and raising them. She had a scarlet tanager that had been knocked down by a stone. After a while, the bird would eat from Eleu's hand. When a reaping machine destroyed a nest of baby indigo buntings, which Eleu naturally took under her wing, the tanager would take the food meant for it and feed the buntings. After two years of domesticity, the tanager flew away one day when Eleu left the cage door open while cleaning the cage. Alfred Victor was a rock collector. Irénée's other two sons, Henry and Alexis, collected insects.

The great tragedy everyone who worked at the gunpowder mills feared daily and which Papa du Pont's final heroic efforts had helped avert less than a year earlier finally occurred on March 19, 1818. The main powder magazine went up, blowing everything within yards of it to bits. In all, forty men died. The damage was estimated at $120,000, and since the total fixed assets of the company were $106,300 at the end of 1815, the explosion could not have left much standing.

Irénée was in Philadelphia trying to raise more money when it happened. His brother Victor escaped by some miracle. His brother-in-law, Charles Dalmas, and his wife Sophie were both injured. Irénée's house was damaged. And life went on. The widows of the dead workers were visited and consoled. Pensions were provided. The mills were rebuilt; the house repaired. Creditors were stalled.

One large creditor was William Grey, from whom Irénée bought saltpeter, used in quantity in the making of gunpowder. Irénée went to him after the explosion and told him he couldn't pay his bill because of the disaster, that he would pay if Grey insisted, but that it would ruin him. Grey assured him that he, Grey, was confident Irénée would pay as soon as he was able and that would be soon enough. Irénée was so grateful he told a daughter that if he ever had another son, he'd name him William Grey du Pont. He didn't.

Madame de Pusy chose this time to whine again about her treatment as a stockholder and instituted a suit against her stepbrother. Irénée paid her an additional $6,000 during the 1820s. He also won a suit brought against him by Bauduy. Adversity, it seemed, would never let Irénée up for air.

His brother became Delaware's first du Pont politician. As early as 1813 the du Ponts had been accused of inspecting the ballots of their workmen before they were cast. Victor denied it. In 1816 Irénée did urge the influencing of workers to vote for Caesar Rodney. A year earlier Victor became a member of the Delaware legislature. From his election in 1820 until 1823, he served in the Delaware senate. When Irénée himself ran unsuccessfully for the state house of representatives in 1828, he urged his workers to vote their consciences, claiming there never was or would be any threat to them or deprivation of their rights.

Irénée was made a director of the Bank of the United States, forerunner of the Federal Reserve System, in 1823, serving through 1825. His brother became a director in 1826. The following year while in Philadelphia, Victor collapsed on the street. He was carried to a nearby hotel, where he died. Irénée was again named director of the Bank, serving until 1830.

Late in November of 1828 Irénée's wife, Sophie, finally succumbed to an illness that had plagued her most of the year. Indeed, she had never really recovered from her injuries sustained in the 1818 explosion. By summer 1828 Sophie was bedridden. Irénée seldom left her side.

With Sophie's death, the melancholy that had been gradually engulfing Irénée over the years grew even more pronounced, the fits of depression more frequent. But he persevered, serving on various commissions, acting as a delegate to the National Republican Convention in December of 1831 and helping to found the Wilmington Fire Insurance Company.

His death on October 31, 1834, was uncanny in its parallel to his brother's nearly eight years earlier. Both collapsed within sight of their hotel while walking the same street in Philadelphia. Both died of heart attacks, breathing their last in their rooms at the United States Hotel.

When Irénée died, the Du Pont Company was roughly $125,000 in debt despite a vigorous business. It was an unlikely base on which to build one of the largest industrial empires in the world, and it would become less likely—the debt would quadruple—before the company finally began to dominate its chosen field.

Chapter Three

Building the Business

Irénée's death left the powder company without a du Pont ready to take over. Into this breach stepped Antoine Bidermann, Irénée's son-in-law, who would not accept the presidency of the company, saying the president should be someone named du Pont. Alfred Victor, Irénée's oldest son, was in his middle thirties. It wouldn't be too long before he was ready.

For three years Bidermann ran the business, bringing Alfred Victor along quickly. Perhaps his most important contribution was the retiring of the critical part of the debt owed French creditors. To get the money for this, he followed Irénée's lead, borrowing from Philadelphia banks. In 1837 Alfred Victor took over, and a new partnership agreement was drawn up, with twenty-six shares divided among Irénée's heirs. Alfred had eight shares; his younger brothers, Henry and Alexis, had five each. Bidermann and Irénée's three remaining daughters—Victorine, Eleuthera, and Sophie—each had two. The shares were valued at $7,000 apiece.

Alfred Victor was not a brilliant businessman. His bent was more scientific and literary, according to his nephew, Henry A. du Pont, son of Alfred's brother, Henry. He was a soft touch, who, like the girl in the Rodgers and Hammerstein song, couldn't say no. He was always guaranteeing notes for people, many of whom were clearly bad risks whose notes would surely become Alfred's obligation. Alfred's concept of the business was a simple one, says a family member, James Q. du Pont, an expert in family history who worked for the Du Pont Company's public affairs department. It could be summed up in two sentences: "Make it safer. Make it better." The two sentences were never separated in Alfred's mind. He was convinced that the company's best work could be better.

In 1839 a visitor to Wilmington was obviously impressed with the company operation. He observed that nearly all of the hundred and fifty employees at that time were Irish and went on to write: "I was much struck with the affection and respect exhibited by the operatives toward their employers. . . . I take pleasure in recording such instances of affectionate regard on the part of the operatives in a large establishment because it is not usual to find it in this country."

Such unqualified approval is especially interesting in the light of some remarks of Alfred's recorded by family historian Bessie Gardner du Pont. She writes that when someone suggested terminating pensions paid to employees' widows, Alfred objected strenuously. ". . . our mills," he said, "with only one well-known exception, have destroyed more lives than any other set of mills in the world; this, of course, comparing the number of hands killed to the amount of powder made." Alfred went on to point out that ". . . the lowest powdermen's wages ever paid in the United States have been at least $2 per week in advance of ours."

Still, a Wilmington newspaper editorial of 1848—in the days before the city's newspapers were owned by the du Ponts —could enthuse: ". . . there has never been a single turn out or strike amongst the men. . . . All difficulties (if there have ever been any) have been settled amicably. . . ."

Writing in 1909 after interviewing old powder workers, Richard Stout may have put his finger on what made the close relationship between the du Ponts and their employees: "One generation succeeded another both of owners and workingmen; as boys, gentlemen's sons and the sons of laborers shared each other's sports in that little village, kept so remote from the outside world; and as they grew up together to manhood they fell naturally into the same relations of mutual respect and loyalty and affection." The devotion of Du Pont employees was "like that of retainers for their lord" in feudal times.

There was another factor in the equation, at least as important. Danger shared. In 1847 an explosion took eighteen lives. When the powder works started up again, a du Pont worked alongside the powdermen at every point of potential danger. As men of widely diverse backgrounds thrown together in time of war develop a special bond from facing death side by side, so the du Ponts and their employees had a special relationship. It was family policy that du Ponts would operate new equipment first to make sure it was in safe, proper working order.

The family's relations with its workers were probably not hurt by its wage policy. While wages were something less than extravagant, they were reasonably stable. The nineteenth century saw the American economy fluctuate rather wildly, with rapid growth followed by sudden recession. From 1827 to 1842, for example, the nation was in the throes of a depression. Wages of cotton workers declined 50 per cent. Wages at the powder works were down 5 or 10 per cent.

By 1850 the du Ponts were Delaware's eighth largest employer with 169 workers on the payroll. The company was third in sales—$375,000 annually. But despite these indications of success, the debt was continuing to pile up. The pressures of running the business were beginning to tell on Alfred, and, at the written suggestion of his brothers and his wife, he retired. The company was $500,000 in the red. Part of the problem was simply that Alfred had been too generous to run the company with the financial restraint then needed.

Alfred's brother, Henry, assumed control and soon began to make things happen. Henry had plenty of help from the outside. The Civil War and America's energetic westward expansion developed an unprecedented demand for the products of the powder works—gunpowder for the war, blasting powder for roads, canals, railroads, mines, and the clearing of fields for farming. In 1850 three powder companies—Du Pont,

Laflin & Rand, and Hazard—produced 65 per cent of the industry's output. The remainder was divided among nearly fifty other firms. Price competition was intensive, and when the Civil War forced the big companies to devote the bulk of their attentions to military business, small mills sprung up locally to meet the domestic demand, furthering the price fights.

Henry, a fearsome figure in his flaming red beard, was well suited to make the most of the opportunities this situation presented. A man of driving energy and prodigious capacity for detail, Boss Henry, as he became known, was not one to delegate responsibility. He ran the show; no one else even knew what the books looked like. The Boss was a stickler for thrift. On his way to the office each morning he used to pick up willow twigs, stuffing them into the stovepipe hat he was seldom without. He would stop at the charcoal house, strew the twigs over a table in front of the workers, and ask that they be charred along with the rest of the willow used for making charcoal. It was his way of dramatizing his insistence that nothing be wasted. Henry had a photographic memory. He knew everyone by his first name. He knew who had been drunk Saturday night, whose wife was pregnant. His reign was despotic, but in the eyes of many, it was a benevolent despotism. Pierre Gentieu, a long-time employee, once claimed he could write a book on the kindness of the Boss.

If his older brother's motto had been "Make it better; make it safer," Henry's might be said to have been, "Make it cheaper; make it quicker." Quality and safety were not abandoned, but Henry understood about profits. In 1854 this attitude may have been in part responsible for a tragedy that could easily have been far worse. Three Conestoga wagons loaded with powder blew up in the streets of downtown Wilmington, killing the drivers but miraculously taking only two citizens' lives. The fastest route to the shipping docks was through Wilmington, but that route was clearly not the safest, and it would never be taken again.

The cause of the explosion remains a mystery. The middle of the three wagons apparently exploded first. The wagons had been stopped. The first one started up. The explosion came as the second began to roll. According to Henry's son, Henry A., the wagons had left the mill a half mile apart with orders to keep that distance, but for some reason had closed together. The concussion from the explosion was felt all the way back at the mills, some several miles away. The public reaction to what many considered a wanton disregard for the public's safety was national in scope.

The year 1857 was a pivotal one for the Du Pont Company. In May, Lammot du Pont, Alfred Victor's son, was granted a patent on his formula for making blasting powder from sodium nitrate, rather than potassium nitrate. A dull enough proposition at first glance, the new formula had dramatic implications. Literally for centuries, the making of powder had depended on saltpeter from India. Now the hitherto useless but abundant saltpeter in Peru—sodium nitrate—could be used. The supply would be much cheaper and more reliable; the product improved. Potassium nitrate would still be needed for military and sporting powder, but for mining, railroads, and other blasting needs, the new powder would do splendidly. For the first time, the du Ponts opened a mill away from the Brandywine, in Luzerne County, Pennsylvania, near the coal mines, to make the new powder. That was the good news for that year.

The bad news befell Alexis Irénée du Pont, Boss Henry's younger brother, who oversaw the mill operations on the Brandywine and whose rapport with the workers was unequaled by any du Pont before or since. Alexis, influenced perhaps by his brother-in-law, Thomas MacKie Smith, was a deeply religious man. He was instrumental in the building of Christ Church, still today the family's principal house of worship. The church may be unique in having a bottle of whiskey embedded in its walls. Alexis was not without a sense of humor, and when he happened to visit the church during construction, he noticed one of the workmen stash the bottle in the wall as he approached. Alexis decided to watch the construction for a while, and the workers had no choice but to seal the bottle into the wall. A year later Alexis would become the first du Pont to be buried from Christ Church.

He was a vigorous, impatient, fatalistic young man. His nephew, Henry A., once recalled that Alexis frequently would wade waist deep through the Brandywine to talk with a man on the other side rather than take the time to walk over one of the bridges. In early 1857 Alexis was showing a clergyman through the powder yards when the visitor remarked on the danger of the business. "Sir," Alexis said, "the man who follows my business should be ready to meet his God."

It was in August that Alexis, apparently on his way to take a look at the progress being made on construction of the Cathedral Church of St. John, detoured through the powder yards. St. John's was Alexis' big project at the time, but business was business. A heavy metal box in a graining mill had to be moved, and Alexis got some men to help him. A spark ignited some loose powder and a sudden explosion killed four men and threw Alexis, his clothing aflame, nearly a hundred feet. Instinct must have taken over. Alexis plunged into the Brandywine to douse his burning clothes, scrambled out, and saw that embers from the fire caused by the explosion were threatening a press mill, one of the most explosion-prone buildings in the yard. Ordering the workers to run, Alexis clambered up onto the roof of the press mill, where a large spark appeared to be the most immediate threat. The mill exploded.

It was Eugene, Alexis' seventeen-year-old son, who found his father, his back broken, one leg mangled, ribs having punctured a lung. Alexis was carried to his home. Doctors from Wilmington and the minister from Christ Church were summoned. The doctors did not stay long; there was nothing they could do. Alexis lived through the night and the next day, saying goodbye to the workers who one by one filed through his bedroom in those last hours. He was forty-one when he died.

The next major crisis that would confront Boss Henry was already brewing as Alexis was buried. The issue of slavery was dividing the nation. Henry's son was a West Point cadet. His first cousin, Victor's son Samuel Francis, was a captain in the U. S. Navy. Both the family and the state of Delaware were divided in their sympathies, although there was little doubt that, put to the test, the family would support the federal government in Washington. Delaware's ultimate position was more in doubt. The southern part of the state had definite Confederate sympathies. It was a ticklish situation. Should lower Delaware prevail, the state would be surrounded by Northern sympathizers and the du Pont powder mills, invaluable to the Southern cause, would become a center of attention, not to mention aggression.

After teetering on the brink of secession, Delaware remained loyal to the Union. The Boss's son graduated first in his class at West Point in 1861. Samuel Francis returned to command the naval squadron blockading Southern ports. The Boss was made a major general in the state militia by the governor.

Although the du Ponts have always adamantly argued that they prefer peace to war, just strictly from a business viewpoint, it cannot be denied that the Du Pont Company's most dramatic prosperity has had a war as its root cause. Family exploits during the Civil War, which was hardly an unprofitable one, have become the stuff of legend.

Unquestionably the best-known du Pont during the war was Samuel Francis. By the middle of 1862 he had been made a rear admiral, and had been the object of a joint congressional resolution thanking him for his squadron's dramatic victory in capturing the forts at Port Royal, South Carolina. The admiral's fame in defeat was perhaps even more widespread than it had been in victory. At the beginning of 1863 Du Pont was ordered to prepare for an attack on

Charleston, South Carolina. In April, using the new ironclads, Du Pont attacked and got nowhere, a destination he had earlier predicted. He refused to renew the attack, despite the urging of both President Lincoln and his Secretary of the Navy. Du Pont told the Secretary that if there was someone around who could capture Charleston, he, Du Pont, would like to be relieved of his command. Politics, interservice rivalries, and personality clashes did little to help matters. Charges and countercharges were made. Du Pont's defeat at Charleston was billed as the worst in naval history. In June he was ordered relieved of his command and returned home generally in disgrace. The national press apparently believed others would have succeeded where Du Pont failed and said so. Two years later Du Pont died an embittered man.

In 1899 the Naval War College held hearings on the Charleston affair in which Du Pont and his successor, Admiral Dahlgren, were exonerated for the failure to take Charleston. Part of the problem was clearly communications between Washington and Charleston. The difficulties of the task set before Du Pont and later Dahlgren were never adequately laid out in Washington. The blame for this depends simply on whom you choose to believe. But the final verdict of the hearings was that Washington expected Du Pont and Dahlgren "to work out an insoluble war problem." The attack on Charleston may have been ill-advised from the beginning; Du Pont apparently thought so, although he perhaps may be accused of not having made those feelings more strongly felt in Washington. As Commodore John Rodgers, who served under Du Pont at that time, testified in 1864, the ironclads alone could never have taken the positions from which the defense of Charleston harbor was mounted, and furthermore, if you lost the ironclads in such an effort, you would lose the blockade. As Rodgers said, the game was not worth the candle. Admiral Du Pont's vindication has been complete. He was a scapegoat for a failure the blame for which belonged in Washington.

On another front, Boss—now General—Henry's son was distinguishing himself as an artillery officer in the Virginia campaigns. He rose to lieutenant colonel, and although his record was somewhat sullied by controversy over the precise role he played in the rather thorough destruction of the Virginia Military Institute, that record was sufficiently remarkable, at least when coupled with some political considerations, to earn for him more than thirty years later the Congressional Medal of Honor. Even later, as a U.S. senator, Henry A. would propose a bill to pay reparations to VMI.

Not all the du Ponts were so eager to play war games. Victor, son of Charles and grandson of the original Victor, paid $750 to purchase a substitute rather than face the Civil War himself. He became instead one of Delaware's most successful lawyers, the start of an elegant tradition. Delaware is a state rich in successful lawyers.

Success was also being enjoyed by the General, who was rather rapidly blurring the distinction between his property and that of the company. In 1864 General Henry reported an income of $110,000. The next highest income in the state that year belonged to a non-du Pont, who reported $47,000.

Perhaps the most enduring family legend to come out of the Civil War involved Lammot du Pont, the thirty-year-old son of Alfred Victor, whose trip to London in the fall of 1861 smacked of elegant cloak-and-dagger diplomacy from the beginning. The Union needed saltpeter. The saltpeter was in London. And London was showing disturbing signs of favoring the Confederacy. In Washington it was decided Lammot should go to England and buy the saltpeter the Union needed but buy it through the Du Pont Company. Amid great secrecy, Lammot sailed at once and proved most adept at his task, virtually cornering the saltpeter market in about a day's work. What happened from here and why is a tale with several versions. There are some points of general agreement: Before he could get his ships under sail with the precious cargo, the British Government embargoed the lot, Lammot returning to the United States and after a quick visit home and to Washington, returning to London, where several days later the ships were released and the saltpeter sent on its way Union-ward. Some sources say Lammot bluffed Lord Palmerston, the British Prime Minister, with a threat of war. Others say the release of Mason and Slidell, two Confederate commissioners taken off a British ship and into Union custody while Lammot was in London the first time, turned the trick. George H. Kerr, who served in later years as Lammot's personal secretary, claims in his book, *Du Pont Romance*, that Lammot told him the real story. Historians doubt it.

According to Kerr, Lammot waited three days during that first trip to London while British officials weighed his cargo night and day in what he thought was a noble effort to accommodate his large order. It turned out, however, that the weighers were attempting to exhaust his credit. When that was finally established as sound, Palmerston issued the embargo order. Lammot finally got in to see Palmerston, who said that a matter of national defense was involved. Lammot's large purchases would leave England without saltpeter. Therefore, Parliament would have to okay lifting the embargo. Lammot argued in vain that since Palmerston had ordered the embargo, he could lift it. Lammot returned to the United States, picked up a letter from Secretary of War Stanton, and took the next ship back to England. Kerr does not reveal the contents of the letter, but says Palmerston read it in Lammot's presence, visibly blanching. The Prime Minister asked for a couple of days, and Lammot told him he was sailing on the morrow and would await word at his hotel.

While Lammot was eating his noonday meal, an envoy of Palmerston's came in and said the Prime Minister would see him. Lammot told the envoy to ask the Prime Minister to wait while he finished his meal, in which he by now had lost all interest. After stalling for a time, he invited Palmerston in, and the Prime Minister said he would delay the sailing of Lammot's ship while the matter was further considered. Lam-

mot told him he could not countenance such an incon-
venience to his fellow passengers and would sail the next day
with or without the saltpeter. Lammot was astonished, Kerr
says, when Palmerston agreed to the release. That afternoon
the saltpeter was on its way to America. This tale, while delightful, describes what would have been unbelievable devia-
tions in diplomatic protocol in those days and is totally without documentary support.

The thirty-year-old chemist from Wilmington outnegotiat-
ing the experienced Palmerston on a matter so vital to the
Union is made more plausible by the likelihood that Stanton's letter was the crucial element in Palmerston's acquies-
cence. Stanton was, after all, the Secretary of War.

Adding further credibility to the story are the contemporary descriptions of this Lincolnesque du Pont, whose contributions to the family enterprise, including the securing of
saltpeter and the invention of the new blasting powder compound, were substantial enough for a lifetime although he
was but thirty.

Lammot joined the company in 1850, but he might rather
have gone fishing. His father told him to take a fishing pole
and walk through the yards on his way to the Brandywine. A
fellow named Charles Le Carpentier was running the saltpeter refinery, but Alfred Victor had heard he might quit.
Alfred told his son Lammot to stroll by the refinery. If Le
Carpentier was there, Lammot could go fishing. If he wasn't,
Lammot should take over. He took over.

Writing about his father many years later, Pierre du Pont
said of Lammot: "He was of commanding voice and figure,
awe-inspiring; yet I remember no unkind or harsh word spoken by him to me. I looked upon him as the personification
of right and justice; yet he never seemed to assume such an
attitude. He and my mother avoided all disputes or disagreements on any subject in the presence of their children."
The one exception Pierre recalled occurred when he was
eleven. His father was sitting outside with some papers, recov-

ering from a bladder illness. One of Pierre's younger sisters was playing nearby when a paper fell to the ground, and Lammot asked the girl to pick it up. She ignored him; he asked again. Still no response. Blows and tears followed. Pierre's mother appeared, tears coming to her eyes. It was "a sight never before seen by me on any occasion," Pierre wrote.

Pierre remembered being fond of the piano, but the one at home was always closed and he never dared open it. Lammot disliked music and was fond of saying, Pierre wrote, that "no man could amount to anything if he smoked cigarettes, wore eyeglasses (pince-nez variety), or played the piano."

His parents, Pierre said, "taught the now old-fashioned ideas of economy. Extravagance and waste deprived others of pleasures and means of livelihood. Thrift and industry served to protect others and to make secure our own welfare."

Lammot died when Pierre was only fourteen, which may account for some of the reverence he accords his father's memory. "I could not hope to be his equal," Pierre once wrote. About that much, at least, Pierre was probably wrong.

A man firm in the courage of his convictions and possessed of the wit and popularity to ensure he would never stand alone, Lammot must have been something of a mixed blessing in the eyes of his uncle, General Henry, who was developing a stranglehold on the company as the Civil War ended that Lammot seemed alone capable of challenging. Lammot had a certain flair for the grand gesture. Shortly after his 1865 marriage, powder workers came to him expressing their fear that a missing nut in a powder press might cause an explosion. Lammot pressed the powder himself, while his wife sat in a rocking chair just 150 yards away. His value to the company could not be denied. He alone stood up to the Boss, but he also remained loyal to Henry and the family business.

The strength of Henry's grip on family and company affairs is suggested by an 1867 tax collector's report listing annual taxes. Henry's were $4,534. Eleuthère Irénée, Alfred Victor's oldest son, and Lammot were next, at $788 and $772 respec-

tively. By a partnership agreement of 1858, the family business
was divided into twenty-six shares valued at $17,000 each.
Henry held twenty of them. Lammot and the second Eleuthère Irénée each held three. That grip would grow still
stronger. In an 1883 letter, Alexis Irénée, son of the Alexis
killed in the 1857 explosion, writes of his older brother Eugene's future and predicts that in twenty years there might be
no du Ponts left on the Brandywine because of diminishing
opportunity there. Uncle Henry's branch of the family, Alexis
wrote, had nineteen twentieths of the company.

That represented a pretty tight grip, and by then required a
large hand. The company had come to dominate the powder
industry. In 1872 Du Pont had 37 per cent of the powder
market; Laflin & Rand accounted for 21 per cent and Hazard
Powder Company 12 per cent, a share that was being eroded
by Laflin & Rand. Early that year, General Henry and Albert
Tyler Rand were ready to engage in an all-out price war. The
cooler heads of Lammot at Du Pont and H. M. Boies at
Laflin & Rand prevailed, and in April the Gunpowder Trade
Association was formed. To the Big Three, which controlled
70 per cent of the market, were added several smaller companies representing 8 per cent. Outside the Association were
the California group with another 8 per cent, and a dozen
more firms who together accounted for the remaining 14 per
cent.

Lammot became the first president of the Association,
which set prices and sales quotas on a regional basis. The
General wasn't satisfied. He still wanted a price war with
Laflin & Rand, but Lammot talked him out of it.

From 1873 through 1879 the nation suffered through a
depression. Du Pont and Laflin & Rand remained solvent.
Few other powder companies did, and the two, operating in
concert through the powder trust and on their own, bought
up the companies going bankrupt. New companies were
urged to join the trust. If they demurred, they found themselves in a price war they had little chance of winning. Such

wars usually led to absorption of the new company. The trust further benefited from the fledgling companies by allowing them to start up in new areas while it watched to measure their potential for survival. If they succeeded, the trust moved in. Thus, the new companies took the risks. A few clever types were able to take advantage of the trust's avarice by starting companies solely with the intention of selling out to the trust at a high price. The ploy frequently worked.

In 1875 Du Pont strengthened its position by purchasing 43 per cent of the California Powder Works. In 1876 Du Pont bought Hazard with $100,000 in cash and $700,000 in notes. Laflin & Rand was equally aggressive. The two companies controlled the industry, owning large blocks of stock in most of the companies they did not own outright.

Commenting on an efficiency study conducted during this period, Lammot said, "We might infer that the theoretical work in making powder was about one hundred kegs per man per day. From my experience it varies from fifty down to four." In different times, that observation might have prompted some hard decisions about productivity, but when you controlled sales quotas and prices, the importance of productivity became rather less compelling.

It was also around this time that Sweden's Alfred Nobel invented an explosive that would change the powder industry—and, indeed, the face of the earth—dramatically. The General was not immediately taken with the promise of dynamite. It was, he was convinced, too dangerous, and a widely publicized fatal explosion of the stuff allowed him to adopt an unshakable I-told-you-so attitude. Lammot was early sure that in dynamite lay the future of the explosives business and argued the point frequently with his uncle. In 1880 the two reached a compromise. Lammot would leave the Brandywine to start a dynamite company. The Du Pont Company would provide some of the money and backing needed. Thus was born the Repauno Chemical Company. Lammot wasted no time establishing its pre-eminence in the high-explosives business. The first year production was 500,000 pounds; the next it was 3 million; and the third year, Lammot withdrew from the Du Pont partnership to devote his full energies to Repauno.

Lammot's heady success was in sharp contrast to the tragedy of his older brother's life. The second Eleuthère Irénée had married Charlotte Henderson, a Virginian. As emotion rose over the issues that were to lead to the Civil War, the young Charlotte was subjected to a merciless scorn by her mother-in-law for being a Southerner, although she never expressed any strong support for the Confederacy. Eleuthère Irénée pleaded with his mother to ease up, but she heeded him not. Charlotte gradually began to lose her sanity. Two trips abroad apparently helped, but upon her return from the second in 1874, an incident involving the girl hired to look after her children undid her for the last time. When Charlotte asked her six-year-old son how the girl had been treating him, he complained of being beaten. He showed his mother the welts on his back, and she became hysterical. Doctors convinced Irénée it would be best to commit his wife to an institution. In 1877, just twenty-nine days after his wife had died without his knowing it in that institution, Irénée succumbed to tuberculosis. He had not spoken to his mother for a dozen years, and although Lammot urged it and his mother asked for it, he would permit no reconciliation even on his deathbed. He was convinced his mother's cruel baiting of his wife had led to her insanity. He could not forgive her.

Lammot's two younger brothers, Alfred and Antoine Bidermann, had abandoned the Brandywine in 1853 to seek their fortunes in Kentucky. They had found them, due in large measure to Fred's brains and industry. By the time their brother Irénée died, the Kentucky prodigals had established themselves as men with whom trifling was ill advised. They may have abandoned their homes, but they did not abandon their families. Fred, in particular, was a favorite uncle among the children of both Irénée and Lammot. Major family affairs, sad or happy, were seldom missed by the Kentucky brothers.

Among the saddest was the death of Lammot in 1884. Life had been good to him. He had a prosperous business, a houseful of children, a devoted wife, and the love and respect of nearly everyone who knew him. He was perhaps a bit arbitrary in his opinions on occasion, but even these were softened with humor. His personal secretary, George Kerr, recalled the visit of a C. Bascom Flood to Lammot's office one day. Upon the fellow's departure, Lammot asked Kerr what he thought of "Mr. C. Bunkum Dud." Kerr was noncommittal. "Well, you take care of him next time he's in," Lammot said. "I can never stand a dude that parts his name on the side." From that day on, G. Harry Kerr became known as George H. Kerr. A similar sentiment about people who part their names on the side has also been attributed to Lammot's more famous contemporary and look-alike—Abraham Lincoln.

Lammot was showing a visitor around the Repauno plant on March 29, 1884, when a workman rushed in to announce strange bubbling in one of the nitroglycerin vats. Lammot wasted no time getting to the scene of the trouble. Ordering the workmen out of the building, Lammot set about trying to cool down the volatile nitro. The explosion that followed left Lammot's body buried under the rubble of the demolished building for hours. His wife, the former Mary Belin, was left with nine children ranging in age from sixteen to two and a tenth on the way.

Like his first cousin, Alfred I., whose father had died seven years earlier, the fourteen-year-old Pierre, Lammot's oldest son, was suddenly and prematurely head of a large family. With Uncle Fred counseling from Kentucky and on visits to the Brandywine, both Alfred and Pierre, who were as different as night and day, shouldered their responsibilities with a maturity far beyond their years.

Shortly after the Civil War, General Henry had enlisted

Lammot's help in attempting to persuade his son, Colonel Henry A., to join the business. The Colonel resisted. He liked the Army life. Finally, his new wife, a New Yorker named Mary Pauline Foster, made it clear to him that Army life didn't suit her, and in 1875 he joined the company, where his father put him to the less than arduous task of reading the office mail. "My father," the Colonel told family biographer Bessie Gardner du Pont, "was unwilling to let any part of the business go out of his hands."

In 1878 the General showed just how complete his dominance of the family and the company was by admitting his two sons, the Colonel and his younger brother William, into the partnership despite a paucity of experience or even demonstrated competence that was unprecedented. There may have been some intrafamily grumbling at this highhanded maneuver, but the will of the Boss was never openly challenged.

The General's acquisitive instincts were finely honed. While the company and the powder trust went about the business of securing their monopoly in the explosives industry, Henry attempted to corner the land market around the Brandywine in his spare time. To this day, the rolling countryside northwest of Wilmington is lined and divided by stone walls Henry had built. He had been nettled by the expense and delay involved in bringing stonemasons down from Philadelphia to repair or rebuild the damage to the mills from explosions and general wear and tear. His solution was to hire a group of masons on a permanent basis, move them to Wilmington, and put them to work building walls whenever there was no work at the mills.

During the depression of the 1870s the General's humanitarian side showed through. Wages for masons fell to $1.75 a day. When Henry heard this, he was paying his masons $2.90. The wage remained unchanged as Henry pointed out that "unfortunately, the price of meat is unchanged."

As the decade of the 1880s drew to a close, the company

prospered but the Boss began to fail. For nearly four decades he had run the company and the family with a steely will that brooked no argument. The company had risen from a sea of red ink and could now boast of a net worth near $12 million. In 1888 the General's sister Sophie, wife of the admiral, had died, leaving Henry the lone surviving grandchild of the original Pierre Samuel. By mid-July the Boss's failing health had forced his son, Henry A., to take over the daily chores of running the business and had caused his nephew Alexis to write a cousin: "His whiskers have turned perfectly white and the muscles of his face have become so weak that he cannot keep his lower jaw in place. He cannot last much longer."

The following month he died. His income from the company from 1837 to his death was $3.8 million. No one was more affected by Henry's death than his cat, Minette. She was inconsolable, going daily to the family cemetery to sit by the General's grave. His widow would send a man to fetch the cat home, but at the first opportunity she would return to graveside. She refused to eat and soon died.

General Henry had not done much to provide for an orderly succession to his place as head of family and company. The firm partners upon his death were his two sons, William and Colonel Henry, and two of his brother Alexis' sons, Eugene and Francis Gurney. As the older of the General's sons and the man who had been in charge of the office while his father had been ill, the Colonel figured he was the obvious choice. Years later he told Bessie Gardner du Pont that during his father's illness he and his father had "discussed the business in such a way that I felt justified in assuming he expected me to succeed him as its head."

The other partners had other ideas. Undoubtedly they felt the Colonel's interest in and knowledge of the business was insufficient to warrant his succession. The Colonel had, after all, been mainly involved with the shipping end of the company's business, working with the railroads, and he seemed perhaps more interested in railroads than explosives. He was, to be sure, now the largest shareholder in the company by far, but that wasn't enough for the other partners.

The Colonel's version of subsequent events as he recalled them in his talk with Bessie du Pont is that he was "much surprised when William came to me a day or two after my father's death and said, 'You cannot be head of the firm. We are four partners. You and I, Eugene and Frank, and Eugene, Frank, and I want Eugene.' I told him that if that was true I was quite willing to accept Eugene, that I had always understood that my father had expected me to succeed him and had instructed me for that purpose, but that I was willing to accept the decision of the other partners. Later on William asserted, I was told, that during my father's illness, he had told him [William] that he wished Eugene to succeed him [Bessie here notes that her husband, Alfred I., told her the same thing], but in view of my own conversations with my father, I did not believe that statement to be true."

In 1890 William resigned from the company. The partnership capital account now showed Henry with $1,360,000, Eugene with $360,000, and Frank with $260,000. Why exactly William chose to resign is unclear. Clearly, he and his brother were not getting along. Indeed, their relationship would grow so embittered that Henry would vow to outlive his brother in order to prevent William's burial in the family cemetery. (He was some twenty years older than William and didn't make it.) William was president of Repauno Chemical Company at the time, a full-time job. He may have wanted to make room for younger partners. Finally, he was having marital problems with his wife and cousin May, and marital problems were not viewed with sympathy in the du Pont family in those days.

William apparently caused the family some consternation by the terms he asked for payment of his shares in the business. That's the Colonel's version, at least, and Bessie writes that her husband told her William had threatened to allow the company's biggest competitor, Laflin & Rand, to use his name. There was an attempt by the other partners to reach a reconciliation with William, but indications are his terms for returning included the forced resignation of his brother, and nothing came of it.

Eugene became the head of the firm, although he probably would have preferred to stay in the laboratory. He was a quiet, studious type for whom the responsibilities of running the company must have seemed awesome. In 1891 a new partnership agreement was drawn. There were four senior partners—the Colonel and Eugene, Frank, and their brother Alexis, who in 1889 had said he was not particularly interested in a piece of the action because his own investments appeared to have substantial potential over the next three or four years. In the interim, that potential had apparently diminished. Two junior partners were added—Alfred I. and Charles I., the great-grandson of Victor, the original E. I. du Pont's brother. The senior partners' capital was $425,000 each. The junior partners had $212,500 invested.

What had caused the Colonel to relinquish his lion's share? About this time he wrote a statement listing four reasons for not joining the new partnership. The first was that it would be "too much to do"; he already had "personal cares and responsibilities" and there was the question of salary. The second was his concern about the "liability of my whole fortune for firm's debts." The third was that he felt the return on his investment in the company was too small, that he would be "working for posterity." Finally, he was convinced "that partnership is against the best interests of individual members of firm and of the family as well."

Unstated in that memorandum to himself but perhaps as compelling a reason as any was the fact that he was about to buy a substantial interest in the Wilmington and Northern Railroad and no doubt needed the cash he would get for selling the large part of his company interest.

The business was rolling comfortably along, which was perhaps a fortunate situation, as Eugene's leadership qualities were best suited to a caretaker's role. By 1890 the powder trust controlled 90 per cent of the blasting powder and 95 per cent of the gunpowder production in the United States. That same year the Chattanooga Powder Company decided to compete with the trust, lasting five years in a price war before submitting. One tactic the Chattanooga company had difficulty combating was the bribing of rail agents, who supplied the opposition with weekly statements of who was getting how much Chattanooga powder at what cost.

In 1890 an explosion rocked the Brandywine, taking thirteen lives and damaging Eleutherian Mills, the original Eleuthère Irénée's home. That year a new pension policy went into effect, paying $500 immediately and $100 for the next five years as well as providing the pensioner with a free house. Working conditions at Du Pont were hardly Elysian in those days, but they weren't much better anywhere else. Although labor trouble was frequent during the 1880s and 1890s, Du Pont had only one short strike headed by a few Irishmen. The leaders were fired. The only other Du Pont labor trouble in those days manifested itself in some barn burnings, which were generally attributed to some stonemasons who had been employed by old Boss Henry. They were apparently disgruntled at being fired by Eugene, who felt the General's old retainer policy exhibited a generosity that was excessive.

The new pension policy was not as handsome as it might appear compared with the earlier one of paying $100 a year. One strong argument in favor of the new policy was the fact that some earlier pensioners had been on the rolls for twenty or thirty years. Still, the worker was not without his advocates among the Du Pont partners. The bond between Alfred I. and the workmen was stronger than any such bond since the first Alexis, and Frank, too, had the workers' interests at heart. In 1891, during a partners' discussion about turning Eleutherian Mills into a club for the workers, Frank urged the proposal's acceptance on his reluctant partners, saying:

"There is probably no works in the United States of as great importance as this home plant that has as poor accommodations for the men employed therein. The quality of the houses is bad; their location is bad; and it may be said the only thing that redeems them is the very low rental that is charged for most of them. Yet with this, the question of social improvement is left in the background."

Frank won his point, and in 1892 Eleutherian Mills opened as a club for the workers with a piano, gym, library, showers, tables for pool, billiards, and cards, and a refreshment stand. Dues were $3 a year, and 177 workers joined the first year. By the end of 1894 there were 261 members.

Eugene, too, showed his concern for his workers in times of crisis. When a bank in Wilkes-Barre, Pennsylvania, with the unlikely name of F. V. Rockafellow & Company, collapsed in 1893, Eugene sent a check to the bank to cover the deposits of Du Pont workers there.

It was in 1890 that Lammot's son Pierre, the man who would have more impact on the development of the modern Du Pont Company than any other, first joined the firm. His cousin Amy, wife of Eugene and aunt by birth to junior partner Charles I., wrote Pierre in February that her husband wanted Pierre to join the firm. Eugene was waiting until the members of the firm were more or less settled on the form of the new partnership before bringing up Pierre, however, and it wasn't until the middle of May that he himself wrote Pierre, a senior at the Massachusetts Institute of Technology, that he had a job.

The company nearly lost its future star a couple of years later. Pierre was working under Frank at Carneys Point across the Delaware River in New Jersey. It was to Frank and Pierre that a patent for making smokeless powder, a major improvement in gunpowder, was issued. But Carneys Point was not an idyllic workplace. Pierre years later recalled spending winter nights there with his cousin Alexis, Eugene's son. "There was no place to sleep at that time," he wrote, "and we crawled in the cotton bin of washed and dried cotton and found it also the sleeping place of many mice, which did not add much to our comfort of the night." More importantly, Pierre was ambitious. He was made superintendent of the Carneys Point plant in 1892, but after more than six years there, he grew restless. In a letter to Pierre in March of 1899 after Pierre quit the company to go to work in Ohio, Frank recalled Pierre's proposition at the time of his resignation as a simple one. Pierre told Frank that either Frank would have to resign or Pierre would.

Years later, in 1945, Pierre would write: "I had become ambitious for the opportunity to go further than seemed to be possible at Carneys Point. I should have welcomed an invitation to go into the (main) office but no offer was made." Just three years after his resignation, the offer came, from a rather unexpected source.

Meanwhile, the powder trust was being forced underground. In 1896 the trust received a legal opinion that it was unconstitutional and responded by going secretive. A letter was assigned to each company in the trust. Only the trust secretary had the code, and he was under orders to burn it if the trust was ever prosecuted. Unconstitutional or not, the trust expanded its scope the following year, entering into an international agreement that divided the world into four territories and spelled out who could sell what where.

The waning years of the nineteenth century were generally happy and prosperous ones for the du Ponts and America. The family remained closely knit; the migrations from the Brandywine were few. One who left was William, younger son of the General, who had suffered through some fourteen years of an unhappy marriage with his cousin May du Pont, of the Victor side of the family, before they were finally divorced in 1892. In those days the most tolerant of the du Ponts viewed divorce with a jaundiced eye. William was the first, although by no means the last, to take this drastic step, and he suffered the ostracism of his cousins for it, an ostracism that was compounded when he married Annie Zinn soon afterward. The widow Zinn was very beautiful and already had a family connection of sorts—her mother's first cousin had married Julia du Pont. Her father belonged to a prominent manufacturing family. But the du Pont sympathy was all with May. William, having thumbed his nose at the family, retreated first to England, then to Virginia, where he moved into Montpelier, the plantation that once belonged to former President James Madison.

The family blood pressure and eyebrows had scarcely been lowered to normal again after William's divorce than the only real public scandal ever visited on the family surfaced. Uncle Fred, Alfred du Pont, the man who had gone west to Kentucky years earlier with his brother Bidermann to seek and find his fortune, died in 1893. He was the richest man in Louisville, and among the most generous. The civic pride of Louisville swelled at mention of his name. His help and counsel had been invaluable to the families of both Pierre and Alfred I. after the deaths of their fathers. It was reported in the Louisville paper that Uncle Fred had died of a seizure at his brother's home; his obituary was a eulogy to a great man. Fred had always eschewed lavish living, content to dwell in a single room at the Hotel Galt while his bank, street railway, coal mines, and paper mill flourished. Everyone liked Uncle Fred.

Two days after his death, the Cincinnati *Enquirer* dropped a bomb whose blast rattled parlor windows along the Brandywine. Uncle Fred had not died of a seizure at his brother's house; he had been shot to death by the madam of Louisville's most popular whorehouse, apparently during an argument over support for a child the woman claimed Uncle Fred had fathered. Publicly, the family and the Louisville papers denied the story. No arrest was made; no prosecution was attempted, but no one sued the Cincinnati paper, either.

The century turned. The du Ponts had come a long way in the hundred years they'd been in America. By all rights, 1902 should have been the year for big celebration, marking the Du Pont Company's centenary. It didn't work out that way. On January 21, company president Eugene du Pont did not show up for work, complaining of a cold. With little warning the cold became pneumonia. Three days later Eugene was dead.

His staunchest defenders would hardly characterize Eugene's presidency as brilliant. But it had been stable through some unsettling times, and his death was untimely in the extreme because there wasn't anyone in the family ready or capable to assume company leadership. The senior partners were Frank, his brother Alexis, and the Colonel. The junior partners, Alfred I. and Charles, were, after all, junior partners.

Frank would have been the obvious choice, but he was battling an illness that would get the best of him just two years later, and he didn't think he could do it. Alexis was a medical doctor and said he wasn't interested, if anyone asked. The Colonel was writing his memoirs and becoming involved in the early beginnings of Atlas Cement Company and U. S. Steel Corporation. He didn't have the time or the inclination. Besides, he'd rather be a U.S. senator. He'd almost gotten there six years earlier in one of the most bizarre political episodes in Delaware history, but the Senate had voted not to seat him, regarding the certificate of election he brought to Washington as perhaps a little tainted from a legal point of view. He was still trying.

The family and the company may have been going through something of what we like to call nowadays an identity crisis. James Q. du Pont, the family historian and company public relations man, once put it like this: "Unless one is very careful; unless you keep yourself solid, rugged, simple, and running lean, you tend to soften. You tend to lose focus. This is what was happening to our company and our family. One of the girls in our family was thinking, 'Look. My husband was killed in an explosion at Wapwallopen. When do we get out of this powder business?' Some of the men were saying,

'What the devil, I've got enough money now. Why don't I just have fun?'"

James Q. contended that Eugene realized what was going on and that that realization was the basis for his decision to incorporate the company three years before his death. By going public, symbolically at least, Eugene perhaps hoped to smooth the path of future transition.

At any rate, as the senior partners mulled over the course of action to take in the wake of Eugene's death, they began to reach the conclusion that sale of the company was inevitable. There was only one buyer with both the money and the industry experience necessary—Laflin & Rand. The decision was made to inquire of Laflin & Rand if it might be interested in buying the Du Pont Company. Price? Twelve million. The meeting of the partners was breaking up when young Alfred I. du Pont, not yet thirty-eight years old, asked if he might say a word or two.

Chapter Four

Two Crises

It was Valentine's Day, February 14, 1902. The other partners had already held several meetings to discuss the future of
the company. Alfred had not attended and may well not have
been asked. As he rose to speak, dressed in the work clothes
he wore as superintendent of the powder mills, some of the
other partners no doubt squirmed a bit. Alfred himself later
admitted he was an impulsive type and not the most popular
member of the younger generation with his elders. The meeting had gone smoothly. Alfred's only contribution had been
to suggest that the partners sell to the highest bidder, rather
than specifically to Laflin & Rand for $12 million. The sugges-
tion had been adopted, probably to keep the peace with
Alfred as much as for any other reason. After all, Laflin &
Rand was clearly the only qualified buyer. That Alfred had
made no other moves at the meeting was considered a good
sign.

Then, in a few seconds, Alfred created an enduring legend.
He told the elder partners he'd buy the company. No one was
particularly impressed. If Alfred had pooled all the resources
at his command, including the shirt off his back, he might
have raised $80,000. "You can't have it," said his cousin
Frank bluntly enough. "Besides, it's cash, you know."

Alfred warmed to his subject. He pointed out that the company faced its current predicament because of a policy that
did not bring younger members of the family along quickly
enough. He claimed the company was his by birthright,
pointing out that he was the eldest son of the eldest son of
the eldest son of the founder. He asked for a week in which
to make a formal proposal. Well, a week wasn't such a long

time to humor Alfred, even if his offer to buy the company was no more than the grandstand play the older partners suspected. With Colonel Henry agreeing to give Alfred a week, the others went along.

The Laflin & Rand plan was not abandoned. Alexis I. talked to Hamilton Barksdale, a du Pont in-law and perhaps the ablest of the younger members of the management team at the company, about accepting an interim appointment as president of the company while a sale to Laflin & Rand could be worked out. It was almost as an afterthought that Alexis told Barksdale about Alfred's offer. Perhaps sensing he was about to be lured into the middle of a family feud, Barksdale declined.

Colonel Henry's recollection of events was set down in a letter to Pierre in 1921. Henry claimed Alfred's initial proposition was not even taken seriously, and that it was only after Alfred had approached Henry privately and told him he proposed to have T. Coleman and Pierre join him in the acquisition that anyone realized there might actually be a chance to keep the company in family hands. Both Pierre and Coleman had already established their abilities as businessmen. Colonel Henry wrote that he considered including Pierre and Coleman a proposition that "differed radically" from one "to buy the business 'at whatever price may be considered just' made by a man whose personal financial condition did not justify it, whose capacity for affairs and business experience was not such as to inspire confidence in those with whom he was trying to deal, and who gave no indication whatever as to what he proposed to do with the property if acquired."

By 1921 the Colonel and Alfred were not on particularly good terms. As a historian, the Colonel had something of a record for self-serving revisionism and might have resented the credit Alfred was getting. But he does have a point: Alfred's proposal, unless at least Coleman was already in the picture, was a bit ludicrous.

Legend has it that once Alfred was assured he would have a

week to come back with a formal plan, he hurried off to
Coleman's house to solicit his participation, and Coleman,
after consulting with his wife and cousin, Alice, called Elsie
by everyone who knew her, said he'd do it if he was made
president and given a free hand in running the company and
if Pierre would join forces with them to handle the finances.

The weight of the evidence leans on the probability that
Coleman and Alfred had pretty well hashed things out before
Alfred made his little speech to the elder partners, and that
Alfred's visit to Coleman after the meeting was to report on
the outcome. His cousin Frank had told Alfred about a week
before the meeting of the plan to sell to Laflin & Rand, and
Alfred had apparently hustled up to New York to try and
raise the $12 million himself. He had been unsuccessful. He
and his older cousin Coleman had been roommates at MIT,
and Alfred had always looked up to Coleman, a rugged, six-
foot-four athlete and magnetic personality who had already
made himself a fortune in his father's and uncle's Kentucky
businesses before he returned to Wilmington to live in 1900.
At least hypothetically, the two cousins had talked about taking over the company. It was undoubtedly at this juncture
that Coleman consulted his wife, whose single sentence on the
matter was, "Well, Coley, you know what it is to work with
your relatives."

Coleman was the oldest of the three cousins, none of
whom had reached forty. Pierre was the youngest at thirty-
two. His recollection is that Coleman called him on the
phone after Alfred had told Coleman about the meeting and
that he made his decision to join his cousins in the course of a
three-minute conversation. But again, the likelihood is that
he and Coleman had discussed the question during a conference the two had had a week earlier in New York. So it was
that the three oldest sons of three brothers whose grandfather
had founded the company moved to take it over. Coleman
was the organization man, Pierre the finance man, and Alfred
the production man.

It did not take long for Coleman to convince the elder partners, including Frank, who had said only days earlier, "Besides, it's cash, you know," that 4 per cent notes for the $12 million would do just as well. To show his heart was in the right place, Coleman offered to give the old partners 28 per cent of the stock in the new company to be incorporated as a result of the purchase. They agreed. Coleman had done it again. He had long held that buying companies was no trick, that the trick was doing it with the other guy's money, and this is just what he did to his older cousins. When one of them asked, "How about a little cash, Coley?" he put on his best gee-I'd-love-to expression and said, "You wouldn't want to take away all our working capital, would you?"

In all, it was a fantastic deal. None of the three young cousins had seen the company books. They were taking the $12 million valuation on the word of their elders, who, for their part, were selling the largest explosives company in the world to three young men under forty who were giving them paper and promises. For a cash outlay of a couple of thousand dollars in legal and printing costs, Coleman, Alfred, and Pierre had bought themselves a large piece of a thriving industry. They figured earnings from the company would cover the interest on the notes and that their organization, finance, and production skills could increase profitability quickly and substantially.

The new company was capitalized at $20 million divided into 120,000 shares. The old partners—Colonel Henry, Frank, Alexis I., and the estate of Eugene—received 6,720 shares each. The junior partners, Alfred and Charles I., got 3,360. As a new owner, Alfred also received 21,600 shares. Pierre got an equal amount. Coleman took twice as much, 43,200 shares. Coleman was named president at a salary of $15,000; Alfred was vice-president at $10,000 and Pierre was treasurer at $10,000. Years later, in notes for a company history he was working on, Pierre would call the purchase from his older cousins "a perfect example of what was known as stock watering."

The sales agreement was dated March 1, 1902. It was the beginning of two decades unrivaled in business history for drama and excitement.

Coleman, Alfred, and Pierre were a well-matched team. Pierre later wrote that both Coleman and Alfred admired Pierre's father, Lammot, and took a brotherly interest in Pierre after Lammot's death "that made an indelible impression throughout my life." Their skills and experience perfectly complemented each other. Coleman had proved his organizational skills in the street railroad business, taking over sick companies and making them well and himself rich. Pierre's financial abilities were fully demonstrated, and Alfred had sent powder mill production from 3,000 to 20,000 pounds a day almost overnight at the start of the Spanish-American War four years earlier. It was not family loyalty that made Coleman insist on Pierre's participation before promising his own. Years later he told a nephew: "I knew that if we were to begin our second hundred years of life, we'd need a third person like Pierre who would be willing to be chained to a desk. I wanted that desk damn near the cash register. I knew I was an extrovert and couldn't sit still a minute. Al was far from an introvert and was a production man at that time. We needed the steadiness of some stick-at-home-base no matter where I was flying around the country. Pierre would do that."

Adding icing to the cake, Pierre brought with him from Ohio a personal secretary named John J. Raskob, who would become an imposing national figure in his own right and who is credited with first proposing that the Du Pont Company make an investment in General Motors.

Why did their older cousins virtually give away the company to the three younger cousins? Several reasons. The alternatives were rather strictly limited. The suggestion to sell to Laflin & Rand was born of desperation. Family pride swelled at the prospect of keeping the firm in family control. And, if the younger cousins defaulted on the notes, the company would then revert to the noteholders. Generations of hard work to build a name and a reputation are not easily relinquished, and if cold, objective analysis might have raised cause for concern, ties of blood quickly submerged doubt.

One du Pont, in what even he recognized as a burst of sentimentality, suggested another reason the older partners wanted to keep the business in the family—employee relations. He contended that the du Ponts were proud of their record in that area and concerned that the well-being of their employees might suffer if entrusted to strange hands. Such a notion smacks of an almost unswallowable ingenuousness. Even the most generous du Pont supporter might be embarrassed to put forth so pure an altruistic motivation. But, understanding that the motivation was by no means an overriding one but simply an additional factor perhaps, a case could be made. From the beginning, the du Ponts were closer to their workers than most employers because of the nature of the business and the du Ponts' participation in all its aspects. In 1902, 106 out of a total of about 250 Du Pont employees had been with the company twenty years or more. These figures count only those working at the mills along the Brandywine. Undoubtedly an even higher percentage of twenty-year men would have been realized if explosions over the years had not taken so many lives. From 1815 to 1907, 393 workers died in explosions at Du Pont facilities, nearly 100 of those deaths occurring along the Brandywine.

Coleman, Alfred, and Pierre wasted no time getting down to work. While Coleman turned his attention to marketing, purchasing, and transportation, Alfred began a tour of the manufacturing facilities. Pierre and Raskob began an analysis of the company inventory and realized almost immediately they had themselves a bargain. Even valued conservatively, the company assets were more like $14 million than $12 million.

The road to improved profitability was clearly marked. It

was called consolidation. The Du Pont Company owned
pieces of many independently operated businesses and several
companies outright, Hazard Powder Company in particular.
Setting up administrative, sales, purchasing, and transportation departments and merging the diverse operations
into one centrally controlled company were the first moves
needed, and at once it became obvious that control of Laflin
& Rand was crucial to success. The two giant rivals together
controlled a large majority of the explosives industry. Each
held blocks of stock in many other companies that if combined would represent controlling interest. On its own, neither company could consolidate the industry.

Fortunately for Du Pont, Laflin & Rand was in the throes
of a management crisis similar to the one through which Du
Pont had just come. The family enterprise was controlled by
older men beginning to relish the prospect of retirement.
Pierre's uncle—his mother's brother, Henry Belin—was asked
to approach Laflin because of his long acquaintance with its
management. He reported that Laflin's owners were receptive
to a take-over. Further talks established an asking price that
was roughly double the current market price, and Pierre and
Raskob balked. Coleman, however, prevailed, insisting the
price was worth it given the potential of the combined companies.

Once again, Coleman, with Pierre doing the figuring, managed to overcome the sellers' prejudice in favor of cash, peddling instead another notes and stock package. For $4.5 mil-
lion in 4½ per cent notes and $1 million in stock, Du Pont
bought 54 per cent of Laflin & Rand. The deal was consum-
mated on August 26, 1902. Six months earlier, the du Ponts
had been ready to sell out to Laflin & Rand. In half a year,
three men all under forty had taken a company, Du Pont, on
the verge of extinction and, with virtually no cash outlay, had
bought control of an industry.

Some tying together of loose ends remained to be done.
There was the California market, which Du Pont owned a big

chunk of but did not control, and a few other details to sweep up, but by 1907, Du Pont controlled 64 per cent of the black blasting, 71 per cent of the blasting, 73.6 per cent of the black sporting, and 64 per cent of the smokeless sporting powder production in the United States. It also controlled 71.5 per cent of the dynamite and 100 per cent of the government ordnance business.

The reorganization the company was undergoing was novel to the business world in a number of respects. Among the most important was Coleman's proposal first made late in 1902 that key employees be permitted to buy stock in the company, an idea older institutions like the railroads and Standard Oil had not yet developed. By 1905 a bonus plan had been worked out, essentially allowing employees to pay for a given number of shares allotted them through the accrual of dividends. In 1904 a pension plan was set up. The du Ponts were early and firm believers in the philosophy of owner management, convinced that employees would make a larger contribution to the success of the company if they had a personal stake in that success. Coleman, Alfred, and Pierre personally extended this belief to younger members of the family, offering $25,000 worth of their own stock to young Alexis I., Eugene, Eugene E., Francis I., A. Felix, Ernest, William K., Irénée, Lammot, and Victor Jr.

It did not take Coleman, Alfred, and Pierre long to realize that the Gunpowder Trade Association was an outmoded and inefficient organization that may well have been illegal as well. In 1903 the company's executive committee, at Pierre's urging, passed a resolution to the effect that "subterfuge or trade deceit" would not be tolerated, a position reiterated in 1905. From the beginning, Coleman suspected that the smaller companies in the powder trust were falsifying sales records to get a larger slice of the pie, a suspicion he soon proved. In March of 1904 Du Pont withdrew from the trust. Companies controlled by Du Pont but not yet fully assimilated followed suit. The Gunpowder Trade Association was defunct, although its burial was not accomplished until the following year.

Marred only by Coleman's occasional battles with ill health, Du Pont fortunes snowballed smoothly along. Legal tangles caused some delays in the consolidating operation, but they appeared relatively insignificant, certainly no cause for excessive concern. True, a few companies controlled by Du Pont continued to give the appearance of independent operation, but these were just hangovers from an earlier period when such practices were more or less usual if not totally acceptable. Their existence could hardly be attributed to criminal intent. Even after the question was first raised— indeed, for the next six years after that—the du Ponts remained sanguine on that score. They had done nothing to leave themselves vulnerable to prosecution, surely not to successful prosecution, they were positive.

In early 1906 a disgruntled former employee—the man Coleman had first picked to head the company's consolidated sales operation, Robert S. Waddell—mounted a virulent crusade against the Du Pont Company, charging it made huge profits because of its monopoly on government business and daily violated the nation's antitrust and restraint of trade laws, doing so with its eyes open. Waddell portrayed Colonel Henry du Pont as the real head of the company and said the Colonel was being sent to the U. S. Senate to look after Du Pont interests. The du Ponts were not overly concerned. "I suppose Waddell goes on the principle that all is fair in war," Pierre wrote at the time, "but I believe he has overreached himself in this attempt to injure us and on that account I think that his article will misfire."

It did not. The nation was growing increasingly concerned about the concentration of economic power and its abuses. Monopoly was not a game; it was a dirty word. The du Ponts could argue and believe all they wanted that theirs was a consolidated business competing on a basis of economic efficiency, but viewed in another—more popular although perhaps not altogether more revealing—light, the explosives industry was being run by an association in restraint of trade controlled by the du Ponts. A little smugly maybe, the du Ponts futilely pointed out that the powder trust was dead and had been for some time. A cosmetic change and no more, replied Waddell and his growing number of supporters.

And still the du Ponts appeared unruffled. They seemed to believe the attack against them was purely political in its motivation. They knew the nation's military establishment valued its relationship with the company, and the du Ponts were not without political clout of their own. Finally, of course, the family considered the charges against it and the company spurious. The government took the du Ponts, and especially Coleman, Alfred, and Pierre, almost completely by surprise when it filed suit in the summer of 1907 charging violations of the Sherman Antitrust Act.

Taking Waddell's claim that Colonel Henry headed the company on faith, a substantial segment of the nation's press began flaying the company and the Colonel, now a U.S. senator, along with Coleman, who was also prominent in national politics as head of the Republican National Committee's Speakers' Bureau. The case dragged on for four years. Despite the bad press, the du Ponts continued to believe they'd win the court case. Public sentiment was not running in their favor. In 1909 Congress almost passed a bill that would have made it illegal for the Navy to purchase smokeless powder from Du Pont. Only a strong, final-hour lobbying effort prevented the bill's enactment.

Among the most damaging aspects of the government's case against Du Pont was the powder trust's international agreement signed in 1897. Not until well after the antitrust attack had been launched did company attorneys advise the executive committee that the agreement was illegal, and it was not replaced by another agreement, covering patents instead of sales territories, until 1907. That first agreement became a cornerstone of the government's case.

In March of 1911 the government won its case against the Standard Oil trust, which was ordered dissolved. The du Ponts considered that case different enough from their own to warrant continued optimism. On June 21 a federal court found Du Pont guilty of having violated and of continuing to violate the Sherman Antitrust Act. The du Ponts were shocked and embittered. The only good news was that the court dismissed the charges against Colonel Henry, buying the argument that the Colonel had effectively severed his relationship with the company in 1902.

As president of the company, Coleman's initial reaction was to ask for a rehearing of the case, but the more he thought about lawyers the angrier he became. In his opinion, they'd already botched the job once and been paid more than $100,000 a year the past few years for doing so. Coleman soon decided he could do a better job himself, especially considering his political connections. The next few months were infuriating and frustrating as Coleman tried in vain to convince the Attorney General of the United States, George Wickersham, that the court had erred. As the election year of 1912 moved into spring, no one had budged. In its decision the court had recognized the impossibility of breaking up the Du Pont Company into all the little firms that had existed prior to the consolidation efforts of Coleman and Pierre and had asked Du Pont to come before it with a solution of its own making that would meet the court requirements, primarily a restoration of competition in the explosives industry. The du Ponts hadn't really given that too much thought yet; they were still considering an appeal. In March Wickersham happened to run into Alfred I. in Philadelphia and told him of the plan to appoint a receiver for the company, whether the court's decision was appealed or not. Pierre, who had realized for six months the need for a settlement, now felt a strong sense of urgency. Any settlement worked out by a receiver would clearly be less advantageous to the family and the company than one prepared in-house.

The Du Pont Company asked the government for a proposal. What would it think fair? The government proved astonishingly accommodating and in almost no time at all, the du Ponts had agreed to create two new companies and provide them with the capacity to supply some 40 per cent of the dynamite and half the black powder business. The government didn't mention assets, and the plan agreed to called for selling the two new companies assets totaling $20 million, while the parent company retained assets of $60 million. The $20 million would be paid for with $10 million in income bonds and $10 million in stock. All the stock and at least half the bonds would be sold or distributed to the parent company's stockholders—essentially the du Pont family. The parent was allowed to retain all the smokeless powder business, at least partially because the military establishment interceded on Du Pont's behalf. The court approved the final decree on June 13, 1912. Thus were born Hercules Powder Company, now Hercules, Incorporated, and Atlas Powder Company, now the American subsidiary of Imperial Chemical Industries. Hercules was about twice the size of Atlas upon the formation of the two.

Waddell, the du Ponts' nemesis, continued to seek retributive justice. He sued Du Pont, claiming his company, the Buckeye Powder Company, had suffered losses of some $600,000 because of Du Pont's unfair competitive practices. He asked treble damages. After two years in court, the du Ponts won a total victory. Coleman was all set to turn around and sue Waddell for perjury, but when it was discovered that both Waddell and his company were broke, the matter was dropped.

Years later Pierre would characterize the conduct of the antitrust case in a letter to a nephew in one vitriolic sentence: "The whole performance was an outrage on proper conduct of law, much of it in the nature of comic opera farce." Coleman considered the government ungrateful from the beginning. At the start of the case, he petulantly pointed out that "our company carried the government during the Civil War when their credit was bad for not only all the company had but for all their borrowing capacity at banks." With all the bitterness the du Ponts harbored toward the government during this time, they could consider themselves exceedingly fortunate. Their company emerged from the proceedings remarkably intact.

The decade from 1906 through 1916 was a highly prosperous one for the Du Pont Company, especially in the latter part of the period, but for the family it was perhaps the roughest ten years in its history. The trouble began in 1906 when Alfred divorced Bessie Gardner. It was not a popular move, although the family's attitude toward divorce may have mellowed somewhat from the universal disapproval with which William du Pont's divorce was greeted more than a decade earlier. William, for one, was able to muster sympathy for Alfred's side. Alfred did little to assuage family feelings when he married his cousin Alicia Bradford Maddox the following year amid a host of rumors that the marriage merely formalized a relationship of rather long standing. Old Colonel Henry was outraged. Pierre felt Alfred had done Bessie no small disservice, and while he remained on more or less friendly terms with Alfred, he became Bessie's financial guardian, straining his relationship with her former husband somewhat. As the family took sides in the affair, brothers and sisters often found themselves in opposition.

Further complicating matters was the business relationship between Pierre and Coleman. While their correspondence reveals a deep affection and respect for one another, their business judgments sometimes conflicted. Coleman, for example, felt that William, more or less exiled from the banks of the Brandywine after his divorce, deserved a repatriation of sorts and a place on the company's board of directors. Pierre was strongly opposed to such a move, afraid, for one thing, that William's return would alienate his brother, Colonel Henry, who would carry his enmity toward William to the grave. As Coleman's health and inherent restlessness kept him away from his office more and more, the weight of Pierre's burdens increased. True, his brothers Irénée and Lammot were beginning to assume added responsibilities, but then the contretemps with Alfred had decreased Alfred's participation in company affairs. The duties of running the Du Pont Company were in Pierre's hands, but the authority seemed vaguely elusive.

As Coleman began to invest in a major way in New York real estate, his cash needs increased. He was, furthermore, convinced that because of his disagreements with Pierre on management questions, particularly in the spring and early summer of 1914, one or the other of them would have to take a back seat and "make noises like a dummy." Coleman realized that neither he nor Pierre would tolerate such a position. Finally, both Pierre and Coleman agreed to the advisability of making a block of stock available for purchase by the company's younger, rising executives. Coleman considered it not quite appropriate that he owned the largest block of stock while growing increasingly inactive in company affairs. One of two solutions to these problems seemed the best course— either Pierre ought to sell out to Coleman, who would resume an active role, or Coleman should sell at least a part of his holdings to Pierre or the company.

In the summer of 1914 Irénée and a group of his cousins and business associates offered Coleman $125 a share for some of his Du Pont stock. He wrote them back, countering that he would buy their stock for $137 a share. As the year drew to a close, Coleman worked out a proposal with Pierre— a proposal with which Alfred and William, who by this time had been elected to the board and was the third member of the finance committee, agreed in principle—to sell 20,700 shares of Coleman's stock to the company for purchase by its younger executives. Coleman was asking $160 a share, which was close to the high at which the stock had sold recently.

In retrospect, the price was a rare bargain, but at the time, it had a speculative nature. Starting that fall, with Russia's entry into World War I, the Du Pont Company had begun to receive enormous orders for powder from the Allies. The profit potential was huge, but its realization depended on the company's ability to expand rapidly enough to fulfill those orders, and at the time, no one was predicting that the war would last for four more years. Knowing the war would not last forever and that when it ended, the company might well be stuck with large orders that would be canceled and production facilities that would no longer be needed, Pierre drove some hard bargains with the Allies, insisting on 50 per cent up-front payment to finance the expansion necessary not with Du Pont but with Allied dollars. This policy substantially mitigated the risk, but it did not ensure profitability.

In August, Coleman's deteriorating health forced a further management reorganization. Irénée was being groomed to take over, but was reluctant at that point. Pierre stayed on as chief executive officer and acting president while Irénée, as chairman of the executive committee, became the operating head. A younger group of managers was given additional responsibilities, a move long advocated by Coleman.

Just how much of the company's prospects were known to Alfred and William in late December of 1914 and their ability to evaluate those prospects given their limited participation in the day-to-day activities of the firm are problematic. At any rate, in a meeting of the finance committee on December 23, Alfred and William turned down Coleman's proposal as presented by Pierre, arguing the price was too high and that $125 a share would be about the most the company ought to be willing to pay. That was, although William and Alfred probably didn't know it, the price at which Coleman had offered to sell his stock to Pierre or buy Pierre's stock the previous August, an offer Pierre turned down because he said he felt Coleman was upset over his disagreements with Pierre on business matters and didn't really want to sell. Pierre was also hesitant at that time to break up a partnership that had been so extraordinarily successful.

Coleman and Pierre were taken aback. Coleman sardonically inquired how much of Alfred's stock Alfred would be willing to sell to the company's younger executives at $125 a share, noting he, Coleman, would be happy to match any offer his cousin made. Nonetheless, Coleman kept his offer open for several weeks. In mid-January of 1915 Pierre and Coleman discussed the possibility of Coleman's making a direct offer to the junior executives but postponed any action until they could get together in person. Coleman was at this time recuperating out west from a serious operation at the Mayo Clinic to relieve complications that had developed after his 1909 gallstone surgery.

On January 23 Pierre and Irénée went to New York to meet Ernest Kraftmeier, an associate of the British Nobel Company, an explosives concern. Kraftmeier had requested the meeting, which Pierre assumed would involve discussion of further Allied purchases from Du Pont. Kraftmeier breathed not a word about purchases. Instead he floored Pierre with the news that rumors abroad had the pro-German investment firm of Kuhn, Loeb having gained control of the Du Pont Company because of the financial embarrassment of one of Du Pont's major stockholders. Kraftmeier said the Allies were much concerned that orders already placed with Du Pont would now be in jeopardy. The embarrassed stockholder was not mentioned by name, but it could only have been Coleman. Quickly Pierre assured Kraftmeier that the rumor had no basis in fact, but the encounter disturbed Pierre, and at a meeting of the company finance committee four days later, Pierre proposed a pooling of the stock held by the committee members—Pierre, Alfred, William, and the absent Coleman—under an agreement prohibiting the sale or pledging of any of that stock without the consent of all four during the duration of the war. The four cousins among them controlled enough stock so that such an agreement would certainly reassure the Allies.

Pooling his stock was not a prospect that appealed to Coleman. He was seriously ill—he had been near death for several days following his operation—and feared that should he die with his stock so encumbered, the effect on his estate might be critical. His real estate ventures promised to demand more capital, another reason for keeping his assets liquid, and it is possible he did not fully understand the details or the reasons behind the pooling of stock proposal and was therefore leery of committing himself. In early February Coleman had a relapse, taking almost a week to recover. On February 17 Pierre and Coleman's secretary, Lew Dunham, had a meeting, prompted by a letter from Coleman to Pierre indicating he might be willing to sell as many as forty thousand of his shares at the prevailing market price. At the meeting, Pierre realized for the first time that Coleman might be willing to sell his entire holdings. Pierre figured he'd need about $14 million.

On February 20 Coleman and Pierre made a deal. Pierre formed a syndicate that included his two brothers Lammot and Irénée; a brother-in-law, R. R. M. Carpenter; John J. Raskob, the man Pierre had brought with him to Du Pont from Ohio; and later his cousin A. Felix du Pont, who was then engaged in the critical work of expanding the smokeless powder production facilities to meet war demands. That same day Raskob had received a commitment from J. P. Morgan's banking firm for up to $10.8 million in loans.

By telegram, Pierre offered Coleman $8 million in cash and $5.8 million in seven-year 5 per cent notes for Coleman's 63,214 shares of Du Pont common and 13,989 shares of preferred, an offer that worked out to $200 a share for the common and $80 a share for the preferred. Coleman wired back that he would rather keep the preferred than sell at $80 and wanted 6 per cent interest on the notes. Pierre agreed to the higher interest and offered $85 for the preferred. Coleman agreed. The notes were to be secured by Du Pont common owned by the syndicate members. The Du Pont Securities Company, which became Christiana Securities Company in 1918, was formed as the legal vehicle through which the transaction would be made. An $8.5 million loan was secured through Bankers Trust Company of New York on behalf of the Morgan interests. The final negotiations were conducted in strict secrecy. The deal was confirmed on February 22, although the final papers were not signed until early March.

Before two months were out, Pierre had given five key Du Pont employees each $250,000 worth of the new syndicate's stock. To another he had given $100,000. To twelve of his relatives he had offered 500 shares—$100,000—in return for 223 shares of their Du Pont stock. He would also give $50 in cash to make up for a quarter share, as the original syndicate's exchange rate had been 500 syndicate shares for 222.75 Du Pont shares. His brothers-in-law—William Winder Laird, H. Rodney Sharp, and Charles Copeland—along with cousins Eugene E. and Henry F. du Pont accepted the offer. Alexis I., Eugene, Francis I., Ernest, E. Paul, Archibald M. L., and Philip F. declined.

With the completion of the syndicate, Pierre held 31,625 shares in Du Pont Securities and his two brothers Irénée and Lammot had 10,953 each. Brother-in-law R. R. M. Carpenter had 5,045, Felix du Pont 5,894, and John Raskob 3,780.

The balance of power within the family had changed dramatically. Pierre and his branch of the family now had control. The destiny of the family and the company was in Pierre's hands. But the price would prove far steeper than the nearly $14 million paid to Coleman, which at any rate would prove to be a steal, for by 1964 that $14 million investment was worth $1 billion.

Alfred and William first heard about Pierre's coup, they later claimed, by reading about it in the Sunday newspaper of February 28. The item had been planted by Pierre after Morgan bankers in New York had reported that rumor of the deal had leaked onto Wall Street. The next day, after waiting until 4 P.M. to hear from Pierre, Alfred asked him to come to his office and told Pierre he assumed the purchase Pierre had just made was for the company. Pierre said no, it was a personal transaction. Alfred told him there was no way he could have financed the purchase without using the credit of the company and therefore the stock should be turned over to the company. Pierre said he didn't see it that way. The next day Pierre received a telegram from William, vacationing in Georgia, who accused Pierre of a breach of faith unless the stock had been purchased for the company. Pierre suspected the telegram was inspired by Alfred, who called a meeting the following day of all the du Ponts who had not participated in the syndicate. Pierre showed up uninvited.

The assemblage beat around the bush for an hour before Pierre finally broke in, asking William to explain his charge of breach of faith. William repeated the contention that the purchase could not have been financed without the explicit or at least implicit use of the company's credit. Pierre said that wasn't so. Alfred asked point blank if Pierre refused to sell the stock to the company. Pierre said yes, he refused.

It didn't take Pierre long to realize that his categorical refusal was a tactical error and he quickly wrote the company's directors a letter in which he withdrew his refusal, promising an open mind on any proposal by which the company might acquire the stock. It was a gesture of more grace than substance. Pierre had a pretty tight grip on the board of directors.

At the directors' meeting of March 6, Coleman's letter of resignation was accepted. Pierre was elected president and chairman of the finance committee. His brother Irénée was elected to replace Coleman on that committee. Felix du Pont was elected a director. The meeting turned to the Coleman stock transaction and turned into what Pierre described as "the hottest meeting ever." Alfred walked out. Pierre had a motion made that the company buy the stock from the syndicate at cost. Then he had the company general counsel come in and explain that because it would require an investment substantially in excess of the company's $7.5 million surplus, such a move would be illegal. The matter was referred to the finance committee.

In a letter to Coleman describing the meeting, Pierre predicted that the finance committee would vote two to one with his abstention to have the company buy the stock. Alfred and William were still on the committee, along with Irénée. The directors would defeat the proposal, Pierre foresaw. And that's just what happened. Only Francis I. was enough persuaded by the arguments of Alfred and William to vote with them in favor of the company's purchase. One other director abstained. The vote was 14–3. Pierre hoped that would be it. Perhaps he had forgotten Alfred's 1902 speech to the older partners when he told them he would buy the company from them. The company was, Alfred had said, his by right of birth. He was the eldest son of the eldest son of the eldest son of the founder. Pierre had denied Alfred that birthright. It was one thing voluntarily to invest it in another, as Alfred had when he agreed to give Coleman a free hand in the new company. But in Alfred's view, Pierre had now stolen it. The battle was just beginning. Before it was over, it would pit brother against brother, husband against wife, neighbor against neighbor, and the family would never again be quite the same.

War of another sort, world war, occupied Pierre's summer, leaving him little time to brood over the emotional wounds opened among the family by the Coleman affair. In September he visited Washington in an attempt to trace rumors he heard to the effect that the Department of Justice was looking into a charge that the syndicate's company, Du Pont Securities Company, was in violation of antitrust laws. The rumor proved true, but the Justice Department did not seem too concerned. Although he couldn't prove it, Pierre was pretty sure that Alfred was behind the complaint, a conviction made stronger by Alfred's refusal to give a yes or no answer when Pierre asked him directly if he was responsible.

Christmas 1915 must have been for the du Pont family a subdued affair at best. On December 9 papers were served on Pierre announcing a suit contesting his purchase of Coleman's stock. The plaintiff was Philip F. du Pont, a somewhat eccentric cousin given to writing poetry and living in relative seclusion in nearby Pennsylvania. He was known as Fireman Phil because of a penchant for chasing fire trucks. Among those named as defendants was Eugene E. du Pont, Philip's brother. Publicly at least, the two never spoke again.

Few believed that Philip had dreamed up the suit solely on his own initiative. Soon his first cousins, the children of F. G. (Frank) du Pont, joined the suit as intervenors. Eleanor du Pont Perot was first, followed by her brothers—E. Paul, Archibald M. L., and Ernest. On January 10, 1916, came the fellow everyone had been waiting for, Alfred I. Two days later another son of Frank du Pont, Francis I., joined in. The lines had been drawn.

No event in the history of the family has ever had the emotional overtones rung by this suit. First, the family had always been a private clan, settling differences quietly within the family and assiduously avoiding publicity both favorable and unfavorable. Shyness was virtually genetic in the family, and now the family's soiled linen would be washed in full public view. That the case ever reached trial is a measure of how deeply and immutably feelings ran. Only the members of Pierre's branch of the family were able to agree on where their loyalties lay in the two matters with which Alfred rent the family fabric—his divorce and the lawsuit. Pierre and his brothers and sisters all supported Alfred's first wife in the divorce matter and Pierre in the suit. But even here, loyalty was not a simple thing. Irénée's wife, for example, was the daughter of Frank du Pont. Four of her brothers and a sister were on Alfred's side in the suit, and three brothers and the same sister had sided with Alfred in the divorce. Pierre's sister, Mary, who married William Winder Laird, lived next door to Ernest du Pont, who sided with Alfred in both affairs. Their children were friends, and Laird helped manage the affairs of E. Paul du Pont's mother-in-law. Paul was on Alfred's side in the suit. Paul's next-door neighbor was Margaretta du Pont Carpenter, another of Pierre's sisters.

The irreparable rift between Philip and his brother Eugene E. was further complicated by their sister, Alice, who sided with Alfred in the suit but whose husband, a man named Ortiz, refused to talk to Alfred. Philip's mother wrote Pierre a letter at the time of the suit's filing expressing great distress at the action of her son and saying she did not even know about the suit until she read of it in the papers or she might have been able to persuade her son to abandon it. While Alfred's sister Marguerite and brother Maurice both sided with him in the suit, Marguerite took Bessie Gardner's side in the divorce and the strength of Maurice's support for his brother was brought somewhat into question as far as the divorce case was concerned when Maurice's wife refused to talk to Alfred's second wife, Alicia.

Alicia's family—her mother was a du Pont—was split down the middle, with Alicia and her brother Edward Bradford, Jr., embracing the Alfred faction while two sisters, Joanna and Eleuthera, who had married Pierre's brother Henry B., went against Alfred in both matters.

The division among the children of Frank du Pont was perhaps ironic. It was, after all, Frank who had been the most skeptical of Alfred's proposal to buy the company back in 1902, but a majority of his children sided with Alfred in both cases. Francis I., A. Felix, Ernest, and Eleanor took Alfred's part in the divorce case, with E. Paul, Archibald, and Irene sympathizing with Bessie. In the lawsuit, only Felix, who had recently been made a director of the Du Pont Company, and Irene, married to Irénée, backed Pierre. The others were all with Alfred, in Eleanor's case at least partly because her husband did some work for Alfred. Again, back fences became dividing lines rather than objects over which neighbors exchanged local gossip. Felix and Ernest were neighbors, for

example. Adding to the emotional complexities of the whole
period were conflicts between sentiment and sense of duty.
The different sides were more or less universal in observing
the Victorian code that essentially dictated that opposing factions decline to speak to one another in public. But family
members today insist that incidents of supposed enemies
chatting in private are legion.

Finally, the family feud must be placed against a background in which cousins grew up playing together and developing strong ties. Becoming adults, many of the men went
to work for the Du Pont Company and here loyalties divided
between those who believed in the old ways of the former
partnership and those who cheered the fast-paced, aggressive
methods of the newer managers. Their jobs depended on how
some family members viewed their company—and therefore
family branch—loyalties. Other family members lived in company-owned houses, a situation that occasionally caused divided loyalties. In the case of Alfred's divorce, family loyalties
sometimes collided with strong moral beliefs.

The case went to trial in late June of 1916. By this time,
Alfred was out of the company. Two days before Alfred
officially intervened in the case, Pierre wrote the company's
board of directors a letter, dated January 8, 1916, in which
he recommended the removal of Alfred. "It is quite impossible that this suit should have been brought without the con-
nivance and co-operation of Mr. Alfred I. du Pont," Pierre
wrote. Francis I. was the only director to vote against Alfred's
removal from the board. Alexis I., son of former company
head Eugene, abstained.

The trial, which lasted three weeks, contested three points
of fact. Alfred I. argued that he and William declined Coleman's offer at the December 23, 1914, finance committee
meeting because they felt the price was too high "at this
time." The phrase in quotes was not a part of the minutes of
the meeting, which were signed by Alfred. He said he
changed his mind about the price between the time of the

meeting and the March 10, 1915, directors' meeting at which the proposal to buy Coleman's stock from Pierre for the company was rejected because in December company powder orders were for about 18 million pounds whereas in early March they had soared to 100 million pounds. The second point Alfred's side tried to prove was that Pierre and his syndicate could not have borrowed the money needed to complete the transaction without the credit of the company behind them and that in any case, the company would be required to meet obligations incurred by the syndicate. The third point involved the extent to which Pierre kept Coleman fully informed on company matters and the finance committee's position toward Coleman's offer during the negotiating period, from late December until late February. On this score, Coleman testified briefly at the trial that he believed he had been well apprised on all matters with which he was concerned. The preserved correspondence between Pierre and Coleman during this period is voluminous.

Undoubtedly a subtle factor in the trial was the Midas-like profitability of the company since the transaction. From January 3, 1915, to June 1, 1916, the company had paid dividends equivalent to 183 per cent of the per share purchase price of Coleman's stock and had $31 million in its treasury with a proposal to pay out $90 a share in additional dividends. Pierre argued that nonetheless, at the time of purchase, Coleman's stock was a risky proposition. Profits would accumulate only if the company fulfilled its contracts and that was no foregone conclusion. There were purchases to be made, construction to be done, production schedules and contract deadlines to be met. There were rumors that Congress might outlaw munition sales or pass a tax on munitions profits.

The testimony was not always rational. Alfred was asked about inquiries he apparently made in New York on the borrowing power of Du Pont stock. "I wanted to know whether or not it would be considered as ample or proper collateral for a loan, and if so, what the relation between its par value or market value and collateral value would be," Alfred testified.

"Is not that the same," he was asked, "as an inquiry as to how much could be borrowed on it?"

Replied Alfred: "No. It is entirely a different thing."

Pierre claimed Alfred had charged him with being, in Pierre's words, "totally incompetent, extravagant and wasteful, and that I would probably wreck the company within three years." Asked if Alfred had not been instrumental in bringing him back to Wilmington and the company in 1902, Pierre replied, "Not that I know of, no." Well, technically, it had been Coleman's phone call, but Alfred's role was surely not insignificant.

Of all the du Ponts who testified during the trial, Francis I., the man who would later found the brokerage firm that would become the second largest in the nation, performed with perhaps the greatest dignity and honor. He had declined Pierre's offer to join the syndicate because it was "against my convictions," he said. Alfred was his friend. But even he lapsed into bitterness for a moment when he was asked if Pierre was the sort of man who would attempt to insult or demean him by a bribe. "I would not care to say what I think about Mr. P. S. du Pont now," he said.

The court opinion, issued April 12, 1917, was a hollow victory for Alfred. The opinion, a supplemental opinion, and an interlocutory decree combined to order the company to hold a special stockholders' meeting to vote on whether or not the company should purchase Coleman's stock. After some haggling over voting eligibility, the meeting was held on October 10. The vote was almost two to one against the company's acquiring the stock, a predictable enough outcome given Pierre's control of the company. The following March the court upheld the vote, and the case was dismissed.

Although as a practical matter, Pierre had won, it was a Pyrrhic victory. His personal copy of the trial transcript is heavily annotated in his handwriting in the margins. His notes provide convincing evidence he believed he was right not only legally but morally. In fifty-eight separate places, he cites "lies" in the plaintiffs' requests for findings of fact and conclusions of law. Two points he makes repeatedly. One is that the directions given Pierre by the finance committee at the conclusion of the fateful December 23, 1914, meeting did not include an order to tell Coleman why the committee was turning down his offer. The other, more salient, point is that at no time was Coleman's offer made to the company for its own purposes but rather in order that the company could help its key executives to acquire the stock. Pierre was sure Alfred had misunderstood his motives.

Alfred did not accept his defeat gracefully, making one last futile appeal to the U. S. Third Circuit Court of Appeals. On March 6, 1919, that court upheld the dismissal of the case. Legally it was over; emotionally it would linger on for years. It had been a struggle of titans. The three principals—Alfred, Pierre, and Coleman—were men who would come to be viewed in the perspective of time passed as legendary, larger-than-life figures, their human foibles and eccentricities forgiven or forgotten, lost among their accomplishments.

If there is a story that remains untold about the family feud, which has been hashed and rehashed over the years in books and periodicals, it is the way in which the family conducted itself in private during those wrenching times. It was determined early—not by any specific gathering of the clan but in a sort of general consensus arrived at snowball fashion —that the poison of the feud ought not to bridge generational gaps. The parents might not speak to one another, but their children should be made to realize that this was not a Hatfield vs. McCoy affair, that someday perhaps they might want to read the transcripts of the trial and decide for themselves where the paths of righteousness led, but that for now, how mother and father felt ought not to influence the feelings of son and daughter.

Thus, the children of Mary and William Winder Laird continued to play with the children of the Ernest and E. Paul du Ponts, for example, although their respective parents never spoke to each other in public. William Winder, Jr., or Chick as he is called by his many friends and acquaintances, remembers playing with Ernest's children although his mother and Ernest didn't speak. He recalls Ed Bradford, Jr., riding his (Laird's) pony. The memory of attending the birthday parties of the children of E. Paul is still fresh in his mind. He and his sisters would be driven to E. Paul's house. "It was always the chauffeur who drove, though," Laird remembers.

Even the most bitter intrafamily falling out was not allowed to carry on through succeeding generations. Although Colonel Henry never forgave his brother William the indiscretion of divorce and an animosity developed between the two that ended only with the Colonel's death, their two sons, William Jr. and Henry Francis, while hardly intimate friends, were always on speaking terms at least.

This effort to keep feuds personal rather than familial, to hold them within the generation that provoked them paid some later dividends. Although Alfred never forgave Pierre despite Pierre's several attempts to hold out an olive branch, most of the other participants in the feud were reconciled. At least part of that reconciliation came about because their children enjoyed one another and eventually dragged their parents into the fun.

The events of 1915 changed the structure of the family radically. Pierre's branch was now in control. Coleman and Alfred had gotten out of the business, although Alfred was still the second largest stockholder in the company. Perhaps the remarkable thing is that the family retained any sort of structure at all in the aftermath of that year.

Chapter Five

Pierre: Star of the Show

The foundation on which is built the public image of the du Pont family as one of fabulous wealth dominating an industry and controlling a state was laid deep, dug by the endurance of the first Eleuthère Irénée and the drive of his son, Boss Henry, and poured by the three young cousins who took over in 1902. But the image did not really take palpable form until World War I. There is no denying that Pierre was its chief architect, not because of any grasp of the public relations art but because it is his name that is associated with the Du Pont Company's extraordinary profitability during the war and its transformation from explosives manufacturer to chemical company afterward. These two factors, coupled with the investment in General Motors, suggested by John Raskob first, but followed through with uncanny judgment by Pierre, leave little room for argument that on the accomplishments of Pierre rests the family reputation today.

But if by the spring of 1915 neither Coleman nor Alfred was any longer active in the Du Pont Company, that did not mean that their stars would shine any less brightly in the financial firmament. No one needed a telescope to track their paths. Indeed, so brightly shone their stars that today their descendants appear dim in that earlier light, even those on whom success has smiled. Of course, rising to fame is far easier than staying on top, let alone clambering to even greater heights.

The modern du Pont family, with its vast numbers and repeating names, can perhaps best be portrayed by breaking it down into six branches. Besides the families of the three cousins who took over the family company in 1902, there are the Henry branch, made up of the descendants of Boss Henry; the Alexis branch, those descending from the Alexis du Pont killed in the 1857 explosion; and the Victor branch, the descendants of the original E. I. du Pont's brother, Victor Marie du Pont. The Pierre branch—or more precisely, the descendants of Pierre's father, Lammot—clearly dominates today's family, both in number and wealth, although individually, members of other branches may rival even the richest members of the Pierre branch, due primarily to the less prolific nature of their forebears.

In the latter days of the nineteenth century, there was little to augur the dominance today of the Lammot (or Pierre) branch. Lammot, to be sure, was highly successful, but he had relinquished his place in the Du Pont Company to pursue his belief that dynamite was the coming material in the explosives business. He had even moved his family away from the Brandywine to Philadelphia.

At the time of Lammot's death, his oldest son, Pierre, was only fourteen. Six years later Pierre joined the Du Pont Company, but he was a restless, ambitious young man, and he didn't think he was moving up fast enough in the family business. He left and went to Ohio. In 1902, of course, he came back, but even then, he was essentially the third man in the three-man partnership that took over the company. Recalling his rise to the top in 1944, some thirty years after the event, Pierre told a cousin he "was forced into prominence largely through Alfred's deafness and Coleman's ill health." That analysis says more about the nature of the man than it does about the circumstances of his move to the front. To put it simply, Pierre was the most successful businessman in the history of the country, if one recognizes the distinction between businessman and entrepreneur. At running a business, Pierre was unsurpassed. He was, to be sure, the right man at the right time in the right place, and he was surrounded by other right men in the right places, but Pierre made it all happen.

Unlike so many others in similar positions, he then stepped aside, early and with grace.

The years of World War I and the decade that followed it made the du Pont family's and company's reputation and fortune. Pierre inherited $49,000 from his father. In 1929 Pierre gave twenty times that amount to charity and paid nearly one hundred times that amount in taxes. In the last half of the nineteenth century, the du Ponts were comfortably well off. By the end of the first quarter of the twentieth century, they had arrived in the realm of the super rich. No one individual gets all the credit, but when it comes to handing credit out, Pierre belongs at the head of the line.

Making profits from World War I was not an exclusive privilege of Du Pont, but the company managed better than most because Pierre saw war business as a danger-fraught affair while other executives were seeing it as a gold mine. War is a temporary proposition, and world war requires a tremendous supply of matériel with no guarantee of how long the demand will last. Pierre, better than anyone else, realized that to supply the Allies with powder would obligate the Du Pont Company to vast expansion of production facilities, facilities that would become obsolete overnight with the war's end. The Du Pont Company did not solicit war business; the Allies came to Du Pont. For Pierre, it was a question of business, not sentiment. If the Allies wanted Du Pont powder, they would have to pay for it. The company had been supplying the U. S. Government's needs for smokeless powder at $.53 a pound and making a profit, although Pierre was not happy about the size of the capital investment that had to be maintained to meet those needs. The first war contract Du Pont signed with the Allies was with the French, who agreed to pay $1.00 a pound with $.50 up front to finance expansion. If Du Pont was going to be stuck with obsolete facilities, Pierre reasoned, someone else was going to pay for them.

It was not quite as harsh or one-sided a bargain as it might first appear. Du Pont placed its production abilities on the line, agreeing to accelerated delivery schedules as part of the contract, schedules few corporations would have been willing to undertake. It paid off. In 1913 the company earned $5.3 million on sales of $26.7 million. In 1916 earnings were $82.1 million on sales of $318.8 million. From 1914 through 1918 Du Pont's gross receipts were more than $1 billion. It paid stockholder dividends amounting to $141 million and retained earnings of $89.3 million. It was with this money that Du Pont launched its diversification program, an effort that would culminate in the Du Pont Company's emergence as the world's largest chemical company. The soundness of the diversification program can also, in large measure, be credited to Pierre.

These were wild years. First, the Du Pont Company had to be geared up for supplying the Allies with powder, a process that saw the personnel in the engineering department alone increase from about 800 to 45,000. In 1915 came the purchase of T. Coleman's stock and the battle with Alfred I. And in September of that year Pierre agreed to join the board of General Motors as a compromise candidate agreeable to both the bankers financing the company and the volatile boss of the company, William C. Durant. Pierre, in fact, became chairman of the board. A little more than two years later, the Du Pont Company invested $25 million of its war profits in General Motors stock. Eugene E. and A. Felix du Pont voted against the purchase. The investment gave Du Pont financial control of General Motors by agreement, with Durant retaining the operational reins.

Meanwhile, the company had developed a five-industry investment plan in anticipation of the war's eventual end. Dyestuffs and allied organic chemicals headed the list, followed by vegetable oil, paint and varnish, water-soluble heavy chemicals, and cellulose and cotton purification. Nothing came of the vegetable oil plan, but the others would become important parts of the business. By far the most important commitment made by the Du Pont Company, especially in light of later events, was that to General Motors. John J. Raskob, who had come to Du Pont as Pierre's personal secretary back in 1902, was the man who convinced Du Pont—and Pierre in particular—that GM was a wise investment. For the first few years of Du Pont's interest in GM, Pierre was not the major Du Pont influence on the auto manufacturer. Raskob, as chairman of its finance committee, was.

A brilliant financier, Raskob proved less formidable as a financial administrator. The information flow and cost controls that were a basic part of the Du Pont operation were missing at GM, in part because while at Du Pont administration was institutional, at GM it was personal, in the form of Durant. Too often, capital allocation was solved by simply giving the various divisions what they wanted and then worrying about how to raise the money. The change-over to peacetime operations and the accompanying expansion to meet the rising demand virtually everyone predicted were expensive. Soon the Du Pont Company's investment had risen to $47 million and its finance committee members were balking at the prospect of increasing this amount. In 1919 a recession caught GM unprepared, with huge inventories and expansion programs. GM's dollar needs continued to escalate, both for capital programs and to finance inventories.

Just when an elaborate scheme to raise additional capital for GM appeared to have solved the company's cash flow problem, Durant dumped an even bigger problem in Du Pont's lap. Durant had been personally trying to support the market in GM stock, which despite his efforts had continued to fall. His string ran out in the fall of 1919 and once again the du Ponts were forced to the rescue. By the early evening of one mid-November day, it became apparent that Durant needed more than $600,000 in cash before the opening of the stock market the next morning and would need an additional $500,000 before the day was out to prevent a collapse in the GM market. Working throughout the night with bankers from J. P. Morgan and Durant, Pierre, Raskob, and Pierre's younger brother Irénée came up with a solution.

It was a highly complicated transaction in several stages. The end result was that Durant resigned, Pierre took over as president of GM, and the Du Pont Company wound up with 38 per cent of GM's stock. While Pierre had been reluctant to take on the presidency of GM, he was finally convinced that no one else was available with both the public stature to renew confidence in the organization and the business acumen to put GM on a sound operational basis. For nearly four years, Pierre worked tirelessly to achieve those goals, and with the help of Alfred Sloan, to whom he turned over the company in 1923, he succeeded, bringing to General Motors much the same operational efficiency that he had brought to Du Pont.

The year before he took the GM presidency, Pierre had turned the Du Pont presidency over to Irénée. Pierre remained as chairman of the board. Du Pont was a smoothly running organization by then, its diversification program well under way with able direction at all levels. In those first years after the war, the Du Pont Company's main strengths were managerial and financial. Most of its diversification program was achieved through acquisition. It was only later—in the 1930s and 1940s—that the company developed the research capability for which it is famous today. Research has always been an integral part of the Du Pont strategy, especially applied research aimed at improving existing products. But the pure research that led to the discovery of nylon was largely the result of the vision and tenacity of Lammot, Irénée's younger brother and successor as president of the company.

Du Pont moved into chemicals rather naturally. The compounds used in the manufacture of explosives had some broad applications in a variety of non-explosive products. The first move, somewhat ironically, was the purchase in 1910 of the Fabrikoid Company, then the largest and most successful producer of artificial leather, a process that employed nitrocellulose (guncotton). More than half a century later, artificial leather, in the form of Du Pont-developed Corfam, would become perhaps the company's largest single product mistake. Between 1915 and 1933 Du Pont bought seventeen companies, not including its investment in General Motors, and became a major factor in four of the five industries envisioned in its original investment list. The man with front-line responsibility for this program was R. R. M. Carpenter, head of the company's development department and the husband of Pierre's youngest sister, Margaretta, called Peg within the family.

During the years of World War I, the du Ponts paid a heavy image price for their large profits on Allied munitions contracts. In 1916 Congress passed a munitions tax that the du Ponts considered unfair in that it singled out powder when a number of other industries were making large profits on Allied war contracts. In 1916 alone, Du Pont paid in munitions taxes an amount equal to its entire profits from the sale of smokeless powder to the U. S. Government in the twenty years since smokeless powder had been developed. Irénée later figured the company paid about 90 per cent of the total collected for the munitions tax and that Hercules, Inc. and the Atlas Powder Company, the two companies spun off from Du Pont by antitrust decree and in which du Pont family members held large blocks of stock, paid most of the rest.

The du Ponts were accused of promoting the war preparedness movement in the United States. Pierre complained bitterly but his complaints fell on unsympathetic ears. Despite the munitions tax, Du Pont made huge profits; no cause for complaint there. And for the most part, Pierre's protestations that firm company policy required both the company and its individual employees to maintain a strict neutrality on the war preparedness issue were simply ignored. Pierre believed that profit was a stronger incentive than patriotism, especially since the United States was not yet at war. Many

Americans considered the company's profits from the war as morally obscene.

Pierre tried vainly to discuss with the government what role Du Pont might be called upon to play in the event of American entry into the war, but such overtures were viewed as warmongering even after the official declaration of war in 1917. It was not until the autumn of that year that the government finally realized the extent to which American participation in the war would reach. A contract under which Du Pont would build and operate huge new powder-production facilities paid for by the government was quickly negotiated, and within a week Du Pont had committed more than $3 million to the project, the largest government contract in the nation's history. At the end of that week, the government canceled the contract. It would be more than two precious months before Du Pont would get another one, and it was in this interim, when it appeared possible that Du Pont would not be involved in new government powder production, that Pierre and Du Pont decided to make the General Motors investment.

The trouble with the government contract, it turned out, was a sentiment rather widely felt in the Wilson administration and perhaps best expressed by Robert Brookings, a member of the War Industries Board, when he said he would "rather pay a dollar a pound for powder for the United States in a state of war if there was no profit in it than pay the Du Pont Company fifty cents a pound for powder if they had ten cents profit in it." Secretary of War Newton D. Baker more or less shared these sentiments, disagreeing with Pierre's interpretation of the risk to Du Pont and the net profit called for in the contract. He labeled the risk virtually non-existent and the profit excessive. He vowed to get the government powder elsewhere and particularly angered Pierre when he told him, in effect, that he thought it was time the American people showed they could do things for themselves. "I thought up to that time I was an American citizen," Pierre said at the time.

In the sense that the Du Pont Company was essentially alone in its capacity to build and operate the necessary powder plants, Du Pont was in the driver's seat. However, the pressure was heavy on Du Pont as well. America was in a state of declared war, and patriotic fever was beginning to run high. The public could all too easily misconstrue the Du Pont position as selfish, greedy, and even traitorous. Du Pont offered to give already drawn plans for the proposed government powder plant to anyone designated as the builder in Du Pont's stead. The government engaged one of the nation's largest engineering and construction firms, Thompson-Starrett, which agreed to build a plant for half the needed capacity. Baker had decided not to deal with Du Pont despite Pierre's offer to submit the matter of recompense to binding arbitration.

But it soon became obvious even to Baker that America would not get the needed powder without the du Ponts. Negotiations were reopened in early January of 1918. A new contract, considerably more favorable to the government, was signed on January 29. Pierre was furious at the Wilson administration's attitude and wanted to go public with the whole story of the negotiations, but cooler heads prevailed, convincing Pierre that such a story could be highly damaging to the war effort and the nation's morale. Instead, Pierre and Du Pont turned their energies toward fulfilling their new contract, which was soon nearly doubled. Du Pont's goal was to come on stream before the rival Thompson-Starrett operation, which had a big head start. By Armistice Day, November 11, Du Pont's plant had produced more than $24 million worth of powder and was well ahead of schedule on construction. Its rival was just beginning production when the war ended. Altogether, Du Pont handled $129.5 million worth of powder business for the U. S. Government and received gross profits of slightly less than $2.7 million. The plants built by Du Pont were built at a unit cost well below that of Thompson-Starrett; if the du Ponts had handled the whole job, it would have cost $13.5 million less than it did, Du Pont's top engineer figured. Thompson-Starrett was not to be blamed, as Pierre was among the first to point out. The firm was to be commended for tackling so large a project with no prior experience. The blame, Pierre felt, lay with those who let the contracts.

With the war's end, Pierre looked forward to retirement. He had wanted to turn the company over to Irénée at the start of the war, but Irénée had said he wasn't ready. Now that argument was no longer valid. Irénée might still be pretty young, but he certainly was not short on experience, and he had a youthful, energetic, and experienced group of managers surrounding him. The old guard that had run the company since 1902 was nearly all gone. On May 1, 1919, Irénée became president of the company and Lammot, his younger brother, became first vice-president and chairman of the executive committee. Pierre contented himself with the chairmanship of the board. The man who molded the modern Du Pont Company was, ironically, its president for a scant four years, having urged the presidency on Irénée even before he himself had officially received the title.

If the Du Pont Company's external activities in those years were spectacular, its internal ones were no less far-reaching. In 1905 the company set up one of the earliest bonus plans on record to compensate managers for extraordinary achievement. The idea was Coleman's, the implementation essentially Pierre's. Coleman and Pierre were as one in believing that executives performed at top capacity when they had a piece of the action, an ownership role in the company rather than just a salaried position. Coleman said he got the idea from Andrew Carnegie's method of handling his steel plant managers. The exact nature of this bonus compensation took some time to work out. A pension plan for employees was an easier matter, perhaps in part because of Du Pont's long tradition of pensioning powder workers' widows. All employees, it was agreed in 1904, who had worked for the com-

pany five or more years would retire at seventy on a pension
to be determined by a formula based on length of service.
Employees in the top salary brackets could elect to work on
past seventy. Employees who became unable to work would
be pensioned if they had twenty-five or more years with the
company. None of which necessarily overwhelms the modern
reader with Du Pont generosity, perhaps, but nonetheless it
represents a pioneer effort for its time.

Coleman and Pierre were also responsible for the administrative organization of the company and the management by
committee concept widely copied in large modern corporations and studied in business schools. Pierre once called Coleman's idea for separating the finance committee from the executive committee and having it report directly to the board
of directors Coleman's single most important contribution to
the company's welfare, a high value indeed considering Coleman's many other accomplishments. It was not, however,
until 1921, under Irénée, that the company underwent its
most significant, far-reaching reorganization.

Perhaps it was the struggle that consumed the company's
founder in his last years, when he found it necessary continually to travel to Philadelphia banks for financing of his
new enterprise, that dictated the financial conservatism of his
descendants. Whatever the cause, Du Pont until recent years
has always looked with a jaundiced eye on the borrowing of
money to finance expansion. The current chief executive
officer, Irving S. Shapiro, is the first to use debt for funding
U.S. operations. The company had always generated the
needed money from earnings in the past, and one of its chief
attractions for investors was its enormous potential borrowing
power.

While Pierre was able to curtail his day-to-day activities in
the affairs of Du Pont and General Motors after 1923, his retirement was hardly hibernation. He kept a close watch on
both companies and important decisions were seldom reached
without his advice and consent more or less right up until the

day he died in 1954. With Du Pont in Irénée's capable hands and GM led by the brilliant Alfred Sloan, Pierre turned his attentions toward Delaware and his estate at Longwood in nearby Pennsylvania.

Never so completely immersed in his business affairs that he neglected what he considered civic obligations, Pierre had used the short hiatus between his resignation of the Du Pont presidency and his acceptance of the GM reins to attempt a reformation of the Delaware public school system. It sorely needed work. Pierre paid for an independent survey of the system by some of the nation's leading experts in the field, who reported in 1919 that Delaware ranked eighth in income tax paid and nineteenth in wealth per teacher but that, outside Wilmington, the state ranked thirty-ninth in spending per pupil, fortieth in teachers' salaries, and forty-fifth in capital expenditures. The state had the worst school attendance in the country. "The schools of Delaware are a state and national scandal," Pierre proclaimed.

A new state education code was drawn and with heavy publicity in its favor generated largely by Pierre, it passed in the spring of 1919 despite growing opposition. As vice-president of the new State Board of Education, Pierre fought hard for the code. That summer he set up the Delaware School Auxiliary Association and put $2 million into a trust for the financing of surveys, the buying of sites, and the construction of schools. By June of 1923 Pierre had put a total of $3.8 million into six trusts for these purposes.

Pierre did more than spend money. As opposition continued to grow toward the new code, he spent the fall of 1919 traveling throughout the state debating the merits of the code and urging its retention. Opponents resorted to vicious personal attacks and charged Pierre with attempting to exercise a "benevolent despotism." Always an almost painfully shy individual, Pierre nonetheless continued to lead the public fight for the code. Results began to show. School attendance in November of 1920 was 85 per cent, up from the 61 per cent of a year earlier. Public expenditures for the school system increased 60 per cent in two years. In 1921 Pierre lost the code battle as the General Assembly passed a law that essentially reverted to 1915. He resigned from the State Education Board, partially in disgust and partially because his new duties at General Motors demanded too much of his time. But if Pierre lost the battle, he won the war. A burgeoning school population and public expectation had created a demand only the state could fill, given the fact that the new law had eliminated county advisory boards and left only local control. What's more, the new law's revenue section provided the state with the power to develop a self-perpetuating maintenance and construction fund for state schools.

In 1925 Pierre publicly complained about inadequate school funding, and the governor responded by appointing him state tax commissioner. The state hadn't been very good at collecting taxes. Pierre set up his own office, made a list of all taxpayers, and began taking those who chose not to pay into court. In less than two years, Pierre was able to tell the General Assembly that the state now had enough money to maintain a modern school system with more than $2 million surplus for school construction without resort to state bond issues.

By this time, Pierre had spent a large fortune in his own money to build schools. Calling him the "one U.S. multimillionaire who has made the public schools his hobby," *Time* magazine in a January 31, 1927, cover story reported Pierre had spent $5 million on Delaware schools. He undertook construction of all state schools for blacks, building with his own funds eighty-six of them. He also built and gave to the state twenty schools for whites and pooled his money with local district funds for twelve other schools. In all, *Time* said, Pierre built model accommodations for 17,300 of the state's 40,000 schoolchildren.

Pierre finally called a halt to this largesse at the beginning of 1927. He saw the state developing a dependence on his generosity and losing its self-respect. The politicians were starting to talk about taking advantage of the job Pierre had done as tax commissioner not to improve the schools but to abolish a $3.00-a-head tax they figured would be a popular deletion among the voters. And so Pierre went on record that his well of generosity was not bottomless. He continued as tax commissioner until 1937, watching with pleasure and pride as Delaware moved from thirty-fourth in literacy among the states in 1914 to tenth in 1934. State support for the school system grew from 35.3 per cent of school revenues in the 1919–20 school year to 85.5 per cent in the 1927–28 year, by far the highest in the country.

Delaware's schools did not occupy all of Pierre's civic mind. In 1918 he established a group called Service Citizens, financing it with yet another trust fund, this for $1.5 million. While many of its efforts were rooted in the educational field, this organization also took an interest in such divergent areas as tuberculin testing of cattle, the operation of an employment bureau, and the standardizing of vital statistics under the State Board of Health. Along the way, Pierre dropped off about $2 million at the local college, which went on, with the help of many of Pierre's relatives, to become the University of Delaware. In 1921 Pierre opened his Longwood Gardens to the public. He built the Kennett Pike, the main traffic artery through "châteaux country," and turned it over to the states of Delaware and Pennsylvania. His wife talked him into lining the pike with trees instead of giving her a pearl necklace. When he turned the pike over to the states, he made them stipulate that the permission of every property owner bordering on the road would be necessary before any billboard could be erected anywhere along the road's right of way. His private philanthropies are virtually incalculable. The son of a nephew once estimated Pierre gave away a billion dollars during his lifetime.

Naturally enough, Pierre attracted his share of the lunatic fringe. For nearly forty years, the letters came in. In 1917 he received a letter from Argentina written by a fellow claiming to be the Diminutive Incarnation of the Identical Universal Spirit who wondered why Pierre had not yet come across with the $1 million to $5 million he'd asked for in his last letter. In 1949 a character calling himself Wilhelm du Pont wrote Pierre about his (Wilhelm's) inheritance. In 1952 an enterprising type wrote that his doctor had prescribed a rich widow for him and asked for the names and addresses of a few. The year 1950 was a good one for kooks. Pierre heard from a fellow who said that if Pierre was the lost colonel to whom he had given directions in Belgium in 1945, then how about a job? If not, the man wished Pierre well anyway. That same year Pierre was offered a rare investment opportunity by an inventor who claimed he had perfected a machine to harvest babassu nuts and promised that the Brazil Government had predicted such a machine would make the nuts a bigger item than coffee beans. If Pierre would put up the needed money to finance his operation, Pierre could have 90 per cent of the babassu nut harvesting machine company. Pierre preserved an entire, fat file of similar correspondence.

Pierre is a puzzling personality. His inner thoughts seem seldom to have been revealed. As the family patriarch for so many years, he was always on the giving end, and the revelations about someone that come from how and for what he asks help or advice are missing. His files that have been preserved are mammoth and comprehensive but say much more about the reactions to him of other people than about him. People, especially family, seemed almost to worship him. His files are filled with letters of thanks that are almost unbelievably saccharine yet sincere. Even his extensive notes for an autobiography that was never written are limited revelations.

Several facets of his character emerge clearly enough. Pierre was exceedingly generous in a way calculated to make his beneficiaries as comfortable in accepting his generosity as possible. His advice seems almost always sound and sympathetic, and despite a schedule that must have exhausted him, he always managed time for those in need. Although he did not marry until he was forty-five and then married a first cousin he seemed to admire and respect more than love in any conventional sense, and although he was without children of his own, he was devoted to family and especially to family history and genealogy, more than once carrying on a lengthy correspondence with a variety of sources just to trace one descendant of an obscure branch of du Ponts. Unlike so many of his contemporary relatives, Pierre was not particularly overwhelmed by the sensual charms of the opposite sex. Flowers and Bach were more his taste. The pipe organ he had installed at Longwood is among the finest of its kind.

Pierre had a quiet but articulate sense of humor. As a child, he was afraid of the dark, of being alone when an explosion rocked the powder mills, of loud noises and thunderstorms. "The worst fright I ever encountered," he wrote in his autobiographical notes, "was when the cook removed her false teeth in my presence and I was alone with her to witness the horror. Had every joint of her body parted, a happening that I fully expected when dissolution once began, I could not have been more terrified." Recalling he was four or five at the time, Pierre added he had "never overcome a dislike for dissociated teeth, even those in my own employ."

At Christmastime Pierre would attend a tree-decorating party given each year by a niece whose house rule was that the first person to break an ornament would be relegated to the bridge table. Pierre loved to play bridge and developed a ritual in which he would arrive, pick up an ornament, and ostentatiously drop it on the hearth in front of the fireplace.

Although Pierre considered his shyness to be a genetic or inherent characteristic, his relative lack of co-ordination and robustness as a boy may have been a contributing factor. He took an inordinately long time learning how to swim and in his notes wrote, "Ball games had no attraction and I never could throw a ball or stone nor judge the direction and position of an object thrown towards me."

Many within the family—and not just his immediate family —called Pierre "Dad" or some equivalent thereof. Perhaps his closest friend was H. Rodney Sharp, who married one of Pierre's younger sisters. Letters from Sharp to Pierre are filled with almost childlike phrases of affection like, "I'm just crazy to see my old Daddy D. . . ." and "I certainly think about you a lot and I hope you won't forget me. . . ." and "I wish that you were right here this afternoon to enjoy this delightful spot with me. Write when you can but I understand when you don't." Sharp, a former schoolteacher, handled Pierre's personal books and records and also worked for the Du Pont Company.

If Pierre had a blind spot, it was in the way he saw the operation of the government, a view about which he could not always remain calm. The height of his dissatisfaction was reached in the 1930s, with his backing, along with that of other family members, of a rather radical right-wing group called the American Liberty League, which also boasted some other substantial industrialists among its membership. The League advertised itself as a defender of the Constitution and individual rights, but essentially it was an anti-Roosevelt, anti-New Deal organization. There were those who thought the League had fascist overtones, and at one point it was marginally connected to an abortive plot to overthrow the Roosevelt administration. The League enjoyed a blessedly brief life. Founded in 1934, it made a lot of noise in the 1936 election, into which the du Ponts poured hundreds of thousands of dollars in a vain effort to beat Roosevelt with Alf Landon. By 1938 the League was moribund. Pierre was no right-wing radical at heart, but he did believe that Roosevelt's policies were mistaken and may have figured that compromise would be achieved more readily from a position somewhat further from Roosevelt's than his (Pierre's) reason might have otherwise dictated.

An old family story tells of how Pierre and an older sister hit upon a clever way to stretch their allowances. They noticed that at the local store if you said, "Charge it on the book," you didn't have to pay and decided to apply this stratagem to the purchase of candy. It worked just fine until the end of the month and the day of reckoning with their mother when the bill came. It was a lesson Pierre never forgot and many years later he would remark, "I wish that an equally wise mother had instilled the same idea into many of the heads of government at Washington."

Pierre seemed always to be doing battle with the government. He never understood the public sentiment against big business, believing that the operations of the Du Pont Company epitomized the free enterprise system at its best. He was dismayed by both the antitrust actions against Du Pont—the 1907 case that caused the Hercules and Atlas spin-offs and the 1950s case that forced the sale of Du Pont-held General Motors stock—and he didn't see anything wrong with the stock deal he made with Raskob after the 1929 crash. He and Raskob simply sold each other several million dollars' worth of stock, establishing losses for each other that they then deducted from their taxes. In January they sold each other back the original stocks. Pierre saw the exchange as a public benefit, arguing that had he and Raskob sold their stocks on the open market, they would have added to the already substantial debacle of the market place. The government saw the exchange as tax evasion, despite the fact that Pierre paid more than $4.5 million in taxes that year, more than anyone else in the country. Based on that figure, the New York *Times* estimated Pierre's income for the year at some $31.5 million.

That figure is made all the more remarkable by the fact that Pierre some five years earlier had set up the Delaware Realty and Investment Company and in effect transferred the bulk of his estate to his brothers and sisters. Pierre put all his Du Pont, Atlas, and Hercules stock into the new holding company along with most of his Christiana and the stock in Longwood, Incorporated. A ridiculously low value of $13.5 million, seemingly based on par value, was put on the properties. The shares in the new holding company were then divided among Pierre's eight brothers and sisters, who agreed to pay Pierre and his wife Alice $900,000 a year for the rest of their lives. Pierre was motivated by three factors. He wanted to see the controlling stock in the hands of those who were running the company and to ensure that control would remain in the family. He figured the tax laws made the transfer a sensible proposition. And he was tired of paying the premiums on his $6 million worth of life insurance, the largest amount held by any individual in the country. In a letter to Alice's brother, Pierre noted the historical niceties involved, pointing out that in 1902 he, Coleman, and Alfred had paid $12 million plus a quarter of the stock in the new company for Du Pont and that in 1915 he and his associates had paid $13.9 million for Coleman's holdings. "It seems logical" to sell his interests for $13.5 million, Pierre concluded.

Just how strongly Pierre felt about the tax laws of the country and their influence on his decision to sell out becomes almost painfully clear in that same letter, where he writes: "A law that practically requires the holding of one-fourth of a large estate in liquid form or the devotion of about one-half of the gross income to paying life insurance premiums seems to me the height of financial stupidity. Now that they are proposing to change this penalty on success to 40% we may as well begin to accustom ourselves to say Lenin City instead of Washington. However, this is not the worst, for, judging from the fate of John Barleycorn, dec'd (?), the accumulation of fortunes will not be stopped by repressive laws. It will soon be a case of satisfying the financial 'bootleggers' who will swarm in our new Lenin City, both inside and outside of the hallowed precincts of the Treasury, where the Mellon crop will be supplanted by something of rank—yes, very rank—growth."

Pierre also saw the laws in another light. He continues: "I often wonder why so many people hang on to their fortunes and property instead of having the fun of watching the distribution process themselves. Under present laws one has no incentive to save or accumulate—in fact, much cause for not doing so—why not then enjoy the dissociation process. I have had much more satisfaction in planning for roads, schools and hospitals, etc., than in continuing the piling up process, and am sure that I shall much more enjoy the further development of the Du Pont interests as an outsider and adviser than as an owner and responsible head."

In another letter to his wife's brother, dated June 12, 1924, Pierre continues to philosophize. "In some ways," he writes, "I would have preferred selling out to the next generation, i.e. to my nieces and nephews, but, as the greater part of them are now quite young, I doubt if time will permit awaiting their development to determine which of the crowd are to be the likely workers in the business." He then goes on to discuss national affairs.

"To my mind," he says, "the worst of our troubles is the one least talked about, i.e. the present utter disregard for law; first, by the lawmakers; second, by the enforcers; and third, by those to whom the law applies. As a cold, hard fact we are rapidly assuming a position where we have no laws because what masquerade as such are either so indefinite that no lawyer or court, let alone an ordinary man, can tell what they mean, or are so impossible of enforcement that it is foolish to attempt obeyance, and the officers and courts refused to enforce literally. . . . This system is bound to lead, and has already led, to bribery and corruption of the worst kind. . . . It is easy to point to a condition where arrests and violations are less frequent when officers of enforcement adopt a system of payments by their victims in order to avoid arrest."

Particularly galling to Pierre was what he saw as wholesale graft resulting from Prohibition, which he saw as unenforceable and infringing on individual rights. "Why should not a group of divorcees get the notion that marriage is a failure and that a system of free love is best, and then put through a bill prohibiting marriage or the claiming of a wife or husband?" Pierre asked.

In the mid-1930s Pierre and the government clashed once again. The forum this time was the Nye Committee hearings. Senator Gerald P. Nye was chairman of a Senate committee investigating war profits. The du Ponts were convinced the whole affair was a politically inspired attempt to embarrass them for their opposition to Roosevelt. Senator Nye called them "merchants of death." The hearings underscored Du Pont's huge profitability during World War I and the fact that from 1918 through 1920 the company paid $1.4 million in income taxes, all of it in 1918. In 1919 and 1920 the company reported net losses based on plant write-offs. Du Pont had gotten the Allies to pay for the building of the plants and the U. S. Government to pay for their dismantling. The hearings also revealed that Du Pont had nearly entered into a contract to sell munitions to Hitler's Germany. A contract was negotiated with an agent, but the Du Pont Company executive committee scrapped it because it was clearly in violation of the Treaty of Versailles. A new contract, adding the clause requiring approval or consent of the U. S. Government, was drawn up, but it, too, was abandoned soon thereafter.

Pierre's role within the family was almost as monumental as his role within the company. He was constantly dispensing advice and money to his relatives, both within the immediate family and among the cousins at large. He was a firm believer in family unity and made a number of peace offers to Alfred trying to mend the rift of 1915. They were in vain; Alfred never quite forgave Pierre, who was not even welcome at Alfred's funeral. He went anyway, staying out of sight. For years his presence remained a secret, but he finally confided to a nephew that he had indeed gone to pay his respects at Alfred's last rites.

If Pierre appeared inaccessible to the public, it was because his office staff did its best to insulate him. Bill Frank, a newspaper institution in Wilmington, recalls that if Pierre was at home, he would answer the phone himself unless he was at dinner, in which case the caller was asked to call back later. Getting through to him at his office was considerably more difficult, Frank says, but sometime between twelve-thirty and one, Pierre would come down from his office into the Hotel du Pont for lunch, and if you lingered in the hotel corridors, you could catch him. He'd always answer your questions, Frank said, despite the stony stares of his luncheon companions, appalled at the effrontery of a newspaperman's interruption.

Still, Pierre never fully overcame his innate shyness. Commenting on its early manifestations in his autobiographical notes, Pierre wrote, "In my classes I generally stood well but I was always relieved when a good standing had been passed over without undue comment." Pierre had a perhaps questionable perspective on those school years. He wrote: "Looking back over my early days I feel sure that I had advantages of education and physical surrounding in advance of the average of the day, but compared to the advantages in schooling of the children of the laboring man of today, mine were pitifully small. This does not mean that I was handicapped, for I count that my inheritance of qualities from my ancestors and the teachings by precept and example of my father, mother and grandmother gave to me advantages that were worth more than my school education."

Pierre was a man of deep convictions, incapable of compromise or even restraint when a belief of his was challenged. His blindness to public sentiment and government action was not from a lack of sensitivity but from an inability to accept that beliefs he held so strongly to be right might not be universally held, might even be viewed with skepticism. So far as Pierre was concerned, such attitudes could exist only through ignorance. When Pierre believed in a proposition, he did not hesitate to say so. In 1919, when enmity between him and Alfred was still at its peak, Pierre wrote Wilmington's city council and the mayor, urging the acceptance of Alfred's offer to widen the city's main street in return for special rights to the property under the sidewalk that Alfred wanted for the vault for his bank. A question had come up as to why Alfred should get special rights when Pierre and the Du Pont Company had done similar work without asking any favors. Pierre's position was simple: Alfred's offer was in the best interests of the city to accept; therefore the city ought to accept. It was a typical attitude. Pierre always was able to separate personal conflicts from value judgments. His special ability was in taking strong personalities with often conflicting views and molding them together into an efficient working team.

While Pierre cut a quiet, unostentatious public figure, his private life-style reflected the enormous wealth he had accumulated. A trivial yet rather mind-boggling example is to be found in a 1934 inventory of his wife's flat silver, which included spoons—two dozen tea, dessert, table, bouillon, chocolate, ice cream, and orange spoons and a mere one dozen egg spoons. The regular staff at Longwood in 1942 included the chef, the second cook, the third cook, four kitchen men, a housekeeper, three housemen, the headwaiter, and the doorman. When Pierre and Alice gave a cocktail party for 275 guests in August that year, the staff was augmented by seven waiters to pass drinks, five waiters to pass canapés, four waiters for the buffet, five waiters for clean-up, and five bartenders.

For a 1923 garden party, Pierre hired twenty-five pieces of Paul Whiteman's orchestra. Preparations for a 1939 supper dance for five hundred at Longwood included the hiring of three men's room attendants and three maids for the ladies' rooms. In addition to the dinner, breakfast was ordered for three hundred at 4 A.M. and arrangements were made to serve one hundred chauffeurs hot dogs, sandwiches, coffee, ice cream, and cake. The debutante parties Pierre threw for some of his nieces are still remembered. Despite a demanding schedule that would undoubtedly require his arising early,

Pierre was always at the door to say goodbye to the last of his guests as they left in the wee hours of the morning.

For a businessman with the national reputation of Pierre, a man who controlled operations at the nation's largest chemical and automobile companies at one time or another and who, it was said, could have had the chief executive's job at U. S. Steel any time he agreed to take it, the family patriarch was remarkably provincial. For the most part, Pierre's vast resources were directed toward Delaware and nearby Pennsylvania. He seemed to figure that if Delaware could not be made into a model state given its small size and relatively unlimited resources, the rest of the world didn't stand much of a chance. Besides the Liberty League, Pierre's only other major venture into national issues was as a relentless champion of Prohibition repeal. The nation wasn't drinking any less as a result of Prohibition, he argued, but it was losing needed tax revenues and fostering crime and racketeering. When Prohibition was finally repealed in 1933, thanks more to the efforts of Pierre's old business ally John Raskob, who had become a primary influence in the national Democratic Party, than to Pierre, Pierre was appointed Delaware's first liquor commissioner, overseeing the licensing and regulation of the liquor business in the state with the same evenhandedness and acumen he brought to all his public endeavors.

In the early summer of 1944 Pierre's wife, Alice, died. Pierre felt the loss deeply but bore it with dignity and largely alone. During the late forties and early fifties, Pierre was absorbed in two major projects—the 150th anniversary celebration of the family's landing on American shores and the federal government's antitrust action to break up the Du Pont hold on General Motors.

The family anniversary reunion, which took place over New Year's weekend of 1950, was a gala the likes of which Delaware had not seen before and is unlikely to see ever again. Planning the party began a year and a half beforehand. In typical du Pont fashion, the private nature of the celebration was emphasized from the beginning. In a letter to the family from the planning committee, dated August 16, 1948, and outlining tentative proposals, du Ponts were exhorted that "every effort must be made to have no publicity about either plans or the actual functions when they take place." Less than a week before the big event, Pierre wrote an Irénée son-in-law, J. Bruce Bredin, arguing strongly against allowing *Life* magazine to photograph the New Year's Day brunch at Longwood, the main event. After somewhat petulantly counterpointing every favorable argument made by *Life* in advancing its cause, even to offering to submit pictures for family approval before publication, Pierre notes that he has "prepared perhaps a dozen men authorized to make arrest of intruders on private property and at least two Pennsylvania state police will be within call. All entrances to the building will be locked against intruders requiring breaking-in or stealth to gain entrance." Pierre's objections were finally overcome, and *Life* was allowed to go on.

With many Delaware cousins and closer relatives helping out with their time and money, more than two thirds of the family mustered in Wilmington for the weekend. Aileen du Pont, a T. Coleman niece, worked particularly hard to ensure the success of the celebration. Among her other tasks was coordinating the funds donated by the family to help defray the expenses of some foreign and less wealthy family members, particularly those in Italy and France. By September of 1949 she could report to Pierre that more than $6,000 had been contributed for this.

Pierre's brother Irénée put on a New Year's Eve dance at his home, Granogue, where double-cutting was encouraged and Meyer Davis played the dance music while the chauffeurs were "warmed and fed in the Granogue basement," according to a program for the weekend mailed to family members. The main event was financed by charging Delaware family members $.50 for each year of their lives. Thus Pierre, two weeks away from his eightieth birthday, paid $40, the most of anyone. All family members had badges color-coded by family branch, and no one got in the door without his badge. A notice informed the family shortly before the big day, "In the event you want a chauffeur or a nurse to go from the lower lobby up to collect your child, please notify Aileen du Pont before noon on Friday, Dec. 30. She will send you a special escort badge for the purpose." As her final contribution, Aileen made six game pies, a dish the original family brought with it on its voyage to the United States. A French cousin sent over special truffles for the pies—which weighed thirty-five pounds each. More than six hundred of the family showed up, out of an eligible number of direct descendants and in-laws estimated at 910 by Pierre. As usual, the financial planning for the affair was impeccable: The books closed on the weekend showing a surplus of $649.17. While a Raleigh, North Carolina, newspaper used the occasion to deplore the lack of a Carnegie Institute or a Rockefeller Foundation in the du Pont family, editorial comment around the country was generally favorable, holding up the family as a shining example of the American Dream come true.

Although it received an occasional reference during the planning for the celebration, the antitrust suit looming in the distance did little to dampen the spirits of the family that weekend. The threat of the suit did, however, cause some questioning about the advisability of having any sort of a major celebration at all. Aileen wrote Pierre wondering if the reunion should be called off and worrying that the government might use the reunion as evidence of family solidarity. In a later letter, Aileen made a more oblique reference to the suit while discussing the reservations some family members had about using a picture of the Du Pont Building on the program. She noted that the building was modern and that the family at the time was trying to prove the separation of the company and the family.

It would be more than a dozen years before the final judgment in the suit would be handed down. Pierre would live to see only the first phase of the process. The government filed its case on the last day of June 1949. Three years later the case went to trial in a Chicago courtroom, and Pierre moved into a suite in Chicago's Drake Hotel. At the age of eighty-two, Pierre retained his sense of humor. On the day he was scheduled to take the witness stand for the first time—as his side's key witness—he stumbled in the Drake lobby and pitched forward onto the carpet. He began to bleed profusely from his nose, much to the concern of his attorneys, disconcerted at the prospect of losing their star witness. But he recovered quickly. Later he was asked what he had hit when he fell. "My nose, of course." He smiled. "How could I miss it?"

Pierre also retained his ability to instill in those working for Du Pont a sense of harmony, of togetherness. Every evening after the day in court, the defendants and their attorneys would be invited back to Pierre's suite for a little bolstering. It was the sort of little gesture that promoted loyalty and solidarity in an unobtrusive way, a gesture that, multiplied thousands of times over the course of a life, provided the foundation on which Pierre's reputation was built.

In May of 1954 Pierre suffered a ruptured abdominal aorta at dinner at Longwood and died in a Delaware hospital that night. During his years with the Du Pont Company, he had presided over a growth that saw Du Pont's assets rise from less than $12 million to more than $2.5 billion, an increase of more than 20,000 per cent. His estate was variously valued in local newspapers at anywhere from $40 million to $100 million despite the fact that he had transferred the bulk of his assets thirty years earlier to his immediate family. Had he lived out the year of 1954, he would have enjoyed vindication. The Chicago court dismissed the government action on December 9. It was a most merry Christmas along the Brandywine, but the family joy proved premature. The government had just begun to fight.

Chapter Six

Two Brothers

Starting with Pierre, the descendants of Lammot du Pont ran things at the Du Pont Company up to World War II. In fact, it would be stretching the point only slightly to argue they controlled the fortunes of the company until 1967. The three chief executive officers during that latter period were Walter S. Carpenter, Jr., brother of a Pierre brother-in-law; Crawford H. Greenewalt, Irénée's son-in-law; and Lammot du Pont Copeland, a Pierre nephew.

Pierre's successor, Irénée, was an urbane, quick-witted fellow whose contributions to the success of the Du Pont Company, while perhaps less spectacular than those of his older brother, were nonetheless impressive and far-reaching. To Irénée fell the task of guiding the company during its transition from munitions maker to chemical giant. With the end of World War I, the number of Du Pont employees plunged quickly from 100,000 to 30,000. Part of Irénée's job was to put those employees who had lost their jobs back to work. He was also shepherd for the company's investment in the organic chemicals industry, begun toward the end of the war, and in 1921 implemented some major organizational changes in the company's management, including the distinct separation of staff and line functions and the transformation of the executive committee to a think tank concerned more or less exclusively with major policy and divested of operational duties. Under Irénée was begun a safety program that made the manufacturing of gunpowder so mishap-free that insurance companies offered Du Pont the same rates as they gave other manufacturers.

After receiving a master's degree in chemical engineering

from MIT in 1898, Irénée went to work in the machine shops of the paper-making division of Pusey & Jones Company in Wilmington—for $2 a week. A year later he, Pierre, and a third man formed a contracting company, drawing up a charter they figured ought to stand up. It was, word for word, the same as the charter for the U. S. Steel Corporation, with only the name of the firm changed. Each of the partners put up $8,000. In 1903 Irénée went to work for the Du Pont Company and organized the construction division of the black powder operating department. By the time Du Pont began supplying powder to the Allies for World War I, Irénée was a vice-president. In 1914 Irénée and several other du Ponts, on Raskob's advice, began to buy personally some General Motors stock. Irénée bought four hundred shares for $27,000. The following year he joined Pierre in the syndicate that bought Coleman's entire Du Pont holdings.

Irénée was a generous contributor as an individual to the war effort and the relief programs for its victims. In 1917 and 1918 he gave a total of $106,920 to the Red Cross, nearly $48,000 to French relief organizations, and $20,500 to United War Work, a consolidation of seven relief groups. He also gave $48,000 to the Delaware Aeronautical School for the training of pilots. With the war's end, Irénée took over. Years later, testifying during the Du Pont-General Motors antitrust trial, Irénée would proudly claim, without being contradicted, that Du Pont was the only major company to live up to every contract it had during and immediately following the war.

In retrospect, success has made the postwar decisions reached by Du Pont obvious. They weren't. The General Motors investment, for example, was a commitment to an entirely new business, albeit one with vast potential, in a company whose future at that point was not at all assured. The du Ponts did their best to minimize the importance they attached to GM as a captive customer for Du Pont products, arguing during the antitrust trial that this was more or less a peripheral consideration. Irénée even went so far as to suggest that Du Pont ownership of General Motors was "an unfavorable influence as far as Du Pont sales were concerned," contending that GM personnel resented Du Pont intrusion and displayed a feistiness toward Du Pont salesmen that would otherwise not have been in evidence. Nonetheless, the conclusion is virtually inescapable that Du Pont invested in General Motors because its executives saw a great future in the auto industry and a ready market. And the company was in an unusual position to take the risk involved. It had the money available, and its stockholders were almost entirely active executives willing and able to gamble.

General Motors was not Du Pont's only gamble in those years. "In my experience," Irénée once said, "the most important decision in the affairs of the company was entering the organic chemical industry during World War I. We had a rocky road. The board [of directors] frequently expressed searching doubts about the wisdom of the decision, giving me some awkward moments, especially as our investment climbed to over $40 million without profits." Eventually, of course, the investment paid huge dividends. Du Pont did not invent either cellophane or rayon, but under Irénée, the commercial development of these two products was brought to a fruitful conclusion. Irénée once said his greatest contribution to Du Pont was that he "provided optimism whenever it was necessary."

Another postwar venture was abandoned early. Du Pont entered the explosives export business after the war and got out soon thereafter. Asked why during the antitrust trial, Irénée provided a five-word answer: "We didn't make any money."

Because he was the most publicly articulate of the three brothers who controlled Du Pont's destiny through so much of the first half of the twentieth century, Irénée was frequently quoted. He said the safety progress made by the company during his years with it gave him the most personal satisfaction, citing his father's death in a nitroglycerine explosion and his desire to minimize the likelihood of a recurrence. The safety program begun under Irénée was so successful that the company injury rate went from 20.3 per million man-hours to 0.35 by 1957. He once told an interviewer that success was based on three things: 1) It's nice to be friendly with your competitors. 2) Business fails when it doesn't make money. 3) Sometimes a man has to swear at his colleagues to drive home a point. Irénée called his roll-top desk "an unsurpassed device for end-of-the-day cleanup." He believed the three most useful inventions of the industrial age to be the Bessemer steel process, the sewing machine, and the telegraph. He didn't say what he thought were the least useful, but friends speculated that he would have picked the automatic gearshift for cars as one and television, at least before his children gave him a set, as another. Once asked what the most useful of future scientific contributions might be, Irénée suggested a pill or medicine of some kind that would reduce or eliminate the need for sleep. His detractors jumped on that answer as an indication of the greedy businessman's desire to increase labor productivity, an analysis that sells an imaginative and provocative answer to a potentially trite question way short.

It was Irénée more than any other du Pont who was responsible for putting together the family syndicate that accumulated some 18 per cent of the stock in U. S. Rubber, the corporate predecessor of Uniroyal. During the antitrust trial, he claimed, with somewhat more audacity than credibility, that his initial purchases of U. S. Rubber and those of his younger brother, Lammot, were purely coincidental, that Lammot's actions had been unknown to him. His simple explanation of the fact that the syndicate was made up of du Pont family members was, remember, that when you looked around for folks willing to risk $1.2 million you saw mostly relatives.

Irénée made his first purchase of U. S. Rubber stock in 1913, but it was not until 1927 that the family syndicate made its move. That was the year after Lammot took over the presidency of Du Pont and Irénée became vice-chairman of the board, a position he considered tantamount to retirement. A dozen du Ponts and a couple of associates formed the syndicate, which in the late twenties purchased about 30 per cent of the rubber company's stock, a percentage that had been reduced to about 18 per cent by the time of the antitrust suit in 1952. In 1929 the syndicate took Du Pont executive Francis B. Davis, Jr., and installed him as president of the rubber firm. That same year the family formed Rubber Securities Corporation, to which it sold its U. S. Rubber stockholdings to crystallize a paper loss in the stock for tax purposes. In the antitrust suit, the government contended the new corporation was formed at least in part to ensure continued syndicate control of the rubber company, quoting an Irénée letter to that effect. Rubber Securities was dissolved in 1938 because the U. S. Rubber Company was then flourishing and the family felt that U. S. Rubber stock was a more liquid investment than the stock of its holding company.

Not untypical of the du Pont family's relationship with the government in those days was Irénée's 1932 confrontation with the Internal Revenue Service. He had sold his Rubber Securities stock to his children's trusts. The IRS said it was a gift. Irénée went to court, not to argue, but to establish once and for all whether his action constituted a sale or a gift. Calling it a gift was fine with him, but he feared another administration would come along, say he "put in the fix for my advantage," and call the transfer a sale. When the court realized that both sides—Irénée and the IRS—wanted the same thing, it accommodated them, declaring the action a gift.

The government's antitrust suit attempted to show that with Du Pont control of the rubber company came a dramatic increase in tire sales to General Motors. The government seems to have had a point. Before 1931 U. S. Rubber tire sales to GM were minimal. Davis testified he may have told the du Ponts that U. S. Rubber had not had much luck selling GM tires in 1929 and 1930. In 1931 GM and U. S. Rubber signed a contract in which GM agreed to buy 50 per cent of its new equipment tires from U. S. Rubber. In 1927 the rubber company's sales were $193 million, on which it netted $1 million in profits. In 1947 sales were $580 million, with profits of nearly $22 million. By 1949 GM was using U. S. Rubber tires on 64 per cent of its Buicks, Oldsmobiles, Pontiacs, and Cadillacs, on 50 per cent of its Chevrolet cars, 55 per cent of its Chevy trucks, and 55 per cent of its GMC trucks and coaches. In 1953 Irénée testified that his opinion, first stated in 1934, that U. S. Rubber ought to sell its tire division still held.

The du Ponts may have reached their peak in terms of the clout they held within American industry in the late 1920s. The Du Pont Company was coming into its own as a chemical giant. The family was gaining control of one of the major rubber companies. In 1928 Du Pont-voted General Motors shares constituted 52 per cent of the total at the GM annual meeting. The Du Pont Company had become involved with Standard Oil of New Jersey and GM in a joint venture for the production of tetraethyl lead, an octane-increasing, antiknock compound for gasoline. In June of 1927 Du Pont bought 114,000 shares of U. S. Steel, about 1 per cent of the total. Not long after the Justice Department announced it was looking into that purchase, Du Pont sold the steel stock, Pierre contending that the investment was strictly to put a short-term Du Pont cash surplus to work. Maybe so, but it was not inconceivable that some people at Du Pont had their eyes on control of yet another major corporation in a basic industry.

The tetraethyl lead venture started out as a disaster. A GM researcher discovered the compound, and Standard Oil and GM formed the Ethyl Corporation to market it with Du Pont as the manufacturer. In May of 1925 Ethyl operations were suspended when thirty-five of forty-five employees at Standard Oil's Bayway, New Jersey, refinery working with the compound became sick. Five died. Tetraethyl lead is highly toxic in concentrated form. Du Pont was forced to stop its production efforts several months later after several mysterious deaths at the Deepwater, New Jersey, plant that was manufacturing the compound along with dye products. Irénée, virtually alone, opposed the suspension. He felt the compound was an important additive and no more dangerous than a number of other chemicals produced by Du Pont. Deepwater was given a new ventilation system, and the U. S. Surgeon General okayed the compound for use in gasoline in 1926. Production resumed, this time with much more stringent safety regulations. Du Pont could consider itself lucky. It had escaped most of the adverse publicity and national horror that was focused on the Bayway incident, which had received far wider notice.

The Nye Committee hearings of 1934 were the forum for the most severe attack on Du Pont morality ever carried on in public, but it was an attack that never fully captured the imagination of the people. The excess profits picture the committee tried to paint was blurred by Du Pont arguments that once the United States entered the war, taxes paid exceeded profits made by Du Pont on U.S. powder sales. Besides, the powder was needed to prosecute the war, and only Du Pont was able to provide it. The du Ponts suffered a few image setbacks, to be sure, but the three brothers—Pierre, Irénée, and Lammot—frequently gave as good as they got, with Irénée generally conceded to be the star witness on the Du Pont side.

Talking about the government's role in preparing for World War I, Irénée suggested that "everybody did not want to make a mistake which would be chalked up against them. Nobody took the initiative." Irénée took another shot at the government when he said, "You blame the businessman for the Depression; you blame the banker for the Depression. I blame the government for the Depression." He argued that Du Pont was far from being alone in making profits from the war and wondered why Du Pont was being singled out. Privately the du Ponts felt they knew the answer: The attack was inspired by the du Ponts' political opposition to Roosevelt. Through it all, Irénée calmly puffed on his pipe.

It may be that the memo writer in this instance was something of a sycophant, but at any rate into the Du Pont home office shortly after the hearings ended came a note from an employee remarking on reaction to the hearings from trade salesmen at a conference in the northeast. "Comments as to the ability of Mr. Irénée du Pont to blow smoke rings are far more general than any serious expression of opinion on the merits of the investigation."

By the late 1920s Irénée was an extraordinarily rich man, but compared to Pierre, his civic and charitable contributions were relatively small. He was, to be sure, a generous supporter of medical and scientific research, a major benefactor of the Wilmington General Hospital, founder of the Delaware Safety Council, and funder of the Crystal Trust, one of the larger family foundations, which was created under the terms governing settlement of his estate, with assets valued at more than $30 million at the end of 1972. But his public generosity was limited by two factors that were not considerations for Pierre. For one thing, Irénée had ten children, although two of them died at early ages. For another, Irénée had some expensive habits, like his 60-foot yacht, *Icacos*.

His most expensive indulgence was his Cuban estate, Xanadu, which he began developing in 1928 after a visit to Cuba two years earlier. It featured a private landing field, its own nine-hole golf course, a pipe organ said to be the largest in Latin America and fitted with a special player piano-like device for which Irénée had rolls made, and an armada of iguanas, a not altogether lovable lizard for which Irénée developed an affection. All this was cared for by a staff of more than two hundred. Over the years, Irénée's capital investment in this little playground exceeded $2 million. It cost about $125,000 a year to run. In November of 1961 Fidel Castro figured the Cuban people could get more out of the place than Irénée and took it over. Seriously ill by then, Irénée was never told of Castro's trespass. From 1930 on, Irénée, whose nickname within the family was Buss and had been from his childhood, spent months at a time at Xanadu while his family remained in Wilmington, paying him occasional visits. Irénée was seldom alone; he was a generous host.

His wife and cousin, Irene, was a generous correspondent. Irénée seems to have preferred the telephone; Irene wrote letters, asking how "the Pleasure Dome" was, keeping Irénée informed on the doings of his children, urging him to have fun, and telling him that she missed him but was glad he was getting along well. Irene had a gentle sense of humor. In one letter to her husband she describes how the Newfoundland dog of an Irénée niece was found burying its puppies, speculating that the dog might have attended a recent birth control lecture. In the summer of 1947 she wrote Irénée about going marketing at the beach resort of Rehoboth in southern Delaware. She was seventy and it was the first time in her life she had been marketing by herself, without assistance from a chauffeur or family member. She apparently enjoyed the experience.

With eight daughters requiring proper presentation to society, Irénée became perhaps the premier debutante party thrower in Wilmington. Some 1,000 invitations would go out on each occasion. His daughter Eleanor was feted at a not untypical affair at the Hotel du Pont, where 633 guests were served a seated dinner. The hors d'oeuvres included caviar and smoked salmon. The dance music was by Meyer Davis. In all, it was a lavish occasion for which Irénée paid just slightly more than $7,000. But that was 1927. Today such a party would cost many times that amount. Irénée and his wife knew what they wanted and what they didn't want when they gave a party. Before the debut of his daughter Doris, a secretary wrote the musicians hired for the affair: ". . . Also, Mrs. du Pont does not like 'stunts,' such as waving around derby hats and other accentuated 'darky' stunts, and I hope you can make the program accordingly." For years one of the most eagerly anticipated annual events in Wilmington was the fireworks display Irénée had put on every Fourth of July at Granogue. People would come from miles around to sit on the side of a hill and watch. The fireworks were discontinued in 1954.

Irénée also enjoyed some of life's simpler pleasures. He was popular among his nieces and nephews, who used to pile into his old Locomobile for what they christened "Pig Rides." Irénée would drive them all down to the local soda fountain for ice cream. He was fond of mathematical puzzles, and it is said that Barbara, Irénée Jr.'s wife, became accepted early by her father-in-law when she managed to solve one of Irénée's problems in her head.

For several years before he died on December 19, 1963, just two days before his eighty-seventh birthday, Irénée's deteriorating health left him shy of complete control of his faculties. His son and two sons-in-law took over the management of his affairs and soon became embroiled in disagreement over how they should be handled. Among the bones of contention was Xanadu. On Irénée's 1961 federal tax return, Xanadu was claimed as a $1.6 million business loss after Castro's expropriation of the place. The Internal Revenue Service disallowed the deduction, and since Irénée was in the top tax bracket of 91 per cent, he then owed an additional $1.4 million. Tax lawyers figured the government would probably agree to settle on something like a 50-50 basis, but in the interim, legislation was introduced in Congress by Senator John Williams of Delaware allowing tax deductions for all private property confiscated by Castro, not just business property. The legislation became law, but one son-in-law, Ernest N. May, argued that it would be a mistake for Irénée to take advantage of it because it had the look of special-interest legislation. "It may be true that the name of Irénée du Pont was kept out of the legislative process," he wrote, "but how many

Xanadus were there in Cuba? At best the situation was one elephant and some mice." May suggested a potential news story that might develop were Irénée to use the new law:

"LBJ Shows Up Senator Williams/Bobby Baker Case Backfires" was the headline May composed. The story ran, "While talking loudly against influence peddling by Baker and corruption in high places, Senator Williams (R.-Del.) was at the same time promoting unusual income tax relief for the du Ponts of Delaware—the world's richest family.

"Irénée du Pont, the last of the Merchants of Death, died last December, leaving in his $400 million estate a $3 million pleasure palace in Cuba. . . ."

Undoubtedly May was overstating the case, just as he exaggerated the dollar numbers because he figured that was what newspapers tended to do. At any rate, May argued in vain; adverse publicity did not crop up at all until a decade later and then was very minor and for the most part aimed in Senator Williams' direction. Williams has always and firmly maintained his actions were ethical, honorable, and open, and certainly to suggest otherwise would be to ignore his long-standing and widespread reputation as "Honest John" in the Senate.

Although he had long since placed his share of his brother's Delaware Realty and Investment Company stock, the company into which went the major portion of Pierre's wealth, in trust for his children, Irénée left an estate valued at nearly $200 million. Out of that amount, $90.4 million was set aside for taxes, $32.7 million went into the Crystal Trust, and $64.7 million went into trusts for his children. His wife had died two years earlier.

When Irénée stepped down from the Du Pont presidency, he made room for his younger brother, Lammot, a man whose philosophies closely paralleled Irénée's but whose style was rather markedly different. Lammot, who was president of Du Pont until World War II and took over from Pierre as GM board chairman in 1928, rarely if ever flaunted his wealth. As Du Pont's president, he bicycled to work. For recreation, he chopped firewood, claiming it cleared his head. Once a cousin came to call at his house and was told by the maid that she thought the cook knew where to find Mr. Lammot. The cook did. "Yessir," she said. "I've got him down in the cellar sharpenin' knives for me."

At the company, Lammot is most generally remembered as the man who insisted that research was a key to Du Pont success and saw to it that sufficient funds were provided for it throughout the Depression. Under Lammot expenditures for Du Pont laboratory operations increased almost sevenfold. "There are times when it is more important to do research than it is to pay dividends," Lammot said during the Depression. "This is one of those times."

Lammot prided himself on being familiar with the products made by Du Pont. It was said of him that there wasn't one of the company's thousands of products he didn't know. A possibly apocryphal story has it that Lammot personally tried Du Pont's first nylon toothbrush, an item that had cost the company roughly $5 million to produce. He returned it four days after getting it. Its bristles were in shreds, and there are those who contend he used the brush to scrub floors just to rile his researchers. Lammot put great store by his team of executives. "If there weren't a lot of men in the Du Pont Company who know more than I know," he once said, "the company wouldn't last long."

Through the 1930s and 1940s, Lammot frequently spoke out publicly on behalf of American business and the free enterprise system. He would talk on national radio, berating government restrictions on business and urging his listeners to enlist in "the fight to save American industry." He criticized government spending and the use of taxation for reform or punishment rather than revenue. He pointed out that government depends for its existence on taxes paid by individuals and businesses and that without profits, there would be no taxes paid. Stressing the need for working capital, he advocated removing tax and labor legislation from the world of politics. In 1938 he predicted 9 million jobs would become available if industry's confidence in the stability of the economy and the government could be won and announced that Du Pont planned to spend $35 million for expansion despite its estimate of a 23 per cent decline in sales. Taxes are too high, he said in 1939, and increasing business operating freedom will solve tomorrow's problems. A corporation has four duties, he preached: to provide jobs, just pay, a sound place for investment, and an example in good citizenship. In 1940 he intoned, "The customer is the real economic dictator in a democracy such as our own, where competition is the rule and monopoly is the exception."

From 1943 on Lammot's voice could be heard often calling for the elimination of government controls after the war. Early in 1941 Lammot was subpoenaed to testify before the Senate Campaign Expenditures Committee as one of the four largest contributors to the Republican effort in 1940. When the IRS said he couldn't deduct contributions to the National Economic Council as a business expense, he went to court—in a losing cause.

Like his brothers, Lammot believed that the public skepticism about big business was rooted in ignorance. In April of 1939 he said, "Only by complete understanding by the masses of what our American incentive system means to them will it survive." What it meant to Lammot, among other things, was a 96-foot yacht. In those days there was still something patriarchical, if not feudal, in the family's relationship to the company and its employees. In June of 1939 Lammot hosted a company picnic for five thousand employees aboard a large pleasure ship in the Delaware River. The atmosphere was a little stiff at first; no one was dancing to the orchestra Lammot had provided for the occasion. "No use letting the music go to waste," Lammot remarked to no one in particular, and with that, he began to twirl about the deck with the nearest young woman he could find. A spontaneous cheer arose from the employees, and soon the deck was filled with dancers.

Lammot did most of his growing up in one of the more architecturally bizarre houses in Wilmington. After his father's death, his mother moved the family back to the Brandywine from Philadelphia and built a house. She asked each of her children to draw her a picture of the room he or she would like for a bedroom. Some of the children were still rather young, and the pictures produced could hardly have been scale drawings. The architect was then presented with a set of the pictures and told to design a house incorporating the children's desires. Fortunately for the architect's sanity, Mrs. du Pont said she was not particularly concerned with what the layout of the ground floor turned out to be. From the outside, the house looked like a series of architectural gaffes, but the children got their bedrooms and a third-floor playroom where they could bang around undisturbed and undisturbing.

A Lammot grandson, Pierre S. du Pont IV, who was elected Delaware's governor in 1976, remembers his grandfather as being rather formal. "I was closer to my maternal grandfather," the governor recalled. "I could never imagine him [Lammot] taking me out for ice cream." Pete, as the governor is called, says his impression of Lammot was that he was "a giant intellect, very scientific." He remembers Lammot used to make miniature kites from broom bristles, tissue paper, and string and could get them to fly indoors, usually by having someone open a door or a window to create at least the semblance of a draft.

Among Lammot's extracurricular interests were tennis, at which he developed a reasonable proficiency; quality beef cattle, in particular Herefords; and education. He was a cofounder of Tower Hill School, the Wilmington area's prestigious private elementary and high school, along with his brother Irénée and several others, and he endowed a professorship at MIT with $500,000. Lammot also enjoyed a perhaps trivial distinction among chiefs of the Du Pont Company. He is the only Du Pont president or board chairman ever to have been married more than once. He was married four times, with eight children by his first wife, two by his last, and none by the two between.

Defense of the antitrust suit was to have been predominantly a three-man show, featuring the brothers who had run the company since the First World War, but Lammot didn't make it. A long history of circulatory trouble finally caught up with him at his summer home off the Connecticut coast on tony Fishers Island. In July of 1952 he had a heart attack and was moved to a New London, Connecticut, hospital just a week before the Du Pont Company celebrated its 150th anniversary. A second heart attack while he was in the hospital killed him. He was seventy-one. The Wilmington newspapers reported his estate to be valued at $75 million, of which Delaware received some $6 million in inheritance taxes. He had, of course, already distributed the substantial part of his wealth among his children. Death deprived Lammot of a fight to which he was really looking forward. Perhaps even more than his brothers, Lammot considered the government's antitrust suit a severe case of overreaching of authority.

The du Ponts had done legal battle with the government before, but never on a scale such as this. The company had been the object of antitrust action on a number of occasions, and individual family members had fought tax cases before, but this time the government had named as defendants in the case 186 family members, more than half of them under twenty-one. The youngest was eight months, and the du Ponts made some telling public relations points when they had a picture of Lana Bredin, the youngest defendant, playing in her playpen in Florida distributed to newspapers across the country. But if government prosecution of an eight-month-old for restraint of trade appeared a ludicrous proposition, the substance of the government case was serious business. At stake were 63 million shares of General Motors owned by Du Pont. At the time the U. S. Supreme Court ordered the divestiture, the shares were worth more than $3 billion. Christiana Securities held 535,000 GM shares on its own, and individual du Ponts owned additional shares. The U. S. Rubber Company aspect of the case was more or less icing on the government case's cake.

While Du Pont attorneys argued that the government's case was based not on restraint of trade considerations but simply on the size of Du Pont holdings, Willis L. Hotchkiss, prosecuting the case, called the Sherman Antitrust Act the economic equivalent of the Constitution in the socio-political realm. Then U. S. Attorney General Tom Clark said, "This case is directed toward the breaking up of the largest single concentration of industrial power in the United States." By any measure, this was the biggest public battle ever fought by the du Ponts. Its joining must have been a wrenching decision for many of them. Always in the past, with the exception of Alfred I. du Pont's 1915 suit, the family had succeeded in maintaining a low public profile. Their wealth had long been a matter for speculation, but information on which to base such speculation was elusive and fragmentary. Now the government's discovery process was putting on public record the details of what the family had always considered no one else's business. Family member after family member paraded to the witness stand to discuss personal wealth and the way in which it was passed on. The end result was hardly a comprehensive accounting of every du Pont dollar, but for the first time there was an indication of what du Pont wealth meant, not just to those du Ponts who ran the company but to their less public relatives as well.

Page after page of trial transcript appendices listed individual and trust holdings of Christiana Securities: Irénée du Pont, 542,400 shares; Lammot du Pont Copeland, 338,348 shares; Henry B. du Pont, 370,499 shares; a Wilmington Trust account for Margaretta du Pont Carpenter, 230,449 shares. What appears to be only a partial list of the holdings of Christiana in the Lammot branch of the family alone shows nearly 2.5 million shares held in trust accounts and more than 2.7 million shares held outright. The market value of those shares alone at the end of 1977, when the price per share was considerably lower than during the late years of the antitrust suit, was more than $600 million.

Testimony in the suit filled volumes. The intertwined corporate affairs of Du Pont and General Motors, as well as U. S. Rubber, were often hard to follow. Irénée testified he never tried to persuade GM to buy more Du Pont products. In 1927, however, the Du Pont finance committee minutes showed a discussion of whether GM was buying enough from Du Pont. A reciprocity arrangement was suggested, but nothing came of it. In 1918 Du Pont asked its employees to buy from GM. Why not? Irénée testified, arguing that the GM products were good and such buying would enhance the Du Pont investment.

It hardly needed enhancing. As of December 31, 1949, Du Pont listed the cost of its GM investment at $57.6 million. GM dividends paid to Du Pont from 1918 through 1947 totaled $656 million, and, of course, the value of the original investment had increased manyfold. For most of the 1920s and the early 1930s, Du Pont actually owned 38 per cent of General Motors. Pierre testified this additional stock, acquired from Durant at his request, was never considered a permanent investment. Du Pont disposed of this stock, reducing its holdings to 23 per cent, by setting up what was known as the Managers Security Plan for GM executives, a bonus setup not unlike the one already operating at Du Pont. The stock was sold to General Motors for distribution among its executives.

If Du Pont influence at General Motors was pervasive, it was not total, according to Pierre's testimony, in which he gave a number of examples of GM managers acting contrary to his advice. In 1923, for instance, William Knudsen, then head of Chevrolet, consulted with Pierre on the advisability of developing two sources of supply for Chevy's manufacturing material needs, presumably including Du Pont products. Pierre argued against the plan, but Knudsen went ahead with it anyway. Pierre added to Irénée's testimony that GM was a difficult customer, saying the feeling at Du Pont around 1921 was that General Motors executives had an animosity toward Du Pont products. The du Ponts pointed out that in a recent year GM had purchased from some three hundred paint and fifty to seventy-five fabric companies. Du Pont's grip on GM as a customer wasn't exactly exclusive.

The government hammered away at the interlocking directorships among Du Pont, Christiana, Delaware Realty and Investment, and General Motors, arguing that at the top of the pyramid stood a handful of du Pont family members in a position to pull all the strings, and, when they became tired, to pass control on to the next generation. Time and time again, government attorneys would ask du Pont family members how they passed on their stock to their children and what they told the children regarding disposition of those shares. Inevitably the du Ponts replied that they never dictated to their children what could and what could not be done with inherited securities. It was, as usual, Irénée who provided one of the trial's lighter moments when he testified that while he never discussed with his children what to do with the stock they inherited, he did tell his daughter Margaretta once not to throw her Delaware Realty stock certificates away.

"I thought that possibly my children were a little careless about securities," Irénée said, "and she might throw it in the wastebasket. A few similar occurrences have occurred, not with certificates, but with dividend checks, but it developed that they were found misplaced."

The anguish caused the family by the exposure of their private affairs to public scrutiny appeared at first blush to have been worth it. On December 9, 1954, Judge Walter LaBuy dismissed the government action. By then the individual defendants had been pared from 186 to 8—the three brothers, Pierre, Irénée, and Lammot, and five relatives. One was Lam-

mot du Pont Copeland, son of Pierre's older sister. Lammot's
son, Pierre S. du Pont III, was another. A Pierre nephew,
Henry B. du Pont, Jr., was a third. The fourth was Colgate P.
Darden, an Irénée son-in-law. George Edmonds, a Lammot
son-in-law, was the fifth.

The government appealed the dismissal, and in June of
1957 the U. S. Supreme Court ruled a "tendency toward monopoly," held there were violations of the Clayton Antitrust
Act and remanded the case to LaBuy's court for remedy.
Two years later LaBuy ruled that Du Pont could retain its
GM holdings but would have to give up voting rights. Again,
the government appealed, and in 1961, by a 4-3 vote with two
justices who had earlier participated directly in the case—one
on each side—abstaining, the Supreme Court ordered Du
Pont to divest itself of its GM holdings.

Final divestiture was a rather complicated affair carried out
in three stages and completed early in 1965. Slightly more
than one and a third shares of GM were distributed for each
share of Du Pont held. Some du Ponts were required to sell
their holdings in GM also. The GM that would have gone to
Christiana was passed through to Christiana stockholders. A
strong lobbying effort in Washington resulted in special legislation allowing the transfer of base cost from Du Pont to
General Motors for tax purposes. Thus, if a Du Pont stockholder had paid, say, $100 a share for his Du Pont stock and
received $60 worth of GM for each Du Pont share he held,
he could transfer $60 of his Du Pont cost to GM and avoid a
capital gains liability. Had the distribution been taxed as ordinary income the tax bill would have been more than $1 bil-
lion. As it was, the du Ponts did not escape tax liability but
were able to postpone a large portion of it.

Between the time of the government's filing its case and
the final distribution of GM stock, Pierre, Irénée, and Lammot all died. With them died the glory days. The knife edge
of the family's will to triumph had been dulled. Taxes, government red tape, softness among the younger generation,

confusion of purpose, and the more or less certain knowledge that the odds hopelessly defied the scaling of new heights all exercised a subtle enervating force on the family. The will to triumph was gradually replaced by the will to survive. The du Ponts had dreamed the American Dream and had strived to make it come true. Now they were beginning to realize that getting there isn't half the fun; it may be all of the fun. The days of the great achiever were no longer, although to their credit, a handful or more du Ponts have refused to accept that. But even for them, the paths of family success no more lead up through the family company. For years the du Ponts preached the benefits of owner-managers. Today they leave the managing to others; they are owners.

Chapter Seven

Fathers and Sons

Among the living du Pont father-son pairs, two in particular stand out—the Lammot du Pont Copelands, Senior and Junior, and the Pierre S. du Ponts, III and IV. All four at one time worked for the family company, and all four ended their careers there prematurely. In the summer of 1977 the two fathers were in retirement. The younger Copeland was selling jokes, and the younger du Pont was governor of Delaware. All four could rivet an audience with their autobiographies, but only the governor was willing to talk. Nonetheless, their lives have been public enough to allow a good look at the four careers.

Lammot du Pont Copeland, Sr., was the son of Louise and Charles Copeland. Louise was Pierre's older sister. Lammot, known as Mots within the family (or Big Mots, to distinguish him from his son), was an only child, a circumstance that probably makes him the richest living du Pont. A *Time* magazine article in 1964 recounts a story about him at the age of ten, when he entered a family biology contest in which the object was to be the first to find and assemble the bones to form the skeleton of an animal found in the Delaware countryside. Mots completed this difficult assignment by cooking a rabbit in a pot of lye. *Time* revealed Copeland as having been tempted in his youth by the medical profession.

But after graduating from Harvard in 1928, Copeland went to work for the Du Pont Company. His start was inauspicious. An expediter of small orders, he was laid off soon after he started. Just four months later he was back on the payroll, and at the age of thirty-seven, he was elected to the board of directors. Copeland developed an early reputation as the family financial genius. Testifying in the antitrust suit, Copeland recalled how he became involved in the family syndicate then buying U. S. Rubber stock. His family gave him "small amounts of securities," Copeland said, so "as a boy, I had a little bit of money, with which I tried to learn about the investment world, and I used to consult with him on minor investments." The "him" was his uncle, William Winder Laird, who had married another Pierre sister and was a founder of the Laird, Bissell & Meeds brokerage firm. In 1927 at the age of twenty-two, Copeland agreed to go 50-50 with his father on a $1.2 million pledge to the rubber syndicate. His mother had died the year before intestate—an unusual circumstance for a du Pont—and Copeland had come into some money. It would be more than forty years before Copeland would make an investment bad enough to cost him his job, and even then, the circumstances were most extenuating.

Copeland was a businessman's businessman. In 1940 he became a director of Christiana Securities and U. S. Rubber. Two years later he joined the Du Pont board. In 1944 he was elected to the General Motors board. He succeeded Pierre on the board of the Pennsylvania Railroad in 1953, and in 1959 was elected to the board of the Chemical Bank and Trust Company in New York. That same year he was named to the Du Pont Company's executive committee. He was a glutton for work. Upon being named Du Pont's president in 1962, Copeland estimated his work week contained eighty hours. Copeland maintained a low profile as president, rarely meeting with customers, suppliers, other business executives, or government officials. His forte was finance, and he stayed as close to home as he could. His business philosophy was summed up in a statement to *Time:* "When you get to the point where sales are rated above profits, that's not business. That's bureaucracy." Like his predecessors, Copeland believed in the theory of owner management. "It's hard for the professional [manager] to think beyond his own tenure. He will be interested in a safe performance over a decade or so, but an owner-manager may be looking fifty years ahead."

Part of Du Pont's success, Copeland felt, stemmed from what was once "called family tradition [and] now is company philosophy. There's a close feeling in the company. It comes from our policy of promoting from within. You're always dealing with people you know." On a number of occasions, Copeland talked about the importance of interested owners, but he recognized they were not an unmixed blessing. "Incompetent owners have ruined many a business," he once said. At another moment, he waxed a bit personal: "Just because your name is du Pont doesn't make you any smarter than the next fellow," he said. As the years went by, Copeland appeared to grow resigned to the fact that the days of the interested owner were numbered. In general, interested owners were becoming tougher to find because of the growth of indirect ownership through mutual and pension funds. Inheritance taxes were reducing the stake of interested owners. In 1973 he said, "I wish there were more of the younger family members working in the company. There aren't enough, and some of those who do work for the company aren't always good enough to make top management." Copeland and the current chief executive officer, Irving S. Shapiro, are the only two company bosses who rose to the top without scientific backgrounds. Copeland succeeded his father as secretary of the company in 1947 and was himself succeeded seven years later by Pierre S. du Pont III. Copeland was destined to become president of Du Pont earlier than he actually did, according to *Fortune* magazine, but Crawford H. Greenewalt and Walter S. Carpenter, Jr., then president and board chairman respectively, decided to remain at their jobs until the antitrust suit was concluded.

When he was finally named president, Copeland told the New York *Times*, "Mr. Greenewalt and I look at life from a similar point of view." Several years later in another interview with the *Times*, Copeland was asked about the relationship between business and government and said the two were already partners through taxation and regulation. Business Copeland saw as the generator of the national wealth, which government used. He called for a stronger relationship and a better understanding between the two of their objectives, needs, and activities. Copeland was president of Du Pont during a period of great optimism and discovery at the company. Corfam, the artificial leather for which Du Pont had such high hopes, was in its infancy. Symmetrel, a drug that combated certain flu viruses, had been discovered. Du Pont scientists were working on a photographic process for producing positive images without negatives, fostering dreams the photo products division would become another Polaroid. Surlyn, the new supertough plastic, was a reality.

The Copeland years seemed fated for dramatic success. But Corfam proved too expensive for the consumer, who also didn't think the risk of catching the flu was severe enough to warrant taking Symmetrel all the time. The photo process never quite went commercial. Only Surlyn, used among other things as the cover on golf balls to prevent their cutting by golfers with imperfect swings, has made a contribution to earnings. The blame was certainly not Copeland's, but all too many promises went unfulfilled. In 1967 Copeland became chairman of the board, and a new man, Charles B. McCoy, took over the presidency and the chief executive's office.

Despite his grueling business schedule, Copeland managed time for a number of hobbies. He enjoyed shooting and fishing and had a pistol range in his basement. He was a life member of the National Rifle Association. He was devoted to music, both classical and jazz, a devotion that is a little surprising given Copeland's bad hearing, a defect that appears to be genetic among a number of du Ponts and one that undoubtedly contributed to another apparently inherited characteristic, shyness. Those who know him well say Copeland is delightful company, but those who know him well are small in number. Copeland has been a delegate to several Republican National

Conventions, and once said, "I have always felt that people have an obligation to take part in politics." Like so many of his relatives, Copeland once flew his own plane. His philanthropic interests are widely varied. In 1965 he established a $2.1 million trust for the benefit of the University of Pennsylvania, and he has been an active Harvard alumnus. He and his mother were the primary catalysts behind the turning of the old Hagley Yard, one of the Brandywine powder mills, into a park in the 1920s. Copeland has also been a concerned supporter of efforts to stem the world's population explosion.

Lammot du Pont Copeland, Jr.—Little Mots—is the oldest of three Copeland children. In the early 1960s he sold chemicals for Du Pont in the San Francisco area and more or less minded his own business. Then he became interested in the newspaper business. His first effort came to nought, but word got around that he was interested, and before long he was offered a string of weeklies in Southern California with an afternoon daily—the Hollywood *Citizen News*—thrown in for good measure. Copeland bought. In 1963 he added the San Fernando Valley *Times* and along the way picked up three Florida weeklies. Before 1966 these papers were Copeland's main business interests. Part of the reason for his interest in newspapers was his desire for a public forum from which to preach his conservatism. He was a director of the American Conservative Union and a member of William Miller's staff during the 1964 Goldwater-Miller campaign. As chairman of the Citizens Foreign Aid Committee, he urged the House Foreign Affairs Committee in 1968 to end foreign aid and work for victory over communism, not coexistence with it.

Copeland Jr. also dabbled in real estate, buying a 785-acre property near Burbank, California, for $1.6 million on the recommendation of one of his newspaper executives. A proposed joint venture to develop the land had to be postponed, money being scarce and some of the land being hilly and difficult to develop.

While his newspapers battled a cash flow problem, Copeland was back East, having been transferred by Du Pont. A West Coast mortgage broker put Copeland in touch with a fellow named Thomas A. Shaheen, a money broker who had recently gone through personal bankruptcy but nonetheless had some important connections. Shaheen arranged a $3.8 million loan from the barbers' and electrical workers' pension funds, which Copeland guaranteed by putting up more than 27,000 shares of Christiana Securities. Shaheen, a slick operator who has since disappeared (best guess is Lebanon), may have sensed he had a live one. At any rate, soon he was calling on Copeland again, this time with a real estate deal, including sweetheart terms for Copeland. Copeland's associates have said it was this transaction that helped convince Copeland that Shaheen was a valuable guy to know.

Before long, Shaheen and Copeland were piling deal upon deal, many of them handled through a holding company they incorporated and named Winthrop Lawrence Corporation. Real estate, movies, toys, a moving van line, insurance, proprietary colleges, even a car wash, all were part of the new firm's business. The typical deal worked something like this: Shaheen would find a company that needed cash. He'd arrange a loan, which Copeland would guarantee. The recipient of the money would be charged a large fee and frequently had to put up an equity interest in his company. To oversimplify, Shaheen would take the fee and Copeland would get the stock in a company that had to be in trouble to come to them in the first place. That is not entirely accurate as a description of any one deal, none of which exactly resembled any other one, but details aside, that is more or less the essence of what happened. Considering the size and scope of the younger Copeland's enterprises, it is somewhat remarkable that the Wilmington community in which he now lived had little knowledge of what was going on. Like his father, Little Mots is rather shy and has few close friends. The du Ponts have never been publicity seekers.

The first hints of impending disaster began appearing in

the summer of 1970 as isolated individual Copeland creditors began filing suits to recover their losses. In November Copeland filed an arrangement petition under Chapter 11 of the Federal Bankruptcy Act. He listed assets of slightly less than $26 million against liabilities of nearly $60 million. Shortly thereafter, Winthrop Lawrence Corporation followed Copeland into bankruptcy court, saying its assets were $23.5 million against $30.4 million in liabilities.

For the next three and a half years Copeland and his attorneys tried to unravel his tangled affairs, managing to reduce his net liabilities from $34 million to less than $20 million through negotiation, litigation, and, in no small measure, through the waiving by his family—mainly his father—of claims against him. It was a difficult task, especially where Winthrop Lawrence was concerned. Frequently Copeland had to admit he did not know where the money obtained by that company and guaranteed by him went. More than half of Copeland's liabilities involved obligations he incurred on someone else's behalf. Nearly $27 million of those liabilities were the result of Copeland's guaranteeing loans to other people. A list of firms in which Copeland and Shaheen were involved either directly or indirectly reads like a corporate casualty report. A year after Copeland filed his bankruptcy petition, the status of some of those companies looked like this:

Winthrop Lawrence, in Chapter 11 proceedings; Graphic Productions, adjudicated bankrupt; Western Towers, foreclosure proceedings instituted; Mag-Mil Company, reduced to judgment; Massey Junior College, in receivership; Dean Van Lines, operating under a Chapter 11 arrangement; Standard Media, another Chapter 11 case; Delta Food Processing, in bankruptcy proceedings; Transogram Company, in acknowledged financial trouble and having reported a substantial loss for the latest quarter; United International, being audited by the Indiana Insurance Commission and rumored to be a candidate for Chapter 11.

The younger Copeland has never talked publicly about how and why he became so deeply enmeshed with these schemes except to issue through his attorneys a statement shortly after his bankruptcy petition was filed calling himself a victim of Shaheen's wiles. The national economic picture didn't help. The economy was sluggish, and money was hard to come by, although the magic of the du Pont name held together for a long time. At one point, a bank in Dallas loaned Copeland more than $4 million on the strength of his signature without security or collateral. There can be little doubt that Copeland enjoyed his role as financial savior for so many firms, along with the perquisites thereto attached, but it is clear that he did not keep a strong enough grip on his own affairs, convinced perhaps by the silvery tongue of Shaheen that he was in good hands. It is also possible he simply failed to understand that guaranteeing a loan for someone else could be just as demanding on his resources in hard times as taking the loan out in his own name.

The whole affair must have been particularly agonizing for his father. In the year preceding the bankruptcy petition, the elder Copeland loaned Winthrop Lawrence more than $8 million. He also guaranteed all but $350,000 of a $3.7 million loan from the Wilmington Trust Company to his son, securing the guarantee with stock. His son's fall and his own role therein finally caused Copeland to resign as Du Pont's board chairman. He has claimed that he was never given the full picture while being asked for help, but a man of his recognized financial acumen must have suspected that everything was not coming up profits at Winthrop Lawrence. Copeland Sr. has not publicly discussed his role, but it seems virtually certain that acting on his own behalf he would never have acted as he did. His son needed help, and unfortunately it was too late for advice. One can almost visualize Big Mots closing his eyes, gritting his teeth, signing checks, and praying.

The plan of arrangement by which Copeland Jr. was to pay off his creditors was finally dated May 17, 1974. In it, he agreed to pay all debts of $1,000 or less in full, to pay twenty cents on the dollar for all debts from $1,000 to $600,000, and ten cents on the dollar above that. The payments were to be made over a ten-year period, money for the payments to come from Copeland's trust income. It must have been galling to many of his creditors that Little Mots could engage in bankruptcy proceedings while receiving an income from trusts estimated at $451,000 for 1975 and projected at $628,000 in 1984, the last year of payments. But Copeland's trusts were of a variety known as "spendthrift," and were neither attachable nor assignable under the law. In fact, in Delaware, not even bank accounts are attachable, making Copeland's trust income virtually impregnable. The schedule of payments, including more than $650,000 in legal fees, provides for $15,000 a quarter as Copeland's living expenses and anticipates a balance remaining from the difference between payments and income—sort of a forced savings account—of nearly $800,000 at the end of the ten years.

There has often been speculation about why Big Mots didn't simply bite the bullet and bail his son out entirely. Neither of the Copelands has addressed himself to this question, but the most likely answer seems to be simply that it was cheaper, considering the family fortune as a whole, to do it the way they did. The feeling is that if the Copelands had believed Little Mots was solely responsible for the liabilities he incurred, they would quite likely have paid them in full, but they were convinced the younger Copeland had been had and were therefore determined to settle as cheaply as possible. It is true that, theoretically, a straight bankruptcy that simply divided available assets among creditors would have cost less, but such a solution might have provoked some creditors into challenging the spendthrift trust setup. While legally such a challenge probably had but faint chance of winning, rocking the boat, bringing the setup to public attention, was to be avoided if possible.

And now Little Mots keeps busy peddling jokes, as presi-

Lammot du Pont (center) and his new bride took their entire wedding party along on their honeymoon trip to Niagara Falls in October 1865. (Courtesy of Eleutherian Mills Historical Library)

Destiny's children: Henry Belin (left) and Pierre S. in back, William
K. (left), Irénée (center), and Lammot in front. (Courtesy of
Eleutherian Mills Historical Library)

The Tancopanicum Band, with Alfred I. du Pont conducting and his cousin Pierre at the piano. (Courtesy of Eleutherian Mills Historical Library)

T. Coleman du Pont was never one to sit on the fence. (Courtesy of Eleutherian Mills Historical Library)

Roads were one of T. Coleman's consuming passions. (Courtesy of
Eleutherian Mills Historical Library)

Alfred I. du Pont strikes his George Washington pose. (Courtesy of
Eleutherian Mills Historical Library)

Pierre S. du Pont (second from right) poses with brother Irénée (left), sister Peg Carpenter, and Vincent Auriol, president of France, at ceremony during which Pierre received the Croix de Commandeur of the French Legion of Honor in 1954. (Courtesy of Eleutherian Mills Historical Library)

The second Lammot du Pont and his second wife, the former Bertha Taylor, on a bicycle built for two in Florida. (Courtesy of Eleutherian Mills Historical Library)

Louise du Pont poses with bridesmaids just after becoming Mrs. Francis B. Crowninshield in 1900. (Courtesy of Eleutherian Mills Historical Library)

Elaine
duPont
Irving
Woodriff

dent of the Comedy Center, the main distribution vehicle for the prolific output of gag writer Robert Orben, who used to write for Jack Paar, Dick Gregory, and Red Skelton. About three thousand people—lesser comedians, after-dinner speakers, businessmen—subscribe to Orben's service, which turns out several pages of one-liners twice a month. For a while, Orben was even gag writer for that stand-up comic to end all stand-up comics, President Ford. Copeland became involved when Orben's former publisher quit several years ago. Little Mots handles the printing and mailing, with a little help from his children in the envelope-stuffing department. President of the Comedy Center is not exactly president of Du Pont, or even Winthrop Lawrence, and the situation has made for lots of bad jokes in Wilmington. But there is another side, slightly pathetic perhaps yet somehow vaguely courageous: Little Mots picking up the pieces of his shattered self-image and remaking it along more modest lines. In Wilmington, such sympathy as there is has been directed primarily at the elder Copeland. His son, after all, managed maybe the largest personal bankruptcy ever in this country without suffering any particularly dire financial consequences. Some people tend to dismiss the younger Copeland's troubles as the inevitable consequence of mixing ignorance with arrogance. Nonetheless, Little Mots tried to make something of his life and do it on his own. That's more than a lot of his generation of the family, even acknowledging the dismal failure in which the effort culminated.

The story of Pierre S. du Pont III is also one ending in failure. The second son of Pierre's brother Lammot, Big Pete (again, to distinguish father from son), began his career working hard and rising fast at Du Pont. He sold nylon and Neoprene, making regular calls on General Motors and U. S. Rubber. During the antitrust suit, he characterized these two customers as "tough sales." On the side, he dabbled in the stock market. He testified that he was sometimes owner of eight thousand or nine thousand shares of U. S. Rubber and sometimes didn't own any at all. He traded the stock during the 1930s. Pete began working for the family company in 1934 and became a director in 1948. After a stint as company secretary, he was elected vice-president and executive committee member in 1963. Just two years later, he resigned under duress.

Like the Copelands, outside investments did him in. In 1957 Pete first became involved with a movie producer named Samuel Bronston, who gave the world *El Cid* and *55 Days at Peking*. Pete played the role of angel, putting up nearly $7 million from 1957 until early 1965. In March of 1964 Pete acquired control of Samuel Bronston Productions. In June Bronston filed for bankruptcy and at the same time filed a $5.2 million suit against Pete for non-performance as a guarantor. Pete charged the notes he endorsed were for dollars Bronston had said in a letter he'd use for movies, but that the proceeds actually went into an oil venture. Creditors of Bronston movies also began suing Pete, suits that were eventually settled out of court for cash, movie rights, and other considerations over a period of three years. The settlements were not made public but the suits had been filed for a total of $15 million. It has been said within the family that Pete's brothers and sisters came to his rescue, allowing him to retain, among other manifestations of the good life, his seventy-two-foot ketch, *Barlovento II*, his summer home on exclusive Fishers Island, and his sumptuous home in Wilmington, Bois des Fosses. Meanwhile, Pete continues to chase Bronston through the courts. Du Pont won a $3.6 million judgment from Bronston more than ten years ago and is still trying to collect. He recently managed to wrest some paintings away from the beleaguered Bronston, but he said at the time they didn't come close to satisfying the judgment. Early in 1976 the courts threw out a $5 million harassment suit brought against du Pont by Bronston.

These kinds of high jinks are not viewed with favor in the staid boardroom of the Du Pont Company. Besides, Pete needed to devote too much time to his pursuit of Bronston to do his Du Pont job justice, and in January of 1965 he resigned.

Except for his Bronston interlude, du Pont has been rather a model citizen. A hearty, pipe-smoking, publicity-shy archconservative, du Pont has served on the national board of trustees of the Leukemia Society of America and has been active in Planned Parenthood, heading the 1948 Planned Parenthood Federation of America fund drive. He served as general chairman of the local United Fund campaigns in 1959 and 1960. He was president of the trustees of Tower Hill School for twenty-five years, becoming chairman in 1977, and has been active in the Wilmington Medical Center. His work in developing the Methodist Country Home, a mammoth retirement residence, resulted in his being elected to the Methodist Hall of Fame in Philanthropy. He was president of the American Museum of Immigration, which developed the immigration museum at the base of the Statue of Liberty.

Pete's hobbies include sailing and books. He is a frequent competitor in the Newport to Bermuda yacht race and headed the syndicate backing the *American Eagle* in the America's Cup challenge in 1963, putting up $100,000. Two libraries in his Wilmington home are filled with rare and limited-edition books. He once had privately printed a lavish, leather-bound, illustrated genealogical history of his and his wife's families that is almost embarrassing in its ostentation and pomposity.

His son, the governor, is also an avid sailor but these days finds precious little time to indulge. Among contemporary du Ponts, Pete IV is easily the most conspicuously successful. His start was not all that promising. He was a C student at Princeton before serving in the Navy, where, like most officers, he found himself doing some legal work. His first case was defending one of his men who had been arrested for speeding. "He showed me where he had been picked up," Pete recalled during an interview over lunch at the exclusive

Wilmington Club. "He argued that his car couldn't have accelerated fast enough to have been going the speed he was charged with. I prepared a helluva case. Did all the calculations. Turned out my client was lying. The place he showed me wasn't where he was picked up at all. I learned a good lesson. It applies to dealing with the General Assembly, special-interest groups, other politicians. Take nothing for granted."

Pete and his father don't always see eye to eye. Big Pete didn't think law school was a particularly good idea, but Little Pete had developed a strong interest in government policy and the involvement of federal courts in state affairs. He took the law aptitude exam and finished in the top 1 or 2 per cent in the country. "I'd been a lousy student until then," he says. Despite his Princeton Cs, he received early acceptance at Harvard Law School. "It was my own decision to go. I paid my own way."

Instead of practicing law upon graduation, he went to work for the Du Pont Company. His father had always urged him to do so, and his wife told him if he didn't work for the company, he'd always wonder whether he'd made a mistake, pointing out he could always quit if he didn't like it. For seven years he stuck it out. He remembers people in the company used to have the impression that because his name was du Pont, he knew what was going on in the executive suite. "I always felt no one made a move where I was concerned unless it was checked out from well above." He began to feel the company was too much like the military in that promotion was an orderly, slow, regimented process. "Before you could become a lieutenant, you had to be a lieutenant j.g. for so many months." He thought he could do more than he was doing at Du Pont and says he was not particularly overwhelmed by the caliber of the competition within the company. The people at the assistant general manager level and up were impressive enough, he says, but below that he was confident his abilities matched or exceeded those of his peers. He finally decided to quit and go into politics. He went to inform his department head, who told him he was sorry to see him go, that he'd just been discussing a promotion for him. "My impression is that such decisions were not normally made on his level," Pete said. "His level was about twenty levels up from me."

Once again, Pete and his father disagreed. Big Pete frowned on politics as a profession and urged his son to stay with the company. The future governor reminded his father of the story about how Big Pete had once gone to his father, Lammot, and told him of his chance to switch from the technical end of the business to marketing. A big promotion was involved. Big Pete wanted his father's advice as to whether he should take the new job. Legend has it that Lammot told his son he'd be crazy to take it, that technology was where the future of the company lay and marketing would never really matter. The son took the job anyway. "But the parallel is lost on him," says Little Pete.

Pierre S. du Pont IV's initial foray into the political jungle was a pretty tame safari. He ran for the state house of representatives in a district so safely Republican that he ran unopposed. Nonetheless, he spent plenty of money on his campaign developing name recognition, which might seem a little bizarre for a du Pont in Delaware. "The pols told me I couldn't get elected with my name," Pete recalled. "I worked for three months on my opening statement." That statement was received with something less than universal approbation within the family. "Several members of the family called me up angry the next day. 'What's the idea of apologizing for being a du Pont?' they wanted to know. 'That's no way to start a campaign.'" Maybe not, but Pete has never lost an election and tends to lead the Republican ticket every time he runs.

His next move was to Washington as a Delaware congressman. For three terms he served, earning a reputation for efficient constituency services and a model congressman's office. He cast himself as an environmentalist and fought for financial disclosure for elected officials. His strategy at home was to freely admit his wealth, publishing a list of his holdings and the income therefrom, although the list of holdings did not include his trusts, the major part of his wealth. He argued that his wealth made it possible for him to be independent because he didn't have to rely on the favors of special interests for financing. His voting record was such that he was rated above average by lobby groups on both the right and the left.

But a junior congressman in the minority party is not a man destined for great accomplishments, and Pete began to get restless. Viewed by many as a political cul de sac, the governorship began to appeal to du Pont as an office out of which concrete progress could be directed. While politicians sought political motives for his action, du Pont decided to run for governor in 1976, convinced the state of Delaware was a manageable entity that was being mismanaged. He was a political realist, conceding that four years of exposure as governor might well end his political career. He saw a job that needed doing and himself as the man who could get it done. No, he promised, he was not maneuvering himself into a more tenable position from which to run for the Senate. He was simply looking to be governor. A tireless campaigner who seems to thrive on the grind of a full daily schedule followed by four or five appearances at night, du Pont won easily, although he was unable to pull his Republican running mate into the lieutenant-governorship. He was sworn in on January 17, 1977.

Six months later he assessed his progress candidly. "I don't know what you thought was wrong on January 17 in Delaware," he said. "But whatever it was, it still is." He pointed to three stumbling blocks he'd tripped over in his first six months. He underestimated state revenues, allowing his freer-spending opponents to say things weren't as bad as Pete was painting them and be right. Special-interest groups outplayed him in the political game. He singled out education's lobby, noting that he had cut something like $20 million from the state's $450 million budget and not a dime had come out of education, which represents 60 per cent of the budget. Finally, he said, the Republican caucus in the state General Assembly decided to play its own game, displaying no loyalty to the new governor. "I was elected on my own and they figure they were, too," he said. "We need to get together." Another problem, he said, was bogging down in detail work, such as the myriad appointments to boards and commissions a governor must make. Far more often than not the fate of the state does not hang in the balance over who is appointed to, say, the barbers' board, but the barbers take it seriously enough to make the appointment a delicate diplomatic matter. A contentious state senate makes those appointments needing senate confirmation even stickier. After six months in office, du Pont estimated the senate was confirming only about 30 per cent of his appointments.

"Legislative Hall is an unreal world," Pete said. "Every little thing is magnified a thousand times. I must get twenty-five questions a day that are perceived as life-or-death matters. I usually get to maybe three of them. I am now convinced that nothing I do or don't do will stop the world."

Du Pont freely admits he made some early mistakes, but he does not see the situation as unsalvageable. "I was elected by a big majority with generally favorable media coverage and a skeptical General Assembly. I had the opportunity. I missed it." But he was still planning to run for a second term. "I still would run again," he said in July of 1977. "I talked to Teeter [the pollster based in Michigan] the other day. He did the polls that helped me make the decision to run for governor. He said if I liked being U.S. representative, I'd love being governor. I told him I was switching to Yankelovich." Du Pont had not yet lost his sense of humor. But his sense of disillusionment was growing. "I've always hesitated about reaching a hard conclusion that anyone was out, for whatever reasons, to screw up the works, but now . . ."

Being a du Pont in public life in Delaware is at best a mixed blessing, Pete feels. "I'm still asked a lot by voters how I can relate to their problems, never having been poor," he says, "but after about '71 the name problem pretty well disappeared. It seems to be resurfacing some now. I get letters saying things like, 'The only reason you can suggest cutting the school budget is that your kids are in private school,' or, 'Raise taxes, huh? Sure, you can afford it.'" On the other hand, campaigning at church suppers and the like around the state, Pete remembers people coming up to him time and again and telling him something like, "I went to a school built by your namesake." Pete says the mistaken preconceived notions about the family that he found within the company are not unlike those he runs into in politics. As an example, he cites the rumors that began circulating, even finding their way into print, when his wife Elise started going to the University of Pennsylvania law school. People had the du Ponts on the verge of divorce. They had Pete's uncle, Willis du Pont, who lives in Florida and is roughly Pete's age, giving a large sum of money to the university. Pete has grown philosophical about such things. They're part of the legacy, especially when it is combined with a public career, like the question he still gets from media people about what those family meetings at which the policy decisions are made are really like.

The truth is, says Pete, that he is not particularly close to most other du Ponts. "Elise knows more about the family than I do," he says. "My father gave her a bunch of books on the family to read before we were married, and much to my surprise, she read them. Of course, I grew up with my first cousins. Every Sunday we used to go to St. Amour [his grandfather Lammot's home] for supper. The whole family. I suspect they didn't really like it all that much, but they're probably glad about the custom now in retrospect." One cousin Pete singled out was Edmond du Pont, the man who ran Francis I. du Pont and Company and whom Pete considered

one of the "independent thinkers" in the family. "I remember having a long talk with him about working for the
company." Pete's association with his more famous namesake
was not intimate. For one thing, Pete was still a teen-ager
when Pierre died, but Pete's maternal grandfather was a landscape architect who thought of Longwood and its gardens as
Mecca. "Whenever he came," Pete recalled, "we would always go out to Longwood. Longwood and Styers Nursery. I've
never been able to garden since."

Pete is convinced that businessmen don't understand politics. "Uncle Pierre, Uncle Buss, and my grandfather could sit
around, put their not insignificant intellects together, and
come up with a good solution to a problem but they didn't
understand the man in the street," he said. "I guess if you or
I went into a technical lab to direct the placement of equipment, we'd probably come up with an equally silly solution."
He said a friend of his tried to convince him there was a
groundswell building for a state sales tax early in the summer
of 1977. They were having lunch at the Wilmington Club,
where there is a large oval table around which the city's top
executives, lawyers, and the like gather for lunch when they
have no specific luncheon appointment. "I told him, 'Sure
there's a groundswell,' " Pete said. " 'You could go around the
big table polling everyone there and to a man, they'd be in
favor of a sales tax.' But the average worker, the average politician, they're another matter."

While friends and detractors alike characterize Pete as a
full-blooded political animal, he gives the strong impression
that the governor's job will be his last elective office. He says
he envies his father's right to privacy, his ability to tell inquis-
itive reporters to please go away, and figures the future con-
tains three possibilities, which he ranks in no particular order
of preference. One would be to "live like a human being" and
enter the private practice of law, something he says he's always regretted never having tried. A second is to return to
Washington in some administrative, non-elective capacity,

but he says that would require "a President I liked, and at the moment, that doesn't seem too likely." His third option, he says, is to take a year or so out and put his experiences in politics on paper, trying to provide an insight into the operating mechanisms of government. How lobbies work, for example.

Asked to what he attributes the disparities in motivation among his generation in the family, Pete says he doesn't really know. "This will perhaps sound foolish," he said, "but I think maybe it has something to do with Yankee versus Southern blood, heredity and environment." As he elaborates, it is clear he is talking about a visceral feeling more than a carefully reasoned philosophy. The faster pace of life in the North, the traditions of Yankee ingenuity and industry as opposed to the traditions of Southern gentlemanliness. For his own high motivation, he also credits his father. "Father was very strict from a motivational standpoint."

Like most of his contemporaries in the family, Pete does not seem to be overly concerned with the passing of particular du Pont traditions on to his children. The notions of dynasty and destiny are not strong. "I talk to the kids, sure," he says. "I try to tell them to be whatever they want to be, but that they better be good at it."

Chapter Eight

Pierre's Other Relatives

In the early years of the twentieth century, Pierre du Pont lost two brothers. Henry Belin du Pont succumbed to a long battle with tuberculosis in July of 1902, and Pierre immediately took over the guardianship of his only child, Henry B. Jr., who would grow up to become the man most people consider the last of the giants in the family. In 1907 William K. du Pont died of typhus, literally breathing his last in Pierre's arms, and once again Pierre became a surrogate father. Henry B. was twenty-nine when he died; William K. was thirty-two. Pierre had been like a father to them since the death of their real father, Lammot, in 1884, and he would do his best to be a father to their children. Both had shown some early promise. William K. had displayed a rather advanced sense of humor as young as thirteen, when he wrote his mother from boarding school: "When you write next, please send a translation. I spent five minutes over a word and found it was 'the.'" Pierre was very close to his brothers and sisters and must have felt the loss of Henry B. and William K. deeply, but undoubtedly he enjoyed watching their children grow up with his guidance and love. His guardianship was far more than a legal formality.

An exchange of letters between S. Hallock du Pont, William K.'s oldest, and Pierre in November of 1922 on the occasion of Hallock's twenty-first birthday is revealing. Hallock writes:

"As you know, tomorrow is my 21st birthday and your legal guardianship ends. I want to thank you in every possible way for all you have done for me and for mother and the girls as well. It is utterly impossible for me to put my appreciation on paper. I probably know of only a very small fraction of all you have done, and I am rather incoherent at any rate.

"I realize perfectly that all I have, in any sense, I owe to you and to mother. The only way I could begin to repay you would be to go into the company and stick to it after college. I will be only too glad to do this as I have a large amount of family feeling and pride, and it seems a very small thing for one of our name not to do his best to continue the work which the family has carried on for as many generations. As far as I know, that is the only thing you have ever asked me to do, and I will be only too glad to do so when the time comes.

"As you know 'Tech' [MIT] has been, and is, no 'bed of roses' for me, and I am still dubious of ever receiving a degree. At any rate, the way I have my course outlined at present, so as to include advanced organic chemistry and industrial and business subjects, means that I must take three more years here. The courses in dyes, explosives, etc., are supposed to be for ordnance officers only but I am practically sure I will be admitted to them when the time comes.

"After finishing up at the Institute, I would like to go to Oxford or Cambridge for a few years to take history, modern languages and any international and diplomatic relations courses that are offered. I am also looking forward to several years during which I can read to my heart's content, a thing I have missed a lot up here. After that I would like to travel awhile.

"If I follow the above schedule, it will mean not going to work until I am between 25 and 28. However, I am perfectly convinced that I went to boarding school and also to college too young, and I don't want to make the same mistake when I enter the company.

"I am very anxious to hear whether you approve of my plans, as outlined above, and also what you would suggest as to the handling of my estate, which is quite a question to a person who has absolutely no knowledge of such affairs. . . ."

To which Pierre replies:

"I feel very much ashamed of myself that I let your 21st birthday pass without having written you or made other note of the occasion. It is a turning point in a man's life that should be marked by some consideration from friends and relatives, and I had planned several times before the occasion to be sure to write you, but I find that my things left undone are increasing rather than decreasing as time goes on.

"You are to be congratulated on your 21st birthday—not so much for having arrived as for having arrived successfully, with a good foundation for future years. Unfortunately, not a few young men reach manhood with a number of regrets as to the past, but I am sure that you are not among them, and have very little cause to wish that you could do it over. I hope that the next 21 years will leave you as good a score.

"As to your indebtedness to me, there is nothing to think of but to feel your obligation liquidated by helping on the next generation. You cannot escape being called upon if you are among the oldest of a large tribe. I hope that your response will always be prompt and helpful.

"Your plans for the future are ambitious and worth carrying out. I expect, however, and, I might say, hope also that before the plan is carried out, you will feel the call to work which will start you in business. I earnestly hope that this will be with the Du Pont Company, so that your efforts will help carry forward the burden of the fifth generation.

"I realize that the Tech course is one requiring your every effort. While I hope that you receive a degree, I do not think this so important as sticking at the work for the allotted term. The degree itself has no bearing on the amount of learning that sticks in your brain, even though there is satisfaction in receiving the official stamp of approval.

"You have my best wishes for success, not only at Tech, but in the plans for your life, of which I am glad to know that you are thinking seriously at this important time."

Hallock wound up going to work for the company sooner than he had planned, but it was apparently more out of sense of obligation than any driving ambition to succeed in the world of chemicals and high finance. His stint was brief, and then he went private. It is difficult to measure the contributions of the du Ponts like Hallock who actively seek anonymity, but they have unquestionably been substantial and often carried a stamp of individuality—some might even say eccentricity—that added color to the social fabric in a way institutional or governmental charity never can. Hallock's $130,200 trust fund, for example, which gave World War I hero Sergeant Alvin C. York, virtually ignored by his country in his later years, $300 a month. Or Hallock's interest in the blue hen, Delaware's state bird, which preserved it from extinction. By no means was all of Hallock's generosity directed by whimsey. He was a major benefactor of the University of Delaware, in particular the Department of Agriculture, and for years funded the police-sponsored Pushmobile Derby for Delaware children. Hallock had a sense of fair play that sometimes manifested itself in bizarre fashion. One of his sons tells a story about how a Dalmatian dog had been trained to run along under a buggy as it made its rounds along the Brandywine. One day the dog was attacked by a pack of hounds and was killed. Hallock raised bull terriers, and when he heard of the fate of the Dalmatian, he had one of the more ferocious terriers trained to run along under the buggy as the Dalmatian had. Not long afterward, the pack of hounds again spotted the buggy with the dog running along beneath it and attacked. This time they had bitten off more than they could chew. The bull terrier made fast work of the pack and mincemeat of those who displayed the least tardiness in beating a retreat. Plagued by bad health during most of the last third of his life, Hallock avoided public exposure, even to the point of skipping large family functions, but he served long and well on many family foundation and institution boards. He was considered something of a maverick within the family, but he was a maverick with a big heart.

His oldest son, S. Hallock Jr., moved to Florida as a

young man some twenty years ago. Like so many of his relatives, Hal nurtured an interest in aviation, running his own air service business and in 1970 becoming the national commander of the Civil Air Patrol with the rank of brigadier general. By then he had logged more than 10,500 hours as a pilot. He is also a skeet champion.

A second son, William K., has become a nationally recognized figure in the field of wildlife and conservation, having been chairman of the federal Interior Department's fifteen-man advisory board on sports fisheries and wildlife. In 1976 he was presented with the National Recreation and Park Association's national voluntary service award. Among his projects was one that raised $400,000 in the Delaware and Maryland area to save 500,000 acres at the mouth of the Saskatchewan River in Canada from flooding and develop it as a waterfowl habitat. William K. never fully mastered the art of formal education, but when it comes to a subject in which he has an interest, he rapidly becomes an expert. Probably no layman is better qualified to talk authoritatively on the subject of ducks and the Atlantic Flyway in particular and wildlife and conservation in general than this du Pont. Among accomplishments of which he is particularly proud is his chairmanship of a committee under former Delaware governor Russell W. Peterson charged with formulating public policy on Delaware wetlands. Bill orchestrated a public policy of preservation. Among Bill's hobbies is antiques, and here too, his thirst for knowledge about things that interest him has been quenched only by absorbing the history and technique in vast detail. If he disagrees with a dealer about a particular antique but says nothing, it is not out of deference or lack of confidence in his own opinion but from a desire to maintain good relations. Within the family, Bill enjoys a sound reputation for ability. He is a trustee and treasurer of Longwood Gardens and a trustee of the Eleutherian Mills-Hagley Foundation. Both his sense of humor and the strength of his will are reflected in a story about his days in

Army ROTC while at the University of Virginia. He had for some time been an expert pistol shot, but at Virginia there was little opportunity for that and as part of ROTC, Bill began to shoot a rifle. The Virginia ROTC rifle coach was a rah-rah type determined to enlist everyone who could shoot as a member of a team he took to compete against other schools and groups in the area on weekends. He considered the sacrifice of weekend social activities for these excursions to be a small one. Bill did not. As incentive for his shooters, the coach would post the names of those with the best scores in the different shooting categories—perhaps eight or ten in total —all over the rifle range. Bill already had the top score in one or two when he decided he'd cool the coach's ardor for him. He proceeded to capture the top scores for every category. He then resigned from the rifle team.

The youngest of the three Hallock sons is Richard S., who may be the best pure pilot to have come out of the family. He is undoubtedly the only man ever to report for the Air National Guard's basic training program at Lackland Air Force Base in Texas piloting his own Lear jet. Among the warmest and friendliest of the du Ponts, Dick admits flying the Lear into Lackland was a mistake, for which he paid throughout basic training as he was ragged by fellow trainees and officers alike. Dick went on to get his commercial pilot's license and flew for a while with a cargo line. You cannot get an airline pilot's license any sooner than he did. Breezing through flight school in Florida with high honors, he passed the written test when he was twenty-one plus a week. At least 1,200 hours are required for a captain's license. The pilot must be twenty-three and must have passed the written exam less than two years before he takes the flying test. On his twenty-third birthday, Dick took the flying test and received his captain's rating in a four-engine Constellation.

Henry B. du Pont, Jr., was Henry B.'s only child. As the oldest member of the second generation on the three brothers' side of the family, H.B., or Pinky as he was known within the family, had the mantle of leadership draped across his shoulders more or less by expectation. Although his college career at Yale was not particularly distinguished, by the age of thirty-six, after having gone on to MIT graduate school, H.B. was already being touted as the man most likely to succeed his uncle, Lammot, as president of the Du Pont Company. The year was 1934, and young H.B. had just been elected a director of Du Pont.

While H.B. never made it all the way to the top, for most of his late years, he was the du Pont to whom people turned in their time of need. If someone was needed to put life into the Greater Wilmington Development Council, a business-led, save-our-city organization, H.B. was asked. If the University of Delaware needed $100,000 for a research vessel for its new marine studies college, H.B. provided; or perhaps it was $50,000 to fund a water resources study. For thirty years H.B. was president of the Alexis I. du Pont school district board. He was a major figure at the Wilmington Medical Center, and because of the time and money he devoted to making downtown Wilmington a nice place to live and work, two city mini-parks or squares are dedicated to his memory.

"H.B. was the last of the old-time operators," says Governor Pete du Pont. "He was the last of the family for whom the company was really a family business. Those even just six or eight years behind him, my father's generation, had things different. Days when you could get an idea, talk to two or three people, and get it done were over." Chick Laird, a first cousin of H.B., put it slightly differently, talking about freedom of individual action in the old days. "H.B. was perhaps the last of the family who was free enough—and had enough money—to do what he wanted," he said.

In H.B. two family avocations were well developed—yachting and aviation. His fifty-four-foot yacht did not particularly distinguish him within the family but the manifestations of his flying interest were another matter. H.B. caught the flying bug almost by accident. He was working for General Motors in Dayton, Ohio, in 1923 and living in a rooming house along with a former test pilot, Ben Whelan, who H.B. thought was an automobile buff. Before he realized what had happened, H.B. said yes to an offhand question during a washroom conversation about flying lessons, and that afternoon he was flying. In 1927 H.B. moved to Wilmington. He flew home, but there was no airport in Wilmington and he had to leave his plane at what was then the beginnings of the Philadelphia airport. It wasn't long before H.B. had convinced an uncle to lease him a farm field on the outskirts of town and permit a small hangar. In June of 1928 the local newspaper ran a picture of H.B. and his plane, noting he commuted to Texas every weekend to visit his fiancée.

H.B.'s makeshift airfield was the forerunner of Atlantic Aviation, a private plane sales and service organization that has grown to employ more than 1,200 people and become one of the largest businesses in the field. When it was incorporated, the company had more directors than employees. H.B. was also a substantial investor in North American Aviation, producer of the P-51 World War II fighter plane. For years he was a director of the company, which later became North American-Rockwell Corporation.

Although H.B., too, was troubled by the family's genetic deafness problem, although he, too, was inherently shy, circumstances forced him into the public limelight. In the last years of his life he came to be the public image of the du Pont family. Little of significance happened in Delaware without his imprint upon it. A measure of his importance is to be found in the index to *The Company State*, a Ralph Nader-sponsored diatribe about the shabby state of public affairs when one family and one company (Nader's protégés do not concede separate interests here) so dominate a political entity like Delaware. In the index to this book, H.B. rates 10 lines of page references; his closest rival, Irénée Jr., has 4.5 lines. The book was published in 1971. H.B. died in April of 1970. Among his large public gifts at death were more than

$1 million to both the Wilmington Medical Center and the University of Delaware. He also left the Eleutherian Mills-Hagley Foundation $650,000 and the Marine Historical Association of Mystic, Connecticut, $520,000.

H.B. had two sons. Henry B. III lived in Connecticut, worked for a Du Pont subsidiary and inherited his father's enthusiasm for aviation. In 1976 he was killed in a freak airplane accident. The other son, Edward B., is a shy, low-profile du Pont who started out working in the Du Pont Company's treasurer's department. Edward was convinced that you needed technical training to get ahead at Du Pont and had a number of discussions with his father on the subject. His father urged him to stick with the company. He didn't. "The day I quit was probably the most traumatic of my life," he once said. "It was Friday when I told my boss. Then I decided I'd better screw up my courage and go tell the old man before he found out from someone else. He wasn't too pleased." Edward is not exactly a chip off the old block. He is now chairman of Atlantic Aviation and president of the public library's board of managers. He also holds down a middle-level job at the Wilmington Trust Company. He was recently elected a director of the Du Pont Company, an election based more on heritage than merit. Inspired vision and driving ambition are not in him. His most conspicuous adventure was as president of the ill-starred Wilmington Clippers, a professional football team that lost $80,000 in its first year of operation, 1966, which, not just coincidentally, was also its last. Asked several years ago what he saw in his future, what his plans were, Edward shrugged. "Just trying to keep body and soul together," he said.

The next of Lammot's children after Henry B. and William K. was Irénée, who for many years seemed destined not to father a son who would survive him. After three daughters, he had a son who lived only three years. Then he had five more daughters. Finally came Irénée Jr., nicknamed Brip. His childhood was not apparently all that unusual. Many of his sisters married young and moved out, and Brip was not really overwhelmed by females. He was asking normal questions for a young boy about if stories were still being made and where life came from and played baseball down by the barn, preferring an old stick to a nice new bat. He didn't much like football, however, and told his mother he forgot, for some reason or another, to get his uniform. Mom knew what was going on, but let it go. In the middle 1930s, his mother wrote his father that Brip had made a motorcycle cap and was fascinated by sewing machines, or any machine, for that matter. At Dartmouth in 1939 Brip managed three Cs and a pair of Bs, one of them in chemistry. His letters home reflected a cavalier attitude toward spelling. His mother wrote Irénée Sr. wondering if she should take Brip to England, noting that it seemed to have been a good thing for the older children and might help Brip decide what to do with his life. She wondered if Brip was cut out for chemistry. After a tour at MIT, Brip went to work, riding his motorcycle through the snow to his assembly-line job. In 1943 Irénée Jr. fell in love. Early the next year he wrote his father about the things he and his new girl friend had in common—music and an aversion to big cities, for example—and how happy he was.

By legacy as much as by ability or inclination, Brip began climbing the Du Pont ladder. In 1959, at the age of thirty-nine, he was elected to the board of directors. Rumors had him being groomed for the presidency, probably after Copeland stepped down. Perhaps young Irénée wasn't the giant among men that his father and two uncles had been, but wasn't he proving himself a most valuable executive, certainly the most promising du Pont? Well, Irénée Jr. would learn that such things didn't count for as much as they used to and he would be admirably philosophical about it. Asked in 1973 if he'd had any regrets or bitter feelings about having been passed over for the company presidency, Brip said no. "I know my limitations. I as a stockholder would have objected to me as president."

At the time of his retirement as a senior vice-president of the company in the summer of 1978, Irénée told reporters, "I think I've done about as much as I can. One becomes less inventive in that (senior vice-president and member of the executive committee) capacity as time goes by." Commenting on his rise through the ranks of the company during a thirty-two-year career, he added, "But it would be highly unusual for a B.S. chemical engineer to reach the level I did other than by pull."

Besides his chores as the family's top man in the company in the 1970s, Irénée has shouldered his share and perhaps then some of civic obligations, replacing H.B. as a major force in the Greater Wilmington Development Council, heading the state chamber of commerce and serving on boards of or making contributions to myriad institutions and organizations promoting worthy causes. He was elected a life member of the MIT corporation. He served as president of Christiana Securities until its dissolution and was a director of the Wilmington newspapers, owned by Christiana up until the recent merger of Christiana into the Du Pont Company. He attempted to establish an alcoholic rehabilitation house in a tony Wilmington neighborhood, but the residents thwarted the project with the usual not-in-my-backyard arguments. In 1973 Brip was quoted as saying, "I want to make sure this area [the northwest suburbs of Wilmington] remains a nice place to live—even if I do nothing else in my life."

After his father died in 1963, Brip moved into Granogue, his father's magnificent hilltop estate. Brip does not fit easily into the mold of robber baron or country squire. He continues to be fascinated with things mechanical, doing much of the maintenance work himself on the ancient Volkswagen he uses for transportation. When a balloonist landed at Granogue a couple of years ago, Brip had to be rousted out of the cellar whither he had descended for a little do-it-yourself repairwork on the furnace. Brip is an unpretentious, almost apologetic sort with a sense of family tradition strong enough to keep him in harness at the family company and to convince him of the necessity of lavish debutante parties for his daughters but not so strong as to make him totally comfortable in the role of host at these affairs.

In his role as father, Brip has made no concerted effort to steer his children's course through life for them. He seems only to want their happiness, defined perhaps as a freedom from hassle. Several years ago his oldest son was living in Cambridge, Massachusetts, picking up odd jobs in darkrooms and trying to make it as a free-lance photographer. "He takes a damn fine picture. God bless him," Brip said at the time. The son has since returned to Wilmington. One daughter, Cynthia, is a designer of opera sets. There is almost the impression that Brip and preceding generations have earned for Brip's children the privilege of doing what they want.

Perhaps the most devoted family man, in the sense of the large family, among the du Ponts today is William Winder (Chick) Laird, Jr., the son of Irénée Sr.'s younger sister Mary du Pont and William Winder Laird, the stockbroker who used to advise Big Motsy Copeland when he was a young man. Laird has been essentially a private investor, usually with an eye toward making things better rather than just making money. He invested heavily in downtown Wilmington real estate, for example, hoping to help assure its proper development. He is often found helping younger people to get started, giving them advice or a job or financial backing. His activities are not easy to catalogue because he operates privately, behind the scenes, without looking for publicity. His work in public education, even, is known to be extensive, but measuring it is impossible.

Laird is, among friends, a gregarious storyteller with a wealth of family anecdote unmatched among the du Ponts. On the subject of myopia—the literal kind appears to be another quasi-genetic du Pont trait—Chick tells two stories. The first is about a class at Tower Hill, the private school founded by family members. It seems that in this class were perhaps eight cousins, all of whom were nearsighted and only one of whom was able on a given day to remember his or her glasses. The cousins would all sit in a row, and when something was written on the blackboard, whoever had remembered glasses would read and pass the glasses along until the entire row had read the board. The second story involves an early version of the driving simulator, a machine on which you can learn how to drive. It was being sent around the country to test the driving public. The Wilmington area tested out unusually nearsighted, and there was some public speculation that the water supply might be to blame. For the most part, the public reaction was mystification. Finally Irénée Sr. was consulted. He had a ready answer. The fact that du Ponts made up a larger part of the area drivers than they did of the public coupled with the fact that du Ponts have a high incidence of nearsightedness caused the data for the Wilmington area to be misleading.

Among Laird's best stories are those concerning the moviemaking efforts of what he calls the Little Family between 1926 and 1932. The Laird and Carpenter and Irénée and Lammot families all lived reasonably near one another, and their children grew up together, along with an assortment of other cousins. The Little Family was made up of those who were born after 1910; those born before 1910 were considered the Big Family. The movies were the idea of the Little Family and consumed a substantial portion of the family's spare time, imagination, and energy. Laird, who has retained a library of prints of the movies, estimates there is as much as twenty-four hours' worth of film altogether, mostly divided into feature-length divertissements with such beguiling titles as *A Scramble of Eggs* or *Foreign Entanglements*. The latter had a script based on the visit of an English cousin to Granogue and his unfulfilled romance with one of Irénée Sr.'s daughters. The movies were a family production from beginning to end. Only the processing of the film was an outside job. The films all had plot, costumes, and script and were intended as spoofs of the silent films of those days. Watching future scions of the du Pont family cavort about the screen, mugging like mad for the camera, is quite a sight.

The fun the young du Ponts were having in the production of these films was infectious, and before long the parents were becoming involved. Laird is careful not to try and make too big a thing of it, but in a real sense, the moviemakers helped to close family rifts after the Big Feud of 1915. It was not, Laird says, a conscious scheme to mend family ties. In part, it was that the older members of the family realized the crisis was over and were virtually looking for an excuse to get back together. The Lairds and the Ernest du Ponts were talking with each other over the back fence. Francis G. and Felix might never be seen together in public, but occasionally the two would slip off to F.G.'s observatory and stargaze together. In this atmosphere, family members on opposite sides of the feud began working side by side with the youngsters on their movies. For one filming session, Mama Laird—Pierre's sister, remember—took a ride on cousin E. Paul du Pont's yacht, *Theano*. Paul had sided with Alfred I. Clearly, the ill will within the family was dissipating. Among the featured players in *A Scramble of Eggs* is Pierre S. du Pont III, whose early success may have gone to his head in later, less fortunate film enterprises.

In general, Chick Laird is viewed within the family as the Boy Scout, endowed with most of the attending virtues. "Chick Laird is a do-gooder," says young Coley du Pont, a distant cousin and the only man named du Pont currently working for the company. "God bless do-gooders once in a while." Coley, like many in his generation, considers Laird a personal friend.

Laird tells a number of stories about life at St. Amour with Uncle Lammot and his children, of which there was a horde. Many of the stories picture Lammot as not very happy. He was not very happy, for instance, about the pulley rig the kids set up between the third-floor towers at St. Amour with a basket in which they could ride back and forth. He was, Laird suggests, even less happy about the time his son went for a kite ride. Some of the older children had made a large kite and attached a basket to it. Then they had made Reynolds du Pont, who was perhaps as old as four at the time, test pilot, dumping him into the basket and sending the kite aloft.

Despite this rather harrowing experience, Reyn never developed a fear of flying. He was one of those du Ponts who had his own plane, although he didn't do much piloting himself. He was also another du Pont yachtsman. Besides sailing himself, Reyn figured he had spent about half a million up through 1974 backing four challengers in America's Cup races, including *Mariner* in 1974. Photography is another interest of Reyn's and, like his cousin Irénée, he enjoys do-it-yourself projects. For years Reyn was about as public a du Pont as you could find as he spent sixteen years in the Delaware senate espousing the Republican cause and keeping his sense of humor honed. The story is still told around Legislative Hall about the time Reyn began debating the merits of various brooms and other custodial equipment that apparently had to do with some appropriations bill. He knew what he was talking about, he told the senate gathering, because before they fired him, that was part of his job at the Du Pont Company. No doubt Reyn exaggerated his demise at Du Pont, but at any rate, he did leave the company in 1958—he'd started in 1941—to devote full time to politics and government. Besides being a state senator, Reyn was also chairman of the state Republican Committee's finance committee and one of a triumvirate who pretty much controlled Republican politics in the state.

Reynolds' son, Tommy, started following in his father's footsteps, winning election to the state house of representatives in 1972 and gaining the chairmanship of the house natural resources committee. Two pieces of legislation to which he attached his name called for easing the penalties for private marijuana use and lowering the drinking age to eighteen. He was defeated in a bid for re-election and has since moved to Florida to join his father-in-law in the automobile business.

Lammot Jr., Reynolds' older brother, was yet another du Pont better known for his extracurricular activities than for his vocation. He was an assistant vice-president of the Wilmington Trust Company, hardly a distinguished position, but he was also chairman of the Delaware Red Cross from 1936 until his death in 1964—he was fifty-four—except for three years during World War II. Lammot Jr. also owned the early version of the Wilmington Clippers, an American League football team started in 1937 and finally disbanded in 1950. In 1942 Lammot was named the first winner of the Wilmington Jaycees' "Young Man of the Year" award. He was an avid deep-sea fisherman, a pastime well suited to his shy, rather withdrawn personality.

It is a measure of the family wealth that when Lammot Jr.'s son Lammot III divorced his first wife in 1973, it cost him $1.5 million plus child support. Lammot Jr. was one of ten children. Lammot III was one of five. Inheritances had to be divided many times, but it is clear there was still plenty to go around.

By his fourth wife, Lammot du Pont, Reynolds' father, had two sons. The older, David Flett du Pont, turned twenty-one in 1955. At one-fifty in the morning of September 2, just before he was to return to his senior year at MIT, David crashed his Aston-Martin on Fishers Island. He was rushed to Lawrence Memorial Hospital in New London, Connecticut, and as his father had three years earlier, he died there. Only a week before had he drawn up an agreement for the distribution of his estate. Under it, MIT received $1 million for athletic facilities and Delaware health and education services received $3 million. David's younger brother, Willis H. du Pont, became a reluctant public figure in 1967 when he was the victim of the largest Miami robbery ever committed. The thieves entered his $900,000 home on Biscayne Bay and made off with a $1.5 million coin collection. Willis offered $200,000 to ransom the collection and eventually got most of it back. Until Harvard's 1973 loss, the robbery of Willis' coins was the largest coin robbery ever.

The second Lammot, Pierre's and Irénée's brother, had two younger sisters. Bella married Pierre's best friend, H. Rodney Sharp, and Margaretta, known as Peg, married R. R. M. Carpenter. Rod Sharp III, Bella's grandson, is among the more thoughtful of the younger du Ponts today. Now in his early forties, Rod went to work for the company—one of the few in his generation of the family to do so—because he loved to fiddle with computers and "where else was I going to find that kind of equipment to work with?" After resisting for a while, Sharp finally agreed to a transfer into the treasurer's department and began to entertain dreams of one day becoming treasurer or even vice-president. "After a while, that sort of wore off," Rod said several years ago. "Things just didn't seem to be heading in that direction." It wasn't long afterward that Rod had a talk with his father, telling him he felt the section of the company he was in made a game out of doing business and wasn't accomplishing very much. "I told him I would probably have to have another job eventually if I was going to stay with the company." So far, the flame of ambition does not appear to have been rekindled. And yet Sharp is one of the brightest and best hopes among the younger du Ponts as reflected by the fact that he was made president of the Longwood Foundation, the largest of the family foundations, at the age of thirty-eight. For a long time, Sharp was dedicated to community service. "Before we had any kids," he said, "Vicki [his wife] and I were on so many things we didn't have a life of our own. Now I just say no." He is even a bit skeptical about his service to Longwood. "You get cynical about what you can do," he says. "You think about the organization without you and the people like you," he says, "and it seems to me it would manage to get along. Longwood makes me feel kind of silly sometimes, sitting there and spending someone else's money." Sharp sees community leadership—once pretty much the province of the family—as coming in the future either from politicians or corporations encouraging their employees to take active roles.

The Carpenter family is perhaps best-known to the public through R. R. M. Carpenter, Jr., Bobby, and his son, R. R. M. Carpenter III, Ruly, who own the Philadelphia Phillies baseball team. Bobby is a gruff bear of a man with strong opinions, always conservative, and no reticence about sharing them. He has been most frustrated in his capacity as director of the Wilmington newspapers, whose relatively conservative positions are simply not conservative enough for him. He is an avid hunter and has given generously to conservation efforts. Those who know him well say no one has a bigger heart, or a softer one. He is the chief benefactor of the University of Delaware's athletic program, which enjoys something of a national reputation. For years he struggled with the Phillies, whose place in the National League seemed to have more to do with tradition than baseball ability. Several years ago he turned the presidency of the club over to his son, who has turned the Phillies around and made them contenders.

Ruly is a chip off the old block with a bit of polish added. He was an outstanding athlete at Yale, where he played end on the football team and captained the baseball team. He may have entertained early thoughts about playing baseball professionally, but he wasn't quite quick enough to be the best, and as a friend notes, "Ruly wasn't going to settle for anything less than being best." He used to kid his father a good deal about the talent on the Phillies. Once, while still in school, Ruly went so far as to suggest that he played better than some of his father's hirelings. That was too much for Bobby, who arranged a little contest at the team's spring training headquarters in Clearwater, Florida. Ruly took some of the team to back him up in the field and pitched against a Phillies aggregation. He beat them, and rumor has it that his father provided more than one of the losers with a one-way ticket to the minors.

Like his father an avid hunter, Ruly has been described by one shooting companion as "the best wing shot in the state." A quiet, reserved, family-oriented man, Ruly has a quick wit. At the family plantation in South Carolina not long ago, the shooting was a little slow one day. In fact, the birds simply were not flying. After several hours Ruly's reserve of patience became exhausted and he yelled to his companions, "Must this senseless slaughter continue?"

The Carpenter family has produced a number of enthusiastic sportsmen. Among the most notable is Bobby's brother, William K. Carpenter, who was probably the best deep-sea fisherman in the world in his day. The family has even produced a barber, Bobby's sister Irene. Her hobby for years was cutting hair, and she had a well-equipped barbershop set up in her home where the family could have its hair trimmed.

Once again the dispersion and variety within the du Pont family must be recognized. Even within a particular branch of the family, like the Lammot (Pierre's father) branch, any attempt to lump the members together in any meaningful way is frustrated by the facts. They could probably agree on the excess and inevitability of death and taxes, but then who couldn't? The point is that the contrasts in styles, goals, motivations, and manners within the family are far more startling than the similarities.

Chapter Nine

T.C. and Family

At least a part of the reason the Lammot branch of the du Pont family dominates today can be traced to T. Coleman du Pont—his erratic health during the period just before World War I and his restlessness, which was forever driving him to seek new worlds to conquer. Of the three cousins—Pierre, Alfred I., and T. Coleman—who took over the Du Pont Company in 1902, Coleman was undoubtedly the best-known during his lifetime. He was a flamboyant character, the sort of man about whom apocryphal stories have the ring of credibility. It couldn't have happened that way, the listener tells himself, and yet, knowing Coley, it just might have.

Had he in later years enjoyed the robust health of his youth, who knows what legends he might have created? In 1909 he underwent a gallstone operation and never again enjoyed full health, a circumstance that must have gnawed particularly at this man who so often expressed the belief that to succeed one needed ambition, ability, and health. He managed pretty well with two of three.

Thomas Coleman du Pont was born December 11, 1863, in Louisville, Kentucky, the son of Antoine Bidermann du Pont, who had abandoned the Brandywine with his brother Alfred (Uncle Fred) ten years earlier. Several early biographers have described Coleman as growing up without the advantages of his more wealthy cousins, but his uncle was the richest man in Louisville before he'd been there very long and his father's home was a Louisville landmark of magnificence. Coleman went to Urbana College in Ohio. He was six-foot-four, more than two hundred pounds, and could run the 100 in ten flat. He captained both the football and baseball teams and was stroke of the crew. From Urbana, Coleman went to MIT, dropping out after two years to go to work in a Kentucky coal mine owned by his father and uncle. Besides being the bosses' son/nephew, Coleman was good at his job. The workers liked him, and he liked them. Not all the workers, perhaps, fully appreciated Coleman's sense of humor when he sent them each a bag of coal for Thanksgiving that first year, 1883, to commemorate the discovery of a new mine, but Coleman never could resist a practical joke.

Among his earlier jobs at the mines was supervising the transportation of the coal from the mine to the town nearby. It was carried by wagons pulled by mule teams. The roads were terrible. Just outside the mine mouth was a large pothole, and after several teams had gotten stuck in it one muddy day, Coleman had an inspiration. He dumped the next load to come out of the mine into the hole, losing the coal but saving time on all future transport. No wagon was stuck after that, and Coleman had had his first taste of road-building. He would remember that incident some forty years later during the dedication ceremonies for the nation's first divided highway, a road conceived, planned, and paid for by Coleman. It ran the length of the state of Delaware, nearly one hundred miles, took twelve years to build despite a forced scaling down of Coleman's original vision, and cost him more than $4 million, not to mention untold aggravation.

Coleman learned a lot about employee relations in those early days. Strikes hit the mines twice in his first five years there. His experience here may have helped to form, as a son-in-law once wrote, Coleman's philosophy of using incentives to stimulate good work, rather than penalties to punish bad work. The deprivation in the coal-mining regions was such that when Coleman acquired a bathtub not long after marrying his cousin Alice in 1889, people would come from miles away just to gape at it.

Coleman's first venture in politics was the Central City, Kentucky, mayor's race of 1893. He lost and he didn't like it.

Furthermore, he'd done a little informal surveying of the coal-mining field, leading to the discovery that the best-paid man in the business was getting but $4,000 a year in salary. The belief that a man ought to be able to retire early enough in life to enjoy retirement was among the first Coleman developed. When he was sixteen, he decided to make a million by the time he was thirty and retire to raise elk and buffalo, and here he was, thirty already, and still in a business whose top salary was $4,000. It was time to move on.

In 1895 Coleman moved to Johnstown, Pennsylvania, as general manager of a steel business that would later become part of U. S. Steel. He thrived. Before long, he became interested in the street railway or trolley car industry, which must have been among the most sloppily managed industries around in those days. Coleman would find a faltering company and offer to revitalize it in return for a paper consideration. He'd have some new stock printed up, take anywhere from 30 to 60 per cent for himself, and then run the company so efficiently that everyone made money. By the turn of the century, he had made nearly the requisite million. He bought up some farmland in Maryland and Delaware and went into scientific farming on a rather grand scale. It was at this time that Coleman laid one of his rare financial eggs, investing in a Wilmington button factory that was starting up. It never produced a single button. His retirement didn't suit Coleman's restless nature. He told an interviewer in 1918:

"This idea that so many people have that they will have a glorious time after they can retire, and that until then they must simply wrestle along somehow, in a rather joyless fashion, is wrong, as wrong as it can be. If you haven't sense enough, or philosophy enough, to order your life and work so as to get genuine satisfaction and fun out of them as you go along, you certainly will not get any bumper measure of enjoyment when the day comes—if it does come—when you can step out of everything. . . . The retirement idol that so many people set before them is a delusion, a myth. If your work doesn't yield you satisfaction, money never will."

While Coleman's decision to join Alfred I. in 1902 in the purchase of the family company may have been carefully considered, there is little question that Coleman was ripe for plucking, ready to plunge into a new venture, especially if he were given free rein. It wasn't the prospect of piling up a new fortune that appealed to him so much; it was the challenge presented to his business abilities. To breathe new life into an organization, and to do it with someone else's money, was the sort of opportunity Coleman couldn't forgo. In thirteen years —until he officially stepped down from the presidency at the Du Pont Company—Coleman and his cousins built the company business from $10 million to more than $200 million in annual sales. When Coleman took over in 1902, seven clerks populated the main office. By the time he retired, a new office building housed more than three thousand employees.

By 1908 Coleman's interest in the Du Pont Company was waning. The reorganization was more or less complete, although what Pierre called "his [Coleman's] most important contribution" to the company, the concept of putting younger men on the executive committee and having the finance committee report to the board of directors instead of that executive committee, would not be implemented for several years. The government's antitrust suit, instituted the year before, was probably annoying Coleman, even if he did not take it particularly seriously at that point, and his health was beginning to fail him. But the main reason his interest in the company was flagging is that the creation had been achieved. The work still to be done was operational. Coleman fancied himself a creator, not an operator. "I lose interest when it's finished," Coleman always said of his business dealings. It was in 1908 that he first offered to build his highway, envisioning a 200-foot right of way with tracks for trolleys, lanes for cars, heavy motor vehicles, and horses, as well as sidewalks. His idea was to lease the unused outer edges of the right of way to pay for the road's maintenance. The road was not Coleman's first thought for a philanthropic gesture to the state. He had first considered a normal training school for boys, a large hospital, or "erecting a fountain."

Wilmington and Delaware were proving to be ponds too small for a fish of Coleman's size. He was already brigadier general by appointment of the governor and the recognized head of the state's Republican Party. His political activity was not, however, limited to Delaware. From 1904 to 1924 he was a member of the Republican National Committee, becoming head of its speakers' bureau in 1908. The heady excitement and bustle of New York City was starting to lure him ineluctably northward. In 1910 he entered a deal with Charles P. Taft, President William Howard Taft's brother, to build the McAlpin Hotel in New York.

Coleman was a large, expansive, jaunty figure with a personality to match. His charm was captivating; his sense of humor engulfed those around him. In his presence, life had a buzzing quality. New York and Coleman were made for each other. Soon there were plans to build the largest office building in the world, the Equitable Building at 120 Broadway. The contractor tried to talk him out of it, arguing the $30 million cost was too big a gamble, but by now Coleman was rolling. In association with hotelier Lucius Boomer, he acquired control of the Claridge, Martinique, Waldorf-Astoria, and McAlpin hotels in New York, the Windsor in Montreal, the Willard in Washington, and the Bellevue-Stratford in Philadelphia and became involved with the Savarin and Louis Sherry restaurant chains. He bought control of the Equitable Life Assurance Society and its $600 million in assets, only to turn around and mutualize the company at a loss of $2 million. The move was not entirely altruistic, as Coleman was able to refinance the Equitable Building's mortgage while in control of the company. And it virtually all happened within the space of a decade, despite Coleman's serious illness of

1914–15 and the family feud that ensued when he sold his Du Pont stock to Pierre.

Unlike his cousin Pierre, Coleman was sensuously insatiable; he played just as hard as he worked. In New York, the champagne flowed and the parties sparkled well into the wee hours of the morning. As early as 1910, the rumors of the lusty life Coleman led in New York began seeping back to Wilmington. A story—appalling or amusing, depending on the audience—was told of how Coleman, inspecting his hotel suite in the company of an assistant manager, found a pair of negligees hanging in the closet, apparently abandoned by the suite's previous occupant. Removing them from their hangers, Coleman turned to a distressed assistant manager and ordered, "Here. Take these out and have them filled."

Coleman loved jokes and would interrupt even a serious business meeting at the slightest indication anyone present might be interested in seeing his latest card trick. He would serve flannel cakes with pieces of real flannel in them. When a guest of his on a shooting expedition to his Maryland farm complained of the cold during a session in the shooting box privy, Coleman had the seat fur-lined. His relatives did not escape Coleman's acerbic wit. Alfred I. used to tell the story about Coleman's coming into Alfred's office one morning and announcing that the company was going to have to give cousin Felix a raise. Unsure of the need for that particular expenditure, Alfred asked why, and Coleman told him, "Felix made a bright remark this morning." Alfred's own tag line to the story is that the remark turned out not to have been original, making the raise unnecessary after all. Another time, Coleman was sitting in his Wilmington office when he received a telegram from Lammot, Pierre's younger brother, in New York, long-distance telephoning still being a somewhat chancy affair. Lammot had managed to forget the name of his four o'clock appointment and asked Coleman to please advise him. Coleman wired back: NAME YOUR 4 O'CLOCK APPOINTMENT J. P. MORGAN STOP YOUR NAME LAMMOT DU PONT.

Even his wife did not escape. Once, with her husband on a trip in Wyoming, the railroad freight office called to inform her a present had arrived from Mr. du Pont and would she please come down and pick it up? This very proper, petite lady called up the car and went down to the freight office, where she found three live buffalo awaiting her. Sadly, her reaction to this confrontation has not been preserved.

Not all of Coley's tricks amused his wife, Elsie, but his children were invariably entertained, and Elsie tolerated his shenanigans. At his Wilmington home, Coleman mastered the art of carving a roast beef to such a degree that he could cut off a slice and in one motion flip the piece of beef onto the dinner plate of those sitting near him. The juices flew some, perhaps, but it was quite a trick. At one such dinner, the du Ponts were entertaining a most proper Boston matron whose view of Coley's antics was dim and vocally expressed. Nonetheless, Coleman persisted, and soon enough it became her turn to be served. Splat! A piece of prime beef landed squarely on the woman's plate. She turned to Elsie and said something about how she thought she had seen stubbornness in her time, that Boston men were the worst, but, well, she didn't know now. Elsie smiled at her. "In this family, we call it determination," she said.

Coleman's ego was of a size appropriate to the rest of the man. Although he was far too acute to set any serious store by it, he undoubtedly got a kick out of the abortive presidential boomlet on his behalf in 1916, which began when a small story "leaked" out of Washington that his friends were quietly touting him for the Republican nomination. Reporters found Coleman the next day in his new Equitable Building offices, where he donned his "Who me?" mask and said he was not seeking the office but had received "thousands of letters from small-business men and farmers asking that I permit my name to be used." With a top political adviser who had served both Taft and Teddy Roosevelt at its helm, the Business Men's Presidential League opened soon thereafter, headquartered in the Waldorf. Coleman was the League's first choice as a presidential candidate.

Back in Delaware, the political sages were wondering what the hell was going on. Surely Coleman wasn't running for President, and if he wasn't, what was he running for? The possibility that Coleman was simply having a good time didn't occur to these skeptical minds, ever convinced that devious are the ways of the politician. Adding the two of the Presidential League and the two represented by Coleman's suddenly renewed interest in his road project, the politicos came up with four—he was after one of Delaware's U. S. Senate seats, the one held by cousin Colonel Henry. The Colonel was, after all, seventy-eight. Even if he ran again and won, chances were he wouldn't be able to serve out his term. The Colonel ran again, and thanks to Alfred I., in the middle of the family feud at the time and determined to battle "Du Pont interests" more or less wherever they cropped up, the Colonel lost. Coleman would have to wait, if a Senate seat was what he wanted. The White House, of course, was even further away.

Coleman's road, meanwhile, was progressing slowly. In 1913 he had agreed to a hundred-foot right of way, half his original plan, and to pay five times the assessed value of the land five years after completion of the road, thereby removing any profit potential for himself. And still Delaware balked. Some said the road was just an attempt by the du Ponts to bring the lower half of the state more closely under their influence. But mostly the trouble was more basic. Landowners along the proposed route saw opportunity. Here was a rich man who wanted their land and could pay for it. Pay for it he would, they determined. In 1917 Coleman changed tactics, turning the less than a third of the highway that had been finished over to the state highway department and letting the department finish the remainder of the road, for which he agreed to pay up to $44,000 a mile for the sixty-nine miles still to be completed. The highway department had the right of condemnation, which Coleman, as a private citizen, did not.

The road was finally dedicated in 1923. The section from Wilmington to Dover was the nation's first divided highway and was widely hailed as the best road in the country. The state estimated it would take $100 a year a mile to maintain the road. The standard for ordinary macadam roads in those days was $900. Driving that road must have been an ego trip for Coleman. It was a pleasure, too, for anyone else. Coleman was something of a visionary when it came to roads. He was one of the first to recognize the needs of what would become today's auto-enslaved society and as a member of the National Highway Association in the late twenties helped design a proposed fifty-thousand-mile federal highway system that bears a remarkable resemblance to today's network of interstate highways. This similarity is at least in part due to his son's work in carrying through the father's vision. Francis Victor (Frank) du Pont was commissioner of the U. S. Bureau of Roads in the early fifties and has been called, with perhaps more hyperbole than precision, the father of the Interstate Highway System.

With as much justification, Coleman might have been called the father of the modern Massachusetts Institute of Technology. The generally accepted version of Coleman's role in the moving of MIT to its Cambridge campus has him offering to give $500,000 toward purchase of a new campus in 1909 after MIT had been turned down by Andrew Carnegie. Coleman attached two conditions to his proposed gift. One was that the site be enlarged from thirty-five to at least forty-five acres. "Almost invariably when a man comes to me to approve plans for a new factory," he said, "I tell him to double the size of everything, and almost invariably I wish afterward that I had used a larger factor of safety. Technology will occupy a great position in the future and must have room to grow." The other condition was that $1.5 million be raised from other sources.

At the time, MIT was considering a site in Boston. When Cambridge was finally chosen, Coleman went along, goes the accepted version of the MIT story. It was then that George Eastman, founder of Eastman Kodak, agreed to put up vast sums of money for construction.

A livelier version of this story still persists, however, both within the du Pont family and without. Coleman's obituary in *The Technology Review*, the MIT magazine, carries these words: "du Pont was responsible for locating the Institute in Cambridge. In face of the opposition of the Selecting Committee to its location on the Charles [River], he purchased the land personally. When the committee eventually voted to buy the site originally rejected, he presented the deed without their knowing who the donor was. The value of the land meanwhile had increased by $300,000."

This version is more or less the one given by William Winder (Chick) Laird, a du Pont family member with a long-lived interest in family history. He adds that Coleman told the committee, "Here. If you don't want the land, I can always resell it."

Among Coleman's less-well-known activities in the years before 1921 was his chairmanship of the Inter-Racial Council. In 1917 Congress had passed a law sharply limiting immigration, a policy to which Coleman was strongly opposed. Coleman started speaking out and by 1920 was in full swing trying to convince his fellow industrialists that the cheap, unskilled labor represented by immigrants was vital to the American economy. It is unlikely that Coleman was moved by the sentimental knowledge that his great-grandfather was an immigrant; Coleman wasn't the sort of man who would think of himself in those terms. At any rate, his peers didn't agree with the basic premise. Unemployment was climbing, and immigration wouldn't help. Furthermore, increased production was coming to rely not on more workers but greater mechanization. There was a vague fear in the country that poor immigrants would be accompanied by radical, socialist notions,

and when Coleman tried to counter that argument by pointing out that foreign-language newspapers in America pur-
veyed fewer far-leftist doctrines than their English-language
counterparts, someone was unkind enough to note that
maybe the American Association of Foreign Language Newspapers was responsible. Muckraker Upton Sinclair, writing in
1920, claimed that association, headed by Coleman, controlled the advertising in 90 per cent of the foreign-language
papers in the country and thereby their editorial content. In
early 1921 Coleman threw in the towel, resigning from the
Inter-Racial Council.

A few months later he walked through the back door into
the U. S. Senate, the beneficiary of a political deal that drew
wide criticism. In 1920 a man of modest credentials, William
Denny, had been elected governor on the Republican ticket.
From the first, rumors in political circles made Denny Coleman's puppet. One of Denny's first major appointments
when he took office in January of 1921 was that of state chancellor, a vital judicial post. When Coleman went to Washington in the spring and visited with U. S. Senator Josiah Wolcott, the rumor began to spread that Denny would appoint
Wolcott chancellor and name Coleman to the Senate seat
Wolcott would have to resign. It was too blatant a deal to
enjoy wide credibility. But that is just what happened.

During Wolcott's confirmation hearings in the state General Assembly, the fur flew. Even Colonel Henry, long a close
political ally of Coleman's, was filled with righteous indigna-
tion. At least Wilmington's *Evening Journal* newspaper, then
owned by the Colonel, voiced its strident disapproval. Coleman had discreetly slipped out of town and was vacationing
in Colorado. The state senate confirmed Wolcott's appointment by three votes, and on July 7 Denny wired Coleman of
his appointment to the Senate. Coleman was sworn in on
July 26 and for the next sixteen months maintained a low
profile, a stance he must have felt uncomfortable with. But
he wanted to legitimize his Senate office by winning the seat

in election, and he could not afford to annoy any more voters. Because he was an appointed senator, Coleman was required to run in the next general election, in November of 1922, for two Senate vacancies. A short-term election would be held to fill Wolcott's unexpired term, running until the following March, and a regular election would determine who sat in the seat for the full term that ensued.

Coleman ran for both against Thomas F. Bayard, Jr., whose family had long been distinguished in Delaware politics. Bayard was also a du Pont in-law. The vote in both elections was very close, only 60 votes separating the two men in the short and 325 in the long election. Although Alfred I. was avowedly retired from the political arena, the close contest proved irresistible. His work against Coleman undoubtedly spelled the difference as Coleman lost both contests. Alfred opined that the "cancer" of du Pont control in Delaware "has been removed for all time." What's more, he delivered himself of this opinion deadpan. Two years later Coleman was back in the U. S. Senate, riding the landslide victory of Calvin Coolidge back to Washington. Alfred stayed out of that one, causing Pierre's brother Irénée to write Alfred that Coleman in effect owed Alfred the election and perhaps this would prove a step toward mending old family rifts. Coleman, too, wrote Alfred, saying if he could ever be of any assistance to him while in Washington, all Alfred had to do was say the word.

As the Golden Era of the 1920s moved irrevocably toward the stock market crash of 1929, Coleman's string began to run out. His last years could not have been comfortable ones. His name was linked to the Teapot Dome scandal of the Harding administration and the following year he was sued by some Floridians who felt Coleman and his partners had done them dirt in a real estate venture. Nothing came of either incident, but Coleman, suffering from cancer of the throat, was gradually being worn down. In 1928 he resigned from the Senate. An operation in 1927 left him without a voice, although he could manage some speech through a tube in his throat. This giant of a man, who used to distribute $20 gold pieces from the back of his Pierce-Arrow at Christmastime in New York, who never lost his flair for the extravagant gesture, was literally wasting away. This was nothing like the times he'd get so wrought up his stomach couldn't take it and only Elsie, his ever generous wife, could soothe him, grabbing the bag she always kept packed for such occasions and rushing to him wherever he was. Those attacks were fleeting; recovery was a question of when, not if. Now, along with the era on which he left such a permanent mark, Coleman was dying. His daughter Renée and son-in-law John Donaldson went to Maryland to see him in September 1930. Renée was an accomplished lip reader, and Coleman, who hated the mechnical device that allowed him a semblance of deformed speech, had been mouthing his words to her.

"I wish there was something I could do for you," a distracted Renée said to him.

Reaching for pencil and pad by his bed, Coleman wrote: "You can. Get a gun and shoot me." Two months later, a month from his sixty-seventh birthday, he died.

Unfortunately, the great bulk of Coleman's personal papers was not preserved. The man was undoubtedly far more complex than the picture of him that emerges from surviving documents, facts, and legends, which rarely penetrate the surface of his life. He once said, "A man may be measured by the way in which he bears success. Most of us manage to bear adversity, whereas a bumper success often ruins us." How, one wonders, would Coleman have measured himself?

Coleman was one of seven children. Every bit as colorful as Coleman was his younger sister, Zara, who became known as Aunt Zadie within the family, some of whose members may well have pronounced her name "Zany." She became nationally known for her active support of what in those days were radical causes—civil rights, woman's suffrage, the side of labor in labor disputes. Coleman called her Miss Kick because he said she was always complaining about something. "I'd never vote for you," she used to reply. Their affection for each other easily spanned their different views of life.

Throughout the thirties and early forties, Aunt Zadie could be found regularly manning the picket lines in the Boston area. Someone once admired a hat she was wearing and she thanked the person, adding, "I had to find one that was just right for church and for picketing." A niece, nationally known architect Vicky Homsey, recently recalled visiting Zara at her home in Cambridge some years ago. "She was in her late sixties or maybe early seventies," Mrs. Homsey said. "She told me she had to get up at five the next morning to join a picket line for mistreated women workers at a shoe factory and I said something about that being awfully early and did she really have to go. She said yes, 'when I'm there, the police are nice to me, but when I'm not there, the police can get a little rough on the girls.'"

Zara did little to endear herself to her family when she told Bethlehem Steel executives their policies were making labor lose faith in democracy and therefore the workers' willingness to co-operate with management, nor did she score many points when she criticized munitions makers. But she was a lovable character who had helped to raise a number of du Pont children at various times. Her welcome in family circles was warm and secure. Mrs. Homsey remembered a visitor at Longwood, the home of Pierre, who figured Zara had to be fair game for criticism in this bastion of capitalism and began dropping disparaging remarks all over the place only to be cut short by Pierre's icy, "Cousin Zara is one of the most remarkable women in the family."

Of course, Pierre might well have made a similar remark feeling Zara ought to be put away. Toward outsiders, the family always has turned a solid front. Even Alfred I. would defend Pierre in such instances. Mrs. Homsey told of how a fellow, thinking he was perhaps the world's most subtle sycophant, called Pierre a snob who cut people dead without a word. Alfred, for whose benefit this description of Pierre had been offered, asked if Pierre had had his glasses on. The fellow said yes, and Alfred told him, "Well then, you're a damn liar."

Aunt Zadie was a favorite with the Homseys. On one of her visits to their Wilmington home, she disappeared for a while, and Mrs. Homsey, mildly concerned, went to look for her. She found Zara on a hill behind the house playing football with the Homsey boys. She was in her seventies at the time. "Someone has to throw a ball to them," Zadie said a little defiantly. "You never will."

"She was right," Mrs. Homsey said. "Neither Sam [her husband] nor I have ever thrown a ball in fun or anger."

An incurable optimist and unswerving believer in human equality, Zara once predicted she would live to see "a Negro, a Catholic, a Jew, and a woman elected President of the United States." She didn't make it, dying in 1946 at the age of seventy-seven.

Success shied away from Coleman's two brothers almost as dramatically as it clung to him. One—Mrs. Homsey's father, Antoine Bidermann du Pont, Jr.—was plagued by absent-mindedness. He would put two socks on one foot and then tell Coleman he couldn't find one. He would get so wrapped up in the dinner conversation that Coleman was sure he had no idea what he was eating. One night Coleman decided to test the theory. The servants were instructed to pass only the rice to Mr. du Pont while the rest of the family ate a full meal. Mrs. Homsey's father didn't say a word. After dinner, some-one asked him how he'd liked the meal, and he said it was fine, but, funny thing, all he could remember eating was rice. One evening Coleman's brother broke new ground in the ab-sent-minded field. Having finished dinner, the family was passing the coffee around the table. The pot reached Ermie, as he was called, and he began to pour. When the cup was nearly full, he half-turned to a non-existent butler and said, "That's enough, thank you." He continued to pour, the coffee began to spill, and he turned again, more insistent. "I said that's enough." Mrs. Homsey swears the story is true.

Coleman's other brother was the youngest child in the family, Evan Morgan du Pont, about whom it was frequently said that he could lose money almost as fast as Coleman made it. In November of 1904 Pierre and T. Coleman carried on a short correspondence about who should endorse whose notes, agreeing that each would take care of his own side of the family. Pierre, however, had already loaned Evan Morgan a few thousand dollars. Coleman's brother was living in Johnstown, Pennsylvania, where he was involved in such anonymous enterprises as the Pure Water Engineering and Construction Company, the Westmoreland and Cambria Ice companies and the Lawrence Ice and Storage Company, all of whose balance sheets betrayed a teetering on the edge of insolvency. For more than thirty years, Pierre and Evan Morgan corresponded about the money owed the former by the latter. A tone of resignation gradually invaded Pierre's letters; the promise held by the future was ever present in the replies of Evan Morgan. In June of 1937 Pierre gave up, writing off the entire remaining balance. Evan Morgan, a lifelong baseball enthusiast, wrote back thanking him and threatening to go John D. Rockefeller one better by playing baseball instead of golf in his nineties. He promised to pay Pierre someday anyway, but wisely, Pierre chose not to hold his breath.

Coleman's son, Francis Victor (Frank), tried hard to fill his father's shoes, but always looked a little like a child clomping proudly around in its parent's footwear. For all that, Frank du Pont's career was a distinguished one. His most enduring monument, unless one is generous enough to credit him with the Interstate Highway System, is the Delaware Memorial Bridge, which spans the Delaware River just north and east of Wilmington, providing a vital link in the main north-south highway on the East Coast. As chief of Delaware's highway department, Frank began in 1941 to pursue the bridge project and was largely responsible for its planning, engineering, financing, and initial construction phases, which began in 1945 when the state General Assembly approved a $40 million bond issue for the bridge. His role as the state's leading Republican at the time proved a useful asset as he nursed the project through its political stages.

Like so many other du Ponts, Frank early developed an interest in aviation. He was among Delaware's first pilots, training flyers during World War I. In 1919 he was awarded a U.S. patent for a toy machine gun he invented. It proved an invention more fraught with symbol than profit. Frank was an active supporter of the Boy Scouts. But roads and politics were his first loves.

By 1953, when he became commissioner of the U. S. Bureau of Roads, which oversaw the spending of more than $4 billion annually in federal funds, Frank had been head of the state highway department for twenty-three years, longer, he wrote his friend Thomas E. Dewey, than anyone in the United States. In office for just six months, Frank presented his recommendations for the nation's highway program to his boss, the Secretary of Commerce, in the fall of 1953. The Interstate Highway System was first authorized by Congress in 1944, but it wasn't until 1956 that the program really got under way. By this time, Frank was no longer with the Bureau of Roads, of which he was commissioner for two years, nor was he still a special consultant to the commerce secretary, a post he held until January 1, 1956. But his recommendations of 1953 were an important part of the 1956 legislation, which increased the mileage in the proposed system from 40,000 to 41,000 and called for the spending of $24.8 billion to complete the system over the following thirteen years. Eventually the system was expanded to 42,500 miles and scheduled for completion in 1980. It is a measure of the vastness of this highway program that a 1958 cost estimate for the interstate system took 1.2 million man-hours to prepare. By this time, Frank was a member of the Highway Research

Board's executive committee. He was also active in the American Road Builders Association.

Frank's correspondence reveals he was on a first-name basis with a number of the major political and governmental figures of his day. Besides Dewey, he knew Sinclair Weeks, John Foster Dulles, Herbert Brownell, and the perennial candidate, Harold Stassen. He was on both sides of the contribution fence, raising money for the Republicans and being asked for it. Richard Nixon asked for help in his 1950 Senate campaign. (He didn't get it, but won anyway.) About the same time, Frank wrote Pierre and his brothers, Lammot and Irénée, trying to provoke large contributions to the Republicans by pointing out the dangers of a continuation of the Truman administration and the inadequacy of the Republican opposition to that point. In September of 1950 Frank received a telegram signed by a number of prominent Delawareans including Lammot and Frank's most valuable ally in the battle for the Delaware Memorial Bridge, the lawyer R. H. Richards, described by many as the most powerful man in the state in his day. The telegram was part of an effort to raise $350,000 for America's Future "to check and reverse the destruction of the enterprise system by encroaching socialism and the consequent ruinous taxation." Frank responded that he was contributing to the Republicans for this same reason and suggested they do the same. In January of 1949 Lammot's son, Pierre S. III, wrote Frank asking for help for the Committee of Americans, an organization to combat leftist propaganda, particularly on the labor front. The cheapest membership was $500. Frank wrote back, "When you want a contribution for some cause, just let me know whether you want it in the form of a check payable to your good self, or cash, and don't even bother to tell me what it is for." The politics of the du Pont family has always been marked by staunch conservatism and, frequently, an astonishing naïveté, which reached its most embarrassing level, perhaps, in the thirties with the family's support of the American Liberty

League, as radically right wing as any group it criticized was radically left wing.

Frank's son, Eleuthère Irénée (Brud), recalls one time when his father gained an insight of sorts into the mind of the grass-roots populace. An old retainer of the family, Uncle Henry, showed up late for work at the du Ponts' Maryland farm one Sunday morning, the residue of the night before making a strong olfactory impression on Frank, who took to berating the man sternly. "The trouble with you, Mr. du Pont," Uncle Henry said quietly when Frank paused for breath during his tirade, "is you've never been a nigger on Saturday night." Frank could hardly argue the point.

Brud remembers stories of his father tap-dancing his way to a certain limited notoriety in the annual Wilmington Junior League Follies, but says Frank was not the party man Coleman was. At Republican National Conventions, for example, Frank used to drive Wilmington lawyer Jack Kiloran crazy by leaving him in charge of the Delaware hospitality suite, which never closed until well into the wee hours of the morning, and then, having himself had a good night's sleep, expecting Kiloran to rally for breakfast at 7 A.M.

Frank's sister Renée Donaldson traveled with a minimum of impedimenta when she visited Wilmington, Brud said, counting on her sisters to loan her such vital, major items as furs and the like, while her brother attended to her transport needs with a car and driver. Renée's older sisters—Ellen Wheelwright and Alice Buck, wife of the Delaware governor—did not always see eye to eye, and there is the story of how Mrs. Wheelwright once defended Mrs. Buck when someone accused her of having limited taste. Not true, Mrs. Wheelwright countered. Mrs. Buck has a lot of taste—and it's all bad.

Perhaps the worst sin Frank ever committed was against posterity. It was he who destroyed most of his father's papers. At the beginning of 1950 he wrote Irénée du Pont that he had destroyed them after going through them. "Literally . . .

St. Amour, the multi-turreted home in foreground that Lammot du Pont's widow built after his death and which has since been torn down, dominated the family compound in Wilmington where several du Pont families still live. The white house to the right was Irénée's before he built Granogue and later belonged to Walter Carpenter, Jr., the Du Pont Company's first president from without the family. At top right is the home of Lammot du Pont Copeland's parents, since torn down to provide a homesite for Copeland's son, Lammot Jr. (Courtesy of Eleutherian Mills Historical Library)

An aerial view of William du Pont, Jr.'s home, Bellevue, reflects his two main interests—tennis and horses (note the garden shrubbery shaped to resemble various pieces of riding equipment). (Courtesy of Eleutherian Mills Historical Library)

Granogue, the last of the great du Pont estates remaining as a residence, is the home of Irénée du Pont, Jr., son of the builder. (Courtesy of Eleutherian Mills Historical Library)

Some years after Alfred I. du Pont built Nemours with its nine-foot wall—erected, legend has it, to keep out relatives—he employed his son, an architect, to design and build the elaborate formal gardens seen here. (Courtesy of Eleutherian Mills Historical Library)

She certainly doesn't look it, but among Wilmington du Ponts, Emily—the widow of Henry B. du Pont, Jr., and a du Pont by birth as well—is generally considered the matriarch of the family. (Donaghey G. Brown, Wilmington [Delaware] *News-Journal*)

In retirement, the great Kelso has become his owner's favorite
mount. Mrs. Richard C. (Allaire) du Pont and Kelso here enjoy a
Maryland morning. (Photo Communications)

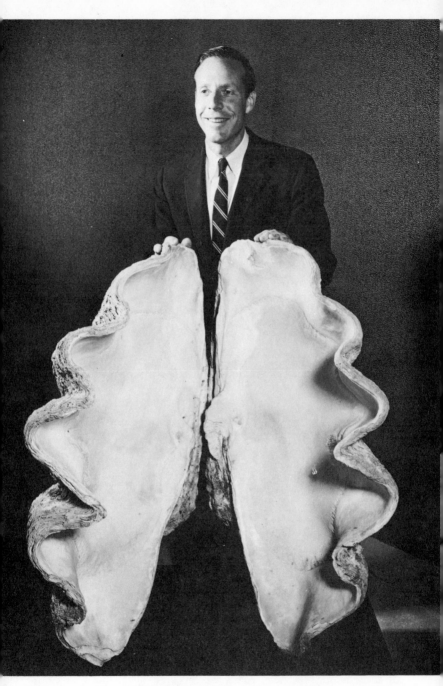

John E. du Pont and friend. John's lifelong interest in natural
history inspired him to build Delaware's Natural History Museum.

Alexis I. du Pont, son of E. Paul, is one of many du Ponts with an active interest in aviation. (Leo S. Matkins Wilmington [Delaware] *News-Journal*)

Irénée du Pont, Jr., is today the only member of the family who is a senior officer in the company his great-great-grandfather founded. (E.I. du Pont de Nemours and Company, Incorporated)

(*Above*) Delaware governor Pete du P[...] once referred to the average Delaw[...] constituent as "Joe Six-Pack," a pu[...] relations gaffe of which he has trie[...] make light and his opponents have t[...] to make much. (Leo S. Matkins, [...] mington [Delaware] *News-Journal*)

(*Left*) It is not easy if your name is Pi[...] S. du Pont IV to project a man-of-[...] people image, but Pete doesn't let [...] stop him from trying occasionally. ([...] Ballenberg, Wilmington [Delaw[...] *News-Journal*)

tons . . ." He gave no reason in that letter for the destruction.

By 1961 Frank's health was starting to deteriorate and he retired from virtually all his activities to his place in Maryland, where the following year he died. He was never quite the dynamic, captivating personality his father was, and at least one close relative feels his biggest personal problem was that he never stopped trying to be like his father, succeeding only in pale imitation. His third wife, Ricky, made a few headlines of her own after Frank's death while hobnobbing with celebrities in Hollywood. For a while in 1964 she was dating Ernest Borgnine, who in 1973 claimed she owed him $25,000 on a note he signed for her. In 1963 she was seen with Bo Belinsky, the colorful baseball pitcher. She was forty-six. He was a good deal younger. "I wish Mrs. du Pont would buy me a ball club rather than a night club," Bo was once quoted as yearning. "I'd like to be a playing general manager."

During an earlier trip to Tinseltown, Ricky had invested in a Marc Lawrence film, *Nightmare in the Sun*. In a resulting lawsuit, she said her investment had been limited by agreement to $250,000, although ultimately it had cost her $420,000. Lawrence boldly claimed she still owed $44,000 on a $50,000 promissory note. The judge went with Ricky, who later won a $466,860 judgment on a claim some of the funds she invested had been diverted to the personal use of a partner in the film corporation. The du Ponts don't seem to have much luck with movie investments.

Coleman's young brother, Evan Morgan, could apparently affect affairs financial just by osmosis. Coleman set up a trust fund for the children of his brother, and ironically, the assets therein "fizzled to almost nothing" soon after Coleman's death, as Evan's son James Q. du Pont remarked to Pierre in a letter. While many of Coleman's investments flourished, his New York real estate ventures did collapse after his death, with both the hotel business and the Equitable Building project going into receivership. When James Q. desired to put an addition on his house, it was Pierre who helped him finance it.

Like so many du Ponts, James Q. was deeply indebted to Pierre. Indian Jim, as he was known to some of his younger relatives ("Did you ever see a smiling Sioux?" one explained), worked summers as a garage mechanic and began adult life trying to earn a living from his favorite hobby, photography. His first job with the Du Pont Company was with the construction crew building a cellophane plant in Iowa. Pierre helped him find his niche at Du Pont, although the idea was James Q.'s. Eventually James developed a national reputation in public relations, traveling the country to talk about the historical du Pont family and company and their influence on current Du Pont policy. In 1948 he wrote Pierre: "If I ever hint that I'd like you to give Helen [his wife] or me the moon, please understand it will simply indicate that I'm trying to normalize my opinion of you by securing at least one sure 'turndown' for the record!"

Among the more distinguished members of Coleman's branch of the family active today is Mrs. Homsey, Coleman's niece. She has recorded a number of firsts for women in the field of architecture and is presently a member of the President's Commission on Fine Arts. "What a feeling of power!" she says. The Commission must approve the plans for everything built in the Washington and Georgetown areas. Coleman's grandson, Brud, is chairman of Delfi American Corporation, a mutual fund management company, and is active in the Delaware Art Museum and the Eleutherian Mills-Hagley Foundation. For diversion, he enjoys a pastime made manly by ex-football player Roosevelt Grier—needlepoint. His wife Minda is a past president of the Delaware Hospital junior board and was chairman of the Delaware Antiques Show. Perhaps as much as any couple, they represent a sort of vague public image of the average du Ponts, wealthy, respectable, and maybe not quite as informed or concerned as they might be about the social and economic problems confronting the society in whose remote upper reaches they live.

The difficulty of pigeonholing the du Pont family today is nowhere better reflected than among the children of James Q., who are today in their twenties and thirties. The eldest is Penny, who has parlayed a Farmington-Bradford Junior College-Yale Drama School education, more than a dozen years' hard work, and an occasional useful connection into a successful career as the host of a television interview show now syndicated to about 250 cities around the nation, although oddly enough her home town of Wilmington is not among them. She lives in New York City, as does the youngest member of the family, Jamie, who may be the only du Pont who has ever discarded the last name. Pursuing an acting career, Jamie adopted the first two names of his grandfather, Evan Morgan, for a while, but has now gone back to his given name, Jamie du Pont. He has done a number of commercials, among them one for Dynamints, and some small television roles. Between these two are Debbie and Coley. She took a not untypical course for a du Pont, marrying a distant cousin, a grandson of Pierre's brother Lammot. Coley has done a rather untypical thing for a du Pont these days—he is working for the Du Pont Company.

Coley, you may recall, is the only person named du Pont now working for the company. He's the young man whose yacht was supposed to have been caught in a storm delaying his start at the Du Pont Company's nylon tire cord plant in Richmond by a day, an unfounded rumor generated out of the magic of the du Pont name. An unassuming, slightly shy, thoughtful young man who inherited unmistakably du Pont physical characteristics if not wealth, Coley was not, as were so many of his ancestors, brought up to work for the company. He was under no pressure from his father to join the company. "He knew kids rebelled against that sort of pressure." In college, Coley was a landscape architecture major. "I was lukewarm about the field when I graduated," Coley recalled. "That's no way to feel starting out on a career." So Coley went back to school, taking some business administration courses at the University of Delaware. "After six and a half years of college, I decided it was time to do something with my life." The Du Pont Company seemed a likely place to start.

The same self-doubt that used to worry his father occasionally disturbs Coley. "My father used to wonder about being a puppet, a court jester, tolerated by the company because he was a du Pont," Coley said not long ago. "I sometimes wonder whether I'm doing worthwhile things. I fall back on the realization that the company would have very good reason to ax me if I wasn't doing a good job. I know I'm highly visible. I guess the name is an asset if you're doing a good job, a liability if you're doing a bad one."

Coley is still not committed as a lifetime Du Ponter. "I want to go as far as my ability and desire will let me. So far, these last five years, it's been great. I have no reason to leave. When I peak in ability, I hope someone will tell me; I'll know myself about desire. I've learned a lot about myself and people in general. There are a lot of preconceived notions that seem to go along with being a du Pont. After a while, it sometimes becomes difficult to distinguish between reality and unreality." Coley is not particularly wrapped up in family tradition or destiny. "I got out of college and thought I'd try it [working for the company]. That's all. I'm amazed at the dedication, the commitment of so many of the middle-management people. Great loyalty. They work all day Sunday if necessary. So far, I don't mind doing that."

Growing up, Coley's friends were determined by who was in bicycle range. He estimates cousins were perhaps 10 per cent of his stable of friends. Two stories made lasting impressions on his youth. The first his father told him when he was twelve or thirteen and concerned a female cousin on her deathbed telling James Q. that what you do in life isn't as important as how you do it and to try and be the best at whatever you do. The second is a recorded message that is part of a display at the Hagley Museum and repeats the advice given his sons by the original Pierre S. du Pont de Nemours about the duties attached to every privilege. Like most du Ponts today, Coley says he does not discuss the family or its role in the company with his cousins and doesn't much care about what is written on the family, "except when I know it's untrue." He feels no particular surge of pride or welling of shame when another member of the family makes headlines for accomplishment or misfortune. The bankruptcy of Lammot du Pont Copeland, Jr., for example, is Copeland's problem. "I can sympathize, of course, but no, I'm not personally embarrassed."

Copeland's troubles do, however, bring up once again the preconceived notions of the public. Coley says sometimes people read about Copeland and think that because Coley is of the same family, "I have the same millions." That is a more understandable mistake than some. Coley was once asked, for instance, about the Alfred I. du Pont Institute, which is surrounded by a high wall with broken glass embedded on top. An acquaintance wanted to know if the story he'd heard about how the du Ponts put all their dumb children there so that the public sees only the smart ones was true. The question was apparently asked in seriousness. Coley could not bring himself to give a serious answer. "I said yes, but there's a hole in the wall in the back."

Coley lives in an unprepossessing stucco house across the street from a sort of du Pont family compound containing the houses of Copeland, the A. Felix du Ponts, and several other cousins. On this particular evening, he had stopped off on the way home and picked up a steak sandwich. From the refrigerator, he had taken a Michelob. The American bachelor dines at home.

At one of his Du Pont Company jobs, Coley recalled finding himself off in a corner with the president of the union, a rather militant sort. "Things were better when your family ran things," the union man had said. "They cared more for the people."

"I told him that Shapiro [the current chief executive officer] was the best thinker, talker, etc. in the company now," Coley said. "And I said I was glad he was there." Shapiro has not always been unabashedly flattering when talking about the du Pont family in public, but Coley is undisturbed. "I'm not as interested in what he says about the family as I am in his business policies, which I admire. I don't know him socially at all."

Like many of his cousins, Coley's future is filled more with unformulated potential than firm plans. His ambitions are modest, informed nonetheless with family pride:

"I just hope," he says, "that when I leave a place where I've been working, people will say, 'He worked hard. He was sort of like the way we imagined a du Pont would be, like the way the guys who made the Du Pont Company great were.'"

Chapter Ten

The Rebel and His Relations

If Pierre gave the du Pont myth its substance, it might be said that Alfred Irénée gave it much of its essence. The most controversial du Pont since the original Pierre Samuel du Pont de Nemours, Alfred has been called the savior of the company and the family rebel, frequently in the same breath. It was Alfred who held the family together in 1902 with his proposal to keep the company in family hands, and it was Alfred who drove the family apart with his lawsuit against Pierre in 1915. It was Alfred who felt the tug of family tradition so strongly that he considered the powder company his birthright, and it was Alfred who in 1910 built a nine-foot wall around his three-hundred-acre estate, had broken glass embedded on its top, and remarked, according to immutable legend, "That wall's to keep out intruders, mainly of the name of du Pont." The essential Alfred was a fighter. Winning was important, but it wasn't the only thing. Maybe it was stubbornness; plenty of people thought so. In any event, compromise was not in Alfred. He tended not to recognize the color gray. Things were black or they were white. Self-respect seemed to demand of Alfred that he fight the things he saw as black. He was accused of being irrationally vindictive, but the accusations were not always made by totally rational individuals.

Alfred's pugnacious proclivities surfaced early. In the games boys play Alfred's supremacy among his contemporary cousins was challenged only when Coleman was visiting from Kentucky. Alfred gravitated toward the children of the powder workers when looking for playmates, in spirit far more akin to Huck Finn than Little Lord Fauntleroy. These early associations grew into deep mutual affection between Alfred during his rise to production supervisor and those boyhood playmates who had grown up to be powdermen. Alfred was the last of the du Ponts to work in the mills side by side with his employees, sharing their danger by day, their camaraderie by night. If some of his cousins concerned themselves with employee relations out of a sense of noblesse oblige or the conviction it was good business policy, Alfred's concern was based on friendship. It was altogether appropriate that Alfred played Santa Claus for the Christmas Eve party given the children of the workers. In at least one large family of workers, the word went out, "Send for the priest and Mr. Alfred," whenever trouble arose. Said another worker, "If Mr. Alfred knew you in Hagley, he knew you on Market Street."

Alfred's parents both died within months of each other in 1877 when he was still thirteen. In his biography of Alfred, Marquis James says the father on his deathbed told Alfred, "I think the old company may need you someday. I just have that feeling." If Alfred remembered those words in 1902, they didn't appear to have affected his attitude toward education in the years more immediately following his father's death. At Andover, Alfred was a mediocre student. A teacher there admonished him one time, noting, "You made 75, a bare pass." To which Alfred replied, "Yes, and if a bare pass was 85, I'd have made that." Alfred once wrote, "A constitutional indifference to marks and a similar desire to have a good time do not afford the best foundation for a shining academic record."

This attitude survived more or less unaltered during a sojourn at MIT. While at MIT, Alfred found a new, vicarious outlet for his now latent pugnacity. He struck up a friendship with John L. Sullivan, then at the height of his early popularity after having won the heavyweight boxing title from Paddy Ryan. John L.'s challenge that he could knock or drink any man under the table was one Alfred wisely declined to take up.

Alfred's concept of a good time was by no means limited to nights on the town with John L. and his cronies. An accomplished musician, Alfred was a regular theater- and concertgoer, traveling to New York and Philadelphia to supplement the musical fare provided by the Wilmington Opera House. After abandoning his education in 1884, Alfred gave rein to his growing fascination with electricity, becoming acquainted with Thomas Edison and visiting his laboratory several times. In the spring of 1886 Alfred's ancestral home—Swamp Hall— suddenly glowed one evening with a brightness hitherto unknown in Delaware. Alfred had wired his house for electricity. Soon his relatives were all clamoring for Alfred to have their houses done. Only old Boss Henry displayed skepticism, admitting Alfred's electricity display was impressive but saying no to its installation in the powder yards. By now, Alfred was working for the company, and soon enough, he'd have his way on the matter of electricity.

His love of music prompted Alfred to start an orchestra, in which he played cornet, clarinet, first violin, or piano as the need arose. At first made up mostly of workingmen, the band eventually was augmented by cousins. Pierre and his brother Lammot sometimes played the piano. Felix might sit in on the cornet. Ernest played slide trombone. In music, as in boxing and electricity, Alfred's interest promoted friendship with a celebrity. He became a warm acquaintance of John Philip Sousa, and each winter would take his orchestra up to Philadelphia to hear Sousa's band.

For a fellow who had lost his parents so early in life, Alfred appeared to be doing rather well for himself as the decade of the 1880s drew to a close. On January 4, 1887, he married Bessie Gardner, a cousin on his mother's side of the family whom he had met the year before when she visited Wilmington at the invitation of Alfred's younger brother Louis. Two years later Alfred's other brother, Maurice, married a vibrant Irish girl to whom Bessie and Alfred took an immediate liking. The newspapers had made much of the wedding, claiming a du Pont heir had married an Irish barmaid, stretching the facts in both cases. Alfred had written Pierre on the subject of Maurice's marriage: "What a blooming idiot Maurice was to do such a thing as that. How scandalized the old people on the Brandywine must be about it." On meeting her, Alfred quickly changed his mind. The same month Maurice was married, Bessie gave birth to their second daughter, named after her mother, but dubbed "Bep" within the family. Early the next year, 1890, Alfred became a partner in the company firm, although he was not yet twenty-six.

Then, slowly, almost imperceptibly, life began to go a little sour on Alfred. Clouds began to cast shadows over his halcyon days. Little things at first. Bessie never could bring herself to share Alfred's interest in music, and eventually his orchestra found someplace besides Alfred's house in which to hold rehearsals. Alfred began to spend an increasing amount of time on other projects, projects sure to hold no interest for his wife. The marriage was in an early stage of decay.

Alfred's family—his brothers and sisters—began to draw apart. According to his biographer James, a large part of the cause behind the split was Bessie's treatment of Alfred and his kin, which they considered rude and intolerable. One cousin, whom Alfred had taken in to live with his family, said she witnessed a number of occasions on which Alfred would leave the dinner table in order to avoid a scene with his wife. Unquestionably, Alfred was not above reproach in this matter; marital discord is never a one-sided affair.

On December 2, 1892, tragedy struck. Alfred's brother Louis, whom a local newspaper had called "the only swell in the du Pont family," had pursued an erratic educational career the previous few years, having renewed his membership in Yale's senior class for three years running without graduating. He had attended Harvard Law School for a year, given up education, and for the better part of 1892 chased the gay life about New York City. He had become a manic-depressive, following periods of high good humor and charm with fits of reticent moodiness. On December 2, in the library of the exclusive Wilmington Club, Louis, twenty-four, shot himself to death.

Within a year, Alfred's Uncle Fred was shot by the madam of Louisville's best bordello and his cousin William had divorced his wife, the first du Pont family divorce and because of that its least popular. Alfred appeared to resent the family's Victorian attitude, which seemed more concerned with the family's reputation than with sympathy for the victims of these tragedies. He was virtually alone within the family in expressing criticism of William's ostracism, both from the family and from the company.

William Randolph Hearst's little war of 1898, otherwise known as the Spanish-American War, provided Alfred with the opportunity to prove his ability as a production manager and prove it he did. The United States has never fought a war in which it was so ill-prepared and ill-equipped. The great production machine simply didn't function properly this time —except along the Brandywine, where Alfred increased production of powder from three thousand to more than twenty thousand pounds a day almost overnight. It was an extraordinary accomplishment that went more or less unnoticed outside the company.

In the winter of 1898 Alfred went to a masquerade party as an Indian. Playing his role to the hilt, he was sneaking around the outside of the house periodically giving forth with a war cry at open windows when he spied his cousin Victor and a friend costumed as Tweedledum and Tweedledee. The sight caused him to convulse with laughter as he sat in the snow. The next day he was in bed with a cold whose congestion was impairing his hearing. A doctor surmised that a broken nose he had suffered twenty years earlier might have been partially responsible for the damage to his hearing, which did not improve. Genetics may also have played a part in his loss of hearing. Whatever the root cause, this rather minor incident in Alfred's life would grow into perhaps his greatest personal loss.

For the time being, it was merely irritating. The next year, Alfred bought a car, Delaware's second. It was a steam-driven Locomobile, which he sold to a Massachusetts man not long afterward. Marquis James reports the man soon wrote Alfred a letter in which he noted the car was "loco all right, but not so mobile." In the following years, Alfred seriously considered leaving the Du Pont Company to go into the automobile business. One thing that may have kept him from making such a move was the birth of a son, Alfred Victor, on St. Patrick's Day, 1900. The son became the eldest son of the eldest son of the eldest son of the eldest son of the founder of the company, and therein lay a family legacy that ought not to be denied.

If 1902 was a year of triumph for Alfred as the deal to buy the company from the older partners was concluded, 1904 was a year of tragedy. Alfred's hearing was gradually deteriorating. For a couple of years, he was able to listen to music with the help of an early hearing aid, but in 1904 even that stopped. The satisfaction, the joy, the solace with which music had filled so much of Alfred's life were gone. "If I had my ears for three hours a day, I would spend two of them playing the violin," he once said, but for the most part, Alfred bore his loss alone, in the shadowy silence that would engulf the rest of his years. That summer, Alfred's family went to Europe. His youngest child, Victorine, was less than a year old. His wife was apparently determined to stay for a while. The two older girls were enrolled in school. Even the pretext of unity, if not harmony, had now been dropped. In November Alfred went hunting at Balls Neck, Virginia, home of a sixteen-year-old who would grow up to become Alfred's third wife, although at this point, courtship was far from Alfred's thoughts. A hunting companion accidentally shot him in the left eye. At the University of Pennsylvania Hospital, doctors said they might be able to save the eye with quiet rest. His wife and oldest daughter returned from Europe. Bessie's visit may have done more harm than good. She went back to Belgium, leaving Alfred depressed. He went home for Christmas, suffered a relapse, and the next day, the injured eye was surgically removed.

Alfred's recovery was slow, dragging on through the following summer. In September Bessie and Alfred formally separated, with Alfred setting up a trust containing $600,000 and providing Bessie and their children an annual income of $24,000, a settlement some of his relatives viewed as at best niggardly. Late the following year Alfred and Bessie were divorced. All the while, the Brandywine rumor mills were almost as busy as the powder mills, and Alfred was the grist. Speculation centered on the precise nature of his relationship with his cousin, Alicia Bradford Maddox, a handsome, spirited, acid-tongued woman who often intimidated those with whom she came in contact and seemed to delight in the fact.

Alicia's father was Judge Edward G. Bradford, whose influence among members of the du Pont family was substantial. Her mother was Eleuthera du Pont, daughter of the Alexis du Pont who died in 1857. George Maddox, Alicia's first husband, was a good-looking Du Pont employee of rather unremarkable ability. Alicia and her father didn't get along. She had always been among Alfred's favorite cousins. What happened from this point depends on who's telling the tale. The gentle version has it that when Judge Bradford took up an active stance in opposition to his daughter's marriage to Maddox, Alfred stepped in to aid his cousin, arranging the wedding and setting up the newly married couple in Louviers, the old residence of Admiral Samuel F. Du Pont. Infuriated, the judge attempted to persuade Coleman, as president of the company, to remove his daughter from Louviers, which the company owned, but was told Coleman and Pierre felt that would only make a bad situation worse. Maddox, who worked under Alfred, received several sudden promotions, the last of

which made Maddox regional superintendent of the Midwest
black powder plants and kept him on the road much of the
time. This, the gentle version has it, was a good thing because
the Maddox match was proving to have been made elsewhere
than in heaven. Alicia spent a lot of time in Europe. When
she was at home, her tongue continually withered those with
whom she came in contact, except for Alfred, who married
her after she obtained a secret divorce on the grounds of de-
sertion. The wedding, on October 15, 1907, did little to cement Alfred's relationship with his cousins.

The not-so-gentle version of this interlude has it that
Alfred began seeing Alicia rather more than perhaps a married man should as early as 1901. He introduced her to Maddox, arranged the marriage, and promoted Maddox all to further his own interests in Alicia and to give appearances a
cosmetic propriety. Maddox finally figured it all out, quit the
company, and, rumor had it, filed suit against Alfred, undoubtedly for alienation of affections. The suit was withdrawn before the filing of a bill of particulars. While Alicia
was supposed to be in Europe, she was actually holed up in
Carlisle, Pennsylvania, less than one hundred miles away.
Thanks to friendly lawyers and a sympathetic judge, she was
granted her divorce on October 8, the week before her marriage to Alfred. The publishing of the circumstances of Alicia's divorce brought forth the suggestion of impeachment
proceedings against the judge, who defended his actions with
élan enough to forestall such a move.

When Alfred got back to the office after his wedding,
Coleman told him he'd really botched his affairs nicely and
had created a situation up with which the family would not
put, as a later British statesman with Coleman's same appe-
tite for cognac might have stated the case. Coleman thought
Alfred ought to sell out to him. Mentioning something about
viewing the family in a hot, far distant region first, Alfred
declined this not ungenerous offer with characteristic vehemence.

The next few years were difficult ones for Alfred. At the office, he was gradually wedged aside. His deafness was given as the reason he no longer served on the finance committee. The production of powder, his specialty, was becoming more and more an impersonal desk job as the company continued to grow, and Alfred was a powder maker, not an administrator. Occasionally he would dream with close friends about shucking his interests in the company and perhaps investing in some facet of the technological revolution then in its early stages. At home, the family, with the exception of Francis I. and his siblings, was sniping and snubbing. Alfred was accused of abandoning his children, each town gossip supplying his or her own reason for Alfred's paternal shortcomings. While some friends said they'd never seen Alfred happier or his home livelier, others felt it was sad that many old acquaintances, cowering before Alicia's acerbic wit, simply stopped visiting after a while. Alicia miscarried, adding yet another item to the long list of Alfred's misfortunes. The intrafamily gossip finally became so vicious on the subject of Alicia and Alfred that the couple filed a pair of slander suits against two of Wilmington's most proper dowagers, one of whom was an aunt to Alicia. The family was appalled. The suits were eventually withdrawn, again before the particulars were made public.

In retrospect, Alfred might have been better off had he moved away from the Brandywine after his marriage to Alicia. His popularity within the family, especially among the younger du Ponts, was substantial, and undoubtedly the members of the family determined to vent their outrage would have expended it more quickly and quietly if the object of that outrage were not in view. Alfred was not particularly enchanted with his work any more, either. But Alfred was a fighter, and Coleman had put him in a position where to leave the Brandywine would be tantamount to quitting, to bowing before Coleman. Instead, Alfred built a fortress within the enemy camp, moving into Nemours, a magnificent chateau he had designed by an architect in New York and erected by a local contractor. Up went the nine-foot wall to discourage visitors.

In early 1911 the family company was reorganized in a move on which Alfred apparently was not consulted. Alfred was relieved of his production responsibilities and became a more or less unattached vice-president. He was, in short, kicked upstairs, although he was returned to the finance committee. In June the company lost its antitrust case, and Alfred, who had disclaimed knowledge of or participation in the alleged violations from the beginning, argued against appealing the case, an argument his cousins found more compelling than did the company lawyers. To the extent that his eloquence influenced Pierre and Coleman to settle rather than appeal—an extent that was probably but marginal—Alfred did the company a great service, especially in light of the settlement later reached.

Once again, Alicia was pregnant. In January of 1912 she gave birth to a daughter, who lived only long enough to be baptized. Alicia never fully recovered from the physical and emotional trauma of this event despite all Alfred could do to distract her. Early the following year Alfred managed to estrange himself from his family even further in what had to be perhaps his most irrational moment. In February he attempted to sneak a bill through the state General Assembly changing the name of his son from Alfred Victor to Dorsey Cazenove du Pont. Characterized as a bill expressing the wish of both parents, it was quickly passed in the state house of representatives and sent to the senate. The next day Alfred's former wife Bessie, through her attorney, said she'd never heard of any proposal to change her son's name and vehemently opposed the bill. It was recalled from the senate, and a hearing was scheduled at which Alfred testified in private, saying he was concerned his son would bring disgrace to the family but refusing to elaborate. In rebuttal, Bessie's lawyer introduced evidence that Alfred Victor, then thirteen, was doing well in school and produced a letter from the boy to his mother asking her to explain why his father wanted to change his name. Stubbornly, Alfred pressed the issue to a vote, mounting a strong lobbying effort based on political considerations in its behalf. The bill was defeated by a vote of 17-15. Alfred's behavior in this matter was viewed with even less charity among family members than was his marriage to Alicia.

The next year, 1914, Alicia, again pregnant, went to Europe, where she was nearly caught in the German juggernaut that swept through France, but managed to escape and return home in September. The following month, she gave birth to a son, Samuel. He died the next day. Life did not seem to be getting any easier for Alfred, and lurking just over the horizon was Alfred's biggest fight. There is no simple answer to why Alfred sued Pierre over Pierre's purchase of Coleman's stock early in 1915. Unquestionably, Alfred believed that Pierre could not have obtained the loan from J. P. Morgan that financed the purchase unless Pierre's position as head of the Du Pont Company was somehow taken into account, thereby, at least indirectly, obligating the company in a transaction Pierre was labeling purely personal. Just as clearly, Alfred believed Pierre and Coleman had put one over on both Alfred and the company's other stockholders. Relations between Alfred and his cousins were strained in those days, and the chance to publicly embarrass them must have been rather appealing. But the question as to why Alfred and William thought $125 was a maximum price for Du Pont stock in December of 1914 and yet made no response to Coleman's admittedly facetious offer to match any shares they'd sell to the company at that price for distribution to key executives—a plan with which both Alfred and William said they were in full accord—has never been answered satisfactorily. It seems just possible that if Coleman was for something, Alfred was against it, especially if Pierre agreed with Coleman.

Alfred and his two cousins simply weren't getting along. In April of 1915 Pierre wrote Alfred: "Dear Sir; It has been reported to me that teams are hauling earth from the old garden at 'Louviers' [the company-owned home in which Alfred had installed the Maddoxes after their marriage] and, in order to do so, are crossing the old lawn and causing damage. While this is reported as being directed by you, I am certain this is the case. I have ordered the work stopped and request that you see that none of your people trespass on the company's property in a way to do damage in the future. Very truly yours . . ." Alfred's reply, if there was one, is unrecorded, but the following July he had his secretary write the company, telling it to keep its personnel off his property. In contrast to this icy exchange are two letters from Alfred to Pierre in the spring of 1905. He writes to Pierre in Paris, "I wish I had been with you to have had the benefit of your Rising Sun [a small Brandywine community] Patois. . . . With my best love. . . ." A month later he writes, "My general health is pretty good, but I lack the old snap which was mine before the [hunting] accident; I doubt, however, that will ever come back. . . ." Obviously, the intervening years saw the relationship between the two cousins deteriorate dramatically.

With the removal of Alfred from the active affairs of the Du Pont Company that resulted from the suit, Alfred began to look for other outlets for his time and money. The first thing he did was buy the Delaware Trust Company, perhaps for no other reason than that he didn't want to leave his fortune entrusted to a bank, Wilmington Trust, controlled by the enemy, his cousins. That same year, for $1 million cash, Alfred bought the Grand Central Palace in New York City. Already he was preparing to take part in the economic rebirth of Europe when World War I should end, envisioning an export-import business on a large scale. He planned to use the Palace as an exhibition hall for goods manufactured in

Europe and South America to stimulate buying interest in the United States.

Early in 1918 Alfred joined forces with a not irreproachable group of opportunists who saw the same potentialities in foreign trade. In a gesture of patriotism, Alfred leased the Palace to the government as a hospital for returning wounded. This forced him to find new office and warehouse space for his new enterprise, which was soon scattered all over New York. By early 1919, concerned that he was losing financial control of these operations, which had grown like Topsy, Alfred first threatened to pull out, then formed the Nemours Trading Corporation to consolidate the businesses, which now included some forty departments engaged in buying and selling everything from automobiles to shoes. The demands on Alfred's capital resources were heavy, but thanks to his interest in the Du Pont Company's share of General Motors, he was able to meet them, and early reports indicated Nemours Trading would show some profits. These reports turned out to be mainly the product of some optimistic accounting.

By the summer of 1919, the period during which this optimism was rampant, Alfred's investment in Nemours Trading was in the $4 million neighborhood. Soon his accountant would discover obligations incurred by the corporation, such as a purchase of unmarketable cotton cloth, that revealed either mammoth stupidity, gross negligence, or worse on the part of the firm's managers. Foreign currency rates of exchange also played havoc with the business, and Alfred was forced to borrow to meet his company's debts. It began to look as if he might be throwing good money after bad. In November his accountant requested $300,000, a note of urgency in his voice. Alfred wrote a check, saying it would have to last. It didn't, and in January Alfred decided to liquidate. He figured he'd be lucky to get out for $5 million. He was right. By the time the trading company's affairs were finally wound up several years later, Alfred had been separated from about

$12 million despite some remarkable work by Ed Ball, of whom more later.

Adding to Alfred's problems during these months was his wife's health. For the past ten years, she had not been the lively lady Alfred married. In January of 1920 she and her cousin Francis I. du Pont traveled to Charleston, South Carolina, for the debutante party of a relative. Alfred was unable to go, having business on the West Coast. As it happened an old friend, whose family Alfred had been visiting in Virginia when he had his hunting accident, was now working at a school in San Diego. Alfred had not seen Jessie Ball, who had been sixteen back in 1904, for fourteen years, but they had kept up something of a correspondence, and Alfred wired her of his impending visit to San Diego. Alfred didn't stay long. A telegram greeted him on his arrival. Alicia had fallen severely ill on her way to Charleston and died the next day. Alfred left a message for Jessie and took the next train back east.

A year later Alfred and Jessie were married. Alfred's friends had been remarking on how well he was taking his financial and personal troubles during 1920. A good part of the reason apparently was the solace provided by the company of Jessie, who had come east in March on a six months' leave of absence from her school and with whom Alfred began spending an increasing amount of time. In the waning years of her life, Jessie would have an annual income of some $10 million, but at the time of her marriage to Alfred, such wealth was a remote prospect at best. Alfred's principal asset at the time was his 75,000 shares of Du Pont, which had not escaped the depression of 1920, falling in value from $25 million to $9 million. Soon the value would go back up, but Alfred could not be sure how much time he had to settle his trading company obligations, and the Internal Revenue Service was pressing a claim for 1915 back taxes. His was a precarious position, but it was one he would survive. In 1922 Alfred received a favorable tax ruling less than a month after he had managed to sell 20,000 of his Du Pont shares to raise the $2 million he would have needed to pay the government in case of an adverse ruling. In 1923 Ed Ball, Jessie's brother, went to work for Alfred and began paring his trading company debts down to size. A rising stock market carried Du Pont Company shares with it, and Alfred was financially well again. The trading company debacle had taken more than half his fortune.

In the mid-twenties, with Jessie acting as an important catalyst, Alfred effected at least a partial reconciliation with his children by his first wife, particularly the three youngest, Bessie, Alfred Victor, and Victorine. The extent of his estrangement was such that he was unaware his son had served as a Marine in World War I. At the Wilmington Horse Show in 1925, he recognized a group of young women as members of the du Pont family but did not recognize his daughter, Vicky, who was among them. The next summer, more or less on the spur of the moment, Alfred decided to set up trusts for each of his four children, providing them with about $12,000 a year in income. He asked as a condition of the trusts that none of them contest his will. They all agreed.

The night of April 22, 1927, was a big night in Wilmington's social life. Irénée du Pont, Pierre's brother, was throwing a big debutante party for his daughter, Eleanor, and at Nemours, Alfred had invited his two youngest, Alfred Victor and Vicky, over for a visit after dinner. He had anticipated that the meeting might be strained and Irénée's party would give his children an excuse to leave. Alfred Victor brought with him his new wife. Vicky brought her fiancé. A little after nine o'clock, the four guests arrived. As Marquis James describes the scene, Alfred went first to Vicky, taking her in his arms—for the first time since 1907, when she was but a child of four. Next he hugged his son, whose name he had attempted to change fourteen years earlier. He kissed Alfred Victor's wife and shook hands with Vicky's fiancé. To this point, not a word had been exchanged. Two hours later the four visitors left, agreeing that the session had not been nearly as arduous as expected.

It was during this time that Alfred began to develop his interest in Florida, which by 1925 was at the height of tenuous prosperity based on wild speculation in real estate. Alfred did not take long to size up the situation. He saw people trying to get something for nothing and figured they'd all go broke. Before long, many of them did. Alfred, ably aided by his brother-in-law Ed Ball, began gradually to move into the vacuum left by retreating speculators. Early in 1926 Alfred bought more than 66,000 acres in northwest Florida for about $800,000. That fall he formed Almours Securities, transferred his assets—all but the Wilmington estate of Nemours—into the new corporation, and took up residence in Florida. The transferred assets amounted to some $34 million. Alfred was greeted by headlines proclaiming his fortune as anywhere from $100 million to $200 million, and it must have seemed as if every schemer and hustler in the state was encamped on his doorstep within the week. Part of Ed Ball's job was to plant himself firmly between these characters and Alfred.

Settling in a mansion he built just outside Jacksonville, Alfred went to work. Banks were among the institutions that suffered most in the sudden end of the Florida land boom, and Alfred's experience with Delaware Trust, which he had since sold to his cousin William, made banking a logical business in which to become involved. Alfred quietly bought control of Jacksonville's third largest bank, the Florida National, within a year of his arrival. By the summer of 1929, Almours Securities had a market value of $150 million. Alfred and Jessie went to Europe for a vacation. Fearing an eventual collapse of the stock market, Alfred had given Ed Ball a power of attorney over Almours. When a big bank in Tampa failed in July, Ball cabled Alfred for approval of a plan to borrow $15 million against some of Alfred's Du Pont stock and put it behind Florida National, announcing the fact to the public. Alfred cabled back for Ball to use his best judgment. The

Tampa bank's collapse was not an isolated incident. That bank pulled several others with it, and all over the state, banks were closing their doors. Ball decided to go ahead, although the run on Florida National had more or less stopped. Two days later it started again. The morning of the third day, tellers greeted customers with a smile. The word was out that Alfred had put up $15 million and it spread. By midday the run had ended.

Now Alfred began to expand, buying the charters of other banks as they went under and making them part of the Florida National chain. The stock market crash on October 29 did not catch Alfred unawares. He had been expecting it, owed no one anything, and was sitting on some $2 million in cash. He wrote his son: "What will be the outcome the Lord only knows, and, due to His usual reticence, it will be impossible for me to get inside information."

One of the ways in which Alfred managed to keep his Jacksonville bank—the flagship, so to speak, of the chain—going was illegal. The bank had a bunch of shaky corporate bonds on its books, most of them quoted at prices less than half what the bank had paid. Many Florida municipal bonds were selling at similar prices, but du Pont figured the corporate bonds were moribund while the municipals exhibited latent recuperative powers. So he had the corporate bonds sold and bought the municipals, exchanging bonds more or less on a one-for-one basis. To balance the books, the municipals were carried at what the corporates had cost originally. For two years bank examiners ignored the practice, but in 1933 they finally told the bank to stop. By this time, Alfred had unloaded about 80 per cent of the bad corporates and improved the bank's position by $2.5 million. Had Alfred been wrong about the relative merits of the bonds or less honorable in his intentions, the bank might have been ruined.

Alfred may also have been skirting the law by holding state office in Delaware while a voter in Florida. Early in 1930 C. Douglass Buck, Coleman's son-in-law and governor of Delaware, had made Alfred chairman of the Old Age Welfare Commission in recognition of his efforts to provide elderly Delawareans with pensions. In 1929 the state senate had defeated an Alfred-backed bill to make such pensions a state responsibility. At the time, only Montana had such a law, and it provided only for local county options. Alfred had hoped to make Delaware the first state to have a statewide program. When the senate said no, Alfred took matters into his own hands, set up an office to gather data on the state's pensionless elderly, and began paying from his own pocket monthly pensions to all the needy he could find. The pensions were not large, averaging about $16 a month. In 1931 a new bill, backed by Buck and Alfred, passed the legislature. That July Alfred sent out the last of his personal checks to the state's old folks. The list of qualified recipients was then about 1,600 strong. From November 1929 to July 1931 Alfred had given away $350,000, not including the expense of starting up the Welfare Office, whose operation the state also took over.

Meanwhile, Alfred Victor had finished schooling in Paris as an architect, returned to Wilmington in 1930 with a partner, Gabriel Massena, and set up a practice. The new firm's first job was on the sunken gardens at Nemours, Alfred Victor's father's estate. Finished in 1931, the magnificent gardens cost the older Alfred $350,000. The firm's second big job was the state welfare home in Smyrna, Delaware, the enabling legislation for which was passed in 1931 with Alfred and Buck behind it. It cost $500,000 and was dedicated in the fall of 1933, Buck having been re-elected governor the year before with Alfred's help.

In a letter to Francis I. du Pont late in 1931, Alfred made one of his rare allusions to the cost of his charity, saying he had spent about $2.5 million "in caring for the interests of others."

By 1934 Alfred had added substantial acreage to his Florida holdings. At that time, he owned more than 300,000 acres, for which he had paid more than $1.5 million, a price that also included a couple of extras—the Apalachicola Northern Railroad, the town of Port St. Joe, part of the town of Carrabelle, and the St. Joseph Telephone and Telegraph Company. At the time of his death in 1935, Alfred's net real estate in Florida was about 280,000 acres. He had bought nearly 150,000 more acres, but he had sold nearly 190,000 to the federal government as part of the Apalachicola National Forest.

Ed Ball had taken a fancy to the Florida East Coast Railway, which served most of the resorts and winter home towns along Florida's Gold Coast as well as an important part of the state's agricultural enterprises inland. In the early thirties the railroad went broke, defaulting on $45 million worth of bonds. Ball figured control of the bond issue was control of the railroad and began buying up the bonds at cheap prices until he had acquired more than $23 million in face value. The railroad would prove to be a gold mine.

When Alfred died of a heart attack on April 29, 1935, two weeks before his seventy-first birthday, he was worth about $60 million, from which state and federal taxes would take nearly $30 million. His will left a number of relatives sums worth up to $750,000 each (the amount to each child and Ed Ball), provided annuities for a group of other people—friends, old people, retainers—and gave Jessie a life interest in the income from the remainder. Nemours, or at least a part of the grounds of the estate, was to be the site for a hospital, either for crippled but not incurable children or for the care of the elderly, first consideration given to Delaware residents. The mansion was not to be part of the hospital. Trustees of the Nemours Foundation, set up by the will, were empowered to contribute to other charities serving children and the aged. In a codicil dated January 15, 1935, Alfred wrote: "It has been my firm conviction throughout life that it is the duty of everyone in the world to do what is within his power to alleviate human suffering. . . ." He expressed the desire that after his bequests to family and others had been provided for, "the remaining portion of my estate should be utilized for charitable needs." Alfred's will and that codicil in particular are currently the subject of what may prove a dramatic legal fight.

Before he died, Alfred had made some peace with most of his relatives. Early in 1920 he and Pierre had exchanged friendly letters on the subject of evaluating Du Pont stock for tax purposes. Coleman had sent Alfred a poignant letter of condolence upon Alicia's death, and Alfred had responded in kind when one of Coleman's sons had died just months later. When Lammot, Pierre's brother, had become president of the company in 1926, he had made a special effort to keep Alfred, the company's second largest stockholder after Pierre or Christiana Securities, fully informed on company matters, and had Alfred lived longer, chances are he might have been restored to the board of directors through the efforts of Francis I., who had approached both Lammot and Pierre on the subject and found them both agreeable. As it was, Alfred and Pierre were never fully reconciled despite several olive branches extended by Pierre. Perhaps the only du Pont who went to his grave without at least some charitable feelings toward Alfred was old Colonel Henry, who died in 1926. The best the Colonel could say about Alfred in those later years was that his behavior wasn't his fault, that he had inherited some of the insanity on his mother's side of the family. No doubt Henry considered his concession on this score as scaling the heights of magnanimity.

Alfred's nephew, Maurice du Pont Lee, whose life was perhaps the most distinguished of the descendants in Alfred's branch of the family, typed a note and taped it in the front of his personal copy of the Marquis James biography of his uncle: "The story of a brilliant, domineering personality, misunderstood by many, loved by those who knew him well, and respected by all." Alfred was more controversial than that, especially within the family. He was the family democrat, a man true to his principles as he saw them. His biggest shortcoming may have been that his vision was sometimes warped by faulty perspective.

If helping the indigent elderly was one of Alfred's chief sources of satisfaction in life, nephew Maurice Lee chose to help the elderly who didn't really need it. A vigorous man well into his eighties, Lee believed that the United States was wasting a valuable resource in ignoring those people over sixty-five who remained able, healthy, and experienced but had been forced into retirement. And these people let it happen, Lee contended. "A lot of us find a convenient palm tree and just sit under it waiting for the undertaker," he once said. "Under these circumstances, he's likely to come promptly." Lee proved by example it didn't have to happen that way, building a national reputation for himself after he retired from the Du Pont Company.

The son of Alfred's sister Marguerite and Cazenove Lee, himself the son of General Robert E. Lee's first cousin, Maurice graduated with an engineering degree from Cornell, helped the Du Pont Company in the expansion of smokeless powder facilities to meet the demands of World War I, was instrumental in the introduction of synthetic dyes from Germany into the United States after the war, served as president of a Du Pont subsidiary, and was among the pioneers in the commercial development of rayon and cellophane. Then, retiring from Du Pont at the mandatory sixty-five, Lee got busy.

Among the first operations he started was Consulting and Advisory Services. Begun in the early 1950s just after Lee's retirement, this outfit offered the counsel of dozens of experts with long experience in a variety of fields to small businesses in need of help. The group made order out of accounting chaos for some firms, streamlined production methods for others, found uses for what once were waste materials of some companies, helped beginning concerns to sort good advice from bad, and even raised loans to send youths with promise to college. In the first dozen years, Lee alone kept records on more than two thousand individuals to whom he had given help. Lee was frequently thanked with the words, "How can I ever repay you?" He had a standard answer: "Help someone else." Just a couple of years before his eightieth birthday, he became involved in JOB (Just One Break), an employment agency for the handicapped and retarded. He claimed in an interview with the Wilmington newspaper on the eve of his eightieth birthday that JOB had already added $500,000 to the state's economy by getting people off relief rolls and onto payrolls. His community activities ranged from preserving and improving the city parks as president of the Wilmington Board of Park Commissioners to helping organize a Wilmington branch of Alcoholics Anonymous. He was a master at persuading his wealthy friends to contribute to the causes he espoused. Those causes included slum clearance, prison reform, and downtown parking, as he became increasingly concerned about the future of Wilmington, which he felt was becoming "an urban wasteland."

He told the newspaper, "When I need money for a good cause, I call some of my wealthy girl friends—and they contribute." Lee died early in 1974, the last of his generation, the grandchildren of Alfred's father, Eleuthère Irénée.

Of Alfred's direct descendants, only Alfred du Pont Dent, second son of Vicky, Alfred's youngest daughter, and Elbert Dent, lives in Wilmington. His mother was the only one of Alfred's children to live out her life in that town. His two older daughters, Madeleine and Bessie, were but occasional visitors once they got married, and his son Alfred Victor moved to Florida in the early 1950s. Vicky, affectionately called "the Duchess," was not a particularly well-known figure about town. Her socializing was limited by the fact that she neither drank nor smoked and disapproved of those who did. Her friends were devoted to her. With reason, she was considered among the most organized individuals in town. She used to call up her friends, skip the niceties of introduction, and plunge straight to the point. Once she called a

friend who was as ardent a fan of the double acrostic in the
Saturday Review as she was. What, Mrs. Dent wanted to
know without so much as a hello, was the name of the bishop
of North Dakota or somewhere. Her friend, active in church
affairs, admitted ignorance. "Well, if you don't know, who
would?" Mrs. Dent snorted. A couple of days later she called
again with the same question. After all, the friend received
Saturday Review from her as a Christmas present each year;
the least she could do would be to supply a bishop's name.
This time the friend said she knew, but wasn't telling because
that wasn't the way to get answers to an acrostic.

Mrs. Dent died early that December—the year was
1965—but the friend had not heard the last of the bishop,
whose name, by the way, was Whipple. "I'll never forget it,"
the friend, a cousin by marriage, said not long ago. "A couple
of weeks after Vicky died, I received a note informing me I
would receive the following year's *Saturday Review*, compli-
ments of Bishop Whipple. Vicky was a very organized lady."

Of the people she loved Mrs. Dent could believe no ill. Her
son Alfred would show up at the house with the effects of the
previous evening's intemperance written all over him, and invariably, Mrs. Dent would blame the appearance of her son
on food. "Must have been something he ate," she'd murmur.
Alfred remembers arguments he and his brother used to get
into with their mother. "She'd sit us down and say she
wanted to discuss the matter fully," he recalled recently.
"She'd ask us to listen to her side first without interrupting.
Then she'd listen to our side, she said. Well, she'd go on and
on and finally she'd finish. Then she'd say, 'But let's not talk
about it any more. You know how these things upset me.'"

Alfred Dent is too young to remember much about his
grandfather, and what he does remember does not always jibe
with the facts. His recollection, for example, is that Alfred I.
left his grandmother while she was pregnant with his mother.
It is true that Alfred I. and Bessie were on rocky terms before
Vicky's birth, but their actual—and still informal—separation

did not occur until the summer of 1904, seven or eight months after Vicky's birth. At any rate, when Dent says his mother never knew his grandfather very well, that he wasn't particularly nice to her, but that she always was loyal to him, Dent is on surer ground. He remembers being told his grandfather had a dog named Yip and used to refer to Pierre as "Yip's cousin Pierre."

Of his uncle, Alfred Victor, Dent has fond memories. He remembers stories of his uncle going to class at Yale in his tuxedo in order to save time getting to New York City for the evening and the professor calling him up in front of the class and writing on the tuxedo with chalk. His uncle may have been the only du Pont ever to work major college football games as a linesman. He was a great sports fan. He married often if not always wisely. After one divorce, a friend asked him, Dent says, "Was the screwing you got worth the screwing you're getting?" Dent has a pair of cuff links inherited from his uncle that have a wife's initials and the marriage date on one side. The other side is blank, and his uncle used to say that side was for the date of his divorce.

In his later years, Alfred Victor would take a drink. Dent always made a point of stopping off to see his uncle whenever he was in Florida, which, in the years before Alfred Victor died in 1970, was frequently enough because Dent had been made a trustee of the Nemours Foundation, located there. "It was a good idea to get to his house before eleven," Alfred said. "After noon, he was a little hard to understand." Alfred Victor died broke, but before his will could be probated, some Du Pont stock he still owned but which was pledged as collateral for a loan went up enough in value to cover the loan and leave a modest six-figure inheritance for his fourth wife. Alfred Victor's sister Vicky was forever worrying about her brother's extravagance, Dent says, recalling that his uncle once called up his mother to tell her she could be proud of him, that he was cutting back on expenses and planned to start saving money. He'd even sold his yacht. "Well," Dent said, "not long afterward, mother finds out that Uncle Alfred has another yacht and she calls him up all worried again and asks him what happened. He apologizes and tells her it wasn't really his fault. 'You see, sister,' he tells her, 'my captain needed a job.'"

Dent is a pretty colorful character in his own right. Not deeply imbued with the work ethic, Dent has an office in his friend's investment business's Wilmington suburb headquarters, and a secretary who will tell you Mr. Dent is not in if you call much before 11 A.M. Since his divorce from his first wife, golf and backgammon have gained if not precedence over at least parity with work. Known to his friends as "the fairway fox," he has a golf swing that provokes more laughter than fear in his opponents, but an appropriately high handicap and a keen gambler's instinct allow him to win his share of bets and then some. Not infrequently, a seemingly offhand remark sparked by an acerbic wit more reminiscent of his stepgrandmother Alicia than perhaps anyone in his family will make the difference in a match, disconcerting an opponent at a crucial moment. If he loses on the golf course, there is always the backgammon table, where friends say his only shortcoming is an overconfidence that results in his taking some long-shot chances because he figures he can outplay whoever sits on the other side of the table. Dent makes no secret of his fondness for alcohol and sometimes gives the impression he is a frustrated musical comedy star, grabbing a microphone in the waning hours of a private party and giving forth a lusty if somewhat tuneless rendition of the title song from *Guys and Dolls*. Once at a luncheon of Wilmington dignitaries to discuss plans for a nursing home whose proposed location would put it in du Pont estate country, Dent performed a special version of the then popular "Downtown" to express his thoughts on an appropriate location for the home.

His interest in backgammon roughly parallels his divorce. "There wasn't too much else to do, so I started going to tournaments." Now he is well known on the circuit. One of his earlier tournament visits was to St. Martin, where he wound up in an important consolation match against a former Miss Holland. The match was played on the beach, and the woman was clothed, so to speak, in a bikini with a transparent top whose only concession to propriety was two little strategically placed strawberries. She told Dent the bikini had been specially made, a revelation to which Dent took no exception. Keeping his eyes on the backgammon board, Dent eventually won and says he almost choked when the guy who was with his distracting opponent allowed that this was the first match he'd ever seen between a real lady and a true gentleman.

His name has provided Dent with a number of stories on himself, which he tells with relish. As a seaman in the Navy he got involved in a poker game. The stakes were modest enough, a $1 or $2 limit, and fortunately the roster did not include Dent's middle name, du Pont. Still, that middle name was not the best-kept secret in his outfit. A chief petty officer happened along and stopped to watch a few hands, wondering out loud after a while how an ordinary seaman making $70 or $80 a month could afford to stay so long in so many hands. A fellow player explained it to him. "This guy owns the Du Pont Company," he said. Another time Dent was seated next to a big name in Philadelphia society at a dinner party. She glanced at the place card that said "Alfred Dent" on it and observed that it must be tough going through life with a name like that. Not the least ruffled, Dent replied, "Not when you put 'du Pont' in the middle."

Backgammon has opened some doors for Dent that even his name might not, including the one at the front of Hugh Hefner's Los Angeles mansion, where he met a long-time idol at a party one night. "There I was talking, actually talking to Groucho Marx," Dent said. "I couldn't believe it. Then Cathy [his wife] comes up and starts pulling on my sleeve.

She finally manages to drag me away a few feet and whispers, 'Get rid of this old man. Joe Namath's in the next room.'"

Dent has little contact with either his brother Richard, who lives in Connecticut, or his first cousins, the children of his mother's sisters. His uncle had no children. Dent does, however, remember hearing about John Bancroft, his aunt Madeleine's son by her first husband, who apparently spent four or five years at the University of Virginia, gave up, told Jessie Ball du Pont, his stepgrandmother, he'd graduated and left. Jessie sent him a check for $3,000 and several years later during a visit to the university inquired if her grandson had made any special honors or won any awards while there, discovering his failure even to earn a diploma.

These days a new—or at least reconditioned—Alfred Dent is making his presence felt, especially in Florida, where he is taking legal action in an effort to loosen the death grip his grandfather's brother-in-law, Ed Ball, has on the Nemours Foundation. For Ball, the accumulation of wealth is an end unto itself, and he's been very good at it. Since Alfred I. du Pont's death, the estate has grown to where even vague estimates of its worth vary greatly, all the way up to $2 billion. The crown jewel among the assets is the St. Joe Paper Company. The foundation owns nearly three quarters of the company, which in turn controls a couple of railroads and more than a million acres of land in Florida and Georgia, among other things. The foundation also has some 700,000 shares of Du Pont and more than a million shares of General Motors. It used to control the Florida National Bank chain until the government forced Ball to give that up. Among the items on the asset side of the balance sheet is $100 million cash.

Dent contends that the foundation has not been run in accordance with his grandfather's will because such a small percentage of its income is being used for the charitable purposes Alfred I. du Pont wished to promote. For one thing, Dent would like to see the foundation sell its interest in St. Joe, which does not contribute to foundation income proportionately to what it represents as a percentage of the assets. In 1975 St. Joe paid out in dividends $4 a share while earning $187 a share. Sale of St. Joe could bring the foundation anywhere from $5,000 to $10,000 a share or a total of $350 million to $650 million, which if reinvested in solid securities could yield $20 million to $50 million in annual income and make the foundation a charitable force with which to be reckoned.

Why has Ball not been challenged before? Two basic reasons. For one thing, Ball is an old man who has confounded the life expectancy charts. "When my father died, Ball was seventy-seven," Dent says. "Now (in the summer of 1977) he's eighty-eight. In another eleven years, he'll be ninety-nine and probably still going strong." For a second, before Jessie died in 1970, foundation income was not a germane issue because any increase in income would simply have gone to her, and with $10 million or so a year already, she hardly needed it. Why now? Dent says he is concerned about his personal liability as a trustee if, for example, the state of Delaware were to sue the foundation on the grounds it was not living up to his grandfather's intent for it. Dent is also concerned about his status as a trustee. He became a trustee only upon expansion of the board, and litigation is now pending on the subject of who is legally a trustee. Dent figures his suit will carry more weight while he is on the board. Unstated but no doubt a factor is Dent's ownership of several hundred shares of St. Joe in his own right. Finally, Dent has a more or less facetious reason for the timing.

"The straw that broke the camel's back," he says, "was when Mr. Ball had us all up to his suite for a drink after a meeting. He was tending bar himself and asked me what I'd like. I saw a bottle of Jack Daniels behind the bar and told him I'd like some of that on the rocks. This was at a time when he should have been trying to get me on his side. He looked at me and said, 'No you won't. That bottle's not open.' That did it."

Dent is taking a chance. He is not rich, at least not by du Pont standards, and legal costs are already forcing him to curtail some of his more expensive habits. His opponent is tough as they come, especially on his home turf, and whatever the reasons Ed Ball clings to control of the foundation, no one, not even Dent, accuses him of seeking personal gain. Ball certainly doesn't need the job; he must be worth around $50 million on his own. He's never taken a dime from the foundation that anyone knows about or even hints at. The stakes are high. For Ball, a life's work. For Dent, added income, a chance to play a key role in developing a huge source of funds for Delaware's children and elderly, and an opportunity to foster a measure of the self-respect his grandfather considered so precious—not necessarily in that order from Dent's point of view.

One cannot help wondering whose side Alfred I. is rooting for, wherever he is. The odds favor his cheering for his grandson, congratulating his old brother-in-law on a magnificent job but trying to convince him that the job is done and the time is come to let go. For Alfred I., the accumulation of wealth was never an end.

Chapter Eleven

Heirs of "the Boss"

Undoubtedly the wealthiest branch of the du Pont family today—on a per-capita basis—is the line descending directly from old Boss Henry, who managed during his lifetime to acquire control of more than 80 per cent of the family business. At the time of his death in 1889, he and his two sons owned about nine elevenths of the company partnership. While their cousins produced offspring by handfuls, the two sons—Colonel Henry and William Sr.—were each survived by only one son and one daughter, and neither of the daughters ever had any children. Although this branch eventually relinquished control of the company, it did not give it away, and the wealth accumulated was inherited by a relatively small number of descendants. This branch is among the more intriguing in the family. By itself, the concentration of wealth here would make it so, but wealth is only one aspect of the fascination.

Colonel Henry is worthy of a biography unto himself. A distinguished Union soldier during the Civil War, he seemed destined both by inclination and ability for a military career, but his wife, a New York socialite of *the* Mrs. Astor's coterie, let him know early that the nomadic life of a soldier was not one she cared to share, and his family urged him to join the company. Although he was the company's largest stockholder for a while after his father's death, he was never too wrapped up in the company's affairs, devoting his time to railroads and Chicago real estate on the business front and developing an active interest in politics and du Pont family history on the side. By 1915 the Colonel was close to retirement. The following year he would run for re-election to the U. S. Senate but would run afoul of Alfred I.'s political machine and lose.

The path to the U. S. Senate was no yellow brick road for Henry, who spent a decade trying to get there before he finally won election in 1906, at the age of sixty-eight. The Colonel made his first bid in 1895, back when the state legislature still elected senators. His opponent for the seat was John "Gas" Addicks, who had moved to Delaware several years earlier after making a large fortune, partially by acquiring franchises to sell illuminating gas in return for political favors. Addicks was a manipulator. He believed everyone had a price and set about to prove it by buying the Delaware legislature. Barely thwarted in his first bid for the Senate in 1892, Addicks was ready in 1895, but he had miscalculated du Pont influence. So, too, had the Colonel. He and Addicks managed to deadlock the state legislature, and for nearly ten years, Delaware was a senator or two short in Washington. Henry actually received a certificate of election from the legislature in 1896, but his method of securing it was sufficiently suspect that the U. S. Senate refused to seat him. The question was whether the president of the state senate, who had succeeded to the governorship upon the death of the incumbent, could vote on the U. S. Senate seat. Henry said no; Addicks said yes; state law said nothing; and legally, Henry's case was weak.

The struggle went on for a decade. In 1905 two compromise senators were finally installed to fill partial terms after the Addicks-Henry war had resulted in no Senate representation for Delaware at all for some two years. In 1906 Henry finally won, with Coleman coming to his aid, spreading money and propaganda about the state in profusion. For the next ten years the Colonel served in the Senate, priding himself on the fact he had the most conservative voting record in that august body.

In 1898 his friendship with President McKinley finally secured the Colonel a prize he would treasure the rest of his life

—the Congressional Medal of Honor for his service thirty-four years earlier during the Civil War. Cynics took two views of the matter, contending either that the medal was a consolation prize to the Colonel after his rejection by the Senate or that with the war against Spain seeming more and more inevitable, the government wanted to be sure of du Pont allegiance. Whatever the motivation behind the award, the Colonel's service record was heroic. More than once the artillery he commanded played a crucial role in battle under dangerous circumstances.

His active interest in du Pont family history reveals the Colonel in another light. The work he did on early family genealogy is an impressive piece of scholarship, but he had a tendency to ennoble the family and ignore historical data, no matter how central, that might diminish the glory of the du Pont name. Thus, for example, he published memoirs of the original Pierre S. du Pont de Nemours, based on original manuscripts he inherited, carefully deleting all reference to the father of de Nemours, Samuel du Pont, as a clockmaker. Henry also made somewhat of a fool of himself courting the noble Pelleports in France, seeking an audience with the Grand Duke of Baden. He justified himself with the contention they were relatives, which stretched a point, at best. The Pelleports were related to the du Ponts through the first Victor's marriage and were hardly consanguinous with Henry's branch of the family. The Colonel's view of more contemporary family history was often colored by his personal relationship with the family members involved.

Brother William suffered from this type of characterization by Henry during the period of the old Boss's death and William's divorce. The Colonel, reminiscing with family historian Bessie Gardner du Pont some years later, recalled that William was in charge of the farm operation at the time and told the men working there that the Colonel wasn't interested in them and was rather inadequate when it came to business. Henry told Mrs. du Pont he had no idea why his brother felt that way and speculated jealousy, adding, "I do not know of what. He was not well educated. His eyes gave out while he was at school." Once the Colonel and Alfred I. started feuding—first quietly over William's divorce and later Alfred's own, then more openly over Alfred's suit against Pierre and his successful political campaign against the Colonel—Henry dismissed Alfred's role in the 1902 company take-over by the younger generation and, in a 1923 memorandum, described Alfred as "that highly unsatisfactory member of our family, whose conduct has been so much and so deservedly condemned." In Henry's revised version of the 1902 affair, he and Alexis kept the company in family hands, when Francis G., Alexis' brother, was for selling out to Laflin & Rand, Du Pont's biggest competitor.

The Colonel frequently mistook in himself disdain for pity, bombast for eloquence. He tended to inflate his stature with self-importance and self-justification, usually convincing himself, if no one else. But family loyalty ensured his prominence among the du Ponts. When it became apparent that the Colonel was rather offended at not being consulted by Pierre during the negotiations to purchase Coleman's stock, a group of younger cousins got together and gave the old man a testimonial dinner. Chick Laird, a nephew of Pierre, recalls there was something of a rivalry between Pierre and Henry as to who was head of the family—not, perhaps, a conscious rivalry, but at least a question in some minds over who was properly the family patriarch.

It is rather typical of the Colonel that he could on one hand claim that when he became senator in 1906 he put his Du Pont holdings in his son's name and went out of his way to keep himself uninformed on company matters in an effort to avoid even an appearance of being influenced as a senator by the company, yet on the other hand could feel slighted when left out of the discussions involving the disposition of Coleman's stock.

Chick Laird tells a nice, revealing story about the Colonel back in those days. Laird and a half dozen or so of his cousins all had vehicles they called "redbugs," described by Laird as "the grandfathers of today's motor scooter." The boys would ride them all over the countryside, and one day they visited Winterthur, the Colonel's home, riding about the driveway and making an awesome racket. Henry came out and asked what the devil those things they were riding were. "Redbugs," he was informed. "Bedbugs?" he asked. Once Henry got the name straight, he wanted to see how one worked. The young cousins showed him and offered him a ride. The Colonel demurred, summoning the butler, who was ordered to test-ride one. When no mishap befell the butler, the Colonel went for a ride. Then he had all the servants called outside, and they, too, took turns riding the redbugs while Henry looked on, enjoying himself immensely.

Henry's brother William is something of a mystery man. Some seventeen years younger than the Colonel, William grew up sheltered and more or less ignored. In other times, his marriage to a distant cousin—May du Pont, sister of Alice, who married Coleman—would have attracted little attention, but in 1878 William's father was the Boss, and he had decreed that there should be no more intrafamily weddings. Boss Henry had no sooner told his sons that he was going to make them partners in the company business than William announced his plan to marry May. His father was unamused. Although William tended to display more interest in spending than making money, he was far from incompetent in business affairs, and his brother Henry sold him short when he told Bessie du Pont that William was in charge of the farms in 1889. William was president of Repauno Chemical Company, the dynamite firm Pierre's father Lammot ran until his untimely demise in 1884, and the Hercules Powder Company, as well as of Hecla Powder Company and Independent Torpedo Company. If William was less than brilliant as a manager, he was nonetheless clever enough to hire brilliant managers, and Repauno continued to prosper. In 1890 William resigned his partnership in the du Pont firm. He and his brother weren't getting along, and neither were he and his wife, which state of affairs wasn't going to make for a happy partnership.

William was married for the second time in 1892 in St. George's Church, Hanover Square, London, one of England's more fashionable churches. He then leased Loseley Park, a stately mansion in Surrey. Later he moved to Binfield Park, near Windsor Castle. Both his children were born in England. He was among the earlier du Ponts to take up yachting, belonging to clubs in both Philadelphia and New York. Indeed, belonging to clubs was something of an avocation in itself for William, who was a member of the Turf, Knickerbocker, Metropolitan, and Downtown Clubs in New York, the Rittenhouse in Philadelphia, and the Wilmington and Wilmington Country Clubs in Wilmington. He was the first of a long line of du Ponts to attend MIT—in 1874–75. He became an important breeder of Jersey cattle upon his return to the United States and Montpelier, which he purchased in 1900. He was a member of the Royal Agricultural Society of England, the Hackney Horse Society of England, and the English Jersey Cattle Society, as well as of the American Hackney Horse Society and the American Jersey Cattle Club. His breeding could hardly be challenged.

Under pressure from Coleman, William was given a seat on the board of directors of Du Pont in 1913, although Pierre opposed the idea. William also joined Alfred I., Pierre, and Coleman on the finance committee. His restoration to company, if not family, good graces did not last long. He sided with Alfred in the big feud and was soon on the outside again. After 1916 William's main Delaware connection became the Delaware Trust Company, in which he joined Alfred, taking over when Alfred moved to Florida. William remained one of the largest stockholders in Du Pont but was without influence in company affairs. It is unlikely that he was particularly disturbed by that situation, but proof of that surmise is difficult to come by.

William was not given to public pronouncements, or very many private ones for that matter. In all the stories, myths, and legends surrounding the du Pont family, William goes unmentioned. He has been the subject of conjecture, especially as the first Brandywine du Pont involved in divorce, but substantive, primary source material on William is in remarkably short supply.

The children of William and his brother Henry were all four intriguing personalities. In both families, the daughter came first, followed by the son. When the Colonel's wife, Mary Pauline Foster, gave birth to her daughter, Louise, in 1877, Aunt Mag—Margaret Ten Eyck (Foster) Smith—wrote Henry: ". . . do not be distressed if the baby is small. I heard today that Henry Ten Eyck . . . was once put in a silver tankard. He now weighs about 250 pounds. I hope your young lady will never equal him in weight." Aunt Mag's hope was more or less in vain, but Louise, who grew up—and out—and married Francis B. Crowninshield and who became a major force in the nation's historic preservation movement, had a sense of humor about it. Addressing a gathering in the early 1950s of the fast-growing National Trust for Historic Preservation in Washington, Mrs. Crowninshield observed that "each year we get bigger and bigger."

While the Crowninshield family was among the more prominent in Massachusetts, the Colonel wasn't altogether convinced his son-in-law's intentions were entirely honorable. David L. Ferguson, a Crowninshield in-law, in a recent book says Henry left Louise a life interest in a trust providing "something like $2 million a year" and provided that the money revert to the du Pont family on her death. When the Brandywine powder mills ceased production in the early 1920s, Henry bought Eleutherian Mills, the home of the original E. I. du Pont, and gave it to his daughter, who promised to live there part of each year and who had it restored. A devoted gardener like so many of her relatives, Louise, along with her husband, had the industrial ruins between the house and the Brandywine turned into classical terraced gardens, which even the caustic Ferguson concedes were regarded as the best of their kind anywhere.

Mrs. Crowninshield had a sharp eye for excellence and beauty and exquisite taste that enabled her interest in preservation and gardening to bear valuable fruit. Conrad L. Wirth, former director of the National Park Service, once said about her that "the old, the beautiful, and the historic legacies from the American past are owned by the nation either in part or largely on account of her interest and help." She was a vice-president of the Garden Clubs of America, at whose headquarters a room is named in her honor, and was a trustee of the National Trust from its inception in 1949 until her death in 1958.

The Crowninshields had three homes. They spent the summers in Massachusetts and the winters in Boca Grande, Florida. In between, they stayed at Eleutherian Mills. Although she never had any of her own, Mrs. Crowninshield loved children. At her summer home by the sea, she used to give visiting kids a fishing pole and get them to drop a line over the sea wall, behind which she had stationed a servant who would tie a present on the end of the line. Her surrogate children were three poodles, a Pekingese, and two parrots. Her husband, the prototype of the leisure yachtsman, was devoted to her and was quoted in a report on his Harvard class's fiftieth reunion as saying, "I am fortunate in being married to an unusually good-tempered wife, one who spends most of her time doing kind things for other people, myself included." One of her few unkind acts, unintentional as it may have been, was putting urine dye in her swimming pool. It was removed after the water around two of Boston's most proper dowagers turned purple one day, as Ferguson tells the story.

In Boca Grande, she was queen. The black servants there were her grateful subjects and would show their appreciation for all she did for them by singing spirituals at poolside during the cocktail hour. Knowing perhaps that she would leave

Boca Grande for the last time the next day, Louise, her health failing, had her chauffeur push her out to the beach the evening before her departure in 1958, where she sat quietly, tears streaming down her face as she watched the sunset over the Gulf of Mexico. Ferguson caps this description by quoting an old servant who had come out to watch Mrs. Crowninshield depart for the North the next day: "There won't be room on her crown for all the stars."

Mrs. Crowninshield inspired affection in those who knew her. This is rather nicely revealed in the acceptance of a dinner invitation written by her cousin Pierre in 1950, his eightieth year. The invitation was apparently a trifle imprecise. "I am not quite sure," Pierre wrote, "if this is the right Saturday or if the dinner is to be held at Eleutherian Mills, Boca Grande, Boyce, Virginia, or perhaps Boston. However, I shall take a sandwich with me and sit on your porch and eat it if I find there is no other provision."

Louise's brother, Henry Francis, was not an impressive youth. Writing his wife in 1889, when Harry, as he was called, was nine, the Colonel appears worried about his son's shyness, his unwillingness "to have anything to do with other boys who are suitable as companions." The Colonel describes Harry as intelligent but more "backward" than his sister. Harry was not much of a hit at Groton, the boys' prep school to which he was sent several years later. Describing him as "the pathetic butt of cruel jokes," Ferguson claims he survived Groton only because he received permission to spend his free hours in a nearby greenhouse after asking for a plot of ground he could use to plant seeds and being turned down. Harry went to work for the Du Pont Company, but, as Irénée du Pont, Jr., recalled in an interview several years ago, "He was a lousy chemist. My father had to fire him." Irénée Sr. did Harry a favor. Beginning in 1927, when he inherited Winterthur from his father, Harry launched a career as collector of American decorative arts and consummate gardener that made him a worldwide reputation. The Winterthur collection of antiques, porcelain, silver, and other decorative art is considered without rival, and the gardens that surround the museum are often favorably compared with those at Longwood, the horticultural paradise created by Pierre. Legend has it that Harry used to walk about his gardens carrying swatches of cloth that he'd spread about to indicate the color flower he wanted in various locations. In the spring, Winterthur bedazzles. In the gardens are more than 235 varieties of azalea alone.

The National Association of Gardeners awarded him its gold medal in 1952, only the fifth time the award had been made in the Association's thirty-eight-year history. One of the others was to Pierre. The Garden Clubs of America gave him their tenth medal of honor awarded in thirty-six years and the citation read in part: "He is conceded by fellow horticulturists to be one of the best, even the best gardener this country has ever produced." Winterthur also ran a model dairy farm stocked with Holsteins. A cousin of Harry's by marriage said recently she remembers getting milk from Winterthur for her children and being told by her pediatrician that the Winterthur milk was the only milk he knew of that was so pure it didn't need pasteurization. Harry once said he figured his milk cost him about a dollar a quart to produce.

What would the old Colonel have thought? He had hoped to send his son to West Point, a wish he was finally persuaded to abandon by Mrs. Francis I. du Pont. At least Harry did not totally ignore business. He served as a General Motors director for twenty-six years.

There are more stories about Harry and his awesome wife, Ruth Wales, than any other member of his generation in the family. Harry was chairman of the committee the then Jacqueline Kennedy formed to help her redecorate the White House. On his first visit there, he almost didn't make it past the guard when he was unable to produce proper identification. He was finally admitted on the strength of his monogrammed billfold. After touring the White House with Mrs.

Kennedy, Harry is alleged to have told her only two pieces of furniture were worthy of White House retention. It was undoubtedly no accident that the two pieces had been a gift of his sister.

Harry's first love was the soil. Asked to pick an occupation for the New Castle County directory, he chose farmer. In 1951 he moved out of the main house at Winterthur into a more modest mansion next door and began referring to himself as "only a visitor at the museum but still head gardener." He had his own nine-hole golf course up until 1963, when he was persuaded to lease most of that property to a group of relatives starting a new, exclusive golf club.

Winterthur, named for the ancestral Swiss home of the mother of its first owner, James Antoine Bidermann, is an enormous palace with by far more rooms than any other du Pont mansion. A family story has it that at dinner one night some young relatives of Harry slipped out of the dining room and began wandering around. They became lost, found a telephone, and picked up the receiver. The switchboard operator asked the youngster on the other end of the line to read her the station number imprinted on the phone and told the kids not to move. Help was on its way. A few minutes later a butler arrived to lead the children back to their parents. He got lost, found another phone, and a second rescue mission was dispatched, this time successfully. Harry had an uncanny recall of Winterthur's inventory and was supposed to have known where everything belonged down to the last Chinese export porcelain ashtray. Once, according to family myth, he bid a suddenly embarrassed dinner guest goodbye by asking her to remove the ashtray in her pocketbook and replace it on the table where she had found it.

More than one story about Harry and porcelain survives today. He once picked up a bowl in the museum to examine it more closely and was admonished by a guard, who told him politely not to touch anything. Another time at a large formal party at Winterthur, perhaps the debut of one of his two daughters, a fully skirted woman standing next to him made a sweeping turn and knocked some priceless piece of export china off a table. Gallantly, Harry smiled, mumbled, "Don't worry about a thing, my dear," and went into a dead faint.

Harry was very publicity-shy. When Mrs. Kennedy paid a visit to Winterthur, the press was barred and had to settle for a photograph of her—Harry refused to pose—taken by a Winterthur photographer, processed, and rushed out to the newsmen waiting at the gate. Guests at Winterthur were frequent and often famous. The legendary Harry was not always the perfect host. Once, for example, the Duchess of Buccleugh, close friend of the Queen Mother, was served a vegetable prepared in a manner she did not readily recognize. She inquired of her host what it was. "Eggplant," replied Harry. "Eggplant?" asked the duchess. "Yes," Harry said shortly, "eggplant," adding only partially under his breath, "Eat it." "Ah," said the slightly flustered duchess, a light finally clicking on. "*Aubergine!*" Upstaged at his own table, Harry stiffened visibly.

In general, guests at Winterthur received royal treatment. Those who spent the night were served breakfast in bed, which was probably just as well because Harry was always up at six or earlier and limited his morning meal to orange juice and milk. Occasionally a guest would take unfair advantage of Winterthur's hospitality and incur the wrath of its hostess, Harry's wife. When a woman staying at Winterthur on the occasion of a big weekend party arrived for Saturday luncheon and announced she simply must have a hairdresser that afternoon, Mrs. du Pont phoned all over the countryside and finally managed to find her one. Mrs. du Pont was not amused at this imposition and told a friend, "She may not know it, but she's been here for the last time." Mrs. du Pont was also not amused by people transparently fishing for an invitation to Winterthur, no matter who they were. The Duchess of Windsor is supposed to have cornered Mrs. du Pont at a New York party and started in on how wonderful she'd heard Winterthur was and how anxious she was to see it. Mrs. du Pont smiled brightly, allowed that all the duchess had heard was undoubtedly true, and urged her not to forget to call ahead for reservations, reminding her that Winterthur was closed on Mondays.

Mrs. du Pont died in November of 1967, and Mr. du Pont lived less than two years after that, dying in April of 1969, just shy of his eighty-ninth birthday. They left two daughters, both of whom were infrequent visitors to Wilmington once they got married. In his will, Mr. du Pont left each of his daughters $750,000—they were both beneficiaries in earlier trusts and their inheritance was more a gesture than a limiting of their financial future—and the bulk of his estate to the corporation that runs the gardens and museum at Winterthur. The corporation also carries on a wide variety of educational, research, and authentication programs in the field of American decorative arts.

William's son and daughter led rather different lives than did their first cousins. What Harry and Louise did for American decorative arts and historic preservation, William Jr. and his sister Marion might be said to have done for horse racing. Marion and William Jr. were both twice married, each choosing a celebrity the second time around. Marion married the actor George Randolph Scott; William married Margaret Osborne, the tennis champion.

For the first half of his adult life, William Jr.'s first love was horses. He was built something along the lines of a jockey, and his home north of Wilmington was elaborately equipped for the training of race horses, an operation he supervised himself, getting up every morning but Sunday at five in the belief that he could not ask an employee to do anything he would not do himself. His showcase for horses was the eleven-thousand-acre Fair Hill estate southwest of Wilmington across the Delaware border in Maryland and spilling over by a few hundred acres into Pennsylvania. There he built his own steeplechase course complete with grandstands. His love of racing led him into racecourse design, a subject on which he became perhaps the nation's foremost authority. He designed more than twenty-five steeplechase and flat racing courses around the country. His racing stable, Foxcatcher Farms, was widely known in racing circles, and when his estate sold fifty-one Foxcatcher horses in 1966, they brought $2.4 million for an average of more than $47,000 apiece.

By the late 1930s William Jr. was developing a growing interest in tennis. He became a proficient player. Wanting others to share his enthusiasm for the sport, he set up a foundation to provide half the cost of building a tennis court to any non-profit institution or organization in Delaware that wanted to build two or more courts. The foundation spent more than $200,000 helping finance construction of more than sixty courts for state schools, Wilmington city parks, the University of Delaware, and others. In the 1940s William hired Bill Talbert as a sort of private tennis professional. In his book, Talbert confesses to having had it pretty soft in William's employ, living "the good life of a country gentleman."

Tennis drove a wedge between William and his first wife, Jean Austin, says one man who knew him well and described his first wife as demanding undivided attention from William. As tennis took more of his time and horses—a passion of his first wife—took less, she grew dissatisfied. "He once told me his life might have been different if he'd married another sister in that family," his friend said. Despite his divorce in 1941 and a sometime reputation among local gossips as having a wandering eye, William loved his family. He was endowed with what a former in-law described as the "sweet" qualities. Not well educated, he possessed a rather undisciplined mind that had its own way of reaching conclusions, but often as not, those conclusions were sound. Under his father's will, he received a life interest in 60 per cent of the income from an estate of about $400 million. Marion got 40 per cent. The principal was to be distributed among their children. Marion, still alive and well and living in Montpelier, has no children. William had five, four by his first marriage and one son by Margaret Osborne, whom he married in 1947 and from whom he was divorced in 1964. When William Jr. died on the last day of 1965, his children received nearly $50 million each from their grandfather's estate.

It was essentially sudden wealth. During his lifetime, William Jr. gave his children only as much as the Internal Revenue Service would allow before subjecting him to gift tax, which usually amounted to $6,000 apiece annually in the years he was married and $3,000 during the six years in the 1940s when he was between marriages. Although he spared no expense when it came to horses and tennis, William Jr. was not an extravagant man in his personal habits. He could frequently be seen lunching alone in the Delaware Trust Company cafeteria, looking more like a man whose income was $6,000 a year than one who in 1960 paid more than $4 million in taxes on his income. Perhaps this philosophy colored his attitude toward his children's finances. At any rate, some handled their sudden wealth better than others.

Of the four William children by his first marriage—two daughters followed by two sons—all but one continue to live in the Wilmington area. The oldest, Jean Ellen McConnell, is an able businesswoman who inherited her father's interest in horses and manages the complex affairs of his Fair Hill estate. She was, rumor has it, somewhat disappointed when her former husband, J. H. Tyler McConnell, was made head of her father's bank, Delaware Trust, having eyed that position for herself. Few deny her ability to have handled the job. The second daughter recently remarried and moved away from the Wilmington area. His son by Margaret Osborne, William III, lives in Texas and is rarely seen in Delaware.

His two other sons—Henry E. I. and John E.—are so different as to belie the fact they are brothers. Henry was christened William Henry but petitioned to have his name changed in 1973. Why his father chose to name two sons

William has never been explained, but it appears that he was suspicious of his oldest son's abilities. Before he died, he set up a holding company for William Sr.'s Delaware Trust stock and divided the shares in the holding company so that his oldest son would receive non-voting shares. In 1972 Henry sued to change the situation. Henry, now married—for the third time—to controversial Martha Verge (Muffin), does not fit the public image of an average du Pont. In some ways, he might be likened to a modern version of Alfred I., although Alfred's success has thus far eluded Henry. He is outspoken, encouraged by his wife, on the subject of the du Pont family's shortcomings and determined to pursue his own course, not infrequently drawing opposition from cousins, only a handful of whom were invited to a debutante party he gave for a daughter several years ago. He and Muffin have spent many thousands of dollars and hours working for prison reform and care of neglected children. The results, however, have been modest, in part because they insist on doing things their own way. Henry lives in regal splendor on an estate in the heart of du Pont country, but he has few visitors among the family. Recently his and Muffin's attitude toward other du Ponts has mellowed somewhat. Muffin, for example, says she used to think the family custom of New Year's calling, in which the women gather in perhaps a dozen houses and the men drive around to visit them all bearing small presents, was phony but now admits she likes it and concedes she is impressed by the generally strong family feeling among the du Ponts. She confesses to enjoying visits to the family cemetery, where she sometimes talks to the headstones. Among her favorites in the family is Alfred I.'s now dead nephew, Maurice Lee. "He understood what I am trying to do," she says.

Henry has managed to run through his inheritance in quick order. While he is reluctant to discuss it, Muffin told a reporter for the Wilmington newspapers a couple of years ago in rebuttal of an earlier article her version of what has happened since 1966. First, she said, there has been a $10 million paper loss on the value of the securities inherited, making the inheritance closer to $40 million than $50 million. Trust funds for Henry's children by two previous marriages took $9 million, she said, while real estate transactions in Delaware, Maryland, and Florida took an additional $6 million to $8 million. Her husband's computer service company, SciTek, went bankrupt to the tune of about $8 million. Henry's only income now, she said, is from five thousand shares of Du Pont and a 1,700-acre farm in Easton, Maryland. When he first came into his money, Henry jumped into the real estate market with both feet and a minimum of good judgment. According to one knowledgeable source, he was buying inland soybean fields in Maryland for more than the smart money was paying for prime waterfront property.

The bankruptcy of his computer company Henry blames on the Mafia, theorizing the Mafia wanted to sabotage a subsidiary, Securities Validation Corporation, which is simply a computer program and a data base for keeping track of lost and stolen securities. Henry is working on reviving that subsidiary, and even his detractors concede he has a good idea. It began in 1968 with the blessing of the New York Stock Exchange as a result of the back office chaos that had developed among the exchange's member firms. In 1975 Congress passed a law requiring the reporting of lost or stolen securities, which before had often gone unreported to avoid public embarrassment of the institutions involved. The Securities and Exchange Commission is currently working on implementation of the law, and Henry hopes to get the job of helping. He already has a data base for $11.4 billion worth of lost or stolen securities and estimates this is but 20 per cent of the total.

The way his service would work is this: People who deal in securities, primarily bankers and stockbrokers, would buy the service. Henry figures he could charge something on the order of $400 a year for a bank and perhaps $10 a year per registered representative. He estimates there are 20,000 banks and

130,000 registered representatives in the country. When stock or bond certificates were presented for sale or transfer, their serial numbers could be run through Henry's computer program and checked against the serial numbers of certificates reported as stolen. As an example of how the service should have worked, Henry cites a California case in which a man took a group of banks for $3 million. He purchased a large amount of stock for which he received certificates. He then wrote the companies involved, claiming he never received the certificates. The old certificates were canceled on the books and a new set issued, which the man promptly sold. He then took the original certificates around to the banks and used them as collateral to secure $3 million in loans. The banks were unable to collect insurance on the loss because the securities they had accepted as collateral were listed with Securities Validation Corporation as having been canceled.

Henry is considered rather rough around the edges, even tacky, by some of the more conservative members of the du Pont clan. He doesn't buy his clothes at Brooks Brothers, and his public behavior is more impulsively brash than quietly polished. He and Muffin are sometimes a source of humiliation to the family. There was the time, for example, when Henry hired a fellow out of prison on parole who had been convicted as an accessory to murder. The man was employed as a butler and chauffeur, managing to get himself accused of robbing a sign shop on the side. Henry and Muffin paid for his lawyer. What's more, it was all in the papers. On another occasion, Muffin sued the very proper Woodlawn Trustees, a non-profit organization charged with developing substantial real estate holdings in accordance with the desires of its founder, William P. Bancroft, who was a wealthy member of a Wilmington textile family. Bancroft said he wanted to see homes for "people of moderate or small means" built once an adequate acreage had been set aside for parks. Muffin didn't think the trustees were doing much of a job and sued them for discrimination, an action viewed by some of the more charitably inclined du Ponts as eccentric. Others were less euphemistic in their characterization.

Henry's younger brother John is among a shrinking number of du Ponts who have the energy and sharply focused interests that give the having and spending of large fortunes some flair and personality. An engaging bachelor who works hard to overcome an innate shyness, John, who lives with his mother on an estate across the Delaware border in Pennsylvania, has used his money to pursue and share two lifelong avocations— natural history and sports. His sport specialty is the pentathlon, which combines swimming, running, pistol shooting, horseback riding, and fencing. His mother's place, a replica of Montpelier set on more than one thousand rolling acres, is an ideal training ground. Some years ago John built a $400,000, fifty-meter, six-lane indoor pool and added a fifteen-station indoor pistol range for good measure. The riding and the running were readily available, and John's fencing coach was at the University of Pennsylvania not far away. Nearing forty, John is now aiming for a possible place on the 1980 Olympic team. He also acts as talent scout for the team, which he managed in the 1976 Olympics. Each year he hosts the triathlon national championships, a competition similar to the pentathlon without riding or fencing. His pool is used by more than two hundred swimmers from high school and college in serious training, including national record holders and Olympians. He recently hired George Haines, coach of more Olympians and national champions than any coach in history, away from the famous Santa Clara Swim Club. His pistol range is used by the Chester and Delaware County and Newtown Square city police, many of whom have been trained by John, who also loans his helicopter to the law-enforcement agencies. He is a detective and special assistant in the Chester County district attorney's office. Law enforcement is his third major interest. "I've worked on some homicides," he says.

His helicopter is no ordinary fair-weather whirlybird. Not more than half a dozen helicopters in the country are so fully equipped with electronics. He can land in zero visibility, John says, the only drawback being that he has to put down at the Philadelphia Airport because his private helipad at home is not equipped to bring him down electronically. It is equipped, however, to put the helicopter away once it's down. The pad is on a track, and John simply pushes a button. Up goes the hangar door and in slides the helicopter.

John's interest in the pentathlon was more or less prearranged for him, although he didn't really know it at the time. After swimming for the University of Miami team, he went west to the famous Santa Clara Swim Club. After a while, he says, it became obvious he wasn't going to make the 1964 Olympic swimming team. One evening he went to the home of Lynn Burke, a 1960 Olympic gold medal winner, and after dinner, her father pulled out an Olympics book, stopped at the pages dealing with the modern pentathlon, and said, "Hey, John. This is for you." Says John, "I didn't even know what it was. Well, Lynn just happened to know the fencing coach at her school and the next day I went with her to meet him and he gave me a note in Hungarian to the University of Pennsylvania coach, one of the best in the world. I went to see him. He read the note and said, 'Good. You want to fence? We start now.' I never found out till much later, but my career had sort of been planned for me behind my back."

It didn't take long for John to become a devotee. "I was already a good swimmer and could ride and shoot pretty well," he said. "And I figured I could learn running and fencing." He was right. He didn't quite make the 1964 Olympic team, but he did win the 1965 Australian championship. Altogether, he has competed in about fourteen countries around the world. "It's been the highlight of my life," he says. His disappointment at not making the 1968 Olympic team must have been severe. The luck of the draw was bad luck for him. He drew a rough horse for the riding event and was nudged off the team.

Most of the time, John gives the impression of being

serious-minded and straightforward, but occasionally an imp-
ish streak surfaces. He says, for example, that the shooting
event in the pentathlon is done with a .22 pistol, but that you
used to be able to shoot whatever handgun you wanted. "I always wanted to use a .45," he confessed. "That would have
shaken up the competition."

John has been a natural history enthusiast for as long as he
can remember. Driving south as a child with his family for
spring vacations, he would frequently prevail upon his parents
to stop along the way so that he could look for snails or whatever under a bridge over the road. "My parents never discour-
aged me," he said. "You might say that was encouragement
of a sort." After a number of years, things started getting
pretty cluttered at home. The garage, barns, even a barn at
his sister's place, all were filled with the collections of birds,
shells, rabbits, and the like John had amassed. In 1957 with
the help of his brother-in-law Tyler McConnell, John set up
the Delaware Museum of Natural History. Eight years later a
building across from Winterthur was started to house John's
collections and the laboratory and office space for his museum staff. From the outside, the building looks like an over-
grown crypt; inside, displays have been designed and en-
gineered with great success to be both educational and
visually appealing. While its shell collections seem to have attracted more publicity, the museum has the best Philippine
bird collection, one of the best Mexican bird collections, and
representative samples from South America and Africa, John
says, adding that the museum's aim is to "supplement, not
compete with, other museums."

In its early years, the museum developed a reputation as
John's toy. Insiders say the museum operated without a
budget, that bills would simply pile up on John's desk until the
quarterly trust fund income checks came in and then the bills
would be paid. In 1976 the museum's expenditures were
about $400,000. Recently John has begun to concentrate on
changing the museum's image, hiring outside management

advice and adding to his board some non-family community members who make the board more widely representative. John thinks of the museum as belonging to the people of Delaware and hopes to attract their more active participation in the museum's programs and its future. Another factor influencing John's decision to broaden participation is the growing burden the museum represents on his financial resources. He is said to be dipping into principal, no longer able to support the museum from income alone.

John is still collecting for the museum from all around the world and says the red tape is so thick that export-import permits alone keep a lawyer busy almost full time. Even at home, to collect, say, birds requires a federal and a state permit as well as notifying the local game warden and obtaining the permission of the landowner on whose property the collector wishes to operate. Every year John takes a three-week vacation, invariably to somewhere in the South Pacific on a collecting expedition. "I enjoy it," he says. "I try to go somewhere that hasn't been explored. You find a hole and jump in."

Up until recently, John has been trying to run a full-scale farming operation on 1,250 acres outside San Francisco, but he is now convinced it can't be done efficiently at long distance and is selling off all but the house he maintains there and three acres. Although he does not give the impression of being particularly political, he reported giving more than $100,000 to the Nixon campaign in 1972 and was quoted in the local newspaper as saying his contributions were inspired by his consideration for "the little people" who would get stuck if the campaign was unable to pay its bills. He said he had been a large contributor before.

Showing a visitor around his mother's place not long ago, John stopped at a complex of barns in two of which were housed his mother's impressive collection of old carriages. "You'll find a lot of interesting collections in the (du Pont) family," he said. "They're usually kept pretty quiet, private."

But there are no nine-foot walls around the farm. That same morning, John's swimming pool was filled with hard-working youngsters under the watchful eye of one of the top swimming coaches in the country, while outside, a small group of University of Pennsylvania ornithology students were preparing a banding experiment. His mother was not in evidence. She had celebrated her eightieth birthday the day before. "She's probably out driving around in one of her carriages," John observed.

Those who know him well consider John somewhat eccentric, a characterization to which he would probably not object with much vehemence. The life he leads is a full one from which he derives no small measure of satisfaction. "I keep busy," he says. "I don't have time to get in trouble."

Marion, John's aunt, who is now in her eighties, divides her time primarily between Camden, South Carolina, and her father's Montpelier estate in Virginia. She is considered the grande dame of the Camden Cup, a prestigious annual steeplechase, and indeed, in some quarters she is considered the grande dame of horse racing. Her most famous horse in recent years was Mongo.

It may be that Marion is the most honored woman in the history of horse racing, in fact. Besides the Camden Cup, she is largely responsible for two other steeplechasing events, the Colonial Cup at Camden and a meeting at Montpelier. As a breeder of horses, she has enjoyed many triumphs. In the last twenty years alone, she has bred more than twenty-five stakes winners, and seven of the top twenty-five all-time money-winning jumpers are descended from her champion sires, Battleship and Annapolis, both sons of Man o' War. In 1938 Battleship became the first American-bred, American-owned horse to win England's arduous, prestigious Grand National. Her Mongo twice defeated the great Kelso, owned by her cousin-in-law Allaire Crozer du Pont, once in 1963 and once in 1964, both years in which Kelso was named Horse of the Year. In 1965 Marion was voted the first recipient of the

F. Ambrose Clark Memorial Award and in 1977 became the first person elected to Virginia's new Equine Hall of Fame. Being the first is nothing new to Marion. In 1930 she was the first woman ever to ride astride her horse, rather than sidesaddle, at the famous Madison Square Garden Horse Show.

When she was first married, she lived in Wilmington in a house her father built for her. Elbert and Vicky Dent—she was Alfred I.'s daughter—then bought the house, and Alfred Dent, their son, lived there until just a few years ago when he sold the place to J. H. Tyler McConnell and his second wife. McConnell's first wife is Marion's niece. The home ownership coincidence was unknown to McConnell when he bought from Dent. Marion grew to know George Randolph Scott through his Virginia connection. Both Scott, the well-known cowboy actor, and Marion's first husband, Thomas H. Somerville, were from the Orange, Virginia, area. Marion and Scott were divorced some years ago. Marion is among the wealthiest women in the country as the beneficiary of 40 per cent of her father's $400 million estate. Because she has no children, that money will go to her five nieces and nephews—the children of her brother William—upon her death.

Chapter Twelve

A Diverse Branch

When Alexis I. du Pont, the youngest son of the Du Pont Company's founder, was killed in the explosion of 1857, he left behind three sons and four daughters and the beginnings of perhaps the most heterogeneous branch of the family. The oldest son was Eugene, president of the company from the death of Boss Henry in 1889 until his own death in 1902. The youngest son, Francis G., was among the best scientists the family ever produced. He was the man who waxed most skeptical about Alfred I.'s offer to buy the company in 1902. His older brother, Alexis I., also a partner in the firm at that time, helped convince Frank to give Alfred I. a chance rather than sell the company to its chief competitor, Laflin & Rand. Alexis was never particularly active in company affairs, however, having been trained as a medical doctor, an occupation he did not formally pursue.

The oldest daughter married the imperious Leighton Coleman, Episcopal bishop of Delaware and a man with whom one didn't trifle, as a fellow clergyman quickly found when he performed a marriage of which the bishop did not approve. Bishop Coleman so harassed the minister who married Willard Saulsbury to May du Pont after her divorce from her cousin William du Pont that the minister fled to Switzerland. Irene, the second daughter, married Edward C. Dimmick. When she died at the age of thirty-two, Dimmick married her younger sister, Joanna Maria. Among the progeny of this slightly obscure strain of the family is a great-great-grandson of Joanna and Dimmick who boasts the most unlikely name in the du Pont family—Byron Crazy Horse Justin Case, occupation undiscovered. The fourth daughter was Eleuthera Paulina, wife of Judge Edward G. Bradford and mother of two daughters who married du Ponts—Eleuthera, who wed Pierre's brother Henry B., and Alicia, Alfred I.'s second wife.

No branch of the family was more torn by the intrafamily feuds over the divorces of William and Alfred I. and Alfred's suit against Pierre than were the descendants of Alexis. Perhaps the most dramatic example of this was the pair of slander suits filed by Alicia and Alfred in an effort to stem the nasty gossip arising from their marriage. One was filed against the widow of Dr. Alexis I. du Pont, who was the brother of Alicia's mother. The other named as defendant the stepmother-in-law of Alicia's younger sister. Neither suit was prosecuted. Dr. Alexis' two sons, Philip F. and Eugene E., did not speak after taking different sides in the Alfred I. suit against Pierre. Francis G.'s children divided six for Alfred and two for Pierre. Today no vestiges of these splits remain, bitter as they must have been. The grandchildren know the roles their grandparents played in those early days of the twentieth century but harbor no ill will. The closest friend of one granddaughter of Philip F., for instance, is a granddaughter of Eugene E.

The Alexis branch is today widely scattered. None of its descendants works for the company, and many have moved away from the Brandywine. The principal figures in this branch are, in the main, descended from the three sons of Alexis.

Eugene, the oldest, has already been treated extensively in earlier chapters. He married a cousin from the Victor side of the family—Victor being the brother of the company's founder—and had two sons and three daughters.

Eugene Jr., the middle child, known within the family as Dirty Gene to distinguish him from his first cousin Eugene E., known as Clean Gene, was a long-time director of Du Pont—from 1917 until his death in 1954—but his real interests lay elsewhere. He was an avid farmer, raiser of hunting dogs, and big-game hunter who used to hold trapshoots at his home, Owl's Nest, outside Wilmington. He would put up prizes for the shoots, which he won himself. At the time of his death, he willed Harvard $600,000 for scholarships, the largest individual gift for scholarships ever received by that university up to that time. He left an estate of $10 million and paid $4.5 million in inheritance taxes to the state of Delaware. To Pelleport, the former home of his sister Amy, which was converted into a convalescent home, he gave more than $1 million.

Eugene Jr. had two younger sisters, Amy and Julie Sophie. Amy never married and moved to California in 1937, twenty-five years before her death in 1962 at the age of eighty-six. Amy established the Unidel Foundation in memory of her father for the support of the University of Delaware. Among other things, the foundation paid for the university's $3.8 million music building, completed in 1973. A devoted horsewoman, Amy continued to ride until she was seventy-eight, giving it up only after being injured in a fall. Julie married a man named James N. Andrews and had four daughters and a son. The oldest daughter's son, C. Coleman Walker, Jr., is one of the few du Ponts who married into another major fortune, taking Julia Armour, of the meat-packing company family, as his bride. The second daughter, Julia, married Alfred E. Bissell, one of the founders of a Wilmington brokerage firm, and is today one of the family's grandes dames.

The two sons of Eugene Jr. wound up not getting along, which is not too surprising considering how different one was from the other. Eugene III, who has been married three times, is at best a rare visitor to Wilmington. He lives in Easton, Maryland, and owns a large plantation in South Carolina. Like his father, he enjoys shooting. Nicholas Ridgely, his younger brother, married a Florida beauty named Genevieve (Bunny) Estes. Under her influence, the couple became perhaps the most social members of their generation in the family, wintering in Palm Beach and attracting frequent mention in the columns devoted to the wanderings and doings of the

Jet Set. Among their friends they numbered Bob Hope and the Duke and Duchess of Windsor. Bunny was often among the contenders for Best Dressed honors and parlayed her impeccable taste, flair for color, and interest in gardening into the presidency of the Garden Clubs of America. Nicky worked for the Du Pont Company for ten years before striking out on his own in a variety of businesses, most of which involved real estate development. In one oil and gas property venture, he and his brother were partners. According to newspaper accounts of a 1966 legal action, Eugene III appeared to be essentially a silent partner. Then, as his money continued to go in faster than it was coming out, Eugene III became a disgruntled partner. Finally, he became a loud partner, suing his brother. He claimed unreasonable management charges levied by the partnership. He claimed he invested without receiving "adequate consideration." He claimed he put up $876,000 from 1957 through 1964 without ever receiving a full financial statement from the partnership. He even claimed his brother had induced him to invest $150,000 in oil wells his brother knew were dry.

Eugene III eventually settled for $2.25 million in 1966. The extent to which Nicky was guilty of the charges never was submitted to determination, but more than one member of the family says in private that Eugene III is not the most likable member of the du Pont clan.

Nicky and Bunny had two daughters. The younger was left weak-legged and nearly blind when her mother caught the measles while pregnant. A quiet but spirited girl, she tended to spend more time with horses than people. Her first marriage did not work out and she is now living a Spartan bucolic existence in nearby Pennsylvania with a second husband. A friend said not long ago she had never seen Vivi, named Genevieve after her mother, happier. It was on their older daughter, Nicole, that the parents had pinned their ambitions. A pretty, sweet, long-legged blonde, Nicole was groomed for marriage to royalty or at very least great wealth.

Her debutante party was among the most elegant of such affairs ever given in Wilmington, which has seen its share of lavish debuts. True, the du Ponts did the same for Vivi, even going so far as to station servants with trays full of glasses of champagne at the bottom of their winding driveway so that guests waiting for the parking service might wait refreshed, but Nicole's party was a showcase for the debutante, and she was dazzling. Her parents were rumored to be sorely disappointed when she fell in love with a Yale man from the Midwest, but they and she survived, and she now lives in New York, traveling comfortably in the right circles with her man from Cincinnati and her parents' somewhat begrudging blessing. Her father died in March of 1977, and her mother now spends most of her time in her former home state of Florida.

Undoubtedly the most famous wedding ever to take place in Wilmington was the one between Nicky's and Eugene III's sister, Ethel, and the son of the then President of the United States, Franklin D. Roosevelt. The courtship of Ethel and young Frank Jr. was not viewed with equanimity by their respective families. The du Ponts had hollered long and loudly against the Roosevelt administration, which had hollered back with charges of economic royalism and other evidences of feisty disagreement. In large part, Roosevelt chose to leave communicating with the du Ponts to his diplomatic wife, who declined an invitation to Ethel's coming-out party on their behalf. In the middle of this storm, Ethel and Frank Jr. grew in their affection for each other, submerging, if not ignoring, the social and political tribulations they were provoking. With a delicate sense of timing, they waited until after the 1936 elections to announce their engagement. The wedding was set for the following June. The President agreed to invade the hostile territory of Wilmington for the occasion.

The presidential visit was an affair not a few du Ponts chose to mark by staying home. "My father disaccepted for our whole family," recalls Frank du Pont's son, Brud. Pierre apparently did not put in an appearance, nor did Henry F. of Winterthur. Still, some one thousand cars arrived for the reception, and the fact that the President did not leave the party until nearly midnight indicates the affair was less strained than it might have been.

One family member who went through the receiving line says he recalls vividly his exchange with Roosevelt. A sudden thunderstorm had come up just as the church was letting out after the wedding. As a result, a number of the guests had been drenched, and parking at the reception had become a rather swampy proposition. Chick Laird, a nephew of Pierre, found himself face to face with Roosevelt—for the first and only time—and being a polite young man decided on the following pleasantry: "Isn't it a shame the rain had to come at just this moment, Mr. President?" Impishly the President looked him in the eye, replying, "Well, I don't know. It seems a fine way to soak the rich."

The marriage ended in a 1949 divorce, and after another unsuccessful marriage, Ethel committed suicide at Grosse Pointe Farms, Michigan, in 1965.

Alexis' second son, the first Eugene's younger brother Alexis, had four children, two sons and two daughters. The eldest, Alice Eugenie, married a somewhat bizarre Belgian named Julien Ortiz, whose rapport with the family was at best erratic. She had two daughters, the older of whom lived until her death in the summer of 1977 on the Eastern Shore in Maryland as Mrs. Harry Clark Boden IV. She was imbued with the family's historic preservation instincts and gave her restored Mount Harmon estate to the National Trust for Historic Preservation. The estate borders on a shooting club preserve, and Mrs. Boden had men patrolling the perimeter of Mount Harmon during shooting season to pick up wounded and dead geese. For a while, she even set up a hospital at the estate, hiring a veterinarian in a fruitless effort to save some of the geese. In an article for a 1977 issue of *Town & Country*,

Sophy Burnham wrote: "Mrs. Boden, as she is wont to point out, was born a du Pont." That, of course, is stretching a point. Mrs. Boden was born an Ortiz.

The younger Alexis' second child was Philip Francis du Pont, a rather eccentric gentleman with a passion for poetry and shooting. Phil's mother, remember, was one of the women sued for slander by Alfred I. and Alicia. Nonetheless, Philip is perhaps best-remembered within the family as the original plaintiff in Alfred's suit against Pierre. Philip was president of Standard Arms Company for a time but business held little fascination for him and he was soon back on his estate just over the Delaware line in Pennsylvania writing poetry and puzzling guests with his unusual eating habits. He had a sink in his dining room at which prospective diners were expected to wash before being seated. When Philip died in 1928, just shy of his fiftieth birthday, he left the University of Virginia $6 million, the largest individual bequest ever left that institution up to that time. His wife, known within the family as Bebe, lived until 1964 and never remarried. A quiet, petite, charming lady, Bebe was an unobtrusive friend of a number of celebrities, including Joan Crawford and the ubiquitous Duchess of Windsor. In 1957 Bebe decided to buy a race horse. Her younger daughter gave her a choice of several two-year-olds, and Bebe paid $6,000 for Tempted, a filly who went on to be the top mare in the country.

Philip's first daughter, Frances, a strong-willed woman with a soft heart, personified an enduring cliché—money can't buy happiness. On the surface it might have appeared that she was among the most fortunate. She owned a prospering boutique outside Wilmington and a string of race horses. She kept an apartment on New York's Park Avenue and frequented some of the city's best restaurants. Her home just across the Delaware border in Pennsylvania was considered one of the most gracious in the area. But beneath this glittering façade lay much tragedy. Her first marriage began in elopement, caused a partial disinheritance, and ended in divorce. Her first daughter, born in 1928, died in a 1971 fire at her Florida home after a life marred by two bad marriages and a long, bitter custody fight over two adopted children of her first marriage. Her other child, another daughter, was not born until 1941. In between, Frances lost several babies through miscarriage or infant death. Her second marriage became a union more of tolerance than love. She died of cancer in 1975. Her second daughter, Carroll, is now married for the second time to a prominent Wilmington lawyer, Edmund N. Carpenter II, son of Walter S. Carpenter, who was president of the Du Pont Company during World War II. Her husband is also the younger brother of W. Samuel Carpenter III, who married a first cousin of her mother. One of Sam's daughters is her best friend, making Carroll both friend and aunt.

Du Pont children are not unlike children everywhere in most respects. They play children's games with other children as often as not unrelated, and they skin their knees and elbows doing so. They get excited about Christmas and vacations, and in general behave as though totally unaware that anything in their lives sets them at all apart from the norm. But Carroll's oldest child, her daughter Ashley, without realizing it, tells some stories beyond even the imaginations of most twelve-year-olds. "You know Louis?" she asks brightly. "He's the elevator man at the Pierre [where her family stays when in New York]. He introduced me to Tatum O'Neal and her father in the elevator. They were really nice. Zsa Zsa Gabor pinched me on the cheek once." Even her mother was envious of Ashley when she returned to their rented villa on the Riviera one summer evening of 1977 after dinner and told her mother about meeting David Niven in the restaurant. Ashley was still an infant when her name appeared in an item in the *Wall Street Journal*. Well-known society orchestra leader Meyer Davis, the item said, would retire, God willing, after playing Ashley's debutante party.

Philip's younger daughter, Jane, married a stockbroker

named Harry W. Lunger and became a prominent figure in horse racing as owner of Christiana Stables. She and her sister were never very close. Frances was a social sort who loved a good party, while Jane was not particularly the party lover, although she enjoyed an evening of poker with friends at home. Jane became a major supporter of the family church and recently gave her twenty-four-room mansion along with forty acres to the Episcopal diocese. She had three sons and two daughters. The youngest son is Brett Lunger, now in his late twenties and trying to make it as a driver on the Grand Prix circuit for racing cars, so far with but modest success. Racing experts vary in their opinion of Brett's abilities, all the way from those who think he has the makings of a champion to those who think he's dangerous—good enough to qualify and compete given decent equipment but not good enough to survive. Brett's stockbroking brother David has been helping him financially as Brett tries to make it in racing without dipping into his own capital. On the side, Brett travels the country lecturing student and civic groups on auto safety, a job no one denies he does very well.

The second daughter of Alexis was Elizabeth Bradford du Pont, who married U. S. Senator Thomas F. Bayard. Mrs. Bayard, long considered one of the family beauties, lived to be ninety-five before she died in 1975. For years she was a vice-regent of the highly prestigious Mount Vernon Ladies' Association, in which post she had succeeded old Colonel Henry A. du Pont's sister, Mrs. A. Lentilhon Foster. She was particularly active in protecting the view across the river from the Mount Vernon mansion from being ruined by suburban sprawl. During her latter years she was one of the senior lady arbiters within the family, exercising a quiet, conservative influence on the younger du Pont women. She became one of the early du Pont Democrats, because her husband was a Democratic senator and, she said, it wouldn't do for him to have a Republican wife. Her position on the Mount Vernon Ladies' Association was partially responsible for what Louise Crowninshield,

Colonel Henry's daughter, used to admit was among her biggest disappointments in life—the fact that she never became a vice-regent. The honor is regional, and during Louise's lifetime, although she maintained several residences, an appropriate vacancy just never occurred. One of Elizabeth's sons is Alexis I. du Pont Bayard, a bit of a family maverick in that he became a significant figure in the Delaware Democratic Party. Du Pont Democrats are a scarce commodity.

The second Alexis' youngest child was Eugene E. du Pont, who became known within the family as Popsy as well as Clean Gene. He was a director of the Du Pont Company for nearly sixty years before he died at eighty-four in 1966, and also sat on the board of Phillips Petroleum from 1917 through 1955. As a Du Pont director, Popsy played a crucial role in pushing through the board a proposal to acquire control of Remington Arms. He was a limited partner in a brokerage firm founded by his son-in-law, George T. Weymouth, who borrowed $300,000 from him to start the company. For recreation, Popsy shot trap and did so well enough to be Delaware state champ.

But for all his genuine accomplishments, Popsy is best-remembered by those who knew him for his sense of humor and its wild manifestations. Once he was over at his neighbor's house when a cement truck drove up. The driver, mistaking Popsy for the neighbor, asked him where he wanted the cement he'd ordered dumped. Popsy probably knew his neighbor was building a barn and wanted the cement for the floor, but an inspiration hit him and he told the driver he was building a new sculpture for the front entrance of the house, asking him to dump the cement just by the front door and apparently managing to keep a straight face while he did so. Another time while perusing the open markets on King Street in downtown Wilmington, Popsy espied one of the scruffiest-looking domestic ducks he'd ever seen and immediately purchased it. Carting it home, he set it loose in nearby Hoopes Reservoir and called a female relative he knew was a bird watcher, saying he'd seen this funny bird on the reservoir and could she identify it. For several days bird watchers stalked the creature, never getting close enough for a positive identification. The newspaper carried a story about it. Finally Popsy shared his secret with one of his four daughters, Murton Carpenter, in a rather oblique manner, calling her up and suggesting that the bird might be hungry for a bit of that standard domestic duck fare—corn.

When Popsy arrived for the funeral service of his cousin Irénée, Pierre's younger brother, in 1963, he was greeted at the church door and helped out of his limousine by the local undertaker, who obsequiously inquired after Popsy's health. A daughter remembers his returning home after the funeral and commenting on this encounter in his inimitable deep, hoarse voice: "He was patting me for size." Popsy was a generous man. He left large sums to the University of Delaware, Harvard, the Wilmington Medical Center, and other institutions. But he was not exactly a soft touch. Once a man of the cloth came to put the arm on him for some building project. The clergyman waxed religious, urging Popsy to join him in prayer. "Now," he said when the praying was done, "don't you feel the hand of the Lord on your shoulder?" Family legend has it that Popsy replied, "No, but when I do, you can be sure I'll put my hand over my wallet." Popsy's sense of humor surfaced early. As a young man he was invited to Winterthur as a companion for his cousin Harry. In those days the place settings at the dinner table included individual porcelain menus on which were written the courses to be served each evening. Sneaking into the dining room before dinner one evening, Popsy carefully inked in prices beside each entry on the menus.

Popsy lost his wife in the 1930s. She had gone to the studio over their garage to do some work and for some never explained reason, had left the car running in the garage below. Carbon monoxide leaked up into the studio and poisoned her.

Popsy's oldest daughter, Deo, inherited his sense of humor

and married a man equally endowed. One Halloween, knowing some practical jokers who were also relatives planned a visit, Deo and her husband, George Weymouth, staged an elaborate drama for the benefit of their unsuspecting guests. As the group drove up, they heard a shotgun blast. Rushing to the door, they were confronted by Deo, staggering down the stairs covered with blood. It was an awful sight. The visitors hadn't even suspected the Weymouths weren't getting along. The blood turned out to be catsup. The Weymouths were quite pleased with themselves.

A number of years ago the Wilmington Trust Company sent Deo a notice that she had overdrawn her checking account, inspiring, so the story goes, Deo's outrage. Grabbing the nearest phone, she called the bank and enlightened its representative on the other end of the line as to the facts of the situation as she saw them, which were: She had plenty of money down there somewhere, and it was perfectly ridiculous of the bank to send her an overdraft notice. She did not expect to get one again. If her checking account happened sometime in the future to run short, the bank should simply transfer money into it from wherever it was the bank kept her other funds and not bother her.

Deo's sister Murton is not without a touch of the family humor herself. When a visitor to the Weymouth home remarked of a portrait painted of George that it was certainly very nice, remarkable likeness and all, but there wasn't any background, it was allegedly Murton who spoke up brightly, "Yes, but then George doesn't have any background."

Popsy's youngest daughter, Nancy Reynolds, is perhaps the most artistically talented du Pont yet to come along. She is an accomplished painter and creator of ceramics whose works' market value seems limited only by the fact that she doesn't need the money. She is also a gourmet cook of no small reputation, a happy circumstance since her husband William G. (Scotty) Reynolds is a connoisseur of wine and food. Thereby hangs a tale. Some years ago Reynolds was in Paris and reserved a table by the window overlooking the cathedral of Notre Dame at the Tour d'Argent one evening for dinner. When he arrived at the appointed hour, the table was already occupied—by a du Pont cousin who had sweet-talked the maître d', the story goes. Apprising Reynolds with an eye much experienced in such matters, the maître d' put Reynolds in the American tourist category, promised to have a table for him momentarily, and invited him to visit the restaurant's wine cellar and choose a bottle he might enjoy with dinner. The wine, the maître d' magnanimously allowed, would be on the house. An hour later Reynolds emerged from the cellar, smiling happily. It had taken a while, but he had found the cellar's prize. The maître d's gesture of apology for having allowed Reynolds' table to become occupied proved to be perhaps the most expensive such gesture he ever made.

For a time, Nancy Reynolds might have had to settle for second place in the family artistic talent department to her nephew, George and Deo Weymouth's son, Frolic, who in the late 1950s after graduating from Yale was developing into a first-rank portrait painter. But Frolic no longer has much time to paint. In the early 1960s Frolic married Ann McCoy, a niece of Andrew Wyeth, and became immersed in the rustic existence of Wyeth country—Chadds Ford, Pennsylvania. Progress was beginning to threaten that existence, and gradually an idea began to take shape in Frolic's head. Somehow there ought to be a way to combine the area's artistic heritage with its environmental one. Of this concept and a bit of forgetfulness was the Brandywine River Museum and its ecological adjunct, the Tri-County Conservancy, born.

The forgetfulness was this. Frolic was looking for a site to house his proposed museum when an old mill bordering on a meadow he already owned along the Brandywine came up for auction sale. Concerned lest he develop a reputation as one of those rich du Ponts going around and buying up everything in sight, Frolic engaged a surrogate bidder for the auction. He figured $100,000 was his top price and arranged to signal his bidder to cease participation when and if the bidding exceeded that level. If the bidder saw Frolic take off his hat, he was to drop out of the bidding. It was a warm, sunny day, and the bidding was spirited. At $100,000, Frolic took off his hat, exposing his prematurely bald dome to the burning sun. A few minutes later, thinking of his hat no longer as a signal but as protection, he put it back on. Up went his bidder's hand and suddenly the mill was going, going, gone to the bidder on behalf of Frolic for $150,000. That was in 1967. The mill is now a handsome art museum wherein hang the works of Howard Pyle, N. C. Wyeth, Andrew and son Jamie Wyeth, and others of what has become known as the Brandywine School of Painting. Adjacent to the museum is an unprepossessing, not to say shabby, structure that houses the offices of the Tri-County Conservancy, the part of the overall project that now takes most of Frolic's time. The organization's main purpose is to preserve and protect the water flowing down the Brandywine. The river is Wilmington's chief source of water supply and also provides many miles of rest and recreation facilities. Limiting industrial growth along its banks, restricting other kinds of development, and ensuring that those industries already using the river do not abuse it keep the Conservancy's small professional staff hopping.

Frolic raises the money, about $500,000 a year for operational expenses. So far, he's managed to keep up, having raised $5 million in the Conservancy's first ten years of operation.

For recreation, Frolic has taken up coaching, driving a team of horses from one of several carriages he keeps while he and friends enjoy the countryside and what Frolic calls "mobile cocktails." He says his interest developed in coaching after he had restored an old farmhouse to live in. "I didn't want cars in the driveway," he explains. "They'd spoil the effect." The logic here is somewhat specious. Frolic does not coach to work every morning; he drives a car. But in a vague, visceral sort of way, what he says makes a certain conceptual sense.

The first Alexis' youngest son, brother of the first Eugene and the second Alexis, was Francis Gurney du Pont, Cousin Frank, the principal advocate of selling the company to Laflin & Rand in 1902. He had seven children—two daughters and five sons—the oldest of whom was Francis I., a brilliant, dedicated scientist and founder of the second-best-known Du Pont Company, the now defunct Francis I. du Pont and Company brokerage firm.

Francis I. was perhaps the closest the du Ponts came to spawning an absent-minded professor. He resigned a Du Pont Company vice-presidency to take charge of the company's experimental station, set up in 1904. His dress gave the impression that he could not be bothered with the distinctions between formal attire, work clothes, and pajamas. He would frequently disappear from a dinner party or a simple evening at home, but his wife always knew where he had gone—to the lab. His career at Du Pont took a marked downward turn when he sided with Alfred in the 1915 feud, which resulted in a more or less mutual alienation of affections between the company and him, but it was not until 1931, in the midst of the Depression, that Francis I. went into the brokerage business, convinced the desperate economic situation was temporary. Testifying years later in a federal suit aimed at loosening Du Pont's grip on General Motors, Pierre's younger brother Irénée recalled that when the brokerage firm first opened, it was called F. I. du Pont and Company. The name was changed soon thereafter to Francis I. du Pont and Company, Irénée said, because much confusion developed in the mails between F. I. du Pont and Company and E. I. du Pont and Company and some people were cynical enough to suggest that the brokerage firm was trading on the similarity of its name to the big Du Pont Company. As was no doubt to be expected, the new brokerage firm emphasized research as the key to sound investment. Francis was first a scientific researcher, with some one hundred patents to his credit.

Francis helped perpetuate the it's-a-small-world syndrome when he married Marianna Rhett, whose father, Colonel Alfred Rhett, had been in command of Fort Sumter during the Civil War when Admiral Samuel F. Du Pont had attempted to capture Charleston. In one of those nice historical ironies, Marianna and Francis I. lived for a while in Louviers, the Admiral's old home. The inherently shy Francis was an unlikely source of scandal in late 1929 when he was sued for alienation of affections by a fellow named Edwin F. Donaldson, whose wife added insult to injury with a suit of her own seeking recovery of $170,000 in securities she claimed Francis I. had given her. The defendant's attorney called the action the "most outrageous and scandalous document ever filed in court." Both suits were eventually settled. In the recovery suit, Francis received a third of the securities and $21,500.

Francis I. had six sons and three daughters. His oldest was Emile F., known within the family as "Chick." Emile's quietly distinguished career with the Du Pont Company began in 1923 in less than auspicious fashion. Emile was working in a rayon plant in Buffalo and, according to his uncle E. Paul, was about to throw in the towel because of the static, unrecognized nature of his employment. The situation was rescued in time for Emile to rise through the employee relations department to become a member of the Du Pont Company finance committee and its board of directors in 1944. His first big job with the company was as manager of its first nylon plant in 1938 in Seaford, Delaware.

Emile was a man of many facets. Within the company, he was perhaps best-known for his work in the company employee safety program pioneered by his cousin Irénée. Perhaps remembering his own experience, Emile also kept an eye on young du Ponts in the company. Emile was also a director of General Motors from 1955 until 1959, when all Du Pont-related GM directors resigned as a result of the government suit to break up Du Pont's control of GM. Outside the company, Emile followed an ever growing number of family footsteps into aviation, obtaining his pilot's license in 1936. He was an avid although private painter and served as president of the Eleutherian Mills-Hagley Foundation, which operates a museum and library dedicated to family and industrial history, from 1958 until his death in 1974. For sport, he enjoyed duck hunting and deep-sea fishing. He was a pioneer of the tag-and-release program for salt-water game fish, experiencing one of his biggest thrills when he landed a marlin that turned out to be a fish he had previously caught, tagged, and released.

In 1962 Emile took his mother for a ride on a jet plane, an event the local newspapers chose to take notice of because Mrs. Francis I. was eighty-six at the time and had not ridden in an airplane since the year after Lindbergh's historic flight in 1927.

Emile's eldest child was named Francis I. du Pont II and nicknamed Nicky. He has followed in both his father's and his grandfather's footsteps, starting out by working for the Du Pont Company and later switching into the investment business as a part of the Delfi American Corporation mutual fund management team along with his cousin Brud, Coleman's grandson. Nicky's son had to be named Francis I. IV because an uncle had already named a son Francis I. III, all of which does little to help outsiders keep the family straight. Insiders find it none too easy, for that matter.

Their oldest brother having chosen a career with Du Pont, it was left to two younger sons of the first Francis I. to carry on the brokerage business. Under Edmond and Alfred Rhett du Pont the firm prospered. Where their father had emphasized research, the sons promoted mass marketing and retail sales. In the late 1960s the company was credited with rescuing several floundering firms caught in the vicious whipsaw that first left brokerage firms drowning in a sea of back-office paperwork, then awash in an excess computer and back-office capacity as trading interest in the market dried up. After one such rescue, Edmond was quoted as saying, "It's not so important that you have money. What's important is that you have money when you need it."

In 1970 Francis I. du Pont and Company needed it, and despite a capital infusion from the du Pont family between October of 1969 and November of 1970 totaling $15 million, the brokerage firm found it did not have it. Its capital ratio had fallen below the minimum requirements of the New York Stock Exchange, creating perhaps the most severe crisis the brokerage business has ever faced. The failure of Wall Street's second-largest broker would have had staggering implications both financially and for public confidence in the system, and there were many late-night and weekend meetings as the brokerage community tried to come up with a solution. To the rescue came Ross Perot, a Texan who had made a huge paper fortune in the computer services business. Perot's interest was essentially threefold. Francis I. was one of his largest customers and he didn't want to lose it. He considered a major voice on Wall Street to be an asset and a good opportunity to secure more business for his computer services. Finally, he claimed that he was motivated by a desire to help keep the free enterprise system afloat. An audit of the brokerage firm's books showed the situation was even worse than had been feared. Chaos ruled in the back office. Perot agreed to extend further financial help, but he drove a hard bargain, the result of which was to force the du Ponts to absorb huge losses.

When the dust had settled, Perot wound up with 91 per cent of the firm in large part because the du Pont family was unwilling or unable to put up another $15 million to protect their original investment. Even had they come up with the money, Perot would have had 51 per cent of the firm. Edmond retired in January of 1971, having lost all of his 25 per cent interest in his father's brokerage business, which he said was worth at least $6 million. His son, Edmond Jr. (Rex), had been made a partner in 1969 at the age of thirty-two and watched his legacy disappear. In a statement issued to the newspapers in May of 1971, Edmond said that except for some real estate holdings, he, his wife, and their two sons, Anthony and Rex, were without funds. The collapse of Francis I. du Pont and Company was remarkably sudden. On July 2, 1970, the firm had reported a net worth of $75 million—more than half of which was in Wilmington dollars.

The troubled times spawned many a rumor. Edmond withdrew from public view for a time, and there were those who said he was recovering from a nervous collapse. Other rumors had Edmond contemplating suits against Perot, but they never materialized. In September of 1971 he was re-elected to the board of trustees of the University of Delaware, a vote of confidence he must have especially appreciated at the time. He and his wife, the former Averell Ross, daughter of the cofounder of the Lybrand, Ross accounting firm, continued their active role in the family church, whose construction had been inspired by Edmond's great-grandfather, the first Alexis.

The summer of 1977 found Edmond and Averell living quietly in a comfortable but hardly grand home in the country northwest of Wilmington. Averell has taken over the time-consuming chore of keeping the family genealogy up to date. She is a warm, bright woman who appears at peace with herself. Edmond is a shy, somewhat subdued man who spends many hours communing with nature and working on the grounds surrounding the house. He has retained a quiet sense of humor and whatever bitterness he may have harbored has mellowed with the passing of time. The couple are very proud of their son, Tony, a talented aerospace engineer in California.

In his mid-forties, Tony is president of Du Pont Aerospace Company, which is not quite as glamorous or lucrative as it might at first sound. In fact, what keeps food on the family table is Tony's other job as chief engineer for Rotoflow Company, a manufacturer of high-speed industrial turbo machinery used in the expansion and separation of gases. Tony says his employers are very understanding about giving him time to work on his own company, which has two major projects in the works. One is an airplane jet fuel he's developed through a coal gasification process that is 55 per cent hydrogen and essentially pollution-free. His company was trying to convince the government late in 1977 to fund a demonstration of the fuel's advantages, working with some Boeing 737s, which Tony claims run better on his fuel than on conventional fuels. The major hurdle he faces is that the fuel, which is basically natural gas, has some storage and handling problems because of the need to keep it very cold. "Cryogenics," Tony explains. His other project is the marketing of a jet airliner he has designed with a thirty-passenger capacity. He argues that airlines could reduce their costs and improve service by using three of his planes instead of one ninety-passenger DC-9, for example. The three planes would fly directly to destinations that DC-9s now serve with one plane making three stops. Tony says that because the planes can operate on shorter runways and take off and land faster than DC-9s, airport overcrowding would not be a problem. At the moment, he describes his company as a three- to five-man operation, but if things go well, he plans to manufacture the planes himself, which would require substantial expansion.

Tony's family had some anxious moments a few years ago when Tony's name appeared on a list of seventy-four prominent American businessmen marked for death by the People's International Court of Retribution, an honor accorded Tony more because of his last name than any role he's played in big business, no doubt. Although he recalls some strange folks lurking around his home back at that time, nothing ever came of his inclusion on the list. He remembers well the day it came out. He was late getting to his office, and when he arrived, he had calls from the Associated Press, United Press International, and the New York *Times*, to all of whom he explained the whole thing must have been a mistake. The criterion for making the list, apparently, had been involve-

ment with companies who polluted, and here Tony was trying to market a pollution-free airplane fuel. Tony says that for
the most part people on the West Coast do not associate him
with his family. The name du Pont rings a bell, but people
seem to think "obviously I wouldn't be working as an engineer if I was a member of *the* du Ponts," Tony says.

The truth is that not only Tony works in his family. His
twenty-five-year-old son helped Tony finance his fuel research
by working on the Alaska pipeline. "There's not much to
spend your money on up there," Tony said. "It's pretty easy
to bank most of it."

Francis Gurney du Pont's second son was A. Felix, a name
that has caused some additional confusion among outsiders
attempting to keep the family straight because the A. stands
for Alexis. Felix was one of the six men who formed the original syndicate headed by Pierre to buy Coleman's stock in
1915 and held the fourth largest interest after Pierre and his
two brothers, Irénée and Lammot. Felix had proved an able
manager as superintendent of the Carneys Point plant and
was then heavily involved in the Du Pont Company's expansion of its smokeless powder facilities to meet the demands of
World War I. He became a director of Du Pont that year
and was the only son of Francis G. to side with Pierre when
Alfred sued over the Coleman deal.

Felix was a man of many interests. He played the French
horn and cornet in the Wilmington Volunteer Firemen's
Band, was a dedicated churchman and an enthusiastic hunter
and fisherman. In 1928 he and his sister Irene, who had married Pierre's brother Irénée, started St. Andrews School, a
small but respected boarding school south of Wilmington.
Felix put up $1 million for construction. His sister financed
the library and provided the school with a substantial endowment. She was also a major benefactress of the Episcopal church, art, music, and Planned Parenthood. Felix was
yet another du Pont with an early interest in the embryonic
stages of aviation, an interest inherited by his children.

There were four children, two boys and two girls, perhaps the most adventuresome siblings ever produced in the family. The eldest was A. Felix Jr., who has retained an avid interest in flying for more than sixty years. At the age of ten, young Felix was already a model airplane buff. He built himself hangars—"like doghouses," he says—in his backyard, even equipping them with electric lights, and the neighborhood children would park their model planes there. As a young man of twenty-two stationed in Texas in 1927 with the Army Air Corps, Felix was quoted in the local Wilmington newspapers as saying, "I want to fly, live as long as I can, and die like a gentleman." In the summer of 1977 he was still flying his own plane and only just beginning to wonder—at age seventy-one —how much longer he'd keep it up.

Felix Jr. spent about a year with the Du Pont Company in the mid-thirties, but flying seemed to be in his blood. For a while he was a test pilot for Fokker Aircraft after General Motors bought the company. He was a vice-president of All American Aviation, founded by his brother. That company is now All American Industries. Allegheny Airlines was spun off from All American after a government ruling that an airline could not be in certain other kinds of businesses. "Maybe we held onto the wrong part," says Felix, contemplating the fact that his family retained control of the engineering division and let go of the airline. Felix was also a vice-president of Bellanca Aircraft, a manufacturer of small planes, and became involved in Piasecki helicopters after World War II in partnership with Laurence Rockefeller. "My father always thought manufacturing was a good business to be in," Felix said not long ago over lunch in the Hotel du Pont, "but he was involved in transportation, too." Felix Sr. had a piece of the old New York, Baltimore, Washington airlines that once flew trimotors between New York and Washington every hour on the hour.

Felix Jr. has long been active in charitable organizations, having been at various times head of the Welfare Council of

Delaware; vice-president of the Curative Workshop, an out-patient physical therapy institution; chairman of the 1960 Cancer Crusade; head of the $1.5 million fund-raising drive put on by the Delmarva Council of the Boy Scouts of America; and a board member of the Franklin Institute, a Philadelphia science museum and educational facility. The last position, Felix says, "was a legacy from Irénée," who was a major benefactor of the Institute. Felix's second wife, Marka, is a nationally recognized figure in the field of mental health. She served two terms as president of the National Mental Health Association and in 1970 was named to the National Advisory Mental Health Council of the U. S. Public Health Service. She has founded the Marka T. du Pont Institute of Human Behavior to further the cause of mental health. When their country home burned down some years ago, the du Ponts gave the 132-acre property on which it was located to New Castle County as parkland. Felix and his family control the Chichester du Pont Foundation, which listed assets of $13.3 million at book value at the end of the 1975 tax year, primarily in Christiana Securities, Du Pont, and General Motors stock. The Foundation's net income for the year was $387,097, and it distributed $389,000.

Felix Jr.'s son Michael became the first du Pont to enter the movie business in a public way, heading for Hollywood in 1960 at the age of twenty-three. He put up $250,000 and landed a small part in a low-budget drama with the faintly ironic title of The Answer. Son Michael has not been "too successful" in the movie game, his father admits. Another son, Christopher, went into the land developing business in Sun Valley, Idaho. Altogether, Felix had four children by his first wife—the two sons and two daughters. One of the daughters, Katharine, married Michael Loening, the son of Felix's second wife by an earlier marriage.

Felix Sr.'s second child was a daughter, Lydia Chichester du Pont, who founded the Children's Beach House in Lewes, Delaware, where handicapped children can spend a couple of weeks of their summers and continue to receive the care they need. The Chichester du Pont Foundation's largest single contribution each year is to this institution. In 1975 the Foundation gave it $155,000. Lydia was a venturesome youth. In 1935 she traveled to the jungles of Venezuela to study a primitive tribe of Goajiros, who were considered to hold the key to some of the missing chapters in the history of civilization. She met a tragic death in June of 1958, literally dying in the arms of her best friend and cousin, Deo Weymouth, who had been driving the car Lydia was in when it was involved in an auto accident.

Richard C. du Pont, Felix Sr.'s third child, like his older brother built model planes as a boy. As an adult, Richard seemed to live life as one continuous flirtation with death. At twenty-one, he and a group of friends were out sailing and were caught in a storm that battered their yacht for four days before they were finally rescued. The following year, 1933, Richard was flying an open-cockpit plane when a snowstorm hit and he was forced to make a virtually blind landing on a ridge in hilly country. That same year his father put up $3,000 as a prize for anyone who could fly a glider from Elmira, New York, to within twenty-five miles of Times Square. Richard set a world gliding record trying to win the money but missed the mark by thirty miles. Once he and his father were up in a glider that was forced to crash-land. All this was a bit much for his older brother. "I only went for one sailplane ride," Felix Jr. recalls. "We had to land in a cornfield. I use a plane for transportation, not recreation."

In the early spring of 1934 Richard and his younger sister, Alice, flew to South America and gave friends and family a scare when they lost communication for a day. The two later explained they had simply spotted a pristine beach along the way and had landed on it for a swim. Richard and his new wife, Allaire, took a trip on the *Hindenburg* in 1936, the year before it burst into flames just before landing at Lakehurst, New Jersey.

Richard's inventive, mechanical mind was forever toying
with new ideas. He was among the early champions of the
flying mail train, using a propeller-driven plane to pull a string
of gliders that could be detached one by one over different
destinations. While fiddling with a fishing pole hooking odds
and ends from the roadside as he drove along in a car, Richard conceived the notion of using a grappling hook suspended
from a plane that could pick up and drop mailbags without
having to land. His brother says the idea might have caught
on except that with the coming of World War II airports
began to proliferate and the concept lost its appeal.

As World War II approached, Richard was generally considered the nation's top authority on gliders. *This Week* magazine called him "the country's outstanding soaring pilot."
The military put this expertise to use, sending Richard to
Italy as a glider consultant. In September of 1943 Richard
was in California to demonstrate a new glider for some military brass. He and five others were towed into the air. Immediately after the tow plane released the experimental glider, it
went into a spin. Unable to pull it out, Richard jumped.
When his parachute failed to open, he plunged to his death.
He was thirty-three. Three others also died; two parachuted
to safety.

His widow never remarried. She lives on an elegant
1,200-acre horse farm in Maryland and is perhaps best-known
as the owner of Kelso, the racehorse who captured the public
fancy, more than $1.7 million in purses, and Horse of the
Year honors from 1960 through 1964. Kelso, a gelding, was
turned into a hunter upon his retirement from racing, carrying his mistress in style across the Maryland countryside as
they followed the hounds. In the summer, Allaire still goes
for long swims in the Bohemia River that runs through her
farm, which is also home to several dozen cats and a dozen
dogs. Her daughter, now Lana Wright, acquired early her
mother's love of horses and keeps hunters on a nearby farm.
Lana was something of a pioneer, being among the first

women ever to compete in the three-day Olympic event for the United States equestrian team.

Her son, christened Richard Jr. but called Kippy, followed his father into aviation. A round, jovial fellow, Kippy's appearance belies a shrewd head for business. He is the family legacy on the board of his father's company, All American Engineering, and owns and runs Summit Aviation, an airfield south of Wilmington. He is among the top Cessna dealers in the country and in 1977 won a trip for himself and his wife to the Paris Air Show for selling Cessna planes. Among his clients in this capacity are the governments of several Latin American countries. An avid outdoorsman, Kippy is an accomplished marlin fisherman and hunter. He dabbles some in real estate development, operating as a silent partner in a Wilmington construction firm and owning a hotel in Haiti and a piece of a project in Providenciales, an island northeast of Haiti in the Turks and Caicos.

Francis G.'s next child after Felix Sr. was Ernest Sr., who after helping the family firm develop gunpowders for World War I, joined his eldest brother, Francis I., in the Ball Grain Explosives Company. Francis set up three companies in the explosives business before starting his brokerage firm. Ernest, like many of his relatives, enjoyed yachting and owned the seventy-four-foot *Edris* as well as the thirty-eight-foot *Ponjola*. He died in 1944 at the age of sixty-three, leaving two sons and a daughter.

The older son was Ernest Jr., dubbed Boodles by some of his cousins. A retired commander in the naval reserve, Ernest saw the World War II assault on Iwo Jima firsthand. He was a beachmaster for the attack, directing small boats with supplies onto the beach and off again with a cargo of wounded. He wrote home at the time, "I haven't even approached doing my share out here," a sentiment based more on emotion than fact. Ernest Jr. retired from the Du Pont Company's employee relations department as an adviser on recreation in 1967 after thirty-eight years with the firm. An unobtrusive, not quite dowdy personality, Ernest, now in his seventies, would look almost sad except for the ever present twinkle in his eyes. He derives his fun from life by quietly helping people on a one-to-one basis, cajoling a drunk he's never seen before, for example, into joining him for a cup of coffee, or consoling a waitress in the hotel who has been caused to be fired by some overly self-important, out-of-sorts customer with a promise of another job and a pension. Or taking a newly elected governor from downstate to dinner because Ernest feels the man is rather lost and tired on his first day in Wilmington. Little things. Each year Ernest has the clowns from the circus flown down from Philadelphia at his own expense to entertain the children at the Alfred I. du Pont Institute.

Ernest's self-effacing, sometimes bumbling style and his propensity for the occasional wee dram have made him the butt of many stories. There is, for instance, the tale of how he was walking his dog one winter Sunday morning and passed a church just as the eleven o'clock service was letting out. He slipped, falling into a ditch by the side of the road. Unable to extricate himself, Ernest was ignored by the parishioners. Finally, the minister approached and asked if he wanted a hand. No, Ernest is alleged to have replied, he'd like a drink. The minister was not an unreasonable man, but considered that first things came first. He helped Ernest out of the ditch and back to his apartment, where in due course the minister produced some bourbon.

Ernest's younger brother is the former sheriff of Cecil County, Maryland. Named after his famous ancestor, the Admiral, Samuel F. Du Pont is the only member of the family today who capitalizes the *D* in Du Pont. In 1973 Sam hired his son Richard as a jailer at $5,500 a year. That same year he requested that his retirement benefits go to his deputies. The next year he was defeated in his bid for re-election. His second wife, Jan, is a good friend of Allaire and has her own racing stable.

Francis G.'s next son was E. Paul. His was a multifaceted

career that began ordinarily enough with the family company, which he left to join his brothers in Ball Grain Explosives. He was also vice-president of Delaware Chemical Engineering Company, another of brother Francis I.'s operations. In 1919 Paul started Du Pont Motors, manufacturing the Du Pont car, a special prize among antique auto buffs today. The Du Pont was a good machine, but the auto business was highly competitive and expensive. Paul had trouble financing his company, and the Depression didn't help matters. Early in 1933 the company went into receivership. In 1930 Paul became involved with the Indian Motorcycle Company. As president of the firm, he enjoyed substantially more success than he did in the automobile venture. From 1935 through 1940 Paul was a partner in his oldest brother's brokerage firm.

Paul was among those who sided with Alfred I. in the suit against Pierre over the purchase of Coleman's stock, a decision he later recanted. In the summer of 1944 Paul wrote several letters to Pierre on the subject. On July 29 he wrote:

". . . Four of my sons are now about past the age I was when all this occurred. They are hardly mature to your and my way of thinking. Had I had a few more years I never would have taken part in the nasty business. You and your brothers were so young when you did such big things; it is not to be wondered at that you had no patience with troublemakers. I am now, at the age of fifty-seven, struggling hard to make success of a manufacturing business and believe me I can appreciate that. The worst of my struggle is it is all my own. I have no associates in the investment who can carry part of the responsibility, and I want my sons to go into the Du Pont Company so I am shying them off.

"I am going through my files to remove any letters from you or your brothers as of that time which may give a bad impression now or later."

Two weeks later he reiterated these sentiments, writing Pierre, ". . . if I had been older I would have had no part in it, for I would not have been moved by Alfred's damnable eloquence."

Paul had six sons. The oldest, E. Paul Jr., was, along with his first cousin Richard, a champion of gliders, believing the skytrain concept had a big future. He had a vested interest in the successful flight of a skytrain prototype to Havana and back in 1938. Paul Jr. worked for the Du Pont Company for twenty-one years, perhaps out of a sense of filial duty as much as anything else. He was an inventor of sorts and was always tinkering with automobiles and motorcycles. He played the violin and dabbled in oil, a venture that caused one of his younger brothers, R. Jacques T., called Jack and named after his great-great-great-grandfather's French mentor, Anne Robert Jacques Turgot, to sue him for $1.5 million.

The suit, which named Chick Laird, a cousin, as co-defendant, claimed that a syndicate formed in 1952 to look for oil and natural gas in the Midwest began costly drilling operations at Paul Jr.'s request without Jack's consent. The whole affair seemed remarkably similar to Eugene III's action against his brother Nicholas. Before it could be settled, Paul Jr. died. The year was 1963 and Paul was fifty-one. The following year, the suit was settled by a dissolution of the syndicate, with Jack paying $160,000 to acquire the syndicate's leases. Jack was also president of an outfit called Ardee Oil Company, which had filed for bankruptcy six years earlier in 1958.

The descendants of Paul Sr. have not made keeping track of who's who in the family any easier. E. Paul Jr., for example, named a son A. Felix IV. Paul Sr.'s youngest son was another Alexis I., called Lex and bearing a striking resemblance to Pierre's father, Lammot, especially since he began cultivating a set of Lammot-like whiskers.

Lex is yet another du Pont taken with aviation. He owns and runs a small airfield in nearby Pennsylvania. In 1973 ambitious plans for a $10 million shopping, office, and recreation complex to be built on two hundred acres adjoining the airport were announced, but to date little has been done. Before he got into the airport business, Lex tried his hand at auto racing, more for fun than profit. In 1960 Lex built an atom bomb shelter at his home, a rather incongruously cautious undertaking for someone who raced cars and flew planes. His passion for antique planes nearly cost him his life when he crashed into an Iowa cornfield with another flying cousin while on an expedition to buy parts for an old plane he had. The two cousins emerged from the plane unscathed.

Francis G. had two daughters, Eleanor and Irene, for both of whom choosing sides in the Pierre-Alfred fight must have been especially wrenching. They wound up on opposite sides, with Eleanor joining most of her brothers on Alfred's side, in part at least because her husband, Robeson Lea Perot, had worked for Alfred. Irene married Pierre's younger brother Irénée, becoming another victim of divided loyalties. Had her hand been called, she undoubtedly would have sided with Pierre, but in her quiet way, she managed to stay pretty much in the background. Her fourth daughter was named after her sister.

Chapter Thirteen

The Underrated Victors

The Victor branch of the family might be called tangential, the product—at least in its relationship to a biography of America's richest family—of a historical and a social quirk. The historical oddity is the tradition of beginning the du Pont story not with the founder of the company but with his father, thereby, perforce, making both the father's sons a part of the tale. The social variant involves marriage custom among the du Ponts, especially in those earlier days. Admiral Samuel Francis Du Pont began this Victor branch tradition with his marriage to a daughter of the original E.I., his uncle. Since then the descendants of the Victor branch have married a number of cousins or—equally within family tradition—promising Du Pont Company executives that ensures the branch's importance despite its relatively modest size.

The Victors, descendants of E.I.'s brother, Victor Marie, whose business fortunes were so uniformly misfortunes, are known within and without the family as "the poor relations." Within the family, the description is faintly facetious. Beginning with Victor Marie's son, Charles I., this branch of the family has produced some talent and some marriages that have assured it at least a measure of success however weighed.

More important in assessing this branch of the family is the fact that Victor Marie might reasonably be called the first American du Pont. Not only was he the first in the family to see the United States; he was also the first to call America home in a more than geographical sense. Had he but money, he would undoubtedly have been a first-rate diplomat, a field for which he demonstrated far greater ability than he did for business.

This first Victor, as different from his younger brother E.I. as is the flirt from the matron, has perhaps been underrated by those assessing his contributions to the du Pont family of today. Those contributions are unquestionably less tangible than those of Victor's brother, but they are not inconsequential. While it is true that the original Pierre S. du Pont, Victor's father, had developed important American contacts like Thomas Jefferson and Ben Franklin, Victor alone had actually lived in the United States before 1800, and his connections were broader and less formal, quite likely to be more useful on a day-to-day basis. If his shortcomings as a businessman were a large drain on his brother and the Du Pont Company during Victor's latter years, Victor was more help to the Du Pont Company in its infancy than he is usually given credit for. It was his social contacts who proved invaluable as business contacts for his brother.

Victor was tall, handsome, and gallant. The discipline his father tried so hard to instill never really took. Victor was at best an erratic scholar as a youth, and although he displayed a flair for charming people and an ability for evaluating a given situation that impressed even his father, too often the man chose the role of hedonist over that of drone. In 1786, at the age of nineteen, he traveled about France allegedly working for his father but frequently writing him with disarming frankness about losing too much at cards or having his work delayed by the temptations of a local carnival. His father was furious. Victor was contrite but unchanging.

In 1787 Victor managed to land a position as secretary to the U.S. minister from France. Helped by some letters of introduction from his father, Victor made something of a social splash in America and spent two essentially fat, happy years before returning to France late in 1789 as the French Revolution churned. Both his father and his father's influential friends soon determined that Victor was too outspoken to remain safely in France, and some money was scraped together to return him to the United States with a promise from the minister that should a job open up, Victor could have it. Just a few months after he finally landed a post, Victor and the minister sailed for France.

It was 1793, and for ten years Gabrielle Joséphine de La Fite de Pelleport had been an orphan. Her father, the marquis de Pelleport, had been captain of the Swiss Guard attending the Comte d'Artois, youngest brother of Louis XVI. Came the Revolution, and Gabrielle was forced to abandon whatever hope she may have held of making a marriage fully worthy of her station. This charming, literate woman and Victor came together through the good offices of a mutual acquaintance and were soon talking love. There were two drawbacks to marriage. One, Victor was a gendarme and as such might any day be called upon to arrest a family member or a friend suspected of anti-Revolutionary activities or thoughts. It was a position neither Gabrielle nor Victor found comfortable. Victor took care of that problem by rubbing spinach juice on his face and feigning an illness that became so severe and prolonged he was finally allowed to resign. His mock illness began on the day Marie Antoinette was beheaded. The second problem was Gabrielle's determination to be married by a priest, a custom upon which the Revolution frowned at the time. Victor managed to find a willing curé, and that problem was taken care of with a secret church wedding followed several weeks later by a more conspicuous, if less satisfying, ceremony performed by a petty municipal officer.

Soon the newlyweds were headed west again, Victor having been appointed secretary of the French legation to the United States. Upon arriving in Philadelphia, the French minister found the consul in Charleston, South Carolina, guilty of incompetence and immediately dispatched Victor to take over. Although Gabrielle never became Americanized to the extent Victor did, the next three years in Charleston were happy ones. In 1798 Victor was named consul general to the United States and headed north to present his credentials to President Adams. The timing was inelegant. Adams was unamused by several recent actions of the French Government and refused to accept Victor's credentials.

So the Victor family boarded the first ship it could find headed for France, where Victor tried to talk his father out of his plan to emigrate to the United States, telling Papa that President Adams "detests you personally." Papa was not to be dissuaded, and most of the rest of the du Pont rise to fame and wealth is an oft-told story.

Still, in light of the rather complete Americanization of the du Ponts, it is interesting to contrast Victor with both his wife and his brother. From Paris, whither he had gone to raise additional capital for his father's ambitious enterprises in 1801, Victor writes his wife: "Here I eat, I work, I am weary, I sleep—but I live only in America . . . because it is the only country that suits me—where I am at home." That was an expression of sentiment uniquely Victor's. Neither his wife nor his brother ever quite felt the same way. His wife, bright and witty, was readily accepted as a desired addition to society wherever the family lived, but she was not pioneer stock and, especially after a sojourn in the wilds of upper New York State, harbored a quiet longing to return to France. Eleuthère Irénée never did come close to mastering English, and had the demands of his business ever let up sufficiently to allow it, he, too, would have welcomed a visit home to France.

While history has made something of a failure out of Victor, the difference, as to degree of success, at least, between him and his brother is undoubtedly exaggerated with hindsight. For one thing, Victor's biggest disaster—his first—was not entirely his fault. Drafts on the French Government payable to Victor's firm simply weren't honored despite their legitimacy and the connections of Victor's father. Napoleon would not pay for the profligacy of his brother Jérôme, who borrowed huge sums from Victor's firm while in the United States. The firm was caught in the middle. Not to loan the funds to Jerome might have endangered its French business just as easily as loaning them proved costly. But despite these setbacks, Victor might have survived in an era of modern communications equipment, for just a few months after Victor closed up shop due to a shortage of cash, word came through that Talleyrand had agreed to loan him 300,000 francs.

The upstate New York interlude seems in retrospect as much an effort to get away from it all and make a fresh start as it was a carefully reasoned, practical business decision. The image of the marquis's daughter, Gabrielle, giving the children piano lessons while wild-looking Indians gaped in the window is not an image one expects to last. Nonetheless, it was Victor's success, not his failure, that led eventually to his leaving New York. He had been sent there by a man named Church, who considered himself the number-one man. Victor's popularity and success led to friction with Church. In 1809 Victor finally heeded his brother's long, continuous plea and joined him on the Brandywine. E.I. helped set Victor up in a woolen mill that never really gained a sound financial footing. The War of 1812 may have saved the powder company for its future destiny, but it simply postponed the inevitable where the woolen mill was concerned. By this time, Victor's son, Charles I. du Pont, was running the mill operation while his father handled the customer relations and sales chores.

In 1815 Victor was elected to the state legislature, the first of a long line of du Ponts to dabble in politics. His election held a special meaning for him in that it was recognition of his U.S. citizenship. Gossip about foreigners on the Brandywine had always been especially hard for Victor to digest. As the years went by, the woolen mill became a real financial burden for the Du Pont Company and E.I., but although Victor repeatedly offered to get out of the cloth business, his brother would have none of it. Perhaps the clearest indication that Victor may not have been quite the inept businessman that history tends to credit him with being is the fact that in the next to last year of his life, 1826, he was named a director of the Bank of the United States, an institution that was to become better-known as the Federal Reserve System.

The four children he left behind when he died were all dramatically different. The eldest, Amelia, was a rather pathetic figure, sweet, to be sure, but with little else to recommend her. Still, she managed to land a husband only to find he was already married under another name back in England. His secret found out, the man fled. The youngest, Julia, had essentially but one claim to fame: She is widely conceded to have been the prettiest du Pont woman ever. Between their two daughters, Victor and Gabrielle had two sons. Charles stayed home and ran the woolen mill. Samuel Francis left the Brandywine and became famous.

Samuel Francis was not yet thirteen when he wrote his mother in 1816, "*J'espère un jour de faire honneur à ma patrie.*" Just a month earlier he had been given an appointment as a midshipman in the Naval Academy, an occasion that had caused Thomas Jefferson to predict in a letter to Samuel Francis' grandfather that the boy might one day be an admiral. The boy was to make of Jefferson a prophet.

Ten years and several ocean voyages came and went. The boy became a lieutenant. In 1829 he faced real danger for the first time when a squall knocked his ship over on its side far enough so that the lee guns were under water. A sister ship was lost in the same squall with all hands. Lieutenant Du Pont wrote home that he was glad to find out he could keep both his nerve and his head in a crisis. The young lieutenant made a rather dashing figure ashore and was not infrequently the object of matrimonial speculation. He broke one engagement. A Baltimore heiress lost appeal for him when her mother behaved in a manner that convinced the future admiral she thought of naval officers as just a cut above other sea creatures—perhaps. Before too long, Samuel Francis began spending more and more time with Sophie Madeleine du Pont, his well-educated, sharp-eyed, articulate first cousin. They were married in June of 1833, and for the next thirty-two years, Sophie became the shore eyes and ears for her seabound husband, his chief adviser and confidante. She would read everything there was about the Navy, ships, sailing, and U.S. and world affairs, keeping her husband up to date. Their correspondence is a study in nineteenth-century elegant literacy.

Meanwhile, Samuel Francis continued to climb the Navy hierarchy, making commander in 1841 and captain in 1855. He was a firm believer in rank and privilege with high standards of probity and fairness he fully expected to find in others. Perhaps his biggest flaw was a thin skin. He was quick to bristle at injustice, particularly if it was aimed his way, and often gave an impression of arrogance in public that may have been more nearly personal discomfort. As a commander, Samuel Francis saw his only pre-Civil War fighting while on the West Coast during the Mexican War. He was good at it and got useful experience in the technique and tactics of blockading. Twice he was offered the superintendency of the Naval Academy, declining both times. Among his more controversial activities was service on the Naval Efficiency Board of 1855, whose recommendations resulted in the retiring or furloughing of 52 per cent of the captains, 40 per cent of the commanders, and 26 per cent of the lieutenants in the Navy, causing many waves and much ill will.

Among the more impressive plumage in his cap was command of the *Minnesota*, one of five steam frigates that ushered in a new age on the sea. It was the *Minnesota* that took William B. Reed to China to negotiate a new trade treaty in 1857. Captain Du Pont was becoming famous. In 1860 the Secretary of State chose Du Pont as official escort for the first Japanese embassy to the United States while it made a three-month tour. Samuel Francis was just about ready to take command of the Philadelphia Navy Yard, a post from which he figured to retire from the Navy eventually, when the Civil War made that subtle shift from whispered possibility to virtual sure thing. Du Pont was quick to pledge his allegiance to the Union and urge all his friends to do likewise. Long an important naval figure in Washington, Du Pont became the senior member of a board charged with studying the blockade problem. The board made a number of well-received recommendations, and then the time for study was over, the time for action at hand.

Samuel Francis' victory at Port Royal discussed in an earlier chapter was unquestionably the zenith of his career. The tactics of his fleet had been masterful, and the victory was the first proof that a naval force could mount a successful attack on a land-based defensive position. Dramatic as the Port Royal conquest was, it satisfied the public's exaggerated expectations of Union triumphs but briefly. Samuel Francis, by now an admiral, was having some supply problems, especially with the coal needed to run his steam ships, and his activities were partially curtailed. The situation at Charleston was unique. Blockading was unusually difficult and the risk of provoking an incident with the French or the British by boarding a wrong ship was greater than elsewhere. The inevitable result was some running of the blockade. The Admiral didn't seem to care, but the Union's pride was hurt.

A series of complex events led up to the fateful Charleston attack and failure. The Admiral became a scapegoat and spent a miserable couple of years at home nursing his wounded dignity. Fortunately his wife had awakened a certain religious fervor in her husband, who had been raised a nominal Protestant as a sort of compromise between his Catholic mother and skeptical father. The Admiral became a strong supporter of Christ Church, the family's Episcopal house of worship. However, it is probably safe to say that the Admiral was not truly at peace with himself until the last three months of his life, during which time he served, at the insistence of Admiral Farragut, on a naval board recommending advancement for officers with outstanding service records in the Civil War. The board was convened in March. The

Admiral caught a spring cold, complications set in, and he died in June.

In some ways, Admiral Du Pont is to the Victor branch of the family what Lammot's son Pierre is to the descendants of Eleuthère Irénée. The star of the show. The Admiral was the only du Pont in the nineteenth century to achieve a national, perhaps even international, reputation. If the end of his career was beclouded by the Charleston failure, he was nonetheless a national hero to many. Full vindication of his role at Charleston eluded him during his lifetime, but his descendants in the Victor branch may now bask in their illustrious ancestor's reflected glory, which is today untarnished thanks to several official inquiries and the publication of the Admiral's correspondence, all leading to the conclusion that the Admiral was asked to accomplish an impossible task that wasn't worth the price.

The most incontrovertibly successful member of the Victor branch was probably Charles I.'s first son, also named Victor, who grew up to be a lawyer. He was admitted to the Delaware bar in 1849 and developed the largest practice in the state. Not the least of his clients was the Du Pont Company. Old Boss Henry depended on Victor's legal judgment heavily and undoubtedly paid well for it. Victor rarely appeared in court, acting mainly as a legal adviser to businesses, but his abilities were well recognized, and more than once he was appointed by the governor as chancellor ad litem—a sort of ad hoc civil judge—because of his ability to handle difficult cases. "He was a complete master of the common law, a specialist without a peer in property law, a legal administrator of genius in business, and a man of sensitive honor, more than probity, in all transactions and relations," said Delaware's Chancellor Nicholson of Victor. *Pro bono publico* had a special meaning for Victor, who, despite the largest practice in the state, always found time for performing unpaid services. Individuals needing help could count on him, and the welfare of the public was always among his foremost concerns. All this made

Victor a prime target of those seeking solid candidates for public life, but Victor wasn't interested. He was influential enough in Democratic politics, but whenever anyone began to send up trial balloons about the possibility of his running for public office—the U. S. Senate, say, or the governor's mansion—he quickly let the air out with a polite but firm no-thank-you.

It is interesting that Delaware's current governor, Pierre S. du Pont IV, who graduated from Harvard Law School, is sometimes billed as the family's first lawyer. The son of Francis I. (Nicky) du Pont II is being touted in some family quarters as the first du Pont to be a practicing lawyer. Are they disowning the Victor branch of the family or are they simply ignorant of their own history?

Victor's eldest son, Victor Jr., also had a quietly distinguished career. He was trained as an engineer, and in 1872 went to work for a railroad company. Two years later a financial panic caused the work on the railroad to be suspended indefinitely. Then Victor Jr. fell seriously ill, and it wasn't until 1877 that he was able to go back to work again, this time in a newsprint paper mill owned by the Du Pont Company in Louisville, Kentucky. He stayed until 1890, most of the time as mill superintendent. Moving back to Wilmington, Victor Jr. became manager of Du Pont's real estate department and a vice-president and director of the company. Like so many of his relatives, Victor Jr. was a shy man who studiously avoided the limelight. He liked to read and tell stories. He was possessed of a charm inherent in so many of the Victor branch. When he died in 1911, he left one child, a son named, of course, Victor.

Helping to cement the Victor branch's ties to the du Pont family was the original Victor Marie's granddaughter Amelia, who married the first Eugene, the man who ran the company after Boss Henry's death. Eugene was, remember, the oldest son of Alexis I. du Pont. Alexis was the youngest son of E.I., the company founder.

Amelia's older brother Victor, the lawyer, had ten children, including six daughters. One of them, May Lammot, will be remembered as the woman who married the Boss's son, William. After their divorce, she remarried a lawyer in her father's law office named Willard Saulsbury. Saulsbury was an independent sort. His father and his uncle had both held U. S. Senate seats from Delaware, and Saulsbury would himself in 1912. He did not endear himself to the family when in 1906 after Coleman's successful campaign on Colonel Henry's behalf to defeat Gas Addicks for a Senate seat, Saulsbury allowed that the difference between Addicks and Coleman was that Addicks did not know how to buy votes like a gentleman. Coleman was not amused, but Saulsbury didn't much care. He used to refer to his in-laws as "that goddamned tribe."

May's sister Ethel married Hamilton Barksdale, perhaps the top non-du Pont executive in the company. Barksdale was the man Francis G. and the other older partners had chosen to open negotiations with Laflin & Rand in 1902 when the possibility of selling the family firm was being seriously considered. Ethel's daughter Greta followed her mother's lead, marrying F. Donaldson Brown, a protégé of Pierre's right-hand man, John J. Raskob. Brown rose to become a member of both the finance and executive committees at Du Pont. Greta's daughter, also named Greta, deviated only slightly from the tradition, marrying Rodney M. Layton, a partner in Wilmington's most prestigious law firm, Richards, Layton and Finger.

Another sister of May, Alice, married her distant cousin, T. Coleman du Pont. Known as Elsie within the family, Alice was in many respects the woman behind the great man. She alone had the ability to soothe Coleman's frazzled nerves and frequently gave him wise counsel. A cousin once described her as having "all the physical appeal of a Greta Garbo and the goodness of a saint." Being married to Coleman undoubtedly required both qualities in large measure.

A fourth sister, Renée, married LeRoy Harvey, a former mayor of Wilmington. She had three daughters and a son, Edmund H. Harvey, who was well known in Delaware for his work in the area of conservation. A non-profit firm he headed, Delaware Wildlands, is one of Delaware's largest private landholders. Renée's oldest daughter, Alice, married William S. Potter, another of Wilmington's top lawyers and long a leading figure in the state's Democratic Party. They had three daughters. The oldest, Polly, was married to a rising Hercules executive, William L. Kitchell II, who died early in 1978. The youngest married Peter M. Sieglaff, who joined his father-in-law's law firm.

The original Victor Marie did not name a son Victor, but from his grandson Victor—son of Charles I.—the line extends unbroken through six generations. Back in the middle 1930s, *Fortune* magazine ran a series of articles on the du Pont family and company and perpetrated the following sentence upon an unsuspecting readership: "His son, the fourth Victor, has the distinction of being the poorest of all the du Ponts." The magazine said the fourth Victor's net worth was estimated at about $1 million, a figure that sounds suspiciously as if it were pulled from a hat. It is virtually certain that Victor was not the poorest du Pont at that time and very unlikely that any of his descendants qualifies for that title today.

The distinction that particular Victor probably does hold title to is Mr. Conviviality. *Fortune* tells the story about how he was once picked up by the Wilmington police and taken to headquarters, where the desk sergeant is alleged to have exclaimed, "My God! Take him home. It's a du Pont!" Victor, the grandson of lawyer Victor, would take a drink. There is a story in Wilmington that a considerate madam at one of the local rest and recreation houses used to take care of him when he became less than ambulatory, calling home and telling whoever answered to come and get him.

But the best story about this Victor involves some of his dowager cousins. These gossipy ladies were riding into town one afternoon when they saw Victor coming out of a local pub with a rather tough reputation as an Irish workers' saloon. The horrified women could hardly wait to tell his father, and at a social function soon thereafter, they approached the elder Victor while one acted as spokesman, couching her words in a transparently hypocritical sympathy. She said they hated to have to tell him this; they knew he would find it hard to believe; but they felt he should know. They had seen his son coming out of the Columbus Inn and you know what kind of a place that is! Old Vic didn't bat an eye. "Well," he told the ladies, "you wouldn't want him to stay in there all day long, would you?" And he turned away to another conversation.

Vic, the son, was not without a sense of humor. He had a job he wasn't too crazy about and one day he popped into his Uncle Coleman's office at the Du Pont Company, announcing that he thought he might like another job. Coleman inquired as to what sort of a job he had in mind, and Victor knew just the thing he'd like. "How about one of those son-in-law jobs?" he asked.

Victor had two sons—Vic Jr. and Charles E.—and a daughter, Emily. The two men have more or less abandoned Wilmington. Victor Jr. lives in Virginia, playing the gentleman farmer role, and Charles after a number of years in California has moved to Jackson Hole, Wyoming. Emily stayed in Wilmington, and the city is most grateful. She is spoken of both within and without the family with affection and respect, an elegant, generous, concerned woman with interests that range from art to animals. Emily may not be in a league with Byron Crazy Horse Justin Case when it comes to quaint names, but thanks to her two marriages, she does bear the name Emily du Pont Smith du Pont. Her second husband was Henry B. du Pont, Jr., the only child of one of Pierre's younger brothers.

Emily's accomplishments are perhaps more modest than H.B.'s, but her personal involvement and dedication have been total. She is or has been chairman of the Delaware Arts Museum, president of the Wilmington Society of Fine Arts, and president of the state SPCA. She has been a strong supporter of the Delaware Historical Society, whose executive director, Dale Fields, has frequently called her his most valued ally. A leading member of the Wilmington Garden Club and various environmental groups, Emily has tried to fit a humanism into these efforts by relating them to the needs of the area's underprivileged. She talks about working to obtain government funds to turn vacant lots in downtown Wilmington into vegetable gardens. She believes that the equal opportunity ideal of the country depends for whatever success it is to enjoy upon the good health and improved education of all children. She is a big booster of neighborhood health clinics and recreation centers, convinced that idleness, the absence of organized extracurricular activities, is a major contributor to delinquency.

What makes Emily special in the minds of the family and the Wilmington community at large is not, however, her ideas on social progress or even her contributions toward that end. It is her infectious enthusiasm coupled with a dignity and a genuine concern that goes beyond a sense of duty or a feeling of noblesse oblige. She brings a grace and a confidence to the projects she undertakes that inspires hope, even optimism. She is special, to put it as simply as possible, because being in her presence makes people feel good.

The Victor branch of the family is unquestionably the most maligned both within and without the family. It is almost as if this branch has just never been able to shake the stigma of failure put upon it by the original Victor Marie. The truth is that this branch has produced as many persons of substance relative to its size as most branches and no more fools than its share.

Chapter Fourteen

The In-Laws

In perhaps no other great American family have in-laws played as important a role as in the du Pont family. The first name that comes to mind in considering du Pont in-laws today is Crawford H. Greenewalt, who married Irénée du Pont's daughter Margaretta and was president of the Du Pont Company from 1948 to 1963, longer than anyone in this century. But in-laws have influenced family affairs virtually since the family arrived in the United States from France in 1800.

Among the earliest of these was James Antoine Bidermann, son of the Swiss banker who invested in the original Pierre du Pont's initial American enterprise. The father became concerned about his investment and sent his son over shortly after the War of 1812 to investigate. Antoine was but twenty-four; yet his grasp of business affairs was already firm. Amid the morass of debt, bickering, and uncertainty he found surrounding the powder mills of E. I. du Pont, Antoine quickly spotted potential—not to mention a desirable bride in E.I.'s daughter Evelina. Bidermann's reassurances to his father helped calm the most important of the du Ponts' restless investors, and when E.I. died, Bidermann stepped in to hold the business together until E.I.'s oldest son was ready to take over. Those were tenuous times for the infant Du Pont Company, and without Bidermann's precocious abilities, the company might have come to a premature end.

From that time forward, in-laws have played vital parts in the growth of the company and the stature of the family. Victor du Pont's son Charles, for example, married twice, each time into one of Delaware's most socially prominent families, adding social acceptability to the family's already growing business reputation. The most valuable contribution of the in-laws collectively has without question been to the Du Pont Company, but du Pont in-laws have been senators, governors, mayors, bishops, university presidents, and a President's son. There is a story told about the family's 150th anniversary celebration for which Irénée Sr. gave a dinner dance. In the receiving line at Granogue, Irénée's Wilmington home, a young man introduced himself to Irénée as William Shakespeare, which just happened to be his name. Another in-law is reputedly the record holder when it comes to individuals suing the Internal Revenue Service over taxes. According to one 1960s Harvard Law School graduate, who himself became an in-law, a class actually studies the cases of J. Simpson Dean, who married one of Pierre's nieces and whose hobby, or at least one of them, became private war with the IRS.

Dean cut quite a dashing figure in his youth. He was twice captain of the Princeton golf team and in 1921 won the intercollegiate championship. His son says Dean could undoubtedly have become a professional golfer but points out that in those days, the profession was not nearly so lucrative as it has grown. Dean developed an ardent interest in horses, both as racing animals and as a means of transport while pursuing the wily fox. Although he was not a stylish rider, he was always able to stay aboard and enjoyed the sport and the breeding of fox hounds. He was a co-founder of Delaware Park, reputedly among the finest race tracks in the country from both a spectator's and a horse owner's point of view. He was joined in this effort by another in-law, Donald P. Ross, who had married the sister of Dean's wife; Alfred E. Bissell, yet another in-law; William du Pont, Jr.; and a man named Baker. Dean became the track's second president. He also started a racing stable, which Ross eventually took over. In recent years racing has held little interest for Dean, who despite his role in its founding, hasn't been to Delaware Park more than a handful of times since 1970.

The in-law game can get rather complicated. For example, J. H. Tyler McConnell married Jean Ellen du Pont, William du Pont, Jr.'s daughter, by whom McConnell had four children, including a daughter, Susan. McConnell remarried, and the brother of his second wife married Susan, all of which makes for some rather confusing relationships.

If Franklin D. Roosevelt, Jr., George Randolph Scott, and Margaret Osborne are the most famous du Pont in-laws—although none of them lasted very long—the most distinguished, at least among those whose careers were outside the Du Pont Company, may be Colgate Darden, Jr., a Virginian who married Irénée's daughter Constance and who has been at various times a congressman, Virginia's governor, and president of the University of Virginia.

Du Pont in-laws have been accused of "out-Romaning Caesar," becoming more conscious of the du Pont traditions and heritage than their spouses, on the one hand, and on the other, they have been accused of being du Ponts when it suits them, innocent bystanders when it doesn't. As usual in such cases, the truth lies somewhere in between. One in-law who could not have been overly impressed by the fact he was marrying a du Pont is Barron U. Kidd, a wealthy Texan who married the sister of Pete du Pont, Delaware's current governor. Tales, perhaps apocryphal, about the Texas guests at the wedding abound. One has it that Barron's ushers flew up to Wilmington in their private plane, bringing their own caddies in the event a golf match was arranged. Another has a Texas house guest admiring his host's split rail fence and inquiring if it wouldn't be too rude to ask the fence's cost. The host replied that it was pretty expensive, about $15 a panel (perhaps eight feet in length), whereupon the guest asked if his host knew where he might find a few miles of it. Not long ago during a visit to Washington, Barron's children expressed a hunger for hamburgers, and Barron sent them off in the chauffeur-driven limousine to McDonald's. Another in-law unawed by the du Ponts was Willard Saulsbury. Saulsbury's family had arrived in Delaware before the du Ponts, and despite the fact that he practiced law out of his new father-in-law's offices, he paid the du Ponts rather less respect than they were accustomed to.

While politicians—like T. Coleman's son-in-law, C. Douglass Buck, twice governor of Delaware, and LeRoy Harvey, who was mayor of Wilmington and married May du Pont's sister Renée—and stockbrokers—like William Winder Laird, who married Pierre's sister Mary, and Hollyday Meeds, another T. Coleman son-in-law—were important enough figures to stand on their own without du Pont support, a large majority of the most influential in-laws worked for the Du Pont Company. Many of them were already well established before their marriages.

Among the ablest in this category was Hamilton M. Barksdale, who married another May du Pont sister, Ethel. It was he of whom the du Ponts thought so highly they nearly made him acting president in 1902 after Eugene's death. He had been smart enough to realize his acceptance would place him in the middle of a potentially explosive family argument and had declined.

At the time, Barksdale was president of the Eastern Dynamite Company, a holding firm formed in 1895 by the merger of three dynamite producers, Repauno Chemical Company, Hercules Powder Company, and Atlantic Dynamite Company. He joined the Du Pont Company when the three young cousins took over, and in 1906 became a vice-president. He was a major contributor to the systematic approach to management adopted by Du Pont and widely copied throughout American industry, playing a key role in the creation of the executive committee, which was one of the first of its kind. From 1902 through 1914 he was in charge of co-ordinating the many newly acquired businesses of the company and established the development department to explore potential acquisitions, reduce company dependence on outside sources of supply, and discover new outlets for products. In the 1911 executive reorganization, Barksdale alone of the executive committee members retained any routine administrative duties. The concept behind the new setup was mainly Coleman's and envisioned the seasoned managers moving up to a policy and long-range planning capacity while delegating the daily operation of the company to the upcoming younger generation. Coleman had wanted to include Barksdale in this group, but Barksdale had pleaded for a chance to run the operations as general manager, and Pierre had taken his side, feeling that Irénée, his younger brother, who would become Barksdale's assistant general manager, wasn't yet ready to run things and would receive valuable training from Barksdale.

Unfortunately, Barksdale had one major weakness, which Coleman had foreseen and Pierre had overlooked. Barksdale could not constitutionally delegate authority and insisted on taking care himself of even minor matters. This shortcoming meant that the young managers under him were not receiving their baptism by fire. A few years later, Coleman, now with Pierre's support, abolished the title of general manager and kicked Barksdale upstairs over his strong protests. Barksdale never did fully understand Pierre's and Coleman's attitude toward him. He died in 1918.

He left behind a son-in-law, thereby also a du Pont in-law, whose contributions to Du Pont and to General Motors in the early days of Du Pont control were perhaps more pedestrian than Barksdale's, but were nonetheless of substantial significance. F. Donaldson Brown, who married Barksdale's daughter Greta, was a financial man and spent his formative business years working with John J. Raskob, the financial wizard Pierre brought with him from Ohio when he returned to the Du Pont Company in 1902. If Raskob was a genius at putting together deals, Brown excelled at developing internal financial procedures, such as uniform accounting. In 1912 Brown devised the return on investment formula still used by Du Pont, with modifications, for measuring the success of an investment. He went to work for General Motors in 1921, carrying through the enlarging and reorganizing of GM's financial offices already begun the previous year by Raskob. In 1924 he joined an enlarged GM executive committee. Working with Alfred Sloan, Pierre's replacement as president of GM, Brown helped devise a set of internal controls and long-range forecasting procedures vital to the practical management of such a vast corporate giant as GM was rapidly becoming.

Three Carpenters also made invaluable contributions to the business of Du Pont. R. R. M. Carpenter, who married Pierre's youngest sister, was one. Walter S. Carpenter, his brother, who married a governess to Irénée's children, was another. As brother of an in-law, Walter Carpenter may not meet strict requirements as an in-law, but, excepting perhaps John Raskob, no man outside the family has ever been more intimately associated with the du Ponts or done more to further their fortunes. Adding some weight to the arguments for his inclusion here is the fact that two sons of Walter married du Ponts. One son, W. Samuel III, was the third Carpenter to make a major contribution to Du Pont.

Sam Carpenter joined the Du Pont Company in 1938, the year he married E. Murton du Pont. He was, one close friend speculates, a man with special motivation, having married a woman with more money than he and being the son of a man who in three years would become the first non-du Pont ever to be president of the family company. Rising rapidly from his initial position as an industrial engineer, Carpenter became the international department's first general manager when the department was elevated to departmental status in 1958. Under Carpenter, the international business of Du Pont flourished beyond company hopes. Some said he possessed the brilliance to run the company but didn't want to play the corporate politics necessary to get to the top. He retired from the company in 1967, and a month later was elected to its board of directors.

Walter's brother, known as Ruly, was among the handful

of men closest to Pierre in the years leading up to and through World War I. While Pierre, and later his younger brother Lammot, kept an eye on him, it was Ruly who headed the company's development department during the period of the company's most rapid expansion. When Pierre was negotiating with Coleman over the purchase of the latter's stock in the company, Ruly was in on the ground floor along with Pierre's two brothers and Raskob. In the final arrangement, Ruly was the fifth largest participant, ahead of Raskob but slightly behind his cousin-in-law A. Felix du Pont. His relationship to Pierre was almost that of son to father. In early December of 1910 Ruly wrote Pierre, addressing him as "Dad" and asking for Pierre's opinion on Ruly's business shortcomings. Ruly already knew of two, he said, citing lack of ambition and appreciation. As a Christmas present, Ruly requested advice from Pierre on this subject each year for the next ten so that he could improve 10 per cent a year. Five years later, in another letter, Ruly thanked Pierre for a raise, promising to continue working for the company despite some feelings he might like to take it easy if he could afford it. Like many of his in-laws, Carpenter was outraged by the federal government's attitude toward Du Pont in the early stages of United States entry into World War I. Du Pont was being criticized for making profits on its war business and as early as 1916 Carpenter suggested that "we write off every pound of military powder capacity we have and consider that we will secure no more of this business."

Ruly's business abilities and perceptions continued to grow. As head of the development department, he voiced some strong skepticism about the advisability of Du Pont's making its initial investment in General Motors, arguing that surely there were other attractive opportunities around better suited to Du Pont's particular skills and expertise, but when it came time to vote, he voted for the investment. When Will Durant, the volatile founder of GM, noted his pleasure with the performance of some Du Pont personnel working on

GM's behalf and asked that two of the men be transferred to GM's New York offices, Carpenter shrewdly pointed out to Pierre that a good part of the reason why these men were so effective was the organization behind them. He likened Durant's request to that of a man who had heard a good orchestra and asked its leader to come and play for him individually. Ruly also played an important role in two other transactions vitally affecting the du Ponts. The first was the setting up of Delaware Realty and Investment Company, the vehicle through which Pierre transferred the bulk of his wealth to his brothers, sisters, and their families in return for an annuity of $900,000. The second was developing the mechanism by which Du Pont sold a vast block of its GM holdings back to GM for distribution to its executives, a transaction that lowered Du Pont's interest in GM from 38 to 23 per cent.

Ruly's younger brother, Walter, grew to become one of the most respected businessmen in the annals of American industrial history. In him were combined a rare acumen, a remarkable memory, and the soft-spoken qualities of a true gentleman. Harold Brayman, hired by Carpenter to build a public relations department at Du Pont, recalls that the 8 A.M. Du Pont starting time was at first hard for him to meet as a former newspaperman who had worked late hours. He hadn't been with Du Pont very long when he came into his office nearer 9 than 8 A.M. one morning. His secretary informed him that Mr. Carpenter had called and asked his call be returned. Brayman got on the phone, answered a relatively simple question for Carpenter, and thought no more of the incident. The next week the incident was repeated. When it happened again, the third week, Brayman began to get a message. Carpenter called a fourth time, at 8:05 A.M., and Brayman was there to take the call. The company's boss had not only made his point but had also learned something about an employee's ability to take a hint.

Brayman says only Pierre rivaled Carpenter in his consideration of those with whom he worked, a trait that bred strong loyalty to them both. The stories of Carpenter's thoughtfulness are legion. Once Pierre hosted a summer's night musical performance at Longwood's outdoor theater, and a car drove in late, after the performance had already begun. A man next to Pierre suggested it might be Carpenter. Just then, the car's lights went out, and Pierre nodded affirmatively. "That's Walter, all right," he said. "Who else would worry about his car's headlights distracting the audience?"

Although no rough edges ever betrayed the fact, Carpenter never finished college. He left Cornell in his senior year to go to Chile for the Du Pont Company and explore the best methods for utilizing the vast nitrate deposits there. As World War I approached, Carpenter went to work with his older brother to determine how Du Pont's huge new capacity for producing smokeless powder could best be used once the war ended. As it became clear that the war would last long enough for Du Pont to build large retained earnings, the Carpenters expanded their investigations to include any and all related businesses in which Du Pont's expertise and production facilities might be put to use. Celluloid was one of the first products looked at, and after some developmental work done at Du Pont's experimental station and an investigation conducted by Walter Carpenter, the company decided to buy "a going concern" in the Celluloid field, finally purchasing the Arlington Company for more than $5 million. Lammot du Pont, Pierre's younger brother, was made president of the company.

Reporting to the executive committee every two weeks, Walter Carpenter began in 1916 in-depth studies of potential future Du Pont businesses. While the executive committee instructed the development department to concentrate its efforts on industries allied to those in which Du Pont already had a stake, by 1917 it was apparent that the enormous human, financial, and organizational resources the company had developed in the course of filling wartime orders might make it advisable to explore other fields as well. The development department's executive committee mandate was two-fold: to determine what industries Du Pont ought to enter into, and, once that decision was made, how best the company might enter them, by purchasing another company, for example, or starting a division of its own.

Carpenter and Pierre disagreed on one field, the dye business, which before the war had been dominated by the Germans. Both the textile industry and the government wanted an American alternative to reliance on Germany after the war for dyes, and Pierre felt Du Pont could handle the job. Carpenter and others were concerned that Du Pont would be unable to compete profitably with the Germans after the war. Hindsight proves both sides were right. Dyes proved to be the toughest of all Du Pont's new projects in which to make a profit, and the company spent millions of dollars before turning the corner. But once the corner was turned, the dye business became a major contributor to Du Pont profitability.

In 1921 Carpenter was made treasurer of Du Pont. Five years later he became Du Pont's financial vice-president. When in 1928 Pierre stepped down as chairman of General Motors, he turned the oversight of Du Pont's GM interests to his younger brother Lammot and Carpenter. In a three-part series on Du Pont, company and family, in the mid-thirties, *Fortune* magazine speculated that Pierre's nephew, Henry B. du Pont, Jr., was being groomed to succeed his Uncle Lammot as the next president of the company. It was still, apparently, inconceivable to the outside world that the company might choose a president from outside the family.

In 1941 Lammot stepped up to chairman of the board, and Walter Carpenter was named president, the first non-du Pont ever to hold that title. It was a choice the family would have little cause to regret. For the next two decades and more, perhaps no name in American business commanded greater respect, especially among his peers. The story of how Du Pont became involved in the Manhattan Project to build the atomic bomb illustrates both Carpenter's attitude about the

role the company ought to have taken and the measure of
acceptance that attitude received at Du Pont.

Leslie R. Groves, who was in charge of the project, tells the
story in his book, *Now It Can Be Told*. On October 30, 1942,
Groves called Willis Harrington at Du Pont and asked him
to come to Washington. Harrington went, taking with him
C. L. Stine, head of Du Pont's experimental station. Groves
outlined the project and asked for Du Pont's help. The initial
reaction in Wilmington was one of reluctance and skepticism. The project was out of Du Pont's field, represented substantial dangers with no assurance of success, and Du Pont already had all the work it could handle. Carpenter, however,
became convinced that the project needed doing and that if
the United States didn't do it, Germany or Japan might get
there first. The executive committee was persuaded. At the
next board of directors meeting, the members sat down
around the huge conference table, a stack of papers in front
of each place, turned face down. In his quiet voice, Carpenter
explained the nature of the undertaking. When he finished,
he told the directors they could look at the papers in front of
them, which explained the project in more detail, before voting. Not one of them did so, before or after the vote, which
approved Du Pont participation.

It was a huge undertaking. Spending was authorized at a
total of $2.3 billion for the project, which was finally com-
pleted for $2.2 billion. The largest part of Du Pont's respon-
sibilities was the Hanford Works, a plutonium plant in the
state of Washington built on a site of nearly 500,000 acres
and costing some $350 million, but Du Pont also built the
Oak Ridge, Tennessee, plutonium semiworks and worked
closely with the scientists at the University of Chicago—Enrico
Fermi in particular—on the research and development phases
of the bomb. The Du Pont Company turned down the government's first letter of intent about the company's participation, Groves says, because it contained a standard fixed fee
clause. Carpenter told the government the company wanted

no profits or patents from its work, perhaps remembering the furor over company profits from World War I. From legal necessity, a fee of $1 was agreed on and paid after V-J Day. Bureaucracy had its day soon thereafter. Government auditors disallowed the full fee because the full time had not run on the contract, and Du Pont was asked to return $.33. "The officers of Du Pont had retained their sense of humor," Groves writes. While Du Pont's efforts on behalf of the Manhattan Project were herculean, they were not without considerable benefit to the company, which enjoyed the knowledge resulting from very costly research, for which the government was footing the bill.

The man most closely involved with the project from Du Pont's end was Crawford H. Greenewalt, son-in-law of Irénée, and the man Carpenter would pick to succeed him as president. Greenewalt was chosen as liaison between the Chicago scientists developing the bomb and the Du Pont engineers building the plants that would produce the materials from which the bomb was made. Groves has nothing but praise for the administrative work performed by Du Pont in connection with the project, work for which Greenewalt was primarily responsible. Groves named Greenewalt, along with Du Pont's chief engineer at the time, Granville M. Read, as the two men without whom the mammoth Hanford Works could not have been completed. With the start of construction on Hanford, Greenewalt was sent to the Columbia River site as technical director, a sensitive, difficult job. The scientists back in Chicago were rather skeptical of this businessman with no training in nuclear physics. They were reluctant to freeze designs for Hanford, preferring to continue the search for improvements. Greenewalt made a quick but intensive study of the nuclear field and soon was talking to the scientists in their own language, convincing them of the urgency to move ahead. He made decisions, risking error to save precious time. Even the scientists were impressed. Fermi once urged Greenewalt to abandon industry for pure research.

Tempted, Greenewalt declined, explaining, "On Fermi's level, my math is the two plus two kind."

Returning to Wilmington in February of 1945, Greenewalt jumped rapidly from job to job, landing in the president's chair in January 1948. In the fourteen years of his presidency, the company maintained a growth rate more than half again that of the chemical industry in general. Operating investment doubled. Sales more than doubled. The number of Du Pont stockholders doubled—to some 220,000. Employment at Du Pont increased by ten thousand.

One of his first tasks as president was the building of the Savannah River atomic plant for the government, called the largest construction project ever undertaken. Du Pont may well have been the only corporation in the country big enough and experienced enough to tackle the job, a fact the government noted obliquely when it filed its antitrust suit against the du Ponts—company and family—General Motors, and U. S. Rubber. Greenewalt's primary responsibility in this affair, once the courts finally and narrowly determined that Du Pont must divest itself of its GM holdings, was to convince Congress of the potentially dire and dramatic consequences that would result were such a divestiture subject to the tax laws prevailing at that time. With the help of the well-known Washington attorney and lobbyist Clark Clifford, Greenewalt succeeded, and Congress passed special legislation mitigating the tax liabilities involved in the divestiture.

Greenewalt earned a reputation for solving problems or, when necessary, putting them aside with a remark like, "Well, I'm not going to bleed and die over that." He has attributed Du Pont success to two factors, sounding as he talks about them just like Pierre or T. Coleman: "First, the realization that an enterprise will succeed only to the extent that all individuals associated with it can be encouraged to exercise their highest talents in their own particular way. Second, the provision of maximum incentives for achievement, particularly in associating the fortunes of the individual with that of the corporation." Those who know him swear by his charm as well as his ability, but he has on occasion been arrogant to the point of rudeness. He once refused to be interviewed by a reporter for the Wilmington newspapers doing a story on the changing role of the du Pont family in the company and the community prompted by the announcement of the proposed merger of the family holding company, Christiana Securities, into the Du Pont Company. He contended he wasn't a member of the family. "I won't wear that cap," he told the reporter. "My wife is as much a Greenewalt as she is a du Pont. This project doesn't appeal to me in the least." Of those asked, he alone refused to be interviewed.

That is, however, at worst a minor blemish in what by any yardstick has been a distinguished career within business and without. Greenewalt was born in 1902. His father was a doctor, his mother a concert pianist. Like so many of his in-laws, Greenewalt received his college education at MIT, where he managed to find time between studying periods to be manager of the boxing and basketball teams and a member of the Tech Show chorus and the Tech Glee Club. He began work at Du Pont immediately upon graduating in 1922. As his early work there involved the graveyard shift at the experimental station watching panels of instruments, he found plenty of time to practice the clarinet, a hobby he has since more or less abandoned along with the cello, which he once took up when a local string quartet found themselves without a cellist. Before becoming involved with the Manhattan Project, he proved himself a more than able scientist at Du Pont, where between 1927 and 1939 his work led to his name's appearing on eighteen patents.

Greenewalt's leisure hours have never been idle. He has an international reputation as an expert on hummingbirds, an interest he developed in a slightly roundabout way. He was growing orchids in a greenhouse off his home and became interested in photography as a way to capture visually the growth of plants. His interest in photography soon dominated and was supplemented by his interest in mechanics and electronics. He became fascinated by birds in flight, especially the hummingbird, and before long he and his associates were developing new equipment, such as stroboscopic lights much faster than those commercially available, to capture the hummingbird in pictures. He has logged more than 100,000 miles traveling all over South America, the American desert, and the Antilles islands during holidays and vacations to photograph these birds. Over a five-year period he photographed more hummingbirds and more different species than any man before him. He has received a number of prestigious awards both as a photographer and as an ornithologist.

Awards recognizing his business and scientific achievements have been no less numerous. Among his noteworthy accomplishments was the development—at the request of Walter Carpenter—of a modern public relations department at Du Pont. For years a combination of inherent du Pont family shyness and a certain naïveté about politics and public affairs had shaped Du Pont Company public policy; the du Ponts believed firmly in what they were doing, its essential rightness and morality, and were mystified by what appeared to be public misunderstanding and hostility. Under Greenewalt and the new director of public relations, Harold Brayman, things began to change after World War II.

During the war, the company was simply too busy to fight the spate of antitrust suits filed by the government over Du Pont dominance of various markets. Brayman recalls Du Pont filing consent decrees or nolo contendere pleas in perhaps a dozen such cases, and Greenewalt used to keep score as to whether Du Pont received more commendations for its war effort or notices of the filing of another antitrust suit. In 1945 the decision was made, Brayman says, to fight all antitrust suits to their conclusion. The big one involving General Motors was the only one Du Pont lost once that decision was made, although a second case, involving ICI (Imperial Chemicals, the British giant), could not be construed as a clear-cut win. Brayman says the co-operation he got from Du Pont's executive committee was unflagging except in one instance, when *Fortune* magazine asked for help on a major Du Pont story several years after the war. The executive committee was still burning from what its members considered had been unfair treatment in the 1930s series of articles and voted against Brayman's recommendation that the company give its okay. Several years later the subject came up again, and the vote was reversed.

Brayman also instituted a policy of answering all public attacks on Du Pont as promptly and effectively as possible. As an example, Brayman cited a Walter Winchell newspaper column excoriating Du Pont on the basis of misinformation. Telegrammed letters to the editor went out immediately to as many as several hundred newspapers, Brayman recalls, giving the facts in the case as Du Pont saw them, and, according to Brayman, several papers dropped the Winchell column. "He never attacked us again," Brayman said.

Government regulation has always been troublesome for Du Pont executives. For the most part, it is not the principle but the practice that causes concern. In general, the feeling is that politics and bureaucracy do not make for good business. In a 1950 *Fortune* magazine article, Greenewalt expressed himself on one aspect of the problem thusly: "It is difficult for business to plan its future and to commit many millions of dollars of stockholders' money in ventures which at some future date may be open to question, not because they have failed, but because they have succeeded."

If Greenewalt has been the ultimate in successful, compatible in-laws, Ernest N. May has been something of a maverick. He married the oldest sister of Greenewalt's wife. May functioned comfortably enough within the system for a number of years before retiring from a mid-level job at Du Pont in 1949. He then devoted most of his time to public service, working mainly in the areas of education and health. In thirteen years, up to 1962, May estimates he spent "at least 22,000 hours of my own time as well as about $250,000 of my own money" on public charities. He became disillusioned. He found that while he had the time and the inclination to be more than a name on the letterhead of the various organizations on whose boards he served, that was not necessarily the case universally. In particular, May was disturbed by what he considered a lack of sound financial practices in the managing of institutions dependent on public funds and the tendency for such institutions—in Wilmington, at least—to rely for their support upon a relatively narrow public base—largely the du Pont family. May began verbalizing these concerns at various board meetings, making a lot of noise, a few enemies, and not much progress. Among his earliest charitable endeavors was an attempt, along with Greenewalt and others, to organize a community chest or United Fund in the 1930s, an effort frustrated until after World War II by several community organizations whose fund-raising machinery was already well oiled.

In 1955 May started the Charitable Research Foundation, devoted to gathering and disseminating financial information about religious, charitable, scientific, literary, and educational institutions in an effort to determine how worthy they were of public and/or private financial support. Public reaction was at first "disheartening," May wrote in a pamphlet he published on his charitable activities in 1975, but eventually, he says, his work received some acceptance, particularly three studies he published on hospital food service, standards for institutional care of the infirm aged, and alumni giving.

May became somewhat alienated from the du Pont family when, as one of three executors of Irénée Sr.'s estate, he made waves about its handling. May had his own ideas about the legal, moral, and responsibility ramifications of his trusteeship, and they were frequently in conflict with the more practical ideas of his fellow executors. An example already cited in an earlier chapter was his disagreement about the treatment of Irénée's Cuba estate, Xanadu, for tax purposes.

A number of years ago May put his Charitable Research Foundation activities on the back burner and turned to what he calls "a long-cherished dream," the establishment of a museum that would demonstrate in two hours the influence of geography on American history. Called Project 400, run by his son Ernest Jr., and tucked away in the nearby Pennsylvania countryside, the museum has yet to capture the public fancy, but those who have made the effort to go through it agree the experience is worthwhile.

It is not, perhaps, a typical du Pont attitude, but May's explanation of why he has devoted so much time to charity is outlined in his pamphlet and is not without its revelations:

"I had before me the examples of P. S. du Pont, Lammot, and Irénée and some other prominent men, particularly H. F. Brown, who had given untold millions to schools and hospitals. Irénée's own personal attitude struck me as most commendable. In retrospect, I see that he gave much more in dollars than he did in thought, but I did not know it then.

"Further, there was the constant driving force of noblesse oblige—the obligation of honorable, generous, and responsible behavior that is concomitant with the privileges of high income (whether earned, unearned, or inherited); a sort of moral obligation to contribute what one could for the public welfare, certainly locally.

"Still further, since I was no longer to spend any of my time and effort toward earning dividends, I felt that the least I could do would be to help those friends and colleagues who actually were producing the dividends; help them to be able to spend these dividends in charity as intelligently and as honorably as possible for the general welfare."

When it comes to charitable activities, du Pont in-laws in recent years may have exceeded their spouses in contributions of time, if not money. The list of du Ponts and in-laws in important roles at local and national levels of charitable organizations is staggering. It could hardly be otherwise, given the vast number of du Pont relatives and the heavy (for obvious reasons) demand on their services. Several in-laws deserve special mention in this light. Marka du Pont, wife of A. Felix, with her work in behalf of mental health and so many other worthy causes, is surely one. Jean K. du Pont, widow of E. Paul, is another. Her work for prison reform and rehabilitation spanned many years, during which she gave generously of both her time and her money. But when it came to giving no in-law could quite rival Jessie Ball du Pont, widow of Alfred I. Her specialty was higher education, although she devoted considerable energy to the Alfred I. du Pont Institute for crippled but curable children, her husband's testamentary wish. The Institute's executive director, Dr. Alfred R. Shands, once said of her: "I am sure there are few who inherited wealth who have spent more time in soundly and intelligently planning for the good this wealth can do than Mrs. du Pont."

It is true that in the years preceding her death in 1970, she had an income in excess of $10 million a year, which makes giving large amounts away no particular hardship. When she died, her estate was estimated at more than $100 million, although she had more or less started from scratch and did not share in the corpus of her husband's estate but only the income. Nonetheless, Jessie made the most of her wealth and in the process became the first woman to invade a number of hitherto exclusively male domains. In 1951 she was the first woman ever named to the Florida Board of Control, which supervises the spending of state dollars for higher education. Five years later the Virginia Chamber of Commerce recognized her accomplishments with a special service award, the first of its kind ever given a woman. In 1959 she became the first woman to serve on the board of trustees of Washington and Lee University. By 1963 Jessie had been awarded thirteen honorary degrees. Her generosity benefited Washington and Lee, Hollins College, and Sweet Briar College, all in Virginia; the University of the South in Tennessee; Stetson University in Florida; and many others. By 1957 she had given Hollins an estimated $1 million. That school, observing its one hundredth anniversary, called her its major benefactor since the school's founding. In 1952 Stetson University called her "the outstanding woman philanthropist in the field of education and charities." Among her more ardent admirers were the young people she sent to college on scholarship each year. In some years they numbered as many as 150.

Her interests were not limited to education. She gave heavily to British war relief efforts during the Second World War. She loved the theater, and endowed awards for distinguished work in radio, a program later expanded to include television. She was dedicated to historic preservation goals, especially as they applied to her native Virginia, and in this was in the company of quite a few other du Pont family members, not the least of whom is Mrs. Lammot du Pont Copeland, the former Pamela Cunningham.

Mrs. Copeland is a woman of many parts. A trustee emeritus of the National Trust for Historic Preservation, she is also honorary first regent of the Gunston Hall Plantation board of regents, a most prestigious if rather arcane position. Her Gunston work was crowned in 1975 by the publication of *The Five George Masons*, a biography she co-authored with some distinction after prolonged research both in the United States and in England. She is a member of the board of trustees at Winterthur and served on the Fine Arts Committee of the Department of State from 1964 through 1974. In 1969 she was named to President Nixon's advisory council on historic preservation and that same year was co-chairman with Mrs. Winthrop Rockefeller of the heralded Renoir retrospective in New York.

Among her hobbies are horticulture, the collecting of Chinese export porcelain, music, and salmon and trout fishing. As you might suspect, her porcelain collection is superb. Of all the women in-laws, Mrs. Copeland is perhaps the most scholarly by inclination. She is an excellent hostess, with an engaging sense of humor and a fondness for people that was especially useful to her shy husband during his years as Du

Pont's chief executive officer. The Copelands are hoping someday to open at least a part of their estate, Mount Cuba, just outside Wilmington, to the public as a botanical garden, but so far they have not been able to resolve some tax and legal problems connected with such an undertaking. Mrs. Copeland's love of music bloomed early. Before her marriage, she was a serious voice student in New York and Paris.

This is but a sampling of the family in-laws, albeit a choice sampling. There are many others who might easily have been mentioned. Alfred I. du Pont's first wife, Bessie Gardner, for example, who devoted so much of her life to preserving and recording the du Pont family's history. Other in-laws have been gold diggers, lushes, and ne'er-do-wells. Each has contributed to the weaving of the family fabric—some mightily—but the du Ponts themselves, at least until recently, have always dominated the tapestry.

Chapter Fifteen

The Company

Although but a handful of the family still works there, the Du Pont Company today bears the family imprint throughout its operations. In places, that imprint is perhaps fading. Overall, however, today's professional managers run the company along guidelines set down many years ago by men named du Pont, the most visionary of whom would be breathless at the size and scope of the old family firm.

The company today has more than 130,000 employees and generates sales approaching $9 billion. At the end of World War I, just after the company's largest period of growth in its history, it had gross capital employed of slightly more than $300 million. Today the figure is near $12 billion. Among the most remarkable aspects of that growth is the fact that the vast majority of it was financed through earnings, not, as has been the case with so many other growth companies, through debt. That is one legacy of the family to the company, one that in recent years has lost its rigidity as a principle. The company does borrow money now, but its executives exercise extreme caution when doing so.

Du Pont's continued emphasis on research and development is another family legacy, at its strongest no doubt when Lammot was president but a crucial part of Du Pont success virtually from the beginning. In 1976 Du Pont spent $353 million for research and development, the largest outlay in the chemical industry. The company put up nearly $2 billion in the 1960s to develop and commercialize new products. Well more than half the company's chemical products today have been developed since 1950. A change is taking place in this area, however, with increasing attention being given to improving existing products and manufacturing processes. Starting in 1977, the company has begun to devote 75 per cent of its R&D resources to improvements, leaving 25 per cent for pioneer research and new ventures. In recent years, the percentages were 66 and 34.

One of the reasons for this de-emphasis on pure research is the rapid shortening of the time period when the results of such research belong exclusively to the discoverer. Nylon, for example, was the sole property of Du Pont for fourteen years after its discovery. Du Pont had Dacron for only ten years; Orlon for four. Nylon has not been a bad deal for Du Pont. In its 1976 annual report, the company noted nylon has accounted for more than $2 billion in net earnings since its synthesis in 1939.

In 1964 *Time* magazine reported that Du Pont research results in between six hundred and seven hundred patents a year. At that time the company employed four thousand scientists and had made millionaires out of more than one of them. "We have never treated scientists as crazy, long-haired guys in the back room," then president Lammot du Pont Copeland was quoted as saying. In the mid-sixties Du Pont was more than three times larger than its closest U.S. competitor in the chemical industry and yet had less than 10 per cent of the market, *Time* pointed out, adding that the chemical industry is the only one that sells to all seventy-nine basic industries in the country. Du Pont has not always been number one. In 1920 Allied Chemical, formed by a merger in that year, was the largest company in the industry.

Besides its vast research capabilities, a number of factors have contributed to the Du Pont success story, all of them family-developed. The du Ponts were important innovators in administration, finance, employee relations and enjoyed a highly beneficial relationship with General Motors during the vital expansion years of both companies, Du Pont and GM. From the beginning, the du Ponts were aware of employee relations simply because the dangerous nature of their business was shared and strong bonds between employer and employee were the inevitable result.

Today those bonds have weakened. The danger has greatly diminished and is no longer shared. The company is a huge, impersonal corporation now. But the policies governing employee relations begun so long ago pertain still, modified often and expanded frequently. Three in particular deserve special attention. The first is labor relations. Du Pont remains largely non-union, at least in the sense that no outside group has yet organized substantial numbers of employees. Shortly after World War I the company began experimenting with employee representation in decisions affecting Du Pont workers at several company installations, but the passage of the Wagner Act in 1935 ended those experiments because it did not recognize employee organizations formed with the involvement of company management. Managers at the various sites told their worker representatives they could no longer work together in this area, and at that point, employees at a number of locations began to organize their own unions. So far these Du Pont plant unions are the only significant labor voice at Du Pont, although for several years now the United Steel Workers have been attempting to organize Du Pont workers, to date with but modest success. Du Pont management likes to think that's because Du Pont workers are already well taken care of. The 1976 annual report states that employee benefits cost Du Pont $781 million that year, "equal to an additional 41.5 per cent of the amount paid in wages and salaries for time actually worked." The multi-billion-dollar Du Pont pension fund is a model of actuarial soundness, and the company recently agreed to base pensions on the three years of an employee's highest pay, rather than the highest five, and in 1977 adjusted pensions of previously retired employees upward by as much as 12 per cent. The company, despite some recent adverse publicity about employee exposure to carcinogens, is recognized as a leader in industrial safety—another family legacy—and in fact, markets its expertise in this field to other corporations on a consulting basis. All of which is not to say that Du Pont employment is blissful, but only to suggest that to date at least, employees have not felt it necessary to rise up in union.

The second policy worthy of especial note covers bonuses. The original plan began in 1905 and was among the first of its kind in American industry. It was the brainchild of T. Coleman du Pont primarily, with the firm support of Pierre. At first it was limited to key executives, allowing them to purchase stock in the company through accrual of dividends on stock set aside for the purpose. By the 1920s the plan had been broadened to cover several thousand employees. From 1905 to 1945 the company paid out nearly $100 million in bonuses. Since the end of World War II, bonuses have become an even bigger part of employee compensation. In 1970, for example, 160 employees shared $721,690 in cash and stock bonuses under Plan A, given for conspicuous service of any nature regardless of company earnings, while nearly 12,000 employees received cash and stock bonuses under Plans B and C for general contributions to company welfare. These bonuses were worth slightly less than $40 million. Since then, the bonus system has been again revised. In 1976, under the Special Compensation Plan, similar to Plan A, 184 employees, none of whom were officers or directors, received $1.1 million. Under the Incentive Compensation Plan, awards totaling $45.8 million were made, including $3.2 million to 25 employees who were officers or directors and $42.6 million to more than 10,000 other employees. In addition, nearly 75,000 shares were optioned at $129.50 a share to 122 employees of whom 19 were officers or directors. A fourth plan allows for the awarding of dividend units, which entitle the beneficiary to cash payments equal to dividend payments, with one unit equaling one share. The payments continue until the beneficiary's eighty-fifth birthday or his death, whichever is later. No dividend units have been issued since 1974.

A program that permits engineers and scientists of particular ability to remain functioning as engineers and scientists without giving up the increased compensation that would come with promotion to administrative positions is the third important aspect of employee relations at Du Pont. In this case, corporate policy has been limited to tacit approval of various department and location plans that began evolving in the late 1940s. Flexible salary policies, allowing for substantial increases without significant changes in responsibilities, are one facet of the plan. The special compensation bonus plan is another. Freedom to work in any fashion a scientist or engineer considers best for him is a third. A classic example of the plan in operation applied to Nat Wyeth, brother of the famous painter Andrew Wyeth, and a brilliant engineer and inventor at Du Pont before he retired several years ago. He was made an engineering fellow, allowing him to give free reign to his creative talents without having to worry about administrative detail. At the time of his retirement, he told a reporter for the local newspapers that he probably spent a third of his time in a pose that might easily have been construed as goofing off by a less understanding employer. He just sat at his desk, doodled, and thought. Du Pont recognizes that in special cases, such activity can produce great benefit for the company.

The administration of Du Pont has long been studied in business schools as a model of efficiency and control. Chief architects of the system were Pierre and Coleman du Pont, with invaluable assistance from Hamilton Barksdale. The key to the system is the operation of the executive and finance committees and the separation of their authority. The executive committee meets each Wednesday and any other times deemed necessary. It is made up of the board chairman, the president, and several senior vice-presidents and serves as the policy-making and supervisory body for all company operations. All major projects from any company department are subject to committee approval, based on a given project's success potential and compatibility with over-all corporate goals and direction. Each member of the committee also serves as "primary liaison" to designated staff and industrial departments and may have responsibilities in an area like environmental affairs or management planning that transcend individual department interests.

The finance committee has eight members, including the president and the chairman of the board of the company ex officio. It meets twice a month to retain a grasp on the company's over-all financial position and to supervise major expenditures. Once a substantial project has been approved by the executive committee from a business standpoint, the finance committee reviews the proposal from a financial view, approving, disapproving, or making a special recommendation to the board.

In these two committees are vested the reins of corporate control, although an executive committee member told *Fortune* magazine back in 1950 that because of his position as thinker, policy formulator, and reviewer, "the only person I can issue orders to is my secretary." That same article contained a prediction gleaned from a cloudy crystal ball. Of the makeup of the executive committee *Fortune* wrote, ". . . nor is it likely to contain a lawyer, for the legal mind is not conditioned to the bold risk-taking by which Du Pont lives." It took twenty years, but in 1970 Irving S. Shapiro, lawyer, joined the executive committee on his way to the chief executive's office.

Each of the ten industrial departments is run by a general manager who has virtual autonomy over day-to-day operations within his department. The executive and finance committees are the connecting link between the departments and the board of directors. By far the largest operating department is textile fibers, which is twice as big as its nearest competitor, plastic products and resins, and eight times the size of the biochemical department, the company's smallest. Textile fibers sales in 1976 were more than $2.5 billion.

At the end of 1976 Du Pont employed 132,000 people, operated in the United States more than 120 manufacturing plants and more than 100 laboratories for research and development, sales service, and on-site work at various locations, and 47 different foreign operations in 34 countries and territories. The company made some 1,700 products. In the chemical business, of course, many products may stem from one raw material.

The basic organizational system in use today was first used in 1921, although the top-level executive and finance committee concepts were already several years along by then. The only major change in the more than fifty years since its inception occurred in 1973 when the board of directors chose to divide top executive responsibility. In the past, the president had been the chief executive officer; the board chairman acted more in an advisory capacity and was generally considered a seat of semi-retirement. Today the chairman acts as chief executive, while the president is the company's chief operating officer. It is a characterization to which both the current chairman and president object as being too simple and glib, but to call the chairman "Mr. Outside" and the president "Mr. Inside" is to draw a more accurate picture than perhaps either is publicly willing to admit.

The du Ponts have always considered financial controls to be very important. While external financial matters at the beginning of the twentieth century received more notoriety, internal financial systems that were developed during those days were equally important to the company's future success. The abilities of T. Coleman du Pont and John J. Raskob to package financial deals were scintillating and vitally affected the course of the Du Pont Company. Financing growth from earnings is a bit of wizardry no one mastered better than Du Pont. But where Du Pont really appeared to develop an edge on the competition was, to be unglamorous about it, in bookkeeping. In the first two decades of this century, Du Pont developed bookkeeping systems that provided management with the data it needed to oversee the business and exercise control. The data were turned out quickly and presented in a format the managers could understand. Du Pont employees were good to begin with, and the company policy regarding incentives made many of them better. Still, on the average company workers probably weren't noticeably superior to their counterparts among the competition. Du Pont had the systems. The systems worked, and the employees looked good.

Perhaps no business relationship between two entities has been more synergetic than that between Du Pont and General Motors before the federal government broke it up. Du Pont provided GM with vital administrative and internal financial help at a crucial time. GM earnings sustained Du Pont dividends in years when Du Pont's own earnings fell, years, for example, like those directly following World War I. The two companies also did a lot of business together, particularly with Du Pont selling to General Motors. The relationship was rather succinctly put by Lammot du Pont in a letter to Fred Fisher dated October 20, 1922: "In view of the stock ownership relations between Fisher Body Corp. [a GM subsidiary], Flint Varnish and Color Works [a Du Pont subsidiary], General Motors and the Du Pont Co., it would seem that Flint should enjoy a large part, if not all, of Fisher Body's paint and varnish business unless some good reason for not having it."

More than once, however, this blunt-instrument approach was resented at GM. Time and again, Pierre and Irénée testified during the antitrust suit of their conviction that GM was a tough customer because its executives were a little feisty about the "stock ownership relations," as Lammot put it. A GM division president wrote U. S. Rubber president F. B. Davis, installed by Du Pont interests, saying, "Now that you have a good foothold in here, it is entirely up to your organization to maintain your position, because from now on, I don't know U. S. Rubber any more than I know the rest of the outfits."

Nonetheless, no one can deny that Du Pont did a lot of business with General Motors. The automotive industry remains a major market for Du Pont products. In 1976 direct and indirect sales to that market accounted for $800 million. Indirect sales would be, for example, fiber sales to tire companies and textile manufacturers for eventual automobile use.

Everyone knows the Du Pont Company is big, but its diversity is sometimes surprising. The company makes sulfuric acid and film used in X-ray machines; it makes fibers for high fashion and bulletproof vests; it makes paint and polyethylene industrial pipe, along with plastic film for packaging blood or candy. It makes something called a thermogravimetric analyzer. Among the company's newer ventures are a clinical analyzer for hospital testing, a process for purifying brackish water, a food-freezing system, and a new process for bonding metals. The company is also working on polymer-based building products. History says one or more of these will make it big. Among Du Pont firsts have been moisture-proof cellophane; nylon, first fiber to be entirely man-made; neoprene, first successful synthetic rubber; Corfam, the leather-like material on which Du Pont lost so much money; Orlon acrylic fiber; Dacron polyester fiber; and Teflon fluorocarbons, material with unusual chemical, electrical, thermal, and surface characteristics.

Since 1926 Du Pont has been in the agricultural chemicals business. It produces a variety of fertilizers, insecticides, weed killers, and fungicides. The company's research in photochemical activity resulted in the developing of the first modern weed killers. As a result of its role in the Manhattan Project to build the first atomic bomb, Du Pont has remained active in the atomic energy field, operating the huge Savannah River plant and laboratory in South Carolina for the Atomic Energy Commission. Among the products from that plant are cobalt-60, used in cancer treatment and medical research; plutonium-238, used as fuel for a number of different power units in space; and californium-252, also used in cancer treatment as well as radiography and mineralogical exploration.

The technical and scientific capabilities of the Du Pont Company are awesome. In its laboratories, scientists accelerate chemical reactions 1,000 times. Substances are subjected to force 100,000 times the force of gravity. Cell tissues are sliced as thin as two millionths of an inch. Research looks at how proteins form, the corrosion process of metals, the affect of light on living cells, and what makes a material adhesive. New ways to synthesize substances, prevent infectious disease, store information, remove salt from sea water inexpensively, and transmit electricity without generating heat have all attracted the attention of Du Pont scientists. In a single year, Du Pont lawyers may file as many as eight hundred patent applications.

While Du Pont is modifying its approach to research somewhat by reducing its emphasis on pure research and concentrating more on improving existing products and processes, much of the glamour that attaches to the Du Pont name in industry can be traced to the decision to allow company scientists some freedom to pursue pure research. That decision, made in 1927, the first year of Lammot du Pont's presidency, resulted in one of the basic discoveries of modern chemical science—how little molecules can be put together to make big ones. On this foundation were nylon, synthetic rubber, polyester, and acrylic fibers built.

Among other Du Pont discoveries was the first fast-drying automobile paint. Now that may not sound like much to get excited about, but in the early days of the auto, finishes were a major problem. For one thing, they tended not to last very long before they began to chip and peel. For another, the finishes in use before 1923 took a long time—two to four weeks—to dry, producing a major bottleneck in the manufacturing process. Duco lacquers, introduced in 1923, were being used by every major auto maker by 1925 because not only did the stuff dry within a matter of hours rather than weeks, it was also an all-weather finish that did not chip or peel.

Du Pont research has also come up with the first synthetic influenza drug, new plastics, new films, new fibers, the isolation of enzymes involved in the synthesis of plant protein from nitrogen in the air, and a photographic process that doesn't use negatives. It is interesting that Du Pont does very little business directly with the consumer but sells instead to other manufacturers in other industries. This is partly the nature of the chemical industry, but it is also true that Du Pont has tried to boost its consumer business without conspicuous success. Outside paint and a few car products, Du Pont's consumer efforts have largely been failures. Corfam is the most obvious example, but it is by no means the only one. Symmetrel, a drug that taken regularly immunizes the taker from Asian flu, is another. Antifreeze is a third. The company seems better off peddling a product in its first usable form to another industry rather than trying to develop a finished product.

A substantial part of Du Pont's business is in providing technical help to its customers. The nature of the business is such that Du Pont is not only bringing new products along all the time but also must show its customers why the product is better and how to use it because so much of Du Pont's product line is "state of the art" from a standpoint of technological sophistication. Du Pont also helps its customers solve problems that may be unrelated to Du Pont products. The site for much of this work is Chestnut Run, 170 acres outside Wilmington that could be described as a microcosm of American industry. Here more than two thousand scientists, engineers, administrators, and technicians using nine laboratories duplicate the operating conditions and equipment of a wide variety of industries so that they can better understand the technologies and problems of their customers.

Few companies with as little direct consumer contact as Du Pont has can boast of a trademark with as wide public recognition as the Du Pont oval. Partly this is the result of its longevity. In early 1906 G. A. Wolf was commissioned to design a trademark for the company and was quoted as saying, "My thought at once turned to an oval, and I found that the name lent itself admirably to that particular shape." For a year, nothing much happened. Then Wolf's design began appearing on some labels. Comment was favorable, and the design was adopted for all Du Pont products. The only change from the original Wolf design has been the removal of a ribbon that ran through the name with "Established in 1802" on it.

The Du Pont Company today is of a size and diversity that pretty well assure it of cyclical behavior. If the economy is good, the company's sales and earnings will reflect that—and vice versa. In the mid-seventies the company's performance has been hamstrung by its heavy commitment to fiber business, which has suffered from a simple problem, overcapacity. In the 1960s fibers were the business to be in, with polyester filament leading the way. For that product alone, there were 18 manufacturers around the world in 1963 and 119 by 1973. In a normal year, fibers account for about 40 per cent of Du Pont sales. Their contribution to earnings has been lagging badly, but Du Pont management is convinced the fiber business will rebound, and when it does, Du Pont will be in the strongest position to take advantage of it.

Meanwhile, what Du Pont now calls its CPS business—chemicals, plastics, and specialty products, or in other words, all non-fiber products—has been booming, helping to offset the fiber lag. While Du Pont, like the rest of American industry, must deal with the phenomenal growth of government regulation (and pay for it), the company has thrived despite such setbacks as the government's taking the lead out of gasoline and the threatened ban on fluorocarbons. One area in particular is contributing more and more to Du Pont's growth: health care. The company realized sales in this field in 1976 of more than $300 million. A majority of that was for

X-ray film and equipment, where Du Pont has long been a factor, but other areas are now contributing significantly to the company's growth. Besides the automatic clinical analyzer to speed hospital testing and improve its accuracy, the company has been moving into the biomedical instruments business since 1963 and expects sales to double by 1981. Some Du Pont fibers are being used in certain surgical procedures, and others are used in hospital garments and operating room supplies.

But the drug business appears to offer the most potential for growth. In 1969 Du Pont purchased Endo Laboratories, providing Du Pont with marketing experience and some good drugs, including anticoagulants, narcotic analgesics, and cough-cold medicines. Research in this field has since contributed a drug that cancels the effect of a narcotic and relieves respiratory depression. A new tranquilizer has also been marketed. An injectable analgesic, which relieves pain but is not subject to narcotic controls, was in final clinical testing at the end of 1976, and work was being done on other analgesics, antiarthritics, psychotherapeutics, urinary antibacterials, and antiviral and cardiovascular drugs.

Increasingly these days, the top executives at Du Pont are being diverted from their task of running a business to address themselves to social questions. This is not unusual in industry today, but Du Pont's questions are more personal, more immediate than most. The company is a multibillion-dollar, multinational operation headquartered in a small city in the second smallest state in the Union. It has always been a family enterprise, and that is still the public conception despite rather dramatic developments within the company that make it clear the family no longer runs things, except in theory. The current board chairman, Irving S. Shapiro, is generally considered one of industry's main public spokesmen nationally, and Du Pont vice-presidents, public affairs people, and scientists are constantly shuttling between Wilmington and Washington communicating their concerns to the government on a wide variety of issues, including environmental control, federal regulation, and industrial safety. The company's Metroliner bill for rail tickets between New York, Wilmington, and Washington must be in six figures.

At home is where the company must exercise the greatest delicacy. Delaware is a quaint political entity. Although politicians frequently deplore in public the domination of the state by "Du Pont," the population in general seems to prefer having them around to not having them and realizes how different, and probably worse, things would be if "Du Pont" had picked, say, Vermont instead of Delaware. Surprisingly, Delawareans are no better informed about things Du Pont than the public at large. There is, for example, a very definite distinction today between the family, the individuals within the family, and the company, but it is a distinction the public declines to recognize. This puts company executives in the position of appearing to act for the family because in acting for the company, they are, in the public mind, also acting for the family.

As the family withdraws from its active control of the company and its domination of community and civic affairs, a void is left that is largely unperceived by the public.

The company admits to trying to pick up some of the slack within the community left by the family's inability in the face of declining individual wealth and growing, more complex problems to meet what have historically been considered its community obligations. The company is, however, limited in what it can do because it serves several masters. Company officers point out that they have a primary obligation to their stockholders. It is true that many of these are Du Pont family members, but the family is a minority. Lavishing company largesse upon Wilmington and Delaware would not be looked upon with favor by stockholders outside the state. The company must also see to the well-being of its employees, not out of any sense of love for its fellow man, but purely as a matter of good business practice. Finally, community reaction to the prospect that the company might take a more active role is not unmixed. The company must balance on a narrow ledge with the abyss of interference and control on one side and the chasm of unconcern and bad corporate citizenship on the other.

The population of Delaware is about 600,000. Du Pont employs about 24,000 in the state, a tenth of the entire state work force. Some 23,000 Delawareans own stock in Du Pont. The socio-economic implications are obvious, and everyone is aware of them. The consensus is that the company copes in a generally fair-minded if undramatic way with its problems in these areas, for the most part playing strictly by the rules. Sometimes cries of anguish and frustration rise up against Du Pont. Usually the voices belong to the have-nots lamenting the disparities between their chances and those of Du Pont, a legitimate enough lament, but not one Du Pont alone can begin to rectify.

The impression one gets about Du Pont as a place to work is that it's not all that much fun. The pay is reasonably good and the benefits are high, but Du Pont is a rather structured, serious business with little room for frivolity or irreverence. Fun is for those sometime weekends when you aren't at the office making sure the guy next to you isn't using his Sundays to play one-upmanship on you.

Du Pont is a huge corporation, but the impression is that no small detail escapes those who need to know it. The information and control systems that help keep Du Pont managers on top of the situation are sophisticated and well oiled. Extravagance in any form is not brooked. There is a story, told a few years ago in a *Time* magazine article, that Du Pont was in the throes of a belt-tightening program when one bright fellow suggested eliminating the lemon wedges from the shrimp cocktail. The company is in the somewhat unusual position of owning the Hotel du Pont, which is part of the company headquarters building complex. The suggestion met with approval. The company saved $200 a year. The story may be fantasy; the company image it reflects is not.

Chapter Sixteen

A Way of Life

The du Ponts are different from you and me, F. Scott Fitzgerald might have said. Yes, Ernest Hemingway would have replied, they have more money. Both, of course, were right. Money, in the last analysis, is what sets the rich apart, but money is more than just a commodity one possesses. Wealth is a way of life, tending to breed complacent mediocrity because its children are born secure, unmotivated, and, as they grow older, conscious of the sanctity of the family name and the shame of scandal. But wealth also breeds opportunity, freedom, and privilege. Those few with the brains and the stomach for it can make big waves in whatever sea they choose.

Several factors set the du Ponts apart from other wealthy families of the United States. The two most important are the pace at which they accumulated their wealth and their sense of family. A third important factor is their heritage. It is interesting—and not a little sad—that none of the three has anything like the significance for today's family that it did a quarter century or a generation ago.

Unlike most rich American families, the du Ponts could at no time have truly been considered nouveau riche. They began modestly well off and with established social standing upon their arrival in America, struggled with some heavy debt for several decades, and then gradually grew from comfortable to wealthy. It is true that the family fortune rocketed to previously undreamed-of heights during and shortly after World War I, but the family was already well established, influential, and wealthy enough by then. Most of America's legendary family fortunes were built more or less from scratch in a few short years by one man sometime after the Civil War and before the turn of the century, the era of the Robber Barons. The du Ponts participated in this era and its ethics. The Gunpowder Trade Association was no consumer affairs group. But there were two basic differences between the du Ponts and other American tycoons. At the time the GTA was formed in 1872 the du Ponts were already the largest firm in the industry. Indeed, if old Boss Henry du Pont had had his way, the gunpowder trust might never have been formed. He was ready to fight price wars to enlarge the Du Pont share of the market, and those would have been wars in which he would have been highly favored. The other difference is that the powder business in those days was growing steadily and handsomely enough but not with the eye-catching dazzle of some other industries like oil, steel, and railroads. If the family leaders had been prescient enough to abandon the trust at the first inkling of federal displeasure with such organizations as Rockefeller's Standard Oil, Du Pont might easily have dodged the antitrust suit that came its way in 1907.

In most of America's rich families, one can point to a single individual as the source of the wealth. This is not true of the du Ponts.

The heritage of the du Ponts and their sense of family go hand in hand. The du Ponts may have been immigrants seeking freedom from persecution and a land of opportunity when they arrived at the turn of the nineteenth century, but they had a head start on most immigrants. They came with a staggering load of baggage that included some less than essential items, including one of the largest libraries ever brought to America by an immigrant family. The President of the United States, Thomas Jefferson, was their friend. The family patriarch had been an important figure in France, although subject to the vicissitudes that plagued everyone who was the least conspicuous in France during its revolution. Even so pretentious a descendant as Colonel Henry A. du Pont could be proud of his heritage, as long as no one mentioned the watch-making background of his great-grandfather.

The du Ponts' sense of family began at the beginning, with the 1784 ceremony at Bois des Fosses, the du Pont country home, in which the father gave Eleuthère Irénée a sword and made him and his brother, Victor Marie, pledge eternal allegiance. Down through the generations the importance of family tradition was instilled in the du Pont children. Du Pont in-laws became caught up in it as well.

Mrs. Henry du Pont, wife of the Boss, wrote to her son, Henry A. du Pont, in 1867: "I earnestly hope that my own du Ponts will be in every respect worthy of their ancestor [Pierre S. du Pont de Nemours] and that they will bear in mind what a precious inheritance of talents and honourable name they have received from [him]. . . . When I read how earnestly your great-grandfather enjoins it on all his descendants to strive to raise still higher our family column, I pray fervently that it might at least always retain its present fair and beautiful form. Sometimes I fear that our present life may have a narrowing effect on us all in our different positions and I am sure that we all have need to be watchful to counteract the effect of routine and too great concentration of purpose, which though good in itself, if carried too far must narrow the mind into one little circle."

Two years later Mrs. du Pont again wrote to her son, remarking upon the death of Amelia du Pont, daughter of Victor, at the age of seventy-four: "I trust that all the prestige of the family will not pass away with the old members of it and that the younger ones will all strive to live up to the example of the great and good ones who have gone before, so that the family name may be more and more illustrious and not grow tarnished as years roll on."

The correspondence of Pierre, especially after he became the family's twentieth-century patriarch, is filled with references to family tradition and the responsibilities that go with being born a du Pont. In the mid-thirties Irene, wife and cousin of Irénée and therefore sister-in-law to Pierre, could write her husband about how her brother Felix feared a splintering of the family and pointed to Eugene E.'s hermit-like family life. Irene's clear implication was that her brother had a point. Although the geographical and numerical spreading of the family has splintered some of these feelings and instincts, they are by no means fully dissipated. It was not long ago that a du Pont in-law, a prominent figure in Wilmington in his own right, said, "I'm not so sure people are right when they say the company is better off with outsiders running it. I think Brip [Irénée Jr.] would do a good job in either [president Edward] Kane's or [chairman Irving] Shapiro's job. He's a real humanitarian, but he knows how to say no. And you don't graduate from MIT without some degree of technical competence."

For a long time that sense of family encompassed the family enterprise. If you were a du Pont, you were most likely going to work for the Du Pont Company. That all began to change after World War I, or even, perhaps, as early as 1915, with the falling out between Pierre and Alfred I. Among the first to recognize what might befall his descendants were they not wary was Pierre, writing in the mid-1920s: "There are, and will be, many of these du Ponts born in a position of wealth that may not require the hard work and continued application which was the lot of our forebears. Perhaps of the two positions the new one is the more difficult and will require greater moral stamina to combat the temptations of wealth and luxury and to carry forward in a becoming manner the family traditions."

It was more than the temptations of wealth and luxury. As the family grew—and in no generation did it grow faster than in the one fostered by Pierre and his contemporaries—it became more and more difficult to maintain the feeling of close-knit loyalty sustained for so long by previous generations. And it was not just the family that grew. The company by the mid-twenties was fast becoming a complex corporate giant.

To keep pace with the industry's and the nation's growth required managerial talent that the family alone could not provide even if every one of its members wanted to work for the company and had the ability to make a real contribution. The company was the best in its field and could afford to hire the best managers available as well as the top scientists. The competition within the company for promotion soon became severe. Where was the incentive for a young du Pont to join the company, spend years learning the ropes—possibly while being transferred all over the country—only to have his rise to the top grind to a halt somewhere at the assistant supervisor level when the competition overwhelmed him? He had everything to lose and not all that much to gain.

Still, it is really only in the last generation that the du Ponts have abandoned the company work force in anything resembling droves. The situation is lamented by both those du Ponts still involved with the company and its current top management. The beginnings of this latest trend appear to have surfaced around the time of World War II. During his presidency of the company Lammot du Pont had once written a letter describing the policy on nepotism thusly: If all other factors were equal, Joe du Pont would be promoted ahead of Joe Doaks, but the name was no automatic ticket to the top if the bearer left ability behind. By 1944 the company had its first non-du Pont president, Walter S. Carpenter, Jr., and the fate of young du Ponts working for the company seems to have started becoming problematic. An indication of the situation can be gleaned from a letter E. Paul du Pont wrote his brother Felix in March of 1944 on the subject. It was a long, thoughtful, revealing epistle and said in part:

"Now I wish to mention first that psychologists are finding out continually that things they thought a while back to be inherited are acquired in early childhood, and again, that many characteristics can be altered later in life. Standing as it does in the realm of pseudo science or near the border line, I am not going to use this as a fulcrum for an argument, though such considerations often back up ordinary common sense. For instance, Irénée told me that he used, as a boy, to walk from school to the train in order to save a nickel toward the purchase of minerals for his collection. When I was going to school in Philadelphia, Father used to give me money for travel as needed, nor did he ever require of me any very strict accounting of the spending of it. I think here is a specific case of Irénée receiving financial training and of my receiving none. I have taken an isolated instance in both cases, but they could, no doubt, be multiplied many times. . . . I mention this to show that I have good reason to believe that there is less in heredity and more in training, which I believe can be made effective at a later date. Any plan for training of young du Pont men should take into account this independent means and the relationship their name creates among employees of the Du Pont Company.

". . . Pierre and his brothers have shown ability which I believe they acquired through early childhood training, of which I have a clue here and there, one of which is mentioned above.

"Now there is something, I feel sure, about this sort of training. It is almost unconscious on both sides. The child and the parent go along happily from day to day, completely oblivious of the process. I can even conceive of the fact that the more perfect the process, the more unconsciously it proceeds, so much the more it is taken for granted. . . .

"Hence, I believe that many young men of the du Pont family could have been training, and that they have not been is the direct result of the fact that Pierre, Irénée, and Lammot have received this unconscious training and know almost nothing of the fact that most people require definite training to fit them for a definite job. And when the job is as big as running the Du Pont Company, it is not surprising that those with ability already developed have been chosen instead of those in whom the development would require a planned program of training.

"As to myself, I was doing fairly well, partly by good luck and partly on account of Coleman, who not only set out to find if 'I could take it,' but gave me from time to time excellent advice and help. Coleman knew where I was, what I was doing, and who was my boss. He had me come to the main office and talked to me—drew me out and gave counsel and admonition at least once a year. It was extremely effective.

"But enough of that. I am to point out the need. Emile was about to give up. He had been rotting in one job in rayon at Buffalo. He was not advanced for the simple reason that, being a du Pont, it was expected by the people where he worked that some direction would be given to them as to what to do with him. I was with the company long enough to have experienced this, and I know that it is real. Receiving no instructions, only an occasional inquiry for a report which elicited little or no comment, they let him rot—until I heard of it and spoke to Irénée. Whereupon he ceased to rot. Irénée did not know where he was or what he was doing when I spoke to him.

"Paul was at the rayon plant, where he had been sent 'to see if he could take it.' Now that is a prime requisite, and I am not talking to decry finding it out. But how about training at the same time? Paul's so-called training at that time consisted in employing him to mop floors and clean the washrooms at twelve dollars a week (the plant was running only three days per week). He was about to leave when his mother told Irénée of his duties and pay. Irénée was incredulous, but must have found out upon inquiry. Victor was put in the treasurer's office in hopes he could learn finance. They had him counting checks. Day after day all he did was to count the physical pieces of paper, not anything whatever where he could exercise judgment. . . .

"When I see what my boy Steve is doing at Indian Motorcycle Company and what Edmond and Rhett are doing in Francis I. du Pont and Company and what Richard accomplished with the army glider program, then I am convinced that the Du Pont Company should not have lost these young men. I am convinced that the way they were, or would have been, treated, either drove them out, or prevented their ever going into the family business."

The letter goes on to talk about some of the obstacles peculiar to a du Pont in his efforts to make it in the company—the possibility of resentment among his fellow employees, the difficulty of adjusting to a subservient role at work so different from his role at home, and the lack of self-restraint that comes from not having to worry about holding onto an unfulfilling job. It ends: "The present situation is that those young fellows who are at work for the company actually advise their young relatives to go into something else, stating that a young du Pont has not the chance of a snowball in hell with the family enterprise. This attitude grows as it rolls, like a snowball on earth."

Several months later Felix replied to his brother, writing, ". . . the subject of finding better and quicker ways of advancing observing younger men in the Du Pont Company is being studied and has already produced some results. It would be a tactical error if Paul [Jr.] should leave until he had waited to see what is ahead." Whatever it was that lay ahead, it seems to have proved inadequate as far as attracting and motivating young du Ponts in a company career.

Over the generations, the du Ponts as a family more closely resemble the Rothschilds than any American family that comes readily to mind. In a book of essays called *The Family in History*, David Landes compares the Rothschilds to a contemporary banking family in Germany named Bleichroder. He refers to Heine's Law: "Jews are like the people among whom they live, only more so." That, Landes contends, describes the Bleichroders, who having become Bismarck's court bankers, attempt to use that success for social acceptance. The Rothschilds, on the other hand, had a sense of family and dynastic distinction that allowed them to preserve an identity, an identity that was further solidified through a tradition of intermarriage. Says Landes, ". . . The Rothschilds knew who they were and where they were from, and therefore, where they were going; by the third generation, the Bleichroders had changed their minds about who they were, or at least who they wanted to be, and had lost their way." Much of what Landes says about the Rothschilds applies equally to the du Ponts, at least through the first 150 years of their American existence.

Landes makes another interesting point that would seem to have bearing on the du Pont situation. "Societies get, on the whole," he writes, "the businessmen and business families they deserve." In other words, the temptation to criticize the du Ponts for their role in the Gunpowder Trade Association monopoly or the profits made from World War I may overlook the fact that the du Ponts were conspicuous during these times not because they broke any social covenants but because, playing within the then prevailing rules, they won the game. There is, and there always will be, a gap between the ideal society in which equal opportunity, justice, and an appropriate sharing of wealth prevail and the practical limitations of reality.

It jars one's sense of justice to observe wealth squandered on lavish living and the pursuit of hedonism, but who is to say that political distribution of wealth results in greater benefit to more people than the economic or capitalist method? Perhaps what Churchill said about democracy applies as well to capitalism.

The du Pont family today is in dynastic decline. Its collective wealth remains staggering, but it has been divided and redivided among more and more inheritors, and the accumulation process has slowed dramatically if it has not ceased altogether. The notable success within the family has become the exception rather than the rule. Will the only victims of this decline be the du Ponts? Maybe, and maybe not.

How much the family has contributed to the society from which it has reaped such vast wealth is hard to assess. Unquestionably, Delaware would be a poorer place. Schools, roads, hospitals, cultural institutions in Delaware have all been helped immeasurably by the family. Many such things wouldn't exist without the du Ponts. The help has been both financial and administrative. Writing in 1973, a bevy of Ralph Nader's people called the University of Delaware the fourth most grandly endowed public-related university in the country and said 40 per cent of that endowment came from the H. Rodney and Isabella du Pont Sharp Trust. Much of the remainder of the endowment comes from the family, as well as a majority of the capital investment in buildings and equipment at the school. This is but one not untypical example among many of the du Pont family's impact on their home state.

Du Pont detractors argue that the family generosity tends to benefit the more affluent white community to the neglect of less-well-off minorities. After all, Longwood Gardens and the Winterthur Museum do not exactly contribute to the improvement of Wilmington's ghetto dwellers. But that charge ignores, or at least slights, family help given the state's hospitals and public schools, not to mention the many agencies set up to help those needing it and funded in large measure with du Pont dollars. The argument may indeed be self-serving, but the family has long contended that the spending of federal money is an inefficient process and that people were better off all around when taxes were lower and private philanthropy played a larger role in meeting the needs of the underprivileged. The problem with that argument is that the underprivileged can make demands of government agencies, which are spawned by the democratic process and funded with taxpayer dollars, that they could not make on private individuals or foundations. Politicians tend to listen to the public voice of the people more attentively than private individuals.

Those arguments aside, the du Ponts have long adhered to a standard of excellence that has made institutions like Longwood and Winterthur unique. Perhaps nowhere in the world can a visitor absorb the cultural heritage of a country from its beginnings as comprehensively in one place as he can at Winterthur. The importance of Winterthur and Longwood is not, however, limited to the places themselves. Through their educational programs, Longwood and Winterthur help train and develop a small but elite group of horticulturists and antiquarians many of whom go on to be recognized as the best in their fields, influencing important programs and institutions throughout the country and bringing to them an excellence they might otherwise lack. The vision and ambition behind these du Pont institutions may pale in comparison with some Rockefeller or Ford Foundation programs to study and solve the world's problems, but the measurable results speak to the efficacy of taking on a manageable project and seeing it to a fruitful conclusion.

The du Ponts are frequently criticized for the lack of a major du Pont foundation to rival the ones of the Rockefellers, Fords, and Mellons, but it should be remembered that by the time the du Pont family was wealthy enough to fund such an institution, it was already a huge, diverse group, the various factions of which preferred to exercise their own generosity rather than contribute to a single family fund. Furthermore, the very size of the family meant that a smaller percentage of its total wealth was available for foundation use because that total was spread among so many more individuals than was the case with most of the other major American fortunes.

Although the point has been frequently argued, most du Pont contributions to the public welfare appear to have been made without strings of self-interest attached. In 1920 Edward N. Vallandigham wrote a letter to Dr. Walter Hullihan upon his election as president of the University of Delaware and put it this way: "Although vast du Pont wealth has much menace to our civic life in Delaware, I have the strongest reason to believe that Pierre du Pont as the almoner of Delaware College and of its public schools is utterly without selfish purpose. I believe that you will in no way be embarrassed by any demand that Mr. du Pont may put upon the college, for I am convinced that he will never interfere with the liberty of teaching."

Delaware's youthful U.S. senator, Joseph R. Biden, Jr., is generally classified as a liberal Democrat, making him on the face of things a potential antagonist of both the du Pont family and the company. A popular speaker on the political dinner circuit, Biden gets around the country a good deal and says that one of the most frequent questions he gets from reporters is how he manages to buck Du Pont interests on such key issues as lead in gasoline and taxes and get away with it. Biden says he meets with the executive committee of Du Pont—as well as those of Hercules and ICI, the other two major chemical firms headquartered in Wilmington—twice a year and that while he doesn't always agree with their positions, he feels he has a good relationship with them. He says he does not make a big public point of fighting the family or the company, rich people or the establishment, but tries to find mutual ground on which they all can agree. He considers the du Ponts "a remarkable family" and feels they have a good public image in general, at least in part because they have built a wall of privacy around their non-public lives. Their private excesses, if there are any, are not a matter of public record, he says.

Biden makes the point that Du Pont influence remains strong and calls it a legacy now based on the public's misconception of the situation. Whether that influence is real or perceived is not an important difference, he says, "unless push comes to shove." Du Pont chairman Shapiro describes the influence of the family on the company today by comparing it with the influence of the Du Pont Company on General Motors back in the days before Du Pont was forced to divest its GM stockholdings. Accountability is the key word, Shapiro says. "The du Ponts know where I am." And they come to see him from time to time. On some occasions, it is to urge him to take a vacation before he becomes a company liability instead of an asset. Other times, they want to talk about the sagacity of the company's changing policy toward debt financing. Not so long ago, a member of the family brought along a business associate of his to discuss debt policy with Shapiro. Needless to say, the associate disapproved of debt financing.

Shapiro says that the family members who sit on Du Pont's board of directors—with the appointment of Edward B. du Pont in January of 1978 there were seven, two of whom were in-laws—do not speak with one voice or one viewpoint. Shapiro declined to discuss in any detail the kinds of contributions family members make to board meetings. But he did indicate that their participation was more than perfunctory. In the past, Shapiro has been less than complimentary in his public pronouncements on the present and future du Pont family and its ability to manage the modern company, but on this particular day, he refused to be drawn into making any disparaging remarks at all.

Nonetheless, the glory days are gone. And not just for the du Ponts. Public policy over the last fifty years has made the maintenance of private fortunes spanning generations more and more difficult. The great Newport, Rhode Island, mansions have become museums. The vast estates of the Vanderbilts, the Astors, the Fricks, the Morgans are being opened to the public or razed to make way for the future. An era is ending.

In 1977 Nemours, the Wilmington estate of Alfred I. du Pont, was opened to the public for the first time. The little people could now gaze in wonder at the seventy-eight-seat dining room table and wander in the basement with its bowling alleys and the billiard room that has cork inlaid in the floor around the tables to make it easy on the players' feet. Here in more halcyon days Alfred employed one fellow whose only job was to pick the dark pebbles out of the white-pebbled paths in the elaborate formal gardens. During the summer, visitors are ushered to the terrace to await their guides and served orange juice from a silver tray—in plastic cups. There is little here now to indicate the special affinity Alfred had throughout his life for the little people. It is not part of the regular tour, but if you stray far enough behind the mansion and to the right, you will come upon a tennis court surrounded by magnificent evergreens. Weeds now poke up through the clay surface. The court has long been abandoned.

Some members of the family continue to fight an impressive rear-guard action against the forces that are inexorably bringing the glamour years to a close. Occasionally still, the strains of Lester Lanin or Meyer Davis waft on an early summer breeze from beneath an elaborate marquee as another du Pont daughter makes her debut at Bois des Fosses or Granogue and the champagne flows. Yet it was only twenty years ago that Secretariat Ltd., a social secretary service that arranges many du Pont parties, could count on perhaps half a dozen such affairs a year. Now one is the more likely number. Partly this is because du Pont daughters are embarrassed today by such a lavish show and prefer a more quiet introduction to society. But part of the reason, too, is that a debutante party done in the style to which the du Ponts are traditionally accustomed is an affair few can afford these days.

Some years ago the Belgian crown prince paid a visit to Wilmington to recognize the contributions of the Du Pont Company, which had several major installations in Belgium, to his native economy. The Lammot Copeland Srs. gave a dinner in his honor, pulling out all the stops. Their chef and his staff worked overtime on the elegant meal, served on the finest export china. The service was gold, the wines vintage, the wine goblets the best crystal. A footman stood behind each chair. When the meal was over, the royal guest rose to toast his hosts. He talked about the highlights of his visit to the United States, his first trip to this country. But his greatest pleasure, he concluded deadpan, was the opportunity he had just realized, the chance to dine for once in an average American home. His timing and delivery were superb. His appreciative audience roared with laughter. It is doubtful anyone there that evening thought anything but comfortable thoughts.

But that sort of extravagance is rare any more. Individual du Ponts are slipping from the ranks of the super rich. To be sure, there are undoubtedly more millionaires in the du Pont family than in any other family in the world; yet the yachts are fewer and smaller these days. A millionaire is comfortable enough, but today he must watch his spending and live with the sure knowledge that his children will have to be even more careful. More and more young du Ponts are being faced with the challenge of going to work for a living. They can still pick their spots without worrying about salaries adequate to feed and clothe their families, and in that, they remain lucky. Nonetheless, it is becoming increasingly difficult to absorb mistakes with impunity.

Most of the family recognizes what is happening and accepts it. None expects—or gets—any sympathy for his situation. There are still some who can argue with impassioned eloquence the merits of inherited wealth and lament the public policy that has so greatly limited it. A majority, however, understand the great good fortune that remains theirs through an accident of birth and cherish the family name. The tradition of New Year's Day calling is still observed, although with a gradually diminishing enthusiasm. Slowly, being a du Pont is becoming secondary to being an individual, a process made difficult by the continuing public preconceptions about what it means to be a du Pont. What is happening to the family is more akin to abrasion than it is to disintegration.

In general, the family is philosophical about its changing circumstances. A. Felix du Pont probably speaks for a majority of the family when he says, "Yes, the dissipation of wealth still goes on. I guess it will until it's all gone."

Acknowledgments

This book would not have been possible without the gracious co-operation of many du Pont family members, who consented to interviews often despite prior unsatisfactory experiences with interviewers who preceded me. In all cases, they were candid and helpful.

I owe a special debt of gratitude to the Eleutherian Mills Historical Library and its staff, all of whom went out of their way to help my research efforts and ensure that I spent a minimum of time spinning my wheels. Research on the du Pont family is probably an easier and more rewarding task than comparable work on any other American family because of the wealth of primary source material here and its accessibility. Without in any way attempting to influence the form this book would take, the library staff gave generously of its time and knowledge. Time and again, one staff member or another suggested a source or an approach that allowed me to escape errors earlier books have made, and in many cases, repeated.

Among previously published material on the du Ponts, I found the Alfred Chandler, Jr.-Stephen Salsbury book, *Pierre S. du Pont and the Making of the Modern Corporation*, particularly helpful. Also the Marquis James biography of Alfred I. du Pont, called *Alfred I. du Pont, the Family Rebel*; and the Ambrose Saricks biography of Pierre S. du Pont de Nemours; and the introduction to the three-volume collection of Admiral Samuel F. Du Pont's correspondence. None of the dozen or so volumes on the du Ponts that I read during the preparation of this book was without some useful insight or information. The task of writing a book about the du Ponts is an awesome one, but much good groundwork has already been laid, for which I was, and am, most grateful.

John D. Gates

Appendix

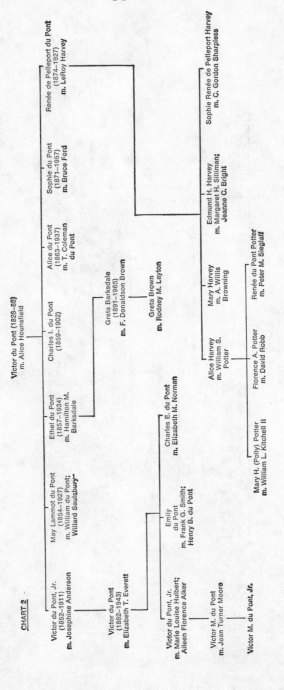

CHART 2

Victor du Pont (1828–88)
m. Alice Hounsfield

Victor du Pont, Jr. (1852–1911)
m. Josephine Anderson

May Lammot du Pont (1854–1927)
m. William du Pont;
Willard Saulsbury

Ethel du Pont (1857–1934)
m. Hamilton M. Barksdale

Charles I. du Pont (1859–1902)

Alice du Pont (1863–1937)
m. T. Coleman du Pont

Sophie du Pont (1871–1957)
m. Bruce Ford

Renée de Pelleport du Pont (1874–1927)
m. LeRoy Harvey

Victor du Pont (1882–1943)
m. Elizabeth T. Everett

Greta Barksdale (1891–1965)
m. F. Donaldson Brown

Greta Brown
m. Rodney M. Layton

Edmund H. Harvey
m. Margaret H. Silliman;
Jeanne C. Bright

Sophie Renée de Pelleport Harvey
m. C. Gordon Sharpless

Emily du Pont
m. Frank G. Smith;
Henry B. du Pont

Charles E. du Pont
m. Elizabeth M. Norman

Mary Harvey
m. A. Willis Browning

Renée du Pont Potter
m. Peter M. Sieglaff

Victor du Pont, Jr.,
m. Marie Louise Hulbert;
Aileen Florence Alker

Alice Harvey
m. William S. Potter

Florence A. Potter
m. David Robb

Victor M. du Pont
m. Joan Turner Moore

Mary H. (Polly) Potter
m. William L. Kitchell II

Victor M. du Pont, Jr.

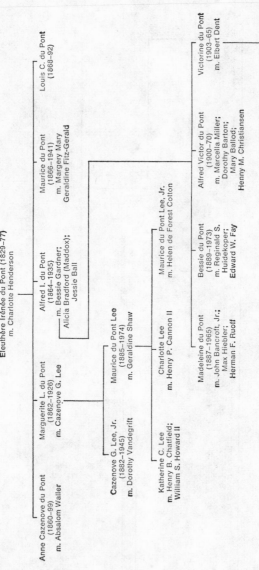

CHART 3

Eleuthère Irénée du Pont (1829–77)
m. Charlotte Henderson

Anne Cazenove du Pont
(1860–99)
m. Absalom Waller

Marguerite L. du Pont
(1862–1926)
m. Cazenove G. Lee

Alfred I. du Pont
(1864–1935)
m. Bessie Gardner;
Alicia Bradford (Maddox);
Jessie Ball

Maurice du Pont
(1866–1941)
m. Margery Mary
Geraldine Fitz-Gerald

Louis C. du Pont
(1868–92)

Cazenove G. Lee, Jr.
(1882–1945)
m. Dorothy Vandegrift

Maurice du Pont Lee
(1885–1974)
m. Geraldine Shaw

Katherine C. Lee
m. Henry B. Chatfield;
William S. Howard II

Charlotte Lee
m. Henry P. Cannon II

Maurice du Pont Lee, Jr.
m. Helen de Forest Cotton

Madeleine du Pont
(1887–1965)
m. John Bancroft, Jr.;
Max Hiebler;
Herman F. Ruoff

Bessie du Pont
(1889–1973)
m. Reginald S.
Huidekoper;
Edward W. Fay

Alfred Victor du Pont
(1900–70)
m. Marcella Miller;
Dorothy Barton;
Mary Ballod;
Henny M. Christiansen

Victorine du Pont
(1903–65)
m. Elbert Dent

Richard Henderson Dent
m. Julie M. Burk

Alfred du Pont Dent
m. Susan L. Wyckoff;
Kathleen Berger

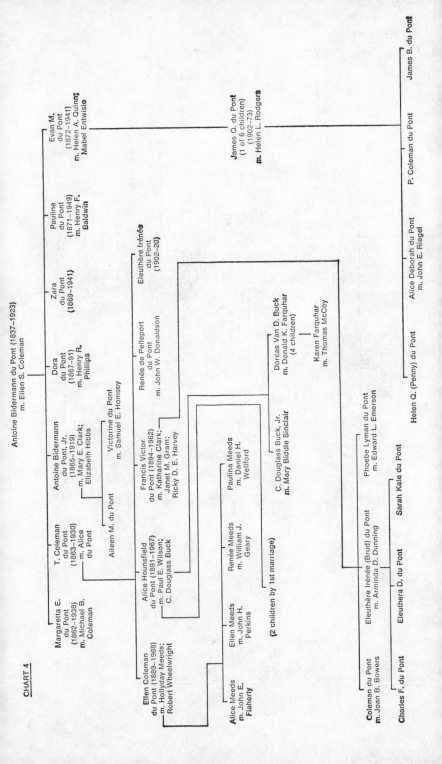

CHART 4

Antoine Bidermann du Pont (1837–1923)
m. Ellen S. Coleman

Margaretta E.
du Pont
(1862–1938)
m. Michael B.
Coleman

T. Coleman
du Pont
(1863–1930)
m. Alice
du Pont

Antoine Bidermann
du Pont, Jr.
(1865–1919)
m. Mary E. Clark;
Elizabeth Hibbs

Dora
du Pont
(1867–91)
m. Henry R.
Phillips

Zara
du Pont
(1869–1941)

Pauline
du Pont
(1871–1949)
m. Henry F.
Baldwin

Evan M.
du Pont
(1872–1941)
m. Helen A. Quinn;
Mabel Entwisle

Ellen Coleman
du Pont (1889–1968)
m. Hollyday Meeds;
Robert Wheelwright

Alice Hounsfield
du Pont (1891–1967)
m. Paul E. Wilson;
C. Douglass Buck

Francis Victor
du Pont (1894–1962)
m. Katharine Clark;
Janet M. Gram;
Ricky D. E. Harvey

Victorine du Pont
m. Samuel E. Homsey

Aileen M. du Pont

Renée de Pelleport
du Pont
m. John W. Donaldson

Eleuthère Irénée
du Pont
(1902–20)

James Q. du Pont
(1 of 6 children)
(1902–73)
m. Helen L. Rodgers

Alice Meeds
m. John E.
Flaherty

Ellen Meeds
m. John H.
Perkins

Renée Meeds
m. William J.
Geary

Paulina Meeds
m. Daniel H.
Wellford

C. Douglass Buck, Jr.
m. Mary Biddle Sinclair

(2 children by 1st marriage)

Dorcas Van D. Buck
m. Donald K. Farquhar
(4 children)

Karen Farquhar
m. Thomas McCoy

Coleman du Pont
m. Joan B. Bowers

Charles F. du Pont

Eleuthère Irénée (Brud) du Pont
m. Arminda D. Dunning

Eleuthera D. du Pont

Phoebe Lyman du Pont
m. Edward L. Emerson

Sarah Kate du Pont

Helen Q. (Penny) du Pont

Alice Deborah du Pont
m. John E. Riegel

P. Coleman du Pont

James B. du Pont

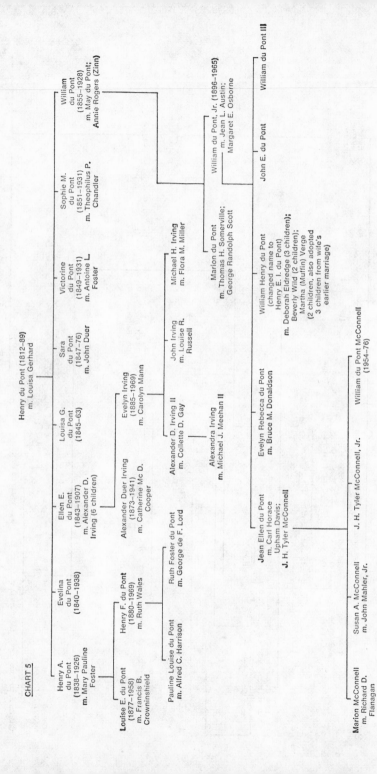

CHART 5

Henry du Pont (1812–89)
m. Louisa Gerhard

CHART 6

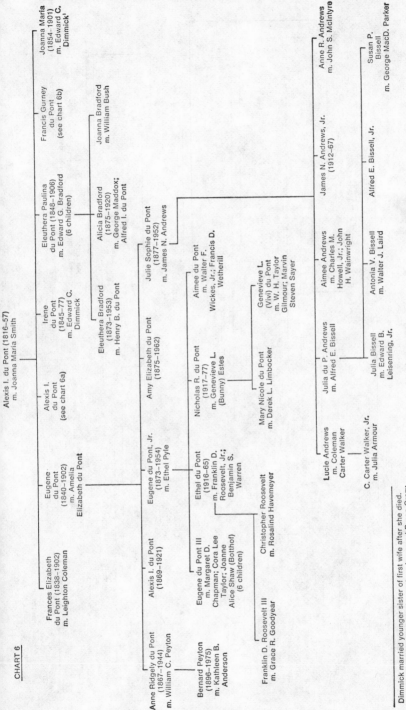

Dimmick married younger sister of first wife after she died.
Younger sister's great-great-grandson is named Byron Crazy
Horse Justin Case.

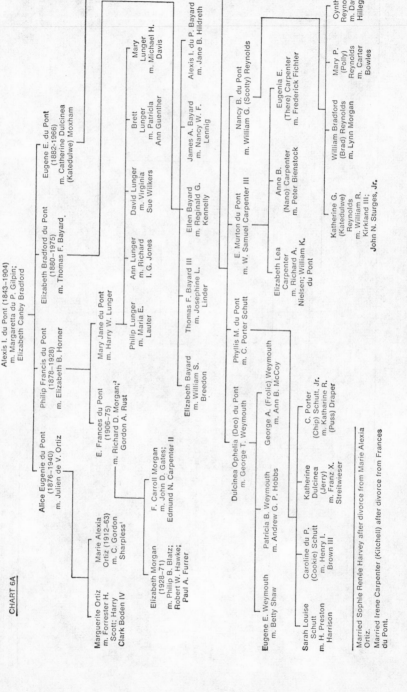

Alexis I. du Pont (1843–1904)
m. Margaretta du P. Gilpin;
Elizabeth Canby Bradford

Alice Eugenie du Pont (1876–1940) m. Julien de V. Ortiz

Philip Francis du Pont (1878–1928) m. Elizabeth B. Horner

Elizabeth Bradford du Pont (1880–1975) m. Thomas F. Bayard

Eugene E. du Pont (1882–1966) m. Catherine Dulcinea (Katedulwe) Moxham

Marguerite Ortiz m. Forrester H. Scott; **Harry Clark Boden IV**

Marie Alexia Ortiz (1912–63) m. C. Gordon Sharpless[1]

E. Frances du Pont (1906–75) m. Richard D. Morgan;[2] Gordon A. Rust

Mary Jane du Pont m. Harry W. Lunger

Philip Lunger m. Maria E. Lauter

Ann Lunger m. Richard I. G. Jones

David Lunger m. Virginia Sue Wilkers

Brett Lunger m. Patricia Ann Guenther

Mary Lunger m. Michael H. Davis

F. Carroll Morgan m. John D. Gates; **Edmund N. Carpenter II**

Elizabeth Morgan (1928–71) m. Philip B. Blatz; Robert W. Hawke; **Paul A. Furrer**

Elizabeth Bayard m. William S. Breedon

Thomas F. Bayard III m. Josephine L. Linder

Ellen Bayard m. Reginald G. Kennelly

James A. Bayard m. Nancy W. F. Lennig

Alexis I. du P. Bayard m. Jane B. Hildreth

Dulcinea Ophelia (Deo) du Pont m. George T. Weymouth

Phyllis M. du Pont m. C. Porter Schutt

E. Murton du Pont m. W. Samuel Carpenter III

Nancy B. du Pont m. William G. (Scotty) Reynolds

Eugene E. Weymouth m. Betty Shaw

Patricia B. Weymouth m. Andrew G. P. Hobbs

George A. (Frolic) Weymouth m. Ann B. McCoy

Sarah Louise Schutt m. H. Preston Harrison

Caroline du P. (Cookie) Schutt m. Henry I. Brown III

Katherine Dulcinea (Jerry) m. Franz X. Streitwieser

C. Porter (Chip) Schutt, Jr. m. Katharine R. (Puss) Draper

Elizabeth Lea Carpenter m. Richard A. Nielsen; William K. du Pont

Anne B. (Nano) Carpenter m. Peter Bienstock

Eugenia E. (There) Carpenter m. Frederick Fichter

Katherine G. (Katedulwe) Reynolds m. William R. Kirkland III; **John N. Sturges, Jr.**

William Bradford (Brad) Reynolds m. Lynn Morgan

Mary P. (Polly) Reynolds m. Carter Bowles

Cynthia Reynolds m. David Hillegas

Married Sophie Renée Harvey after divorce from Marie Alexia Ortiz.

Married Irene Carpenter (Kitchell) after divorce from Frances du Pont.

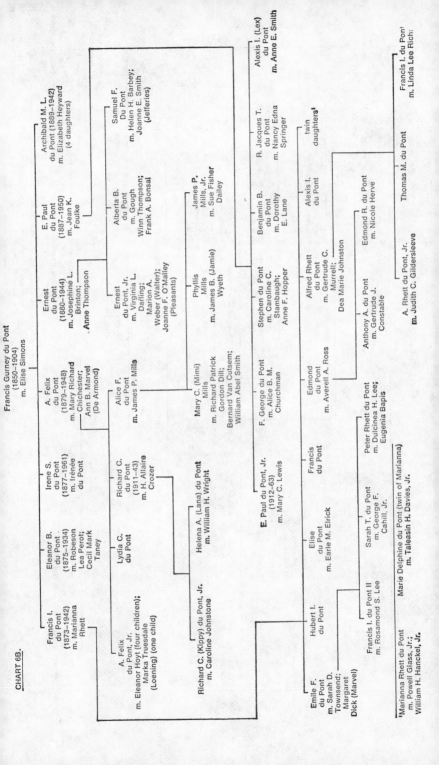

CHART 6B.

Francis Gurney du Pont
(1850–1904)
m. Elise Simons

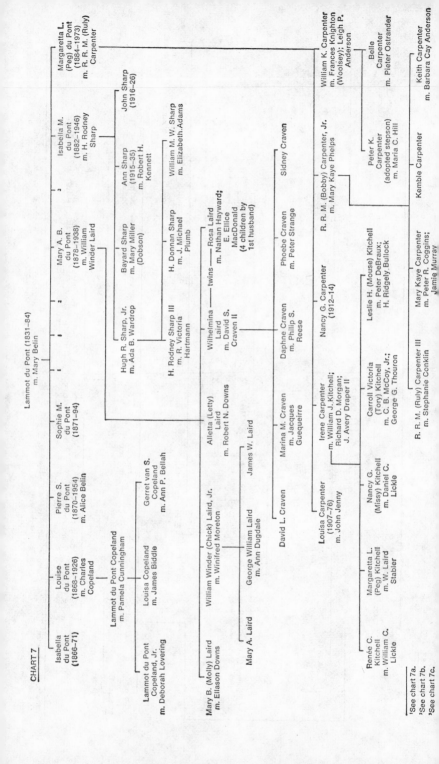

CHART 7

Lammot du Pont (1831–84)
m. Mary Belin

Isabella du Pont (1866–71)

Louise du Pont (1868–1926) m. Charles Copeland

Pierre S. du Pont (1870–1954) m. Alice Belin

Sophie M. du Pont (1871–94)

Mary A. B. du Pont (1878–1938) m. William Winder Laird

Isabella M. du Pont (1882–1946) m. H. Rodney Sharp

Margaretta L. (Peg) du Pont (1884–1973) m. R. R. M. (Ruly) Carpenter

Lammot du Pont Copeland m. Pamela Cunningham

Gerret van S. Copeland m. Ann P. Bellah

Louisa Copeland m. James Biddle

Lammot du Pont Copeland, Jr. m. Deborah Lovering

Mary B. (Molly) Laird m. Ellason Downs

William Winder (Chick) Laird, Jr. m. Winifred Moreton

George William Laird m. Ann Dugdale

James W. Laird

Mary A. Laird

David L. Craven

Alletta (Letty) Laird m. Robert N. Downs

Marina M. Craven m. Jacques Guegueirre

Wilhelmina Laird m. David S. Craven II

Daphne Craven m. Philip S. Reese

twins

Rosa Laird m. Nathan Hayward; E. Ellice MacDonald (4 children by 1st husband)

Phoebe Craven m. Peter Strange

Sidney Craven

Hugh R. Sharp, Jr. m. Ada B. Wardrop

H. Rodney Sharp III m. R. Victoria Hartmann

H. Donnan Sharp m. J. Michael Plumb

Bayard Sharp m. Mary Miller (Dobson)

Ann Sharp (1915–35) m. Robert H. Kennett

William M. W. Sharp m. Elizabeth Adams

John Sharp (1916–26)

Renée C. Kitchell m. William C. Lickle

Margaretta L. (Peg) Kitchell m. W. Laird Stabler

Nancy G. (Missy) Kitchell m. Daniel C. Lickle

Louisa Carpenter (1907–76) m. John Jenny

Irene Carpenter m. William J. Kitchell; Richard D. Morgan; J. Avery Draper II

Carroll Victoria (Tory) Kitchell m. C. B. McCoy, Jr.; George G. Thouron

R. R. M. (Ruly) Carpenter III m. Stephanie Conklin

Nancy G. Carpenter (1912–14)

Leslie H. (Mouse) Kitchell m. Peter DeBraux; H. Ridgely Bullock

Mary Kaye Carpenter m. Peter R. Coggins; Jamie Murray

R. R. M. (Bobby) Carpenter, Jr. m. Mary Kaye Phelps

William K. Carpenter m. Frances Knighton (Woolsey); Leigh P. Anderson

Peter K. Carpenter (adopted stepson) m. Maria C. Hill

Kemble Carpenter

Belle Carpenter m. Pieter Ostrander

Keith Carpenter m. Barbara Cay Anderson

¹See chart 7a.
²See chart 7b.
³See chart 7c.

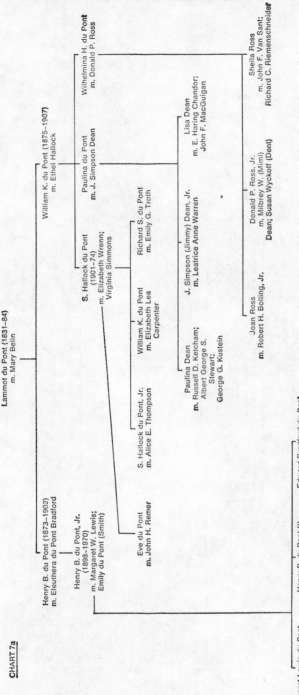

Lammot du Pont (1831–84)
m. Mary Belin

Henry B. du Pont (1873–1902)
m. Eleuthera du Pont Bradford

William K. du Pont (1875–1907)
m. Ethel Hallock

Henry B. du Pont, Jr.
(1898–1970)
m. Margaret W. Lewis;
Emily du Pont (Smith)

S. Hallock du Pont
(1901–74)
m. Elizabeth Wrenn;
Virginia Simmons

Paulina du Pont
m. J. Simpson Dean

Wilhelmina H. du Pont
m. Donald P. Ross

Eve du Pont
m. John H. Remer

S. Hallock du Pont, Jr.
m. Alice E. Thompson

William K. du Pont
m. Elizabeth Lea
Carpenter

Richard S. du Pont
m. Emily G. Troth

Paulina Dean
m. Russell D. Ketcham;
Albert George S.
Stewart;
George G. Kustein

J. Simpson (Jimmy) Dean, Jr.
m. Leatrice Anne Warren

Lisa Dean
m. E. Haring Chandor;
John F. MacGuigan

Joan Ross
m. Robert H. Bolling, Jr.

Donald P. Ross, Jr.
m. Milbrey W. (Mimi)
Dean; Susan Wyckoff (Dent)

Sheila Ross
m. John F. Van Sant;
Richard C. Riemenschneider

Margaret Lewis du Pont
m. E. Newbold Smith

Henry B. du Pont III
m. Joan Wheeler

Edward Bradford du Pont
m. Ruth Ann Vallett

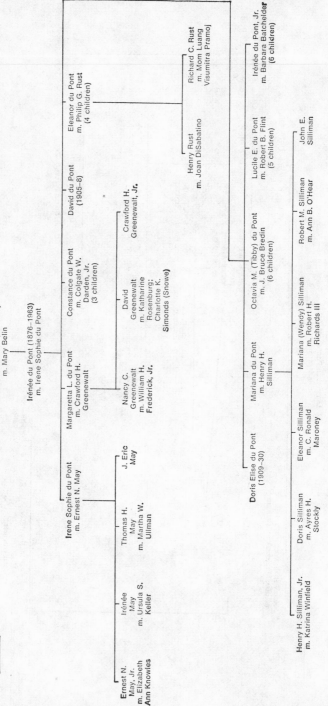

CHART 7c

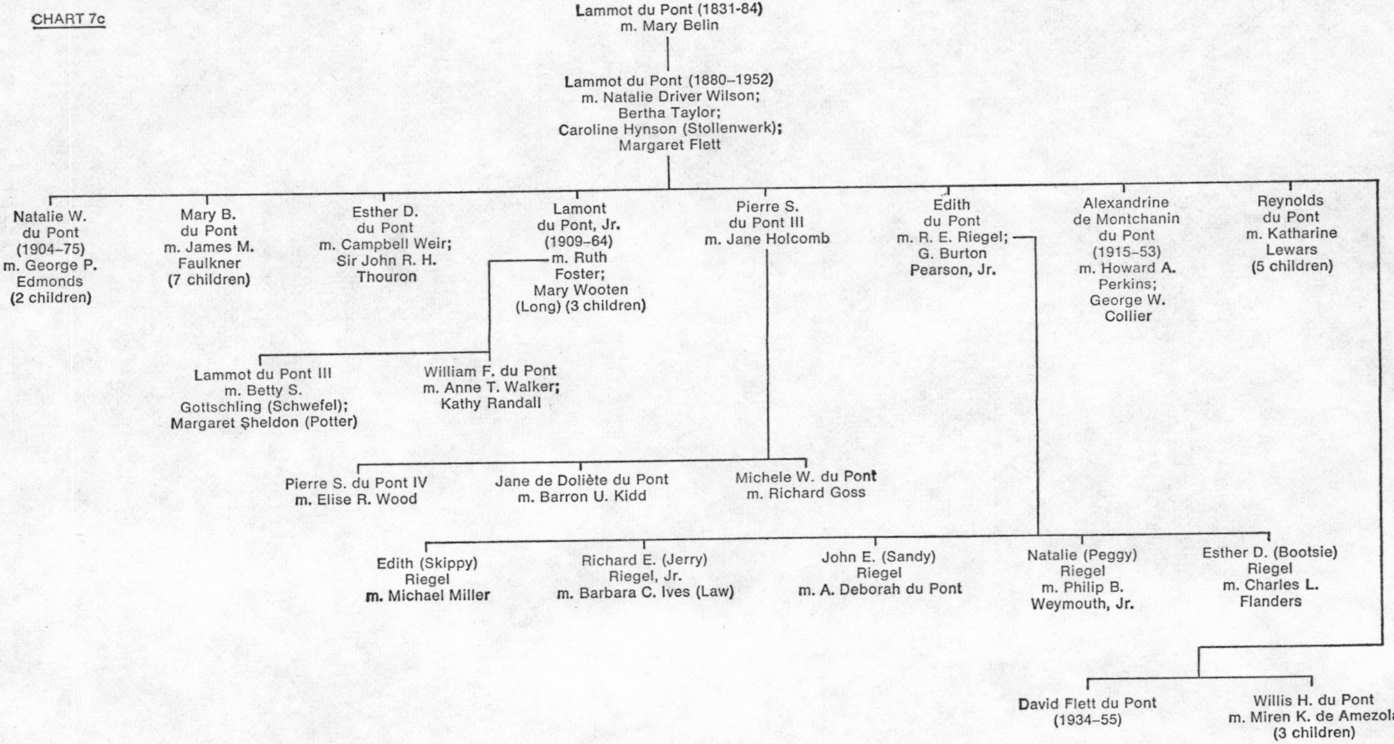

Lammot du Pont (1831-84)
m. Mary Belin

Lammot du Pont (1880-1952)
m. Natalie Driver Wilson;
Bertha Taylor;
Caroline Hynson (Stollenwerk);
Margaret Flett

Reynolds du Pont
m. Katharine Lewars
(5 children)

Alexandrine de Montchanin du Pont
(1915-53)
m. Howard A. Perkins;
George W. Collier

Edith du Pont
m. R. E. Riegel;
G. Burton Pearson, Jr.

Pierre S. du Pont III
m. Jane Holcomb

Lamont du Pont, Jr.
(1909-64)
m. Ruth Foster;
Mary Wooten (Long) (3 children)

Esther D. du Pont
m. Campbell Weir;
Sir John R. H. Thouron

Mary B. du Pont
m. James M. Faulkner
(7 children)

Natalie W. du Pont
(1904-75)
m. George P. Edmonds
(2 children)

Lammot du Pont III
m. Betty S. Gottschling (Schwefel);
Margaret Sheldon (Potter)

William F. du Pont
m. Anne T. Walker;
Kathy Randall

Michele W. du Pont
m. Richard Goss

Jane de Doliête du Pont
m. Barron U. Kidd

Pierre S. du Pont IV
m. Elise R. Wood

Edith (Skippy) Riegel
m. Michael Miller

Richard E. (Jerry) Riegel, Jr.
m. Barbara C. Ives (Law)

John E. (Sandy) Riegel
m. A. Deborah du Pont

Natalie (Peggy) Riegel
m. Philip B. Weymouth, Jr.

Esther D. (Bootsie) Riegel
m. Charles L. Flanders

Willis H. du Pont
m. Miren K. de Amezola
(3 children)

David Flett du Pont
(1934-55)